Shojo Beat

Natsume's BOOK of FRIENDS

STORY and **ART** by
Yuki Midorikawa

VOLUME **6**

Natsume's BOOK of FRIENDS

VOLUME 6 CONTENTS

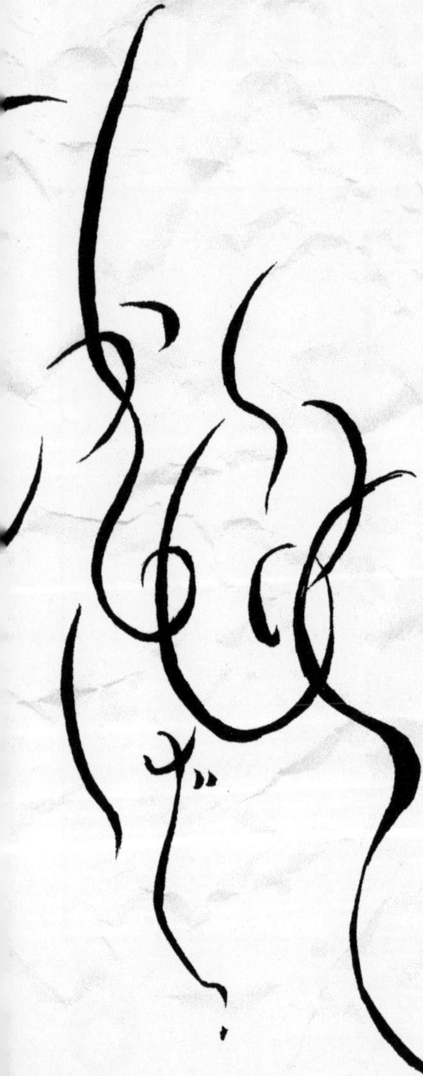

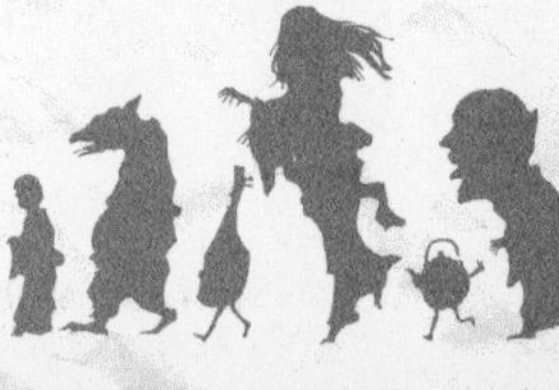

Natsume's BOOK of FRIENDS CHARACTER GUIDE

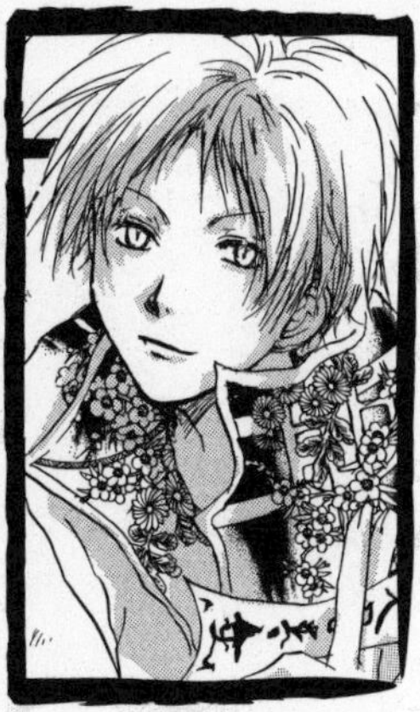

Takashi Natsume

A lonely orphan with the ability to see the supernatural. He inherited the *Book of Friends* from his grandmother and currently lives with the Fujiwaras, to whom he is distantly related.

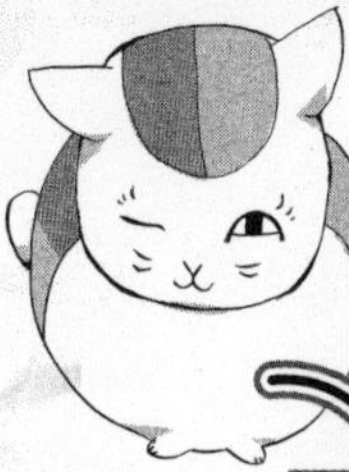

Nyanko Sensei

Natsume's bodyguard, posing as a cat. His yokai name is Madara.

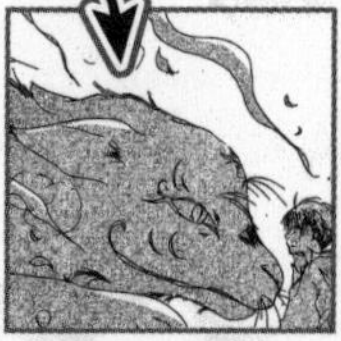

(TRUE FORM)

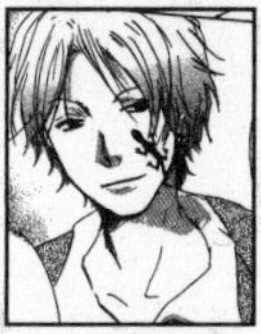

Shuichi Natori

An exorcist and an actor. His gecko tattoo is actually a yokai that lives on his body.

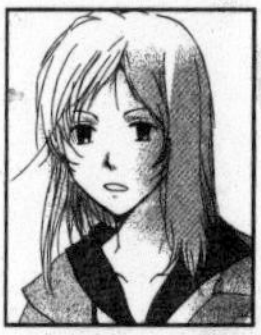

Tohru Taki

A girl who can see yokai when they pass within the spell circles she draws. A big fan of Nyanko Sensei.

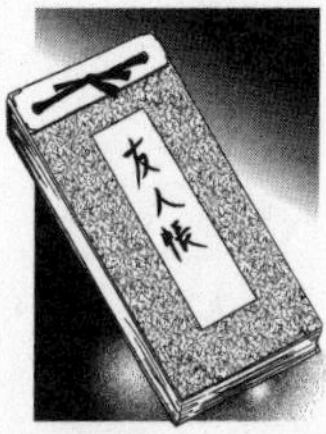
友人帳

The Book of Friends

A collection of contracts put together by Reiko, Takashi's grandmother, that grants her mastery over the yokai who sign.

THE STORY

Takashi Natsume has a secret sixth sense—he can see supernatural creatures called yokai. And ever since he inherited the *Book of Friends* from his grandmother, the local yokai have been coming after him. Takashi frees Nyanko Sensei from imprisonment and promises he will get the *Book* when Takashi dies. With his new bodyguard, Takashi leads a busy life returning names to yokai.

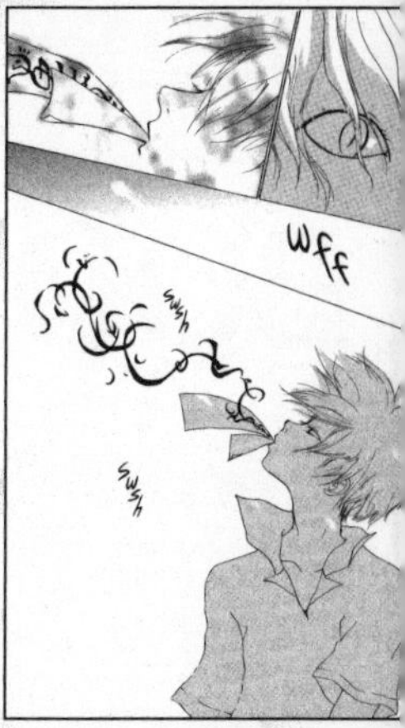
Wff
swish
swish

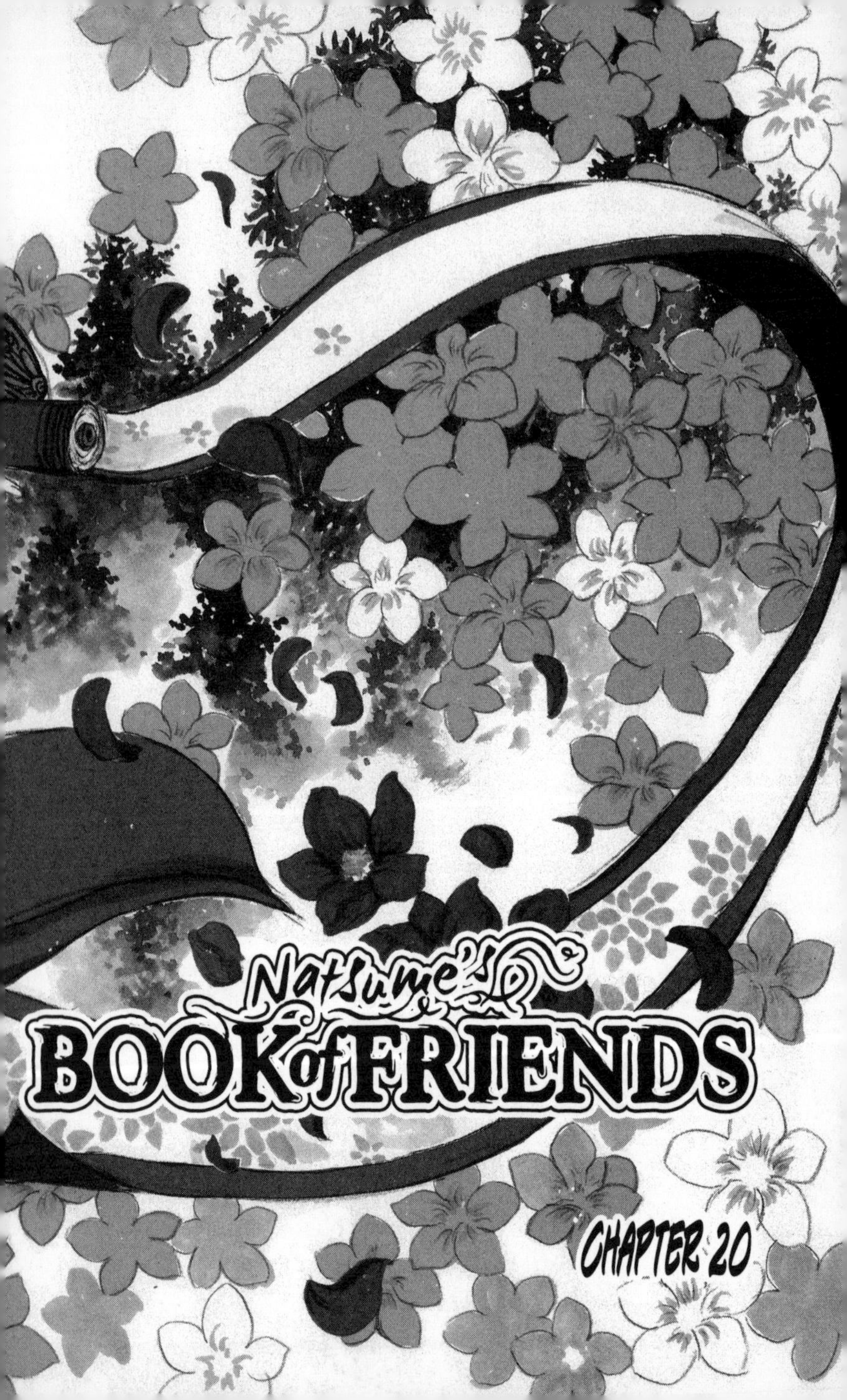
Natsume's
BOOK of FRIENDS
CHAPTER 20

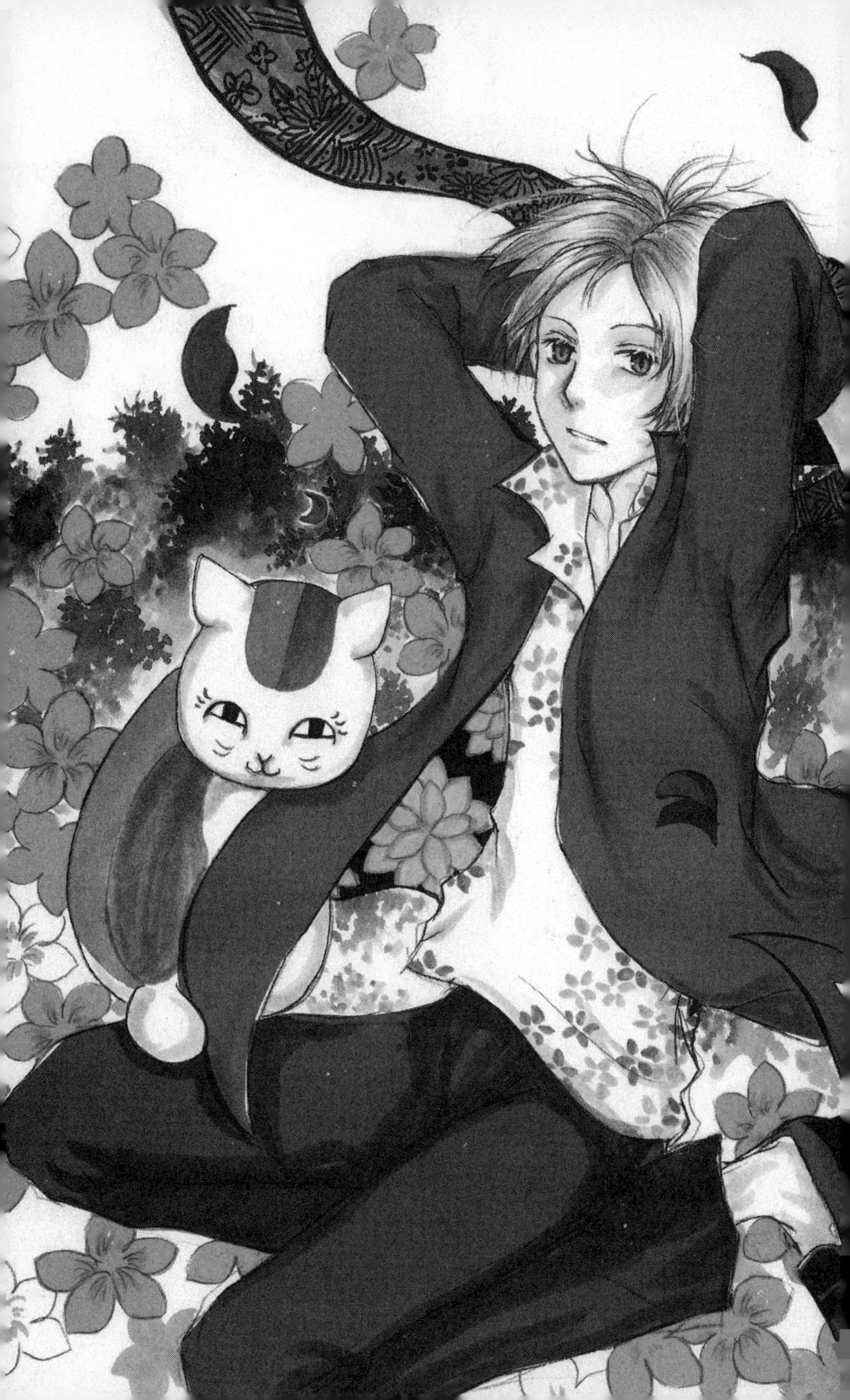

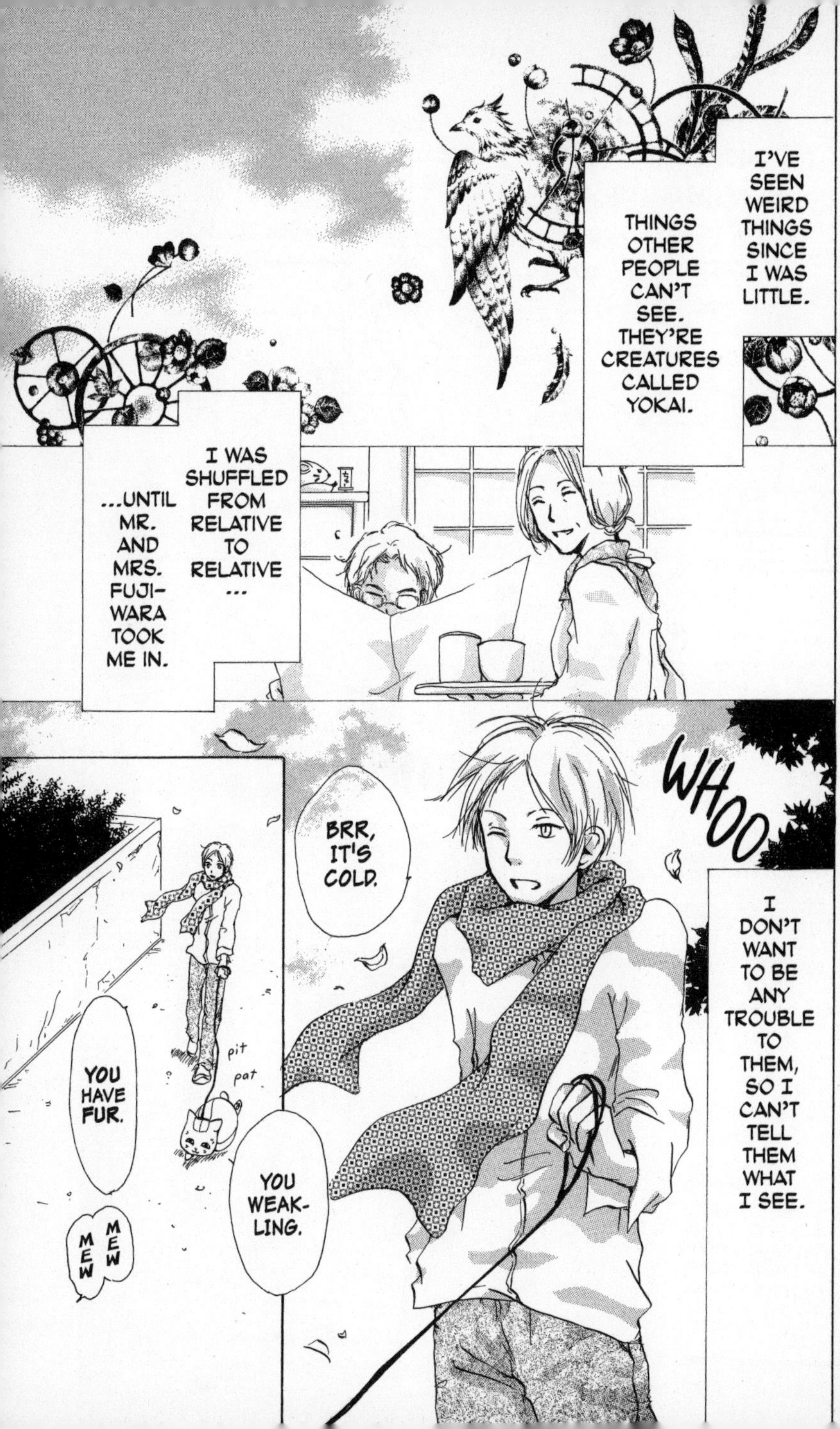
I'VE SEEN WEIRD THINGS SINCE I WAS LITTLE.
THINGS OTHER PEOPLE CAN'T SEE. THEY'RE CREATURES CALLED YOKAI.
I WAS SHUFFLED FROM RELATIVE TO RELATIVE...
...UNTIL MR. AND MRS. FUJIWARA TOOK ME IN.
WHOO
I DON'T WANT TO BE ANY TROUBLE TO THEM, SO I CAN'T TELL THEM WHAT I SEE.
BRR, IT'S COLD.
pit pat
YOU WEAK-LING.
YOU HAVE FUR.
MEW MEW

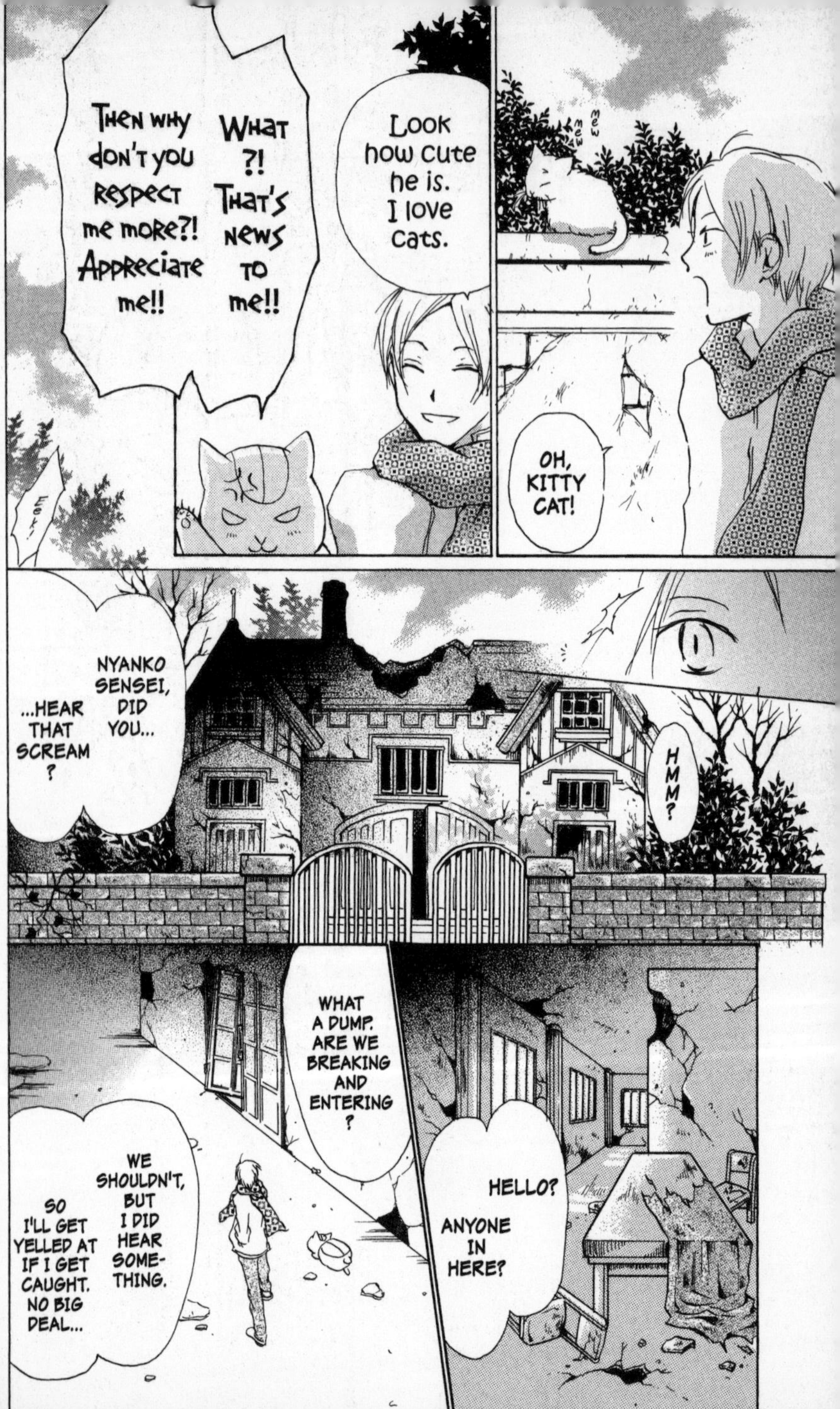
mew mew
OH, KITTY CAT!
Look how cute he is. I love cats.
WHAT?! THAT'S NEWS TO ME!!
THEN WHY DON'T YOU RESPECT ME MORE?! APPRECIATE ME!!
Eek!
HMM?
NYANKO SENSEI, DID YOU...
...HEAR THAT SCREAM?
HELLO?
ANYONE IN HERE?
WHAT A DUMP. ARE WE BREAKING AND ENTERING?
WE SHOULDN'T, BUT I DID HEAR SOMETHING.
SO I'LL GET YELLED AT IF I GET CAUGHT. NO BIG DEAL...

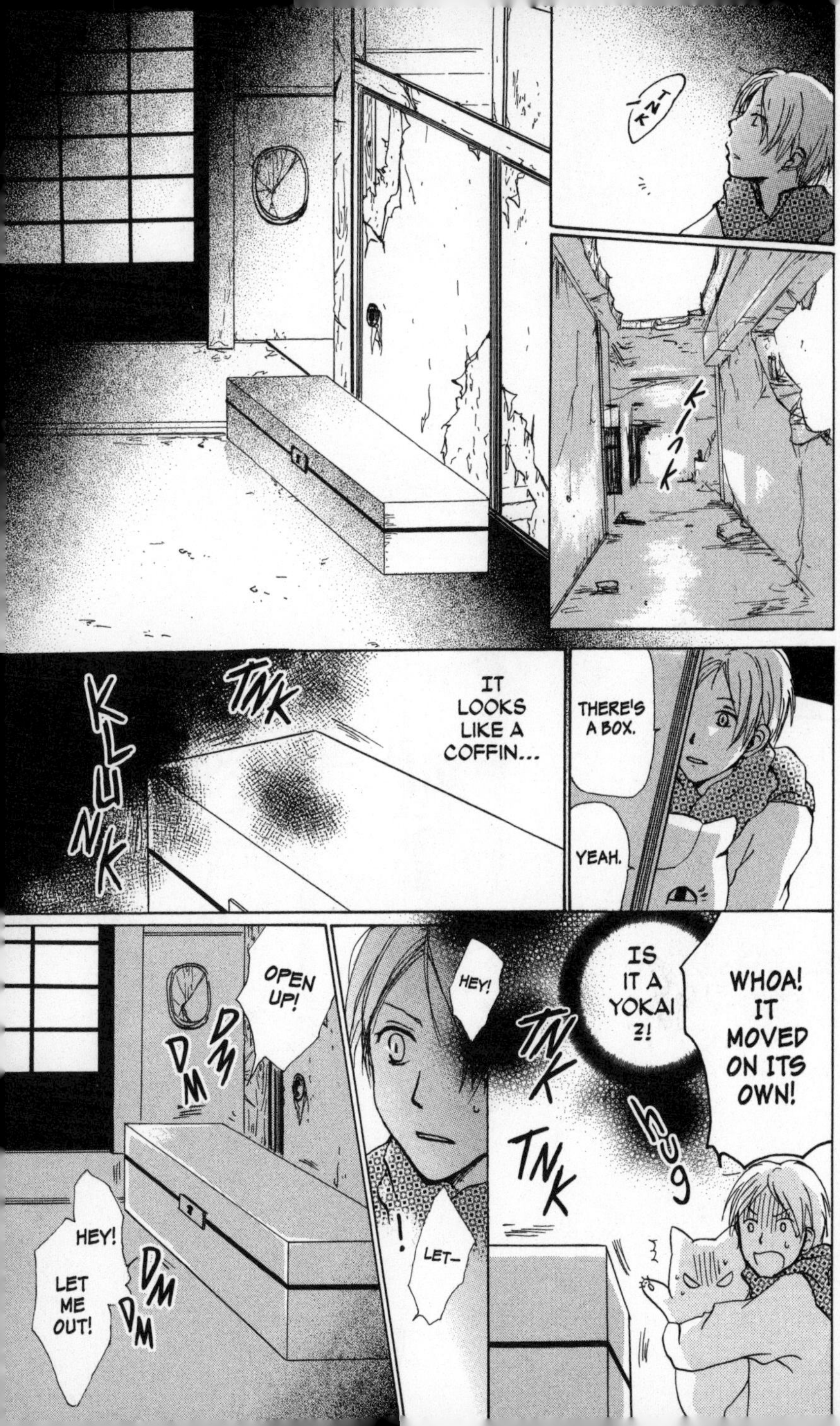
TNK!
KINK
THERE'S A BOX.
YEAH.
IT LOOKS LIKE A COFFIN...
TNK
KLUNK
WHOA! IT MOVED ON ITS OWN!
IS IT A YOKAI?!
TNK
TNK
hug
HEY!
!
LET—
OPEN UP!
DM DM
HEY!
LET ME OUT!
DM DM

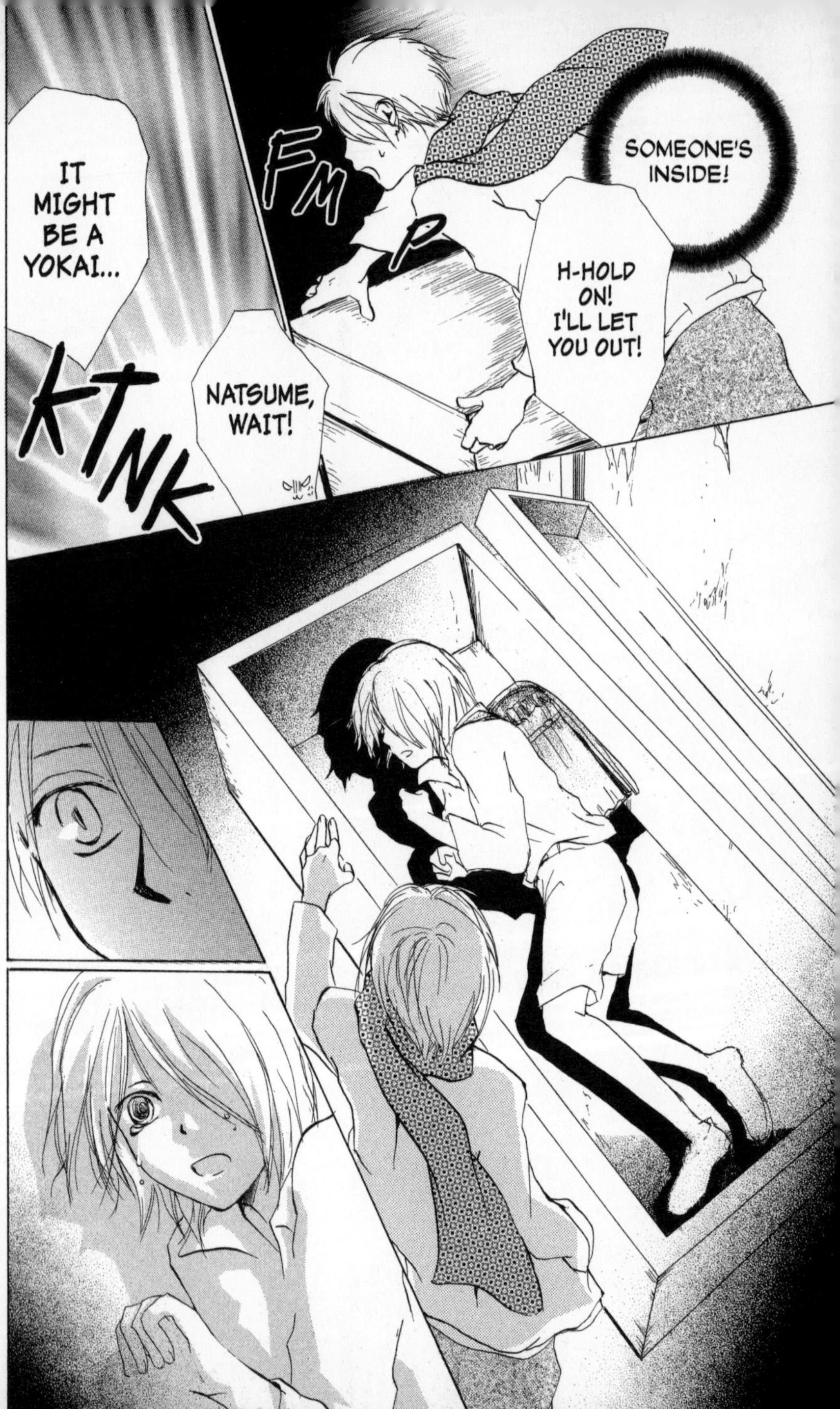
SOMEONE'S INSIDE!
FMP
H-HOLD ON! I'LL LET YOU OUT!
IT MIGHT BE A YOKAI...
NATSUME, WAIT!
KTNK

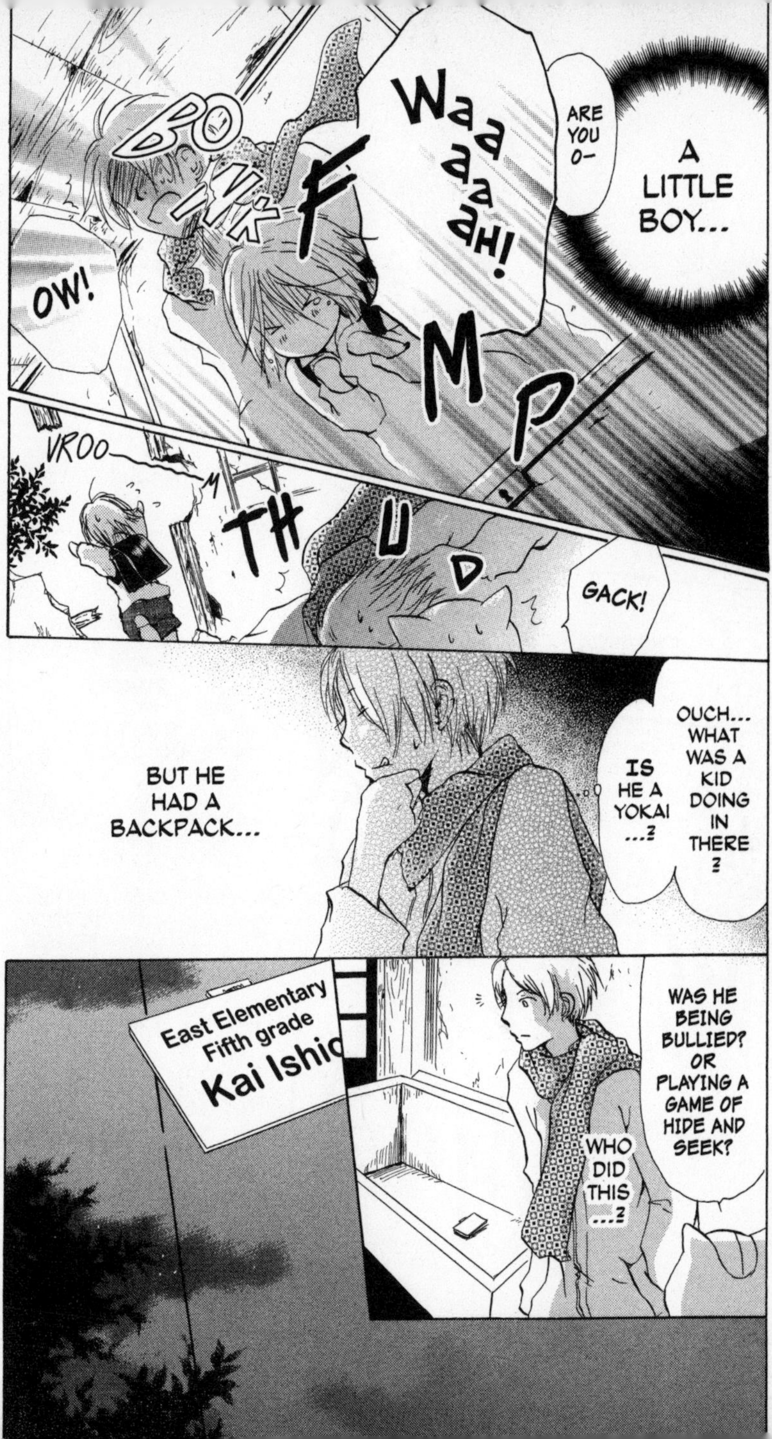
A LITTLE BOY...
ARE YOU O-
Waaaaaaah!
FUMP
BONK
OW!
GACK!
THUD
VROOM
OUCH... WHAT WAS A KID DOING IN THERE?
IS HE A YOKAI...?
BUT HE HAD A BACKPACK...
WAS HE BEING BULLIED? OR PLAYING A GAME OF HIDE AND SEEK?
WHO DID THIS...?
East Elementary
Fifth grade
Kai Ishio

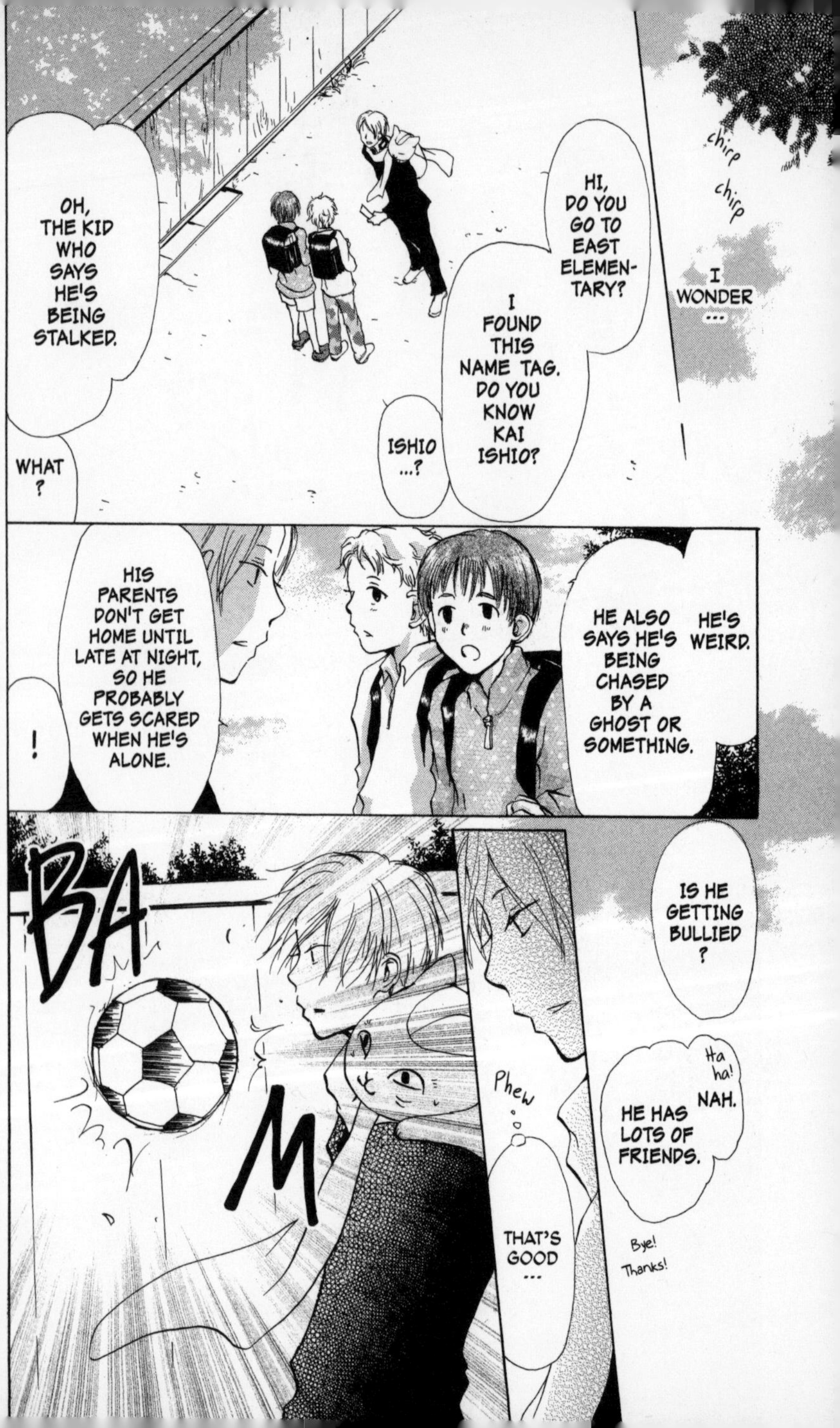
chirp chirp
I WONDER ...
HI, DO YOU GO TO EAST ELEMENTARY?
I FOUND THIS NAME TAG. DO YOU KNOW KAI ISHIO?
ISHIO ...?
OH, THE KID WHO SAYS HE'S BEING STALKED.
WHAT ?
HE'S WEIRD.
HE ALSO SAYS HE'S BEING CHASED BY A GHOST OR SOMETHING.
HIS PARENTS DON'T GET HOME UNTIL LATE AT NIGHT, SO HE PROBABLY GETS SCARED WHEN HE'S ALONE.
!
IS HE GETTING BULLIED ?
Ha ha!
NAH.
HE HAS LOTS OF FRIENDS.
Bye! Thanks!
Phew
THAT'S GOOD ...
BAM

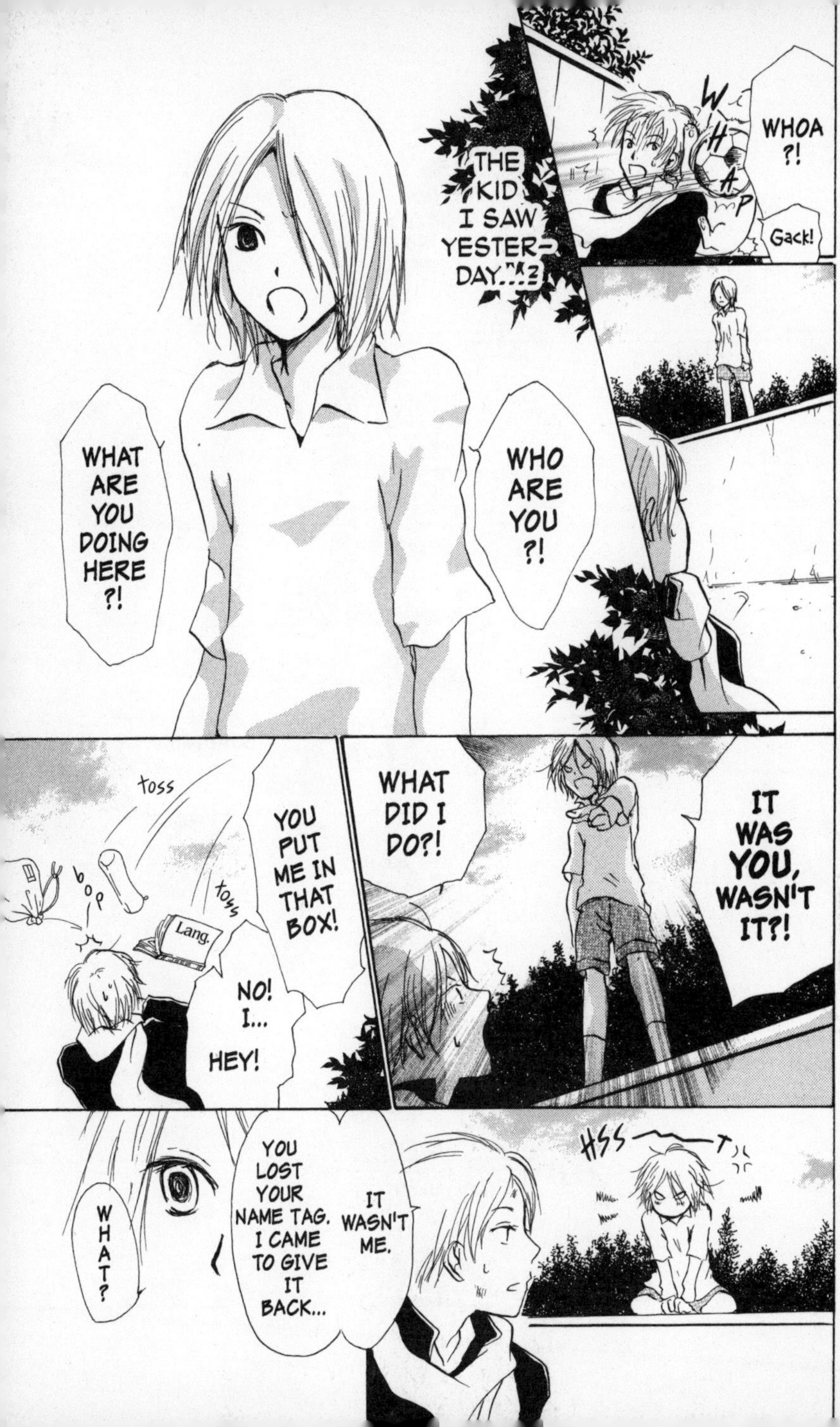
WHOA ?!
WHAP
Gack!
THE KID I SAW YESTERDAY...?
WHO ARE YOU ?!
WHAT ARE YOU DOING HERE ?!
IT WAS YOU, WASN'T IT?!
WHAT DID I DO?!
YOU PUT ME IN THAT BOX!
toss
bop
toss
Lang.
NO! I...
HEY!
HSS
IT WASN'T ME.
YOU LOST YOUR NAME TAG. I CAME TO GIVE IT BACK...
WHAT?

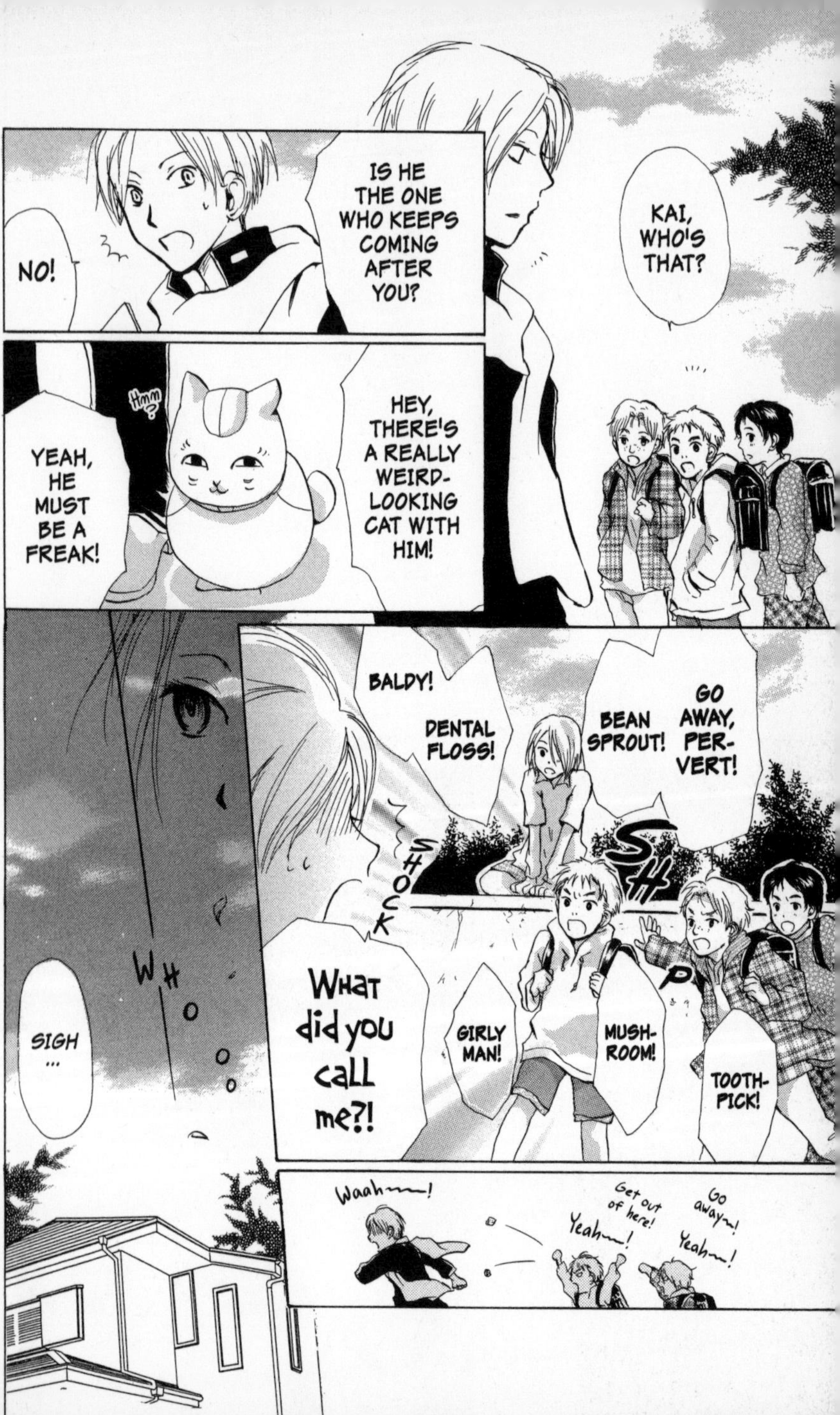

KAI, WHO'S THAT?
IS HE THE ONE WHO KEEPS COMING AFTER YOU?
NO!
HEY, THERE'S A REALLY WEIRD-LOOKING CAT WITH HIM!
Hmm?
YEAH, HE MUST BE A FREAK!
GO AWAY, PER-VERT!
BEAN SPROUT!
BALDY!
DENTAL FLOSS!
SH
SHOCK
P
TOOTH-PICK!
MUSH-ROOM!
GIRLY MAN!
What did you call me?!
WHOOO
SIGH...
Go away~!
Yeah~!
Get out of here!
Yeah~!
Waah~!

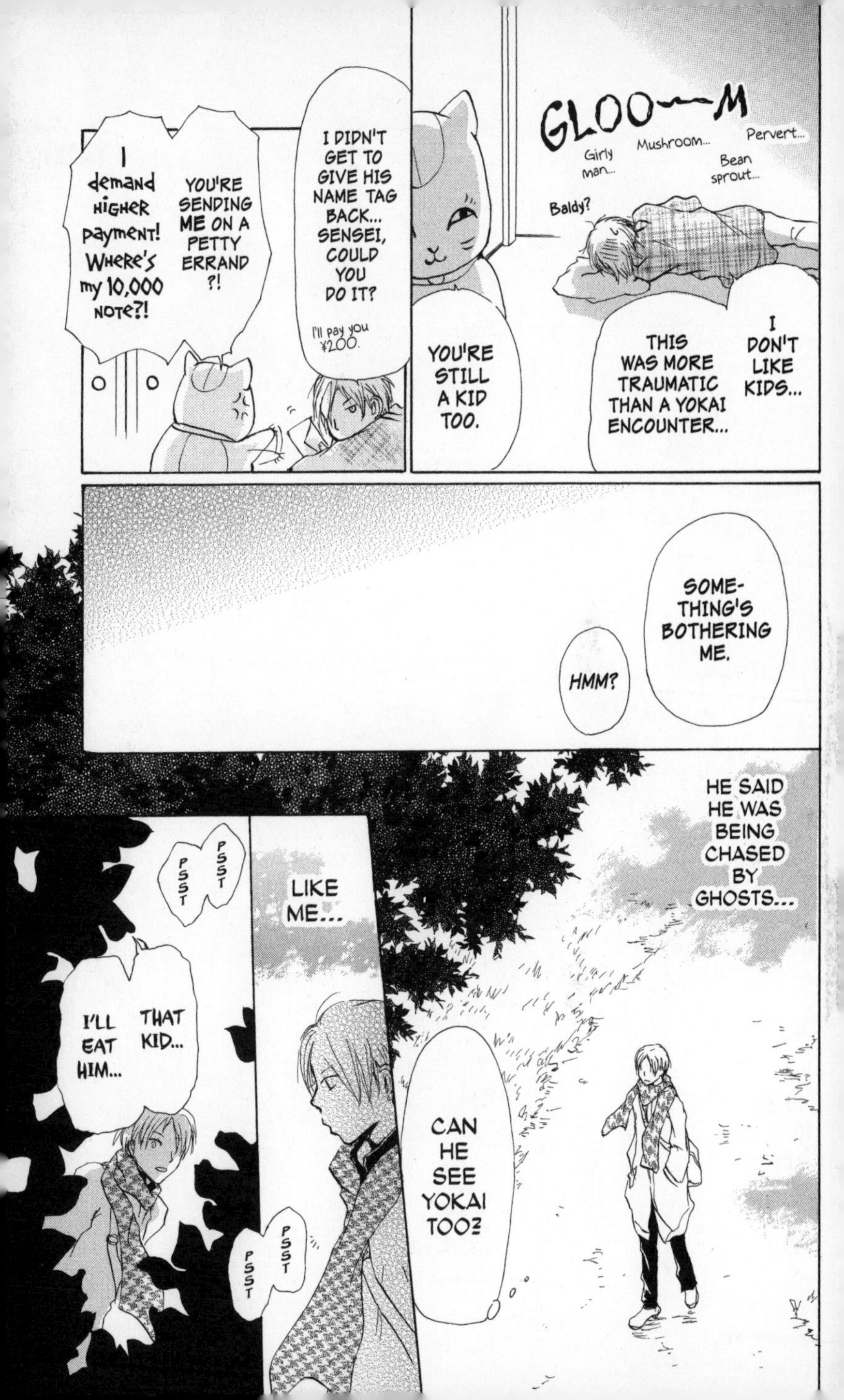
GLOO—M
Girly man...
Mushroom...
Pervert...
Bean sprout...
Baldy?
I DON'T LIKE KIDS...
THIS WAS MORE TRAUMATIC THAN A YOKAI ENCOUNTER...
YOU'RE STILL A KID TOO.
I DIDN'T GET TO GIVE HIS NAME TAG BACK... SENSEI, COULD YOU DO IT?
I'll pay you ¥200.
YOU'RE SENDING ME ON A PETTY ERRAND?!
I demand higher payment! Where's my 10,000 note?!
SOME-THING'S BOTHERING ME.
HMM?
HE SAID HE WAS BEING CHASED BY GHOSTS...
LIKE ME...
CAN HE SEE YOKAI TOO?
PSST PSST
THAT KID...
I'LL EAT HIM...
PSST PSST

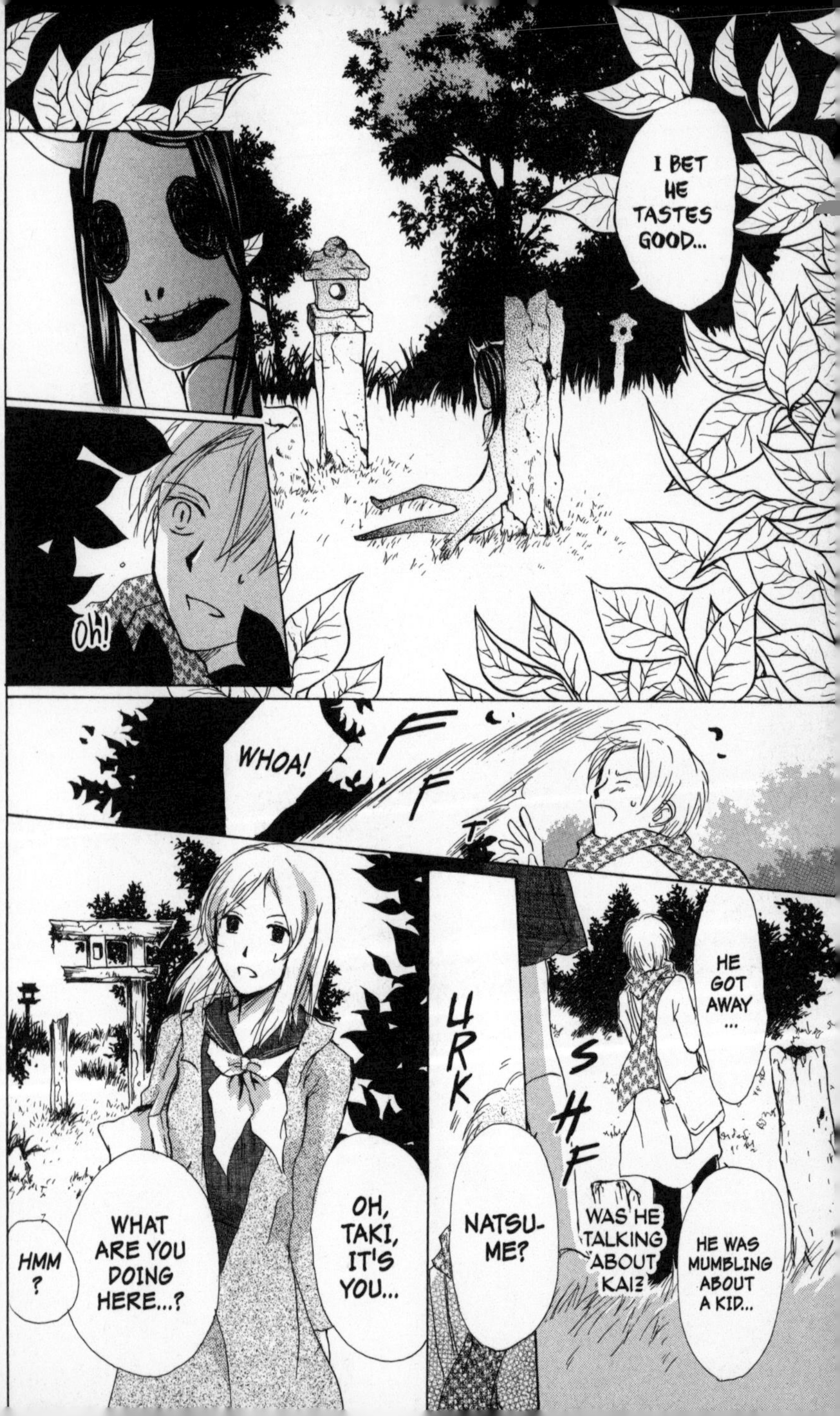
I BET HE TASTES GOOD...
Oh!
WHOA!
FFT
HE GOT AWAY ...
HE WAS MUMBLING ABOUT A KID...
WAS HE TALKING ABOUT KAI?
SHF
URK
NATSU-ME?
OH, TAKI, IT'S YOU...
WHAT ARE YOU DOING HERE...?
HMM ?

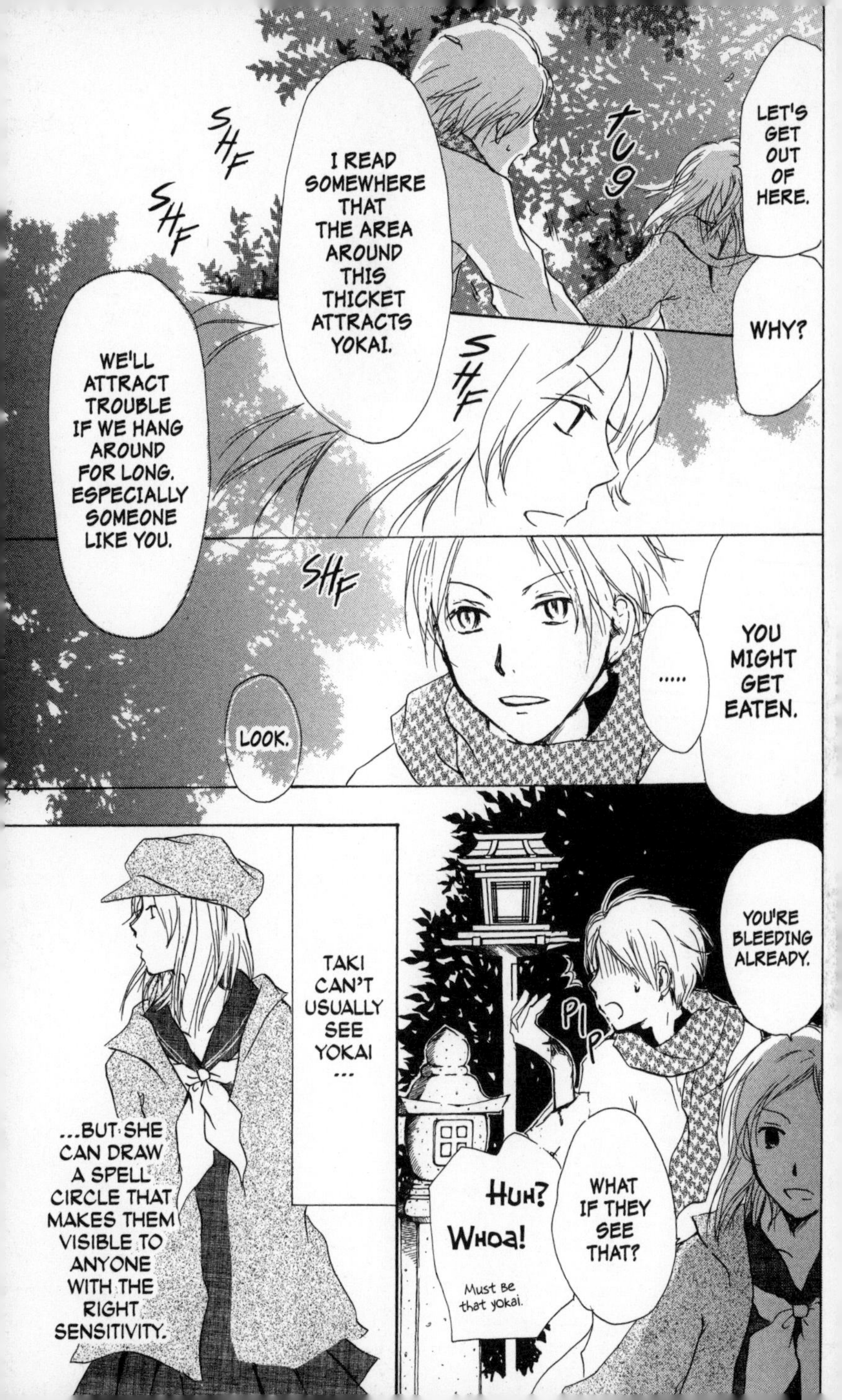
LET'S GET OUT OF HERE.
TUG
I READ SOMEWHERE THAT THE AREA AROUND THIS THICKET ATTRACTS YOKAI.
SHF
SHF
WHY?
SHF
WE'LL ATTRACT TROUBLE IF WE HANG AROUND FOR LONG. ESPECIALLY SOMEONE LIKE YOU.
YOU MIGHT GET EATEN.
.....
SHF
LOOK.
YOU'RE BLEEDING ALREADY.
PIP
WHAT IF THEY SEE THAT?
HUH?
WHOA!
Must be that yokai.
TAKI CAN'T USUALLY SEE YOKAI...
...BUT SHE CAN DRAW A SPELL CIRCLE THAT MAKES THEM VISIBLE TO ANYONE WITH THE RIGHT SENSITIVITY.

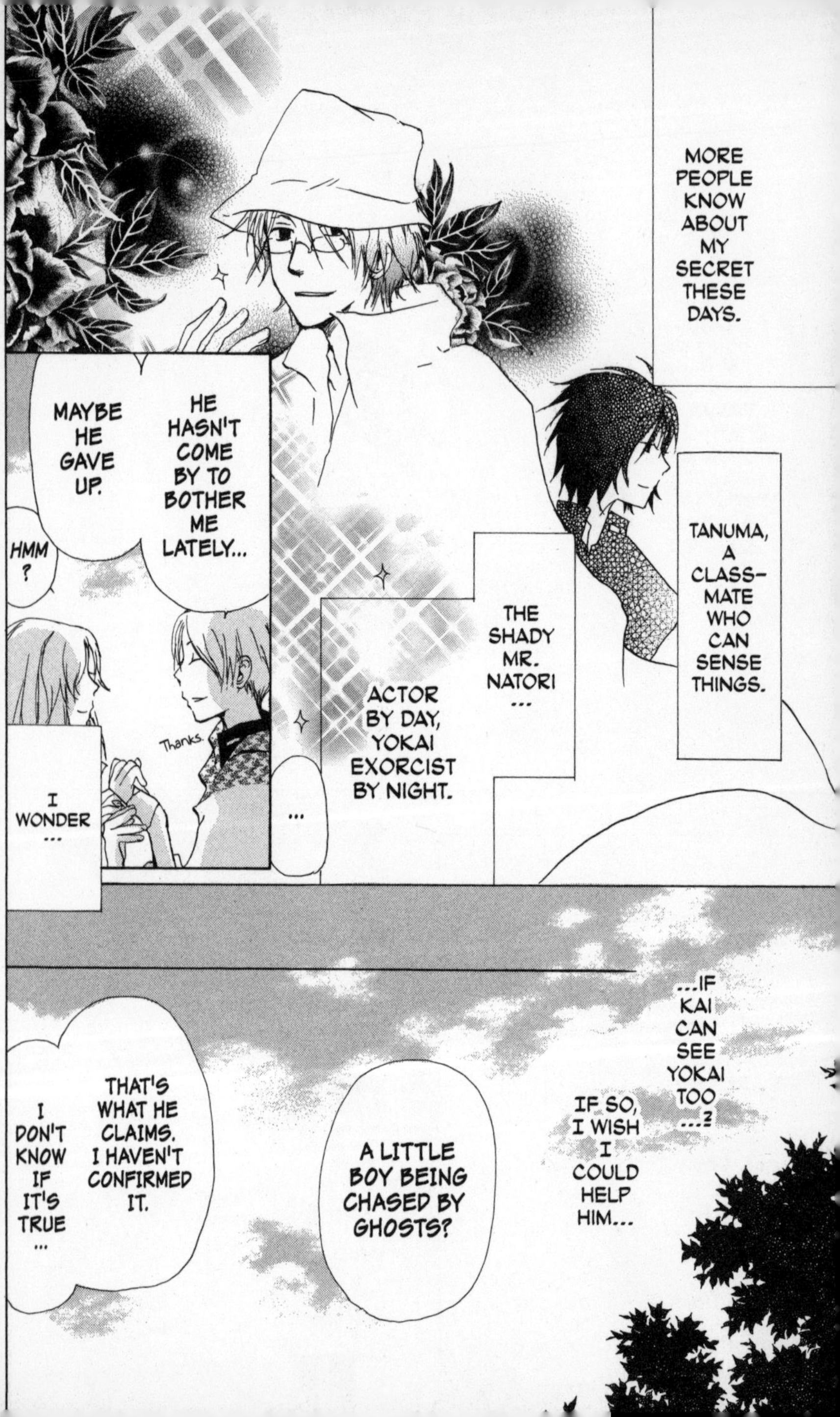
MORE PEOPLE KNOW ABOUT MY SECRET THESE DAYS.
TANUMA, A CLASSMATE WHO CAN SENSE THINGS.
THE SHADY MR. NATORI...
ACTOR BY DAY, YOKAI EXORCIST BY NIGHT.
...
HE HASN'T COME BY TO BOTHER ME LATELY...
MAYBE HE GAVE UP.
HMM?
Thanks.
I WONDER...
...IF KAI CAN SEE YOKAI TOO...?
IF SO, I WISH I COULD HELP HIM...
A LITTLE BOY BEING CHASED BY GHOSTS?
THAT'S WHAT HE CLAIMS. I HAVEN'T CONFIRMED IT.
I DON'T KNOW IF IT'S TRUE...

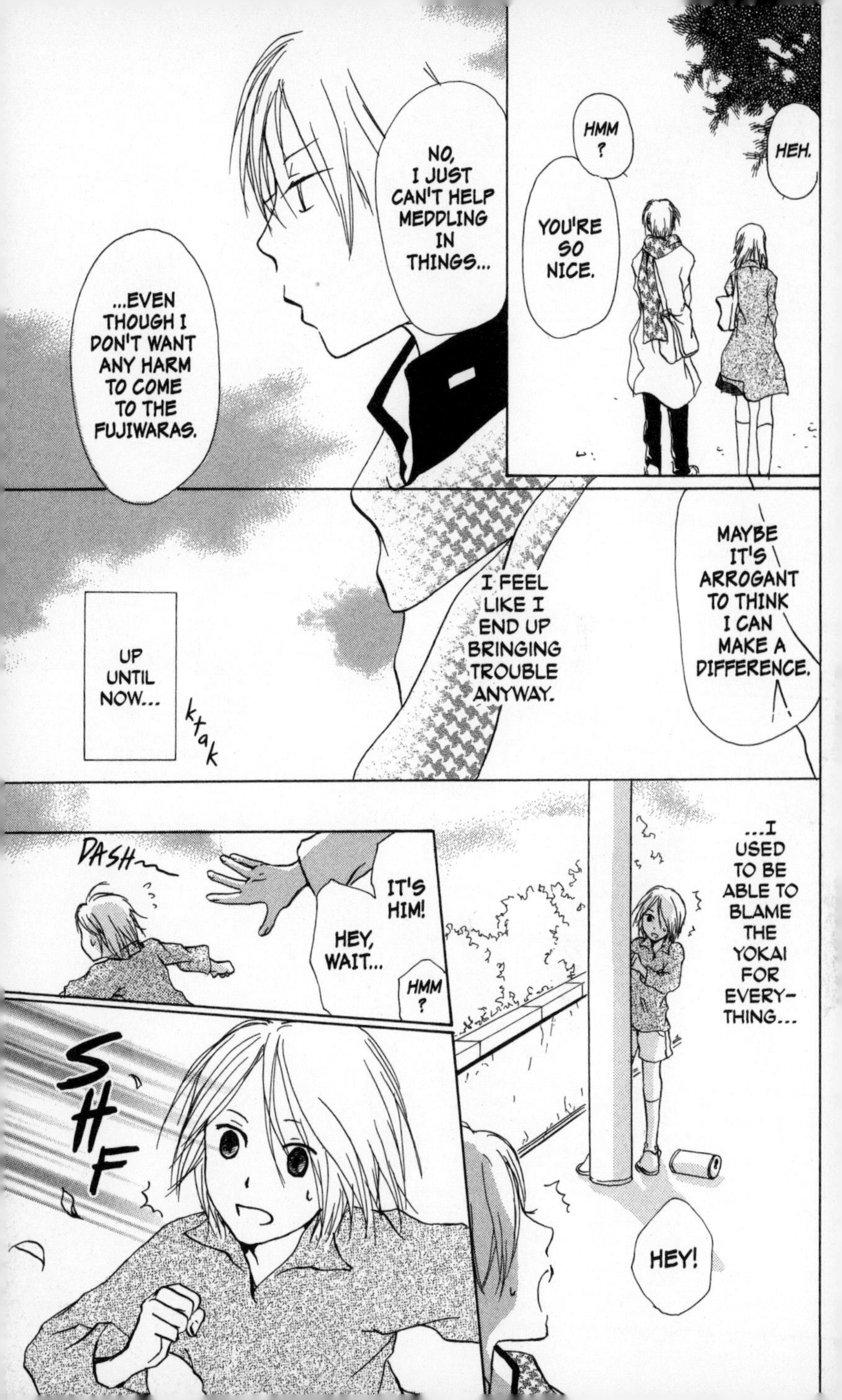
HEH.
HMM ?
YOU'RE SO NICE.
NO, I JUST CAN'T HELP MEDDLING IN THINGS...
...EVEN THOUGH I DON'T WANT ANY HARM TO COME TO THE FUJIWARAS.
MAYBE IT'S ARROGANT TO THINK I CAN MAKE A DIFFERENCE.
I FEEL LIKE I END UP BRINGING TROUBLE ANYWAY.
UP UNTIL NOW...
ktak
...I USED TO BE ABLE TO BLAME THE YOKAI FOR EVERYTHING...
HEY!
IT'S HIM!
HEY, WAIT...
DASH
HMM ?
SHF

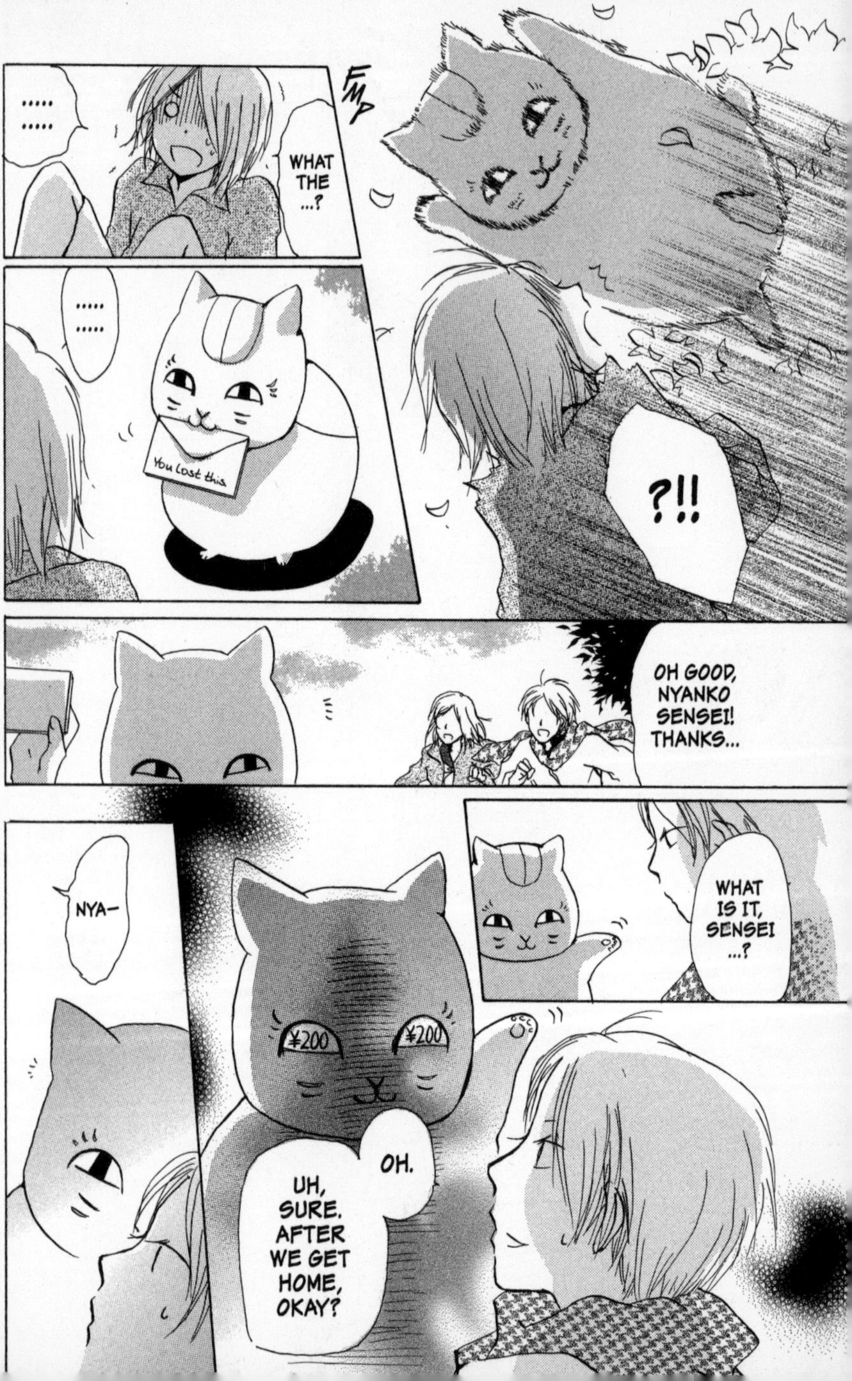
FMP
?!!
WHAT THE ...?
....
....
You lost this
OH GOOD, NYANKO SENSEI! THANKS...
WHAT IS IT, SENSEI ...?
NYA-
¥200
¥200
OH.
UH, SURE. AFTER WE GET HOME, OKAY?

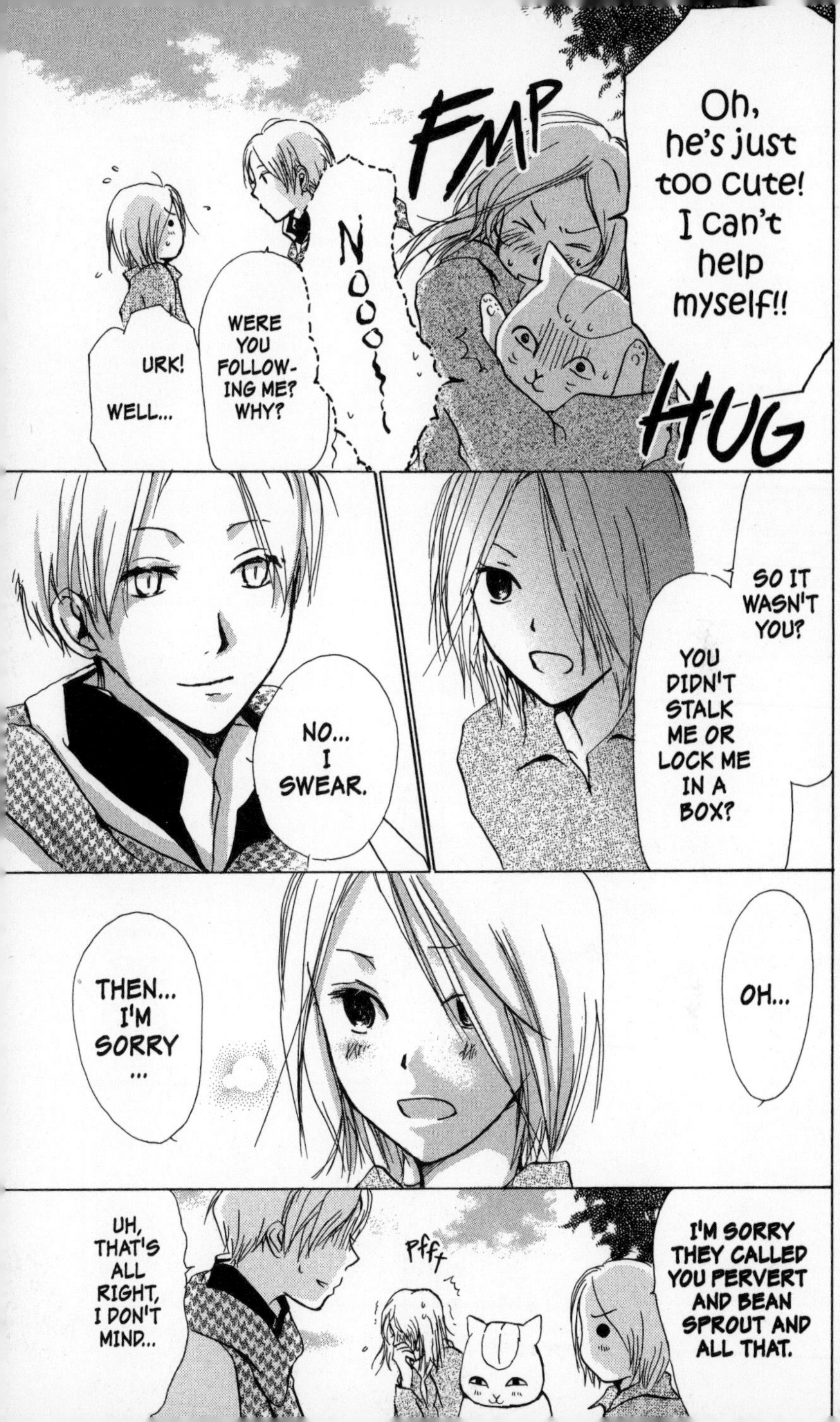

Oh, he's just too cute! I can't help myself!!
FMP
HUG
NOOOO
WERE YOU FOLLOW-ING ME? WHY?
URK! WELL...
SO IT WASN'T YOU?
YOU DIDN'T STALK ME OR LOCK ME IN A BOX?
NO... I SWEAR.
OH...
THEN... I'M SORRY ...
I'M SORRY THEY CALLED YOU PERVERT AND BEAN SPROUT AND ALL THAT.
Pfft
UH, THAT'S ALL RIGHT, I DON'T MIND...

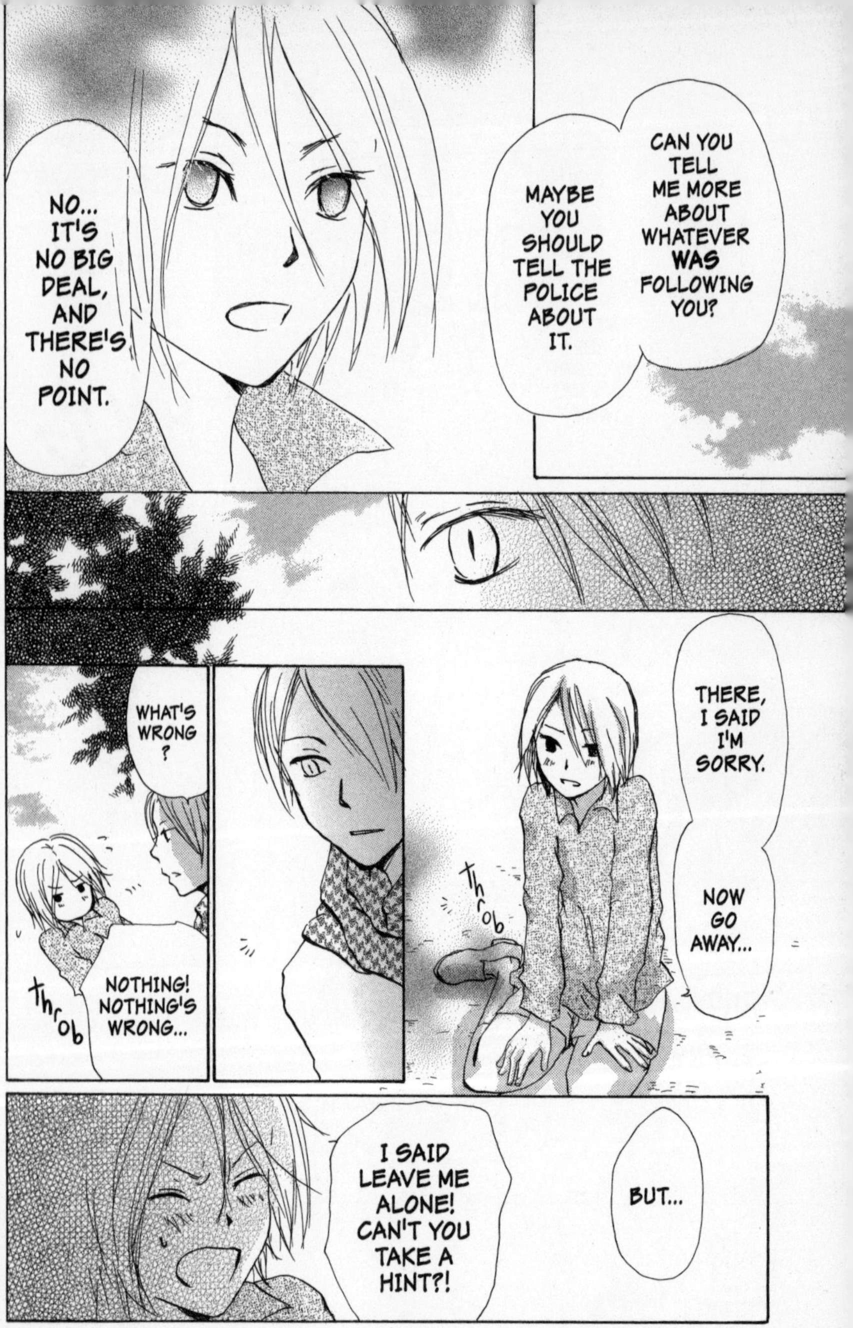
CAN YOU TELL ME MORE ABOUT WHATEVER WAS FOLLOWING YOU?
MAYBE YOU SHOULD TELL THE POLICE ABOUT IT.
NO... IT'S NO BIG DEAL, AND THERE'S NO POINT.
THERE, I SAID I'M SORRY.
NOW GO AWAY...
throb
WHAT'S WRONG?
NOTHING! NOTHING'S WRONG...
throb
BUT...
I SAID LEAVE ME ALONE! CAN'T YOU TAKE A HINT?!

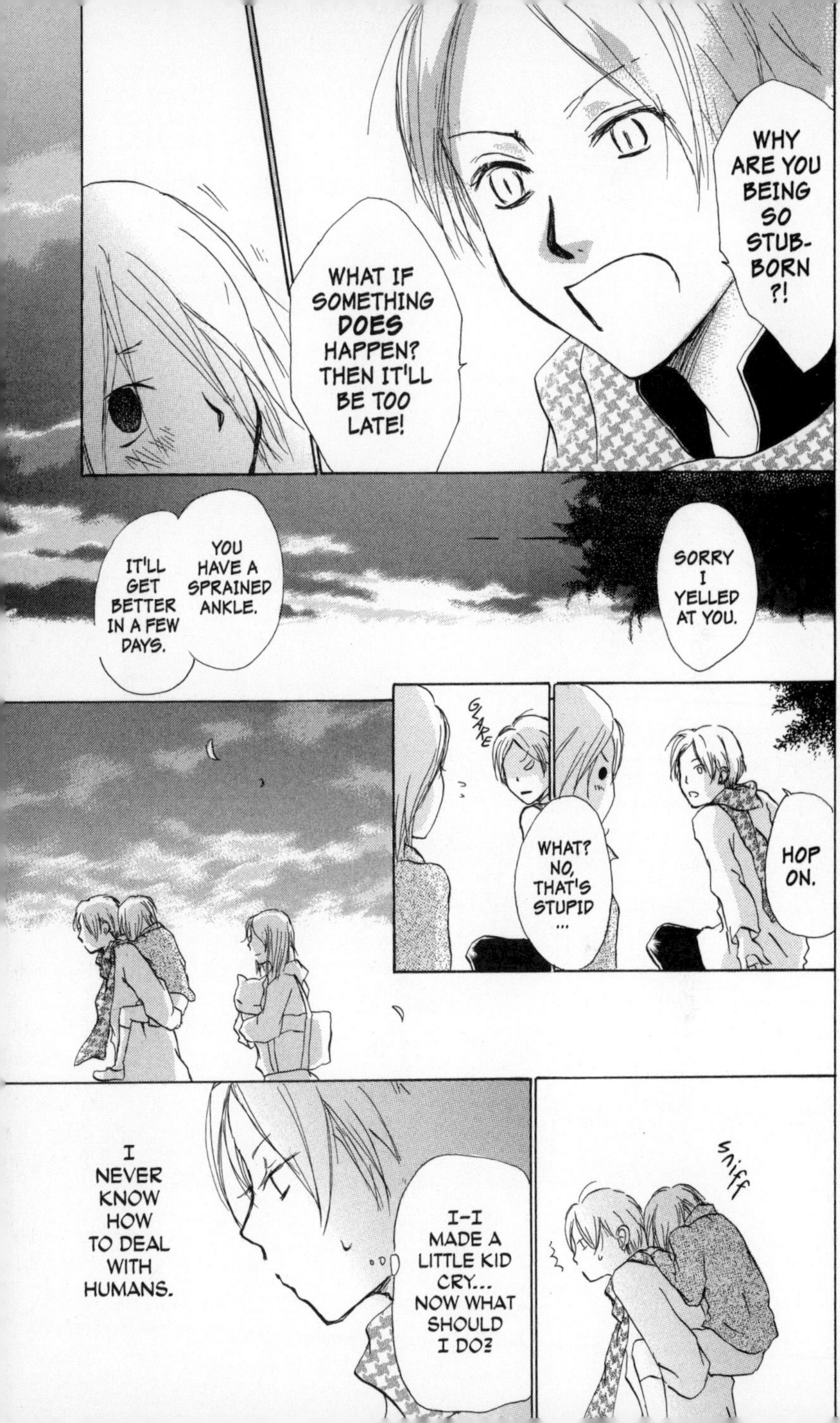
WHY ARE YOU BEING SO STUBBORN?!
WHAT IF SOMETHING **DOES** HAPPEN? THEN IT'LL BE TOO LATE!
SORRY I YELLED AT YOU.
YOU HAVE A SPRAINED ANKLE.
IT'LL GET BETTER IN A FEW DAYS.
HOP ON.
GLARE
WHAT? NO, THAT'S STUPID...
sniff
I-I MADE A LITTLE KID CRY... NOW WHAT SHOULD I DO?
I NEVER KNOW HOW TO DEAL WITH HUMANS.

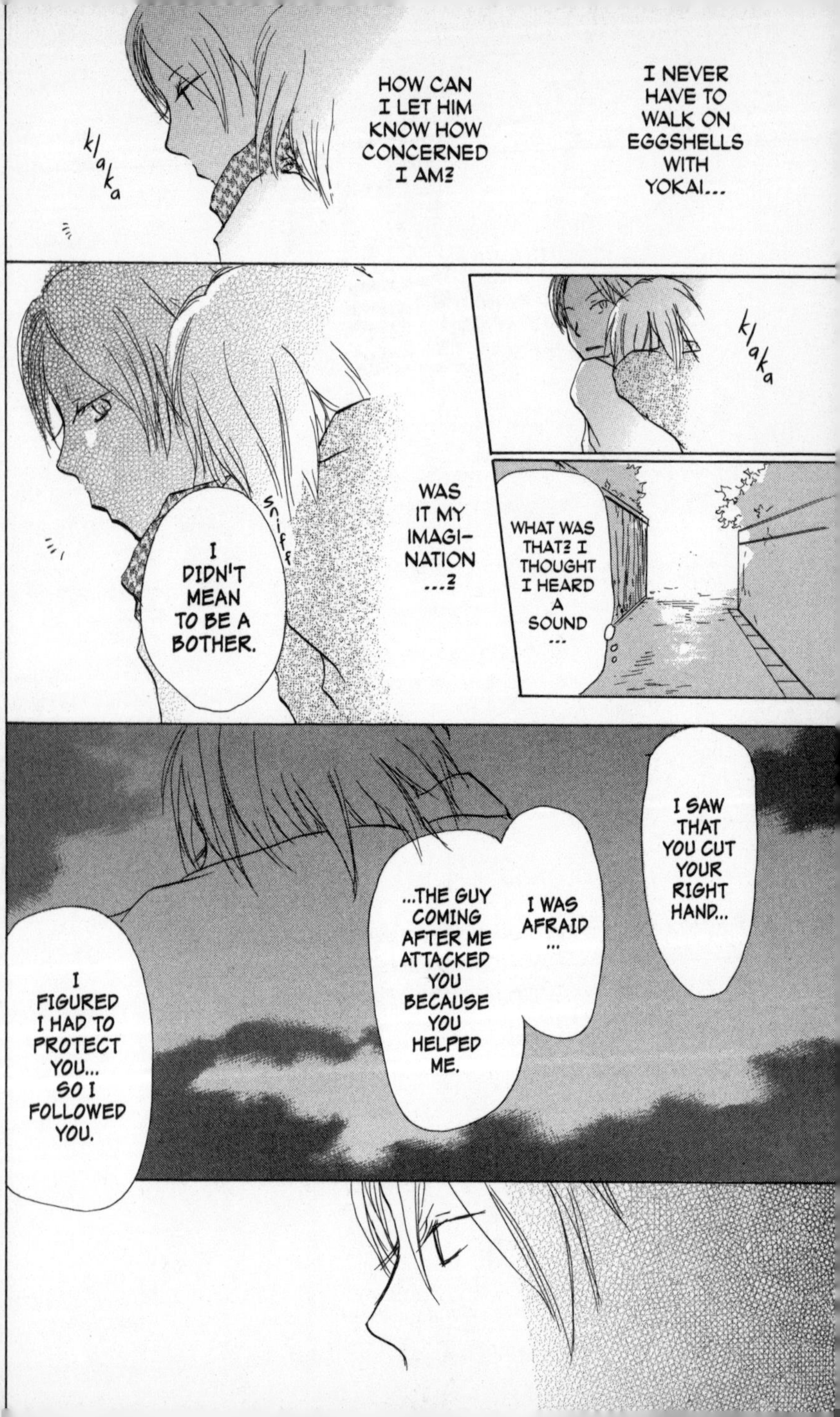
I NEVER HAVE TO WALK ON EGGSHELLS WITH YOKAI...
HOW CAN I LET HIM KNOW HOW CONCERNED I AM?
klaka
klaka
WHAT WAS THAT? I THOUGHT I HEARD A SOUND...
WAS IT MY IMAGINATION...?
sniff
I DIDN'T MEAN TO BE A BOTHER.
I SAW THAT YOU CUT YOUR RIGHT HAND...
I WAS AFRAID...
...THE GUY COMING AFTER ME ATTACKED YOU BECAUSE YOU HELPED ME.
I FIGURED I HAD TO PROTECT YOU... SO I FOLLOWED YOU.

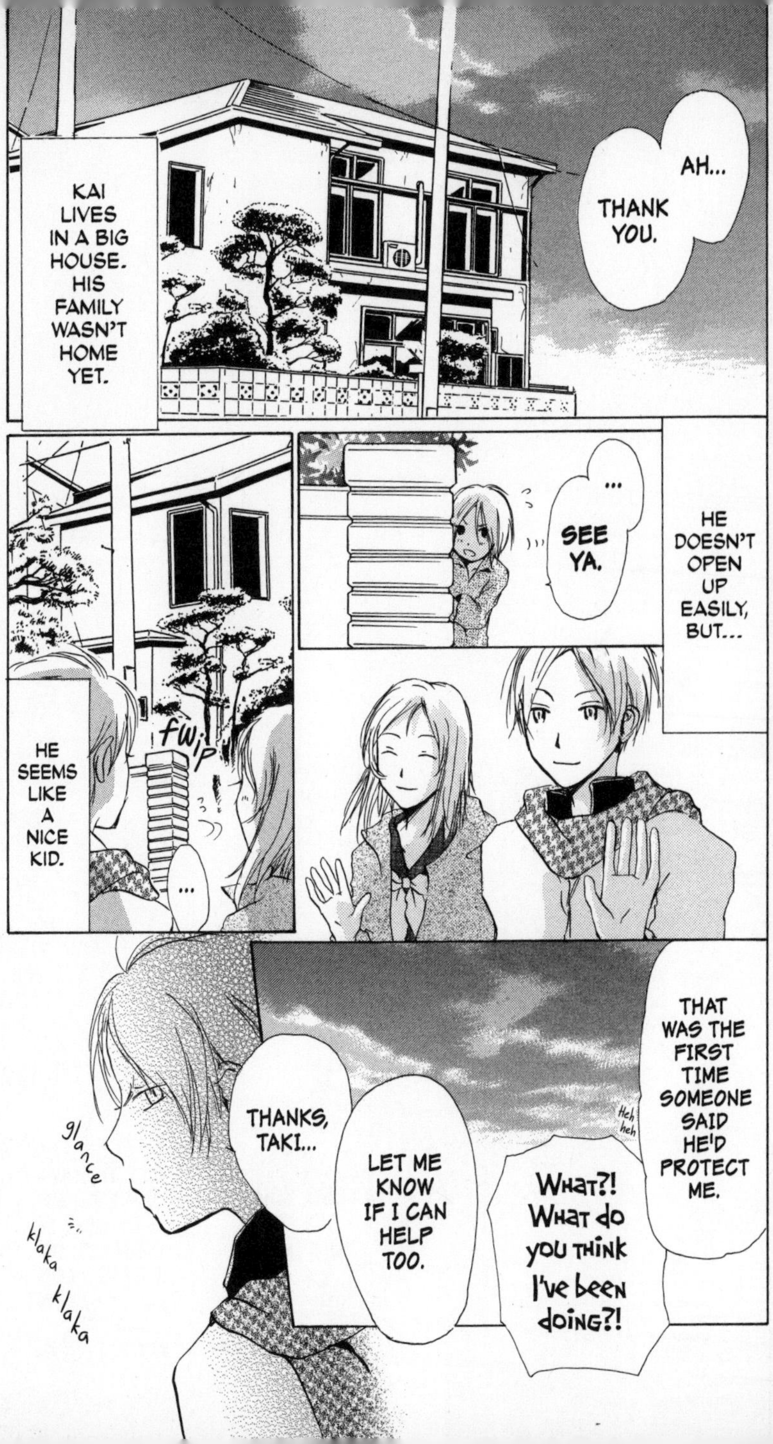
AH...
THANK YOU.
KAI LIVES IN A BIG HOUSE. HIS FAMILY WASN'T HOME YET.
...
SEE YA.
HE DOESN'T OPEN UP EASILY, BUT...
HE SEEMS LIKE A NICE KID.
fwip
...
THAT WAS THE FIRST TIME SOMEONE SAID HE'D PROTECT ME.
Heh heh
What?! What do you think I've been doing?!
LET ME KNOW IF I CAN HELP TOO.
THANKS, TAKI...
glance
klaka klaka

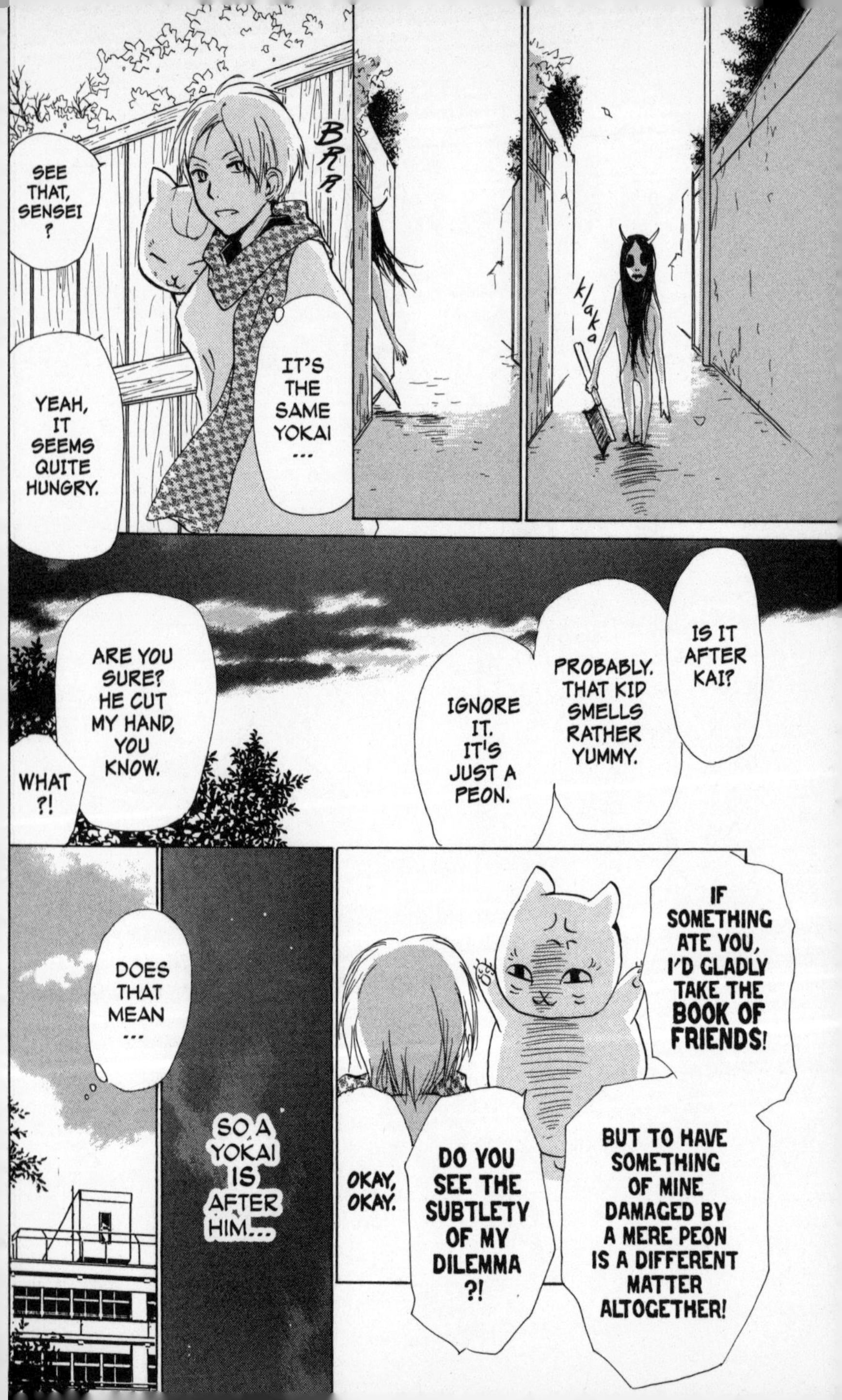

klaka
BRR
SEE THAT, SENSEI?
IT'S THE SAME YOKAI...
YEAH, IT SEEMS QUITE HUNGRY.
IS IT AFTER KAI?
PROBABLY. THAT KID SMELLS RATHER YUMMY.
IGNORE IT. IT'S JUST A PEON.
ARE YOU SURE? HE CUT MY HAND, YOU KNOW.
WHAT?!
IF SOMETHING ATE YOU, I'D GLADLY TAKE THE BOOK OF FRIENDS!
BUT TO HAVE SOMETHING OF MINE DAMAGED BY A MERE PEON IS A DIFFERENT MATTER ALTOGETHER!
DO YOU SEE THE SUBTLETY OF MY DILEMMA?!
OKAY, OKAY.
SO A YOKAI IS AFTER HIM...
DOES THAT MEAN...

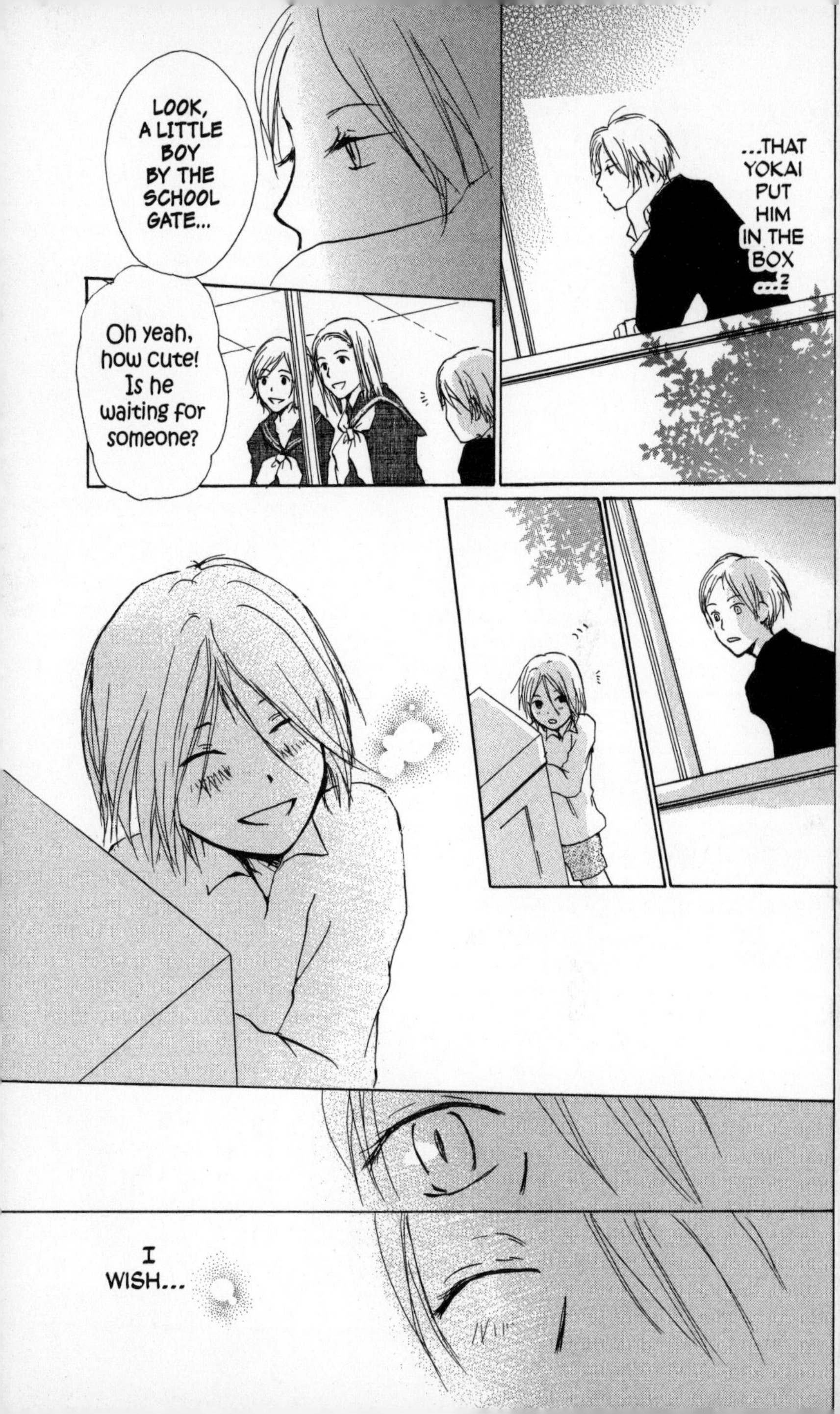
...THAT YOKAI PUT HIM IN THE BOX ...?
LOOK, A LITTLE BOY BY THE SCHOOL GATE...
Oh yeah, how cute! Is he waiting for someone?
I WISH...

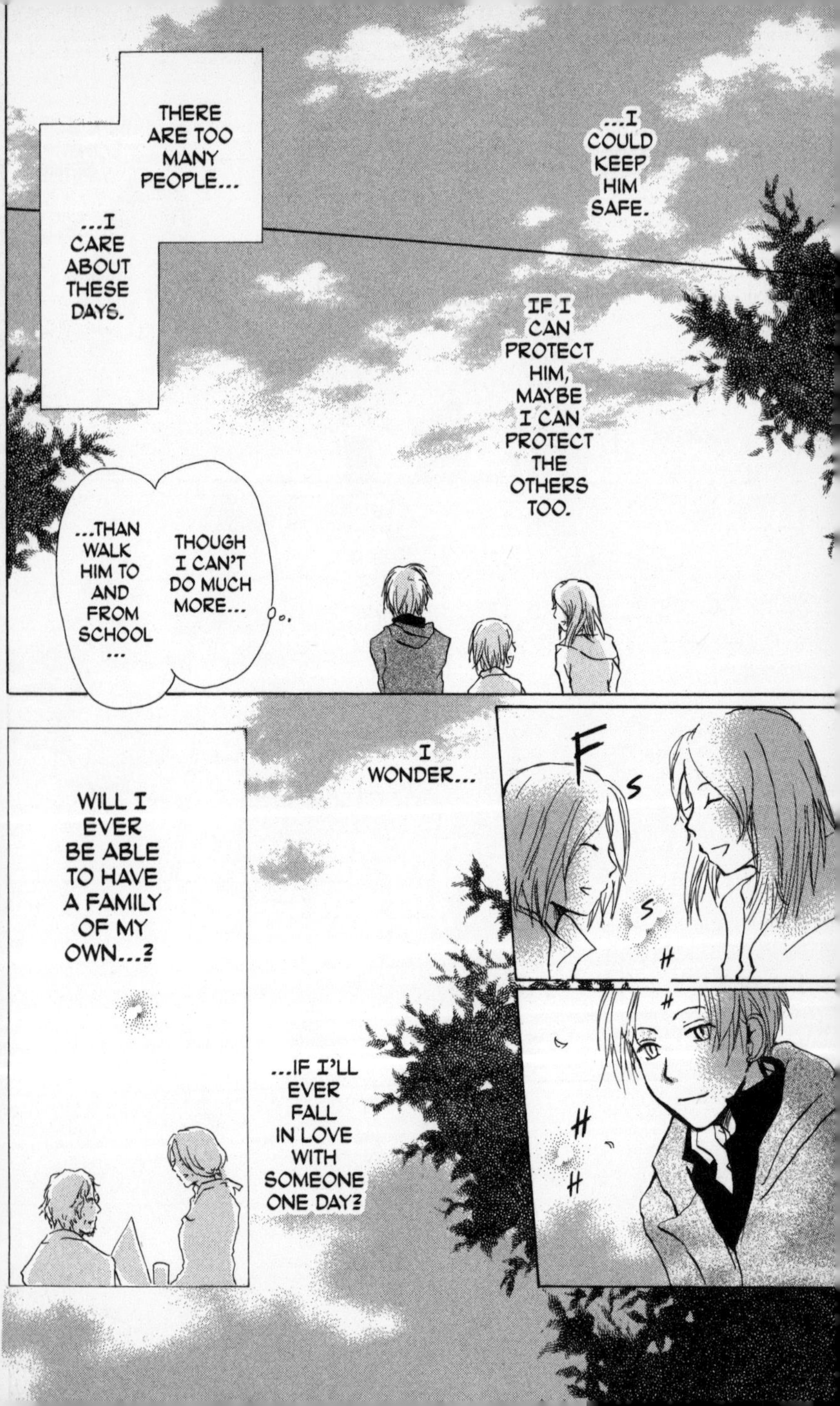
...I COULD KEEP HIM SAFE.
IF I CAN PROTECT HIM, MAYBE I CAN PROTECT THE OTHERS TOO.
THERE ARE TOO MANY PEOPLE...
...I CARE ABOUT THESE DAYS.
THOUGH I CAN'T DO MUCH MORE...
...THAN WALK HIM TO AND FROM SCHOOL...
FSSHHHHH
I WONDER...
...IF I'LL EVER FALL IN LOVE WITH SOMEONE ONE DAY?
WILL I EVER BE ABLE TO HAVE A FAMILY OF MY OWN...?

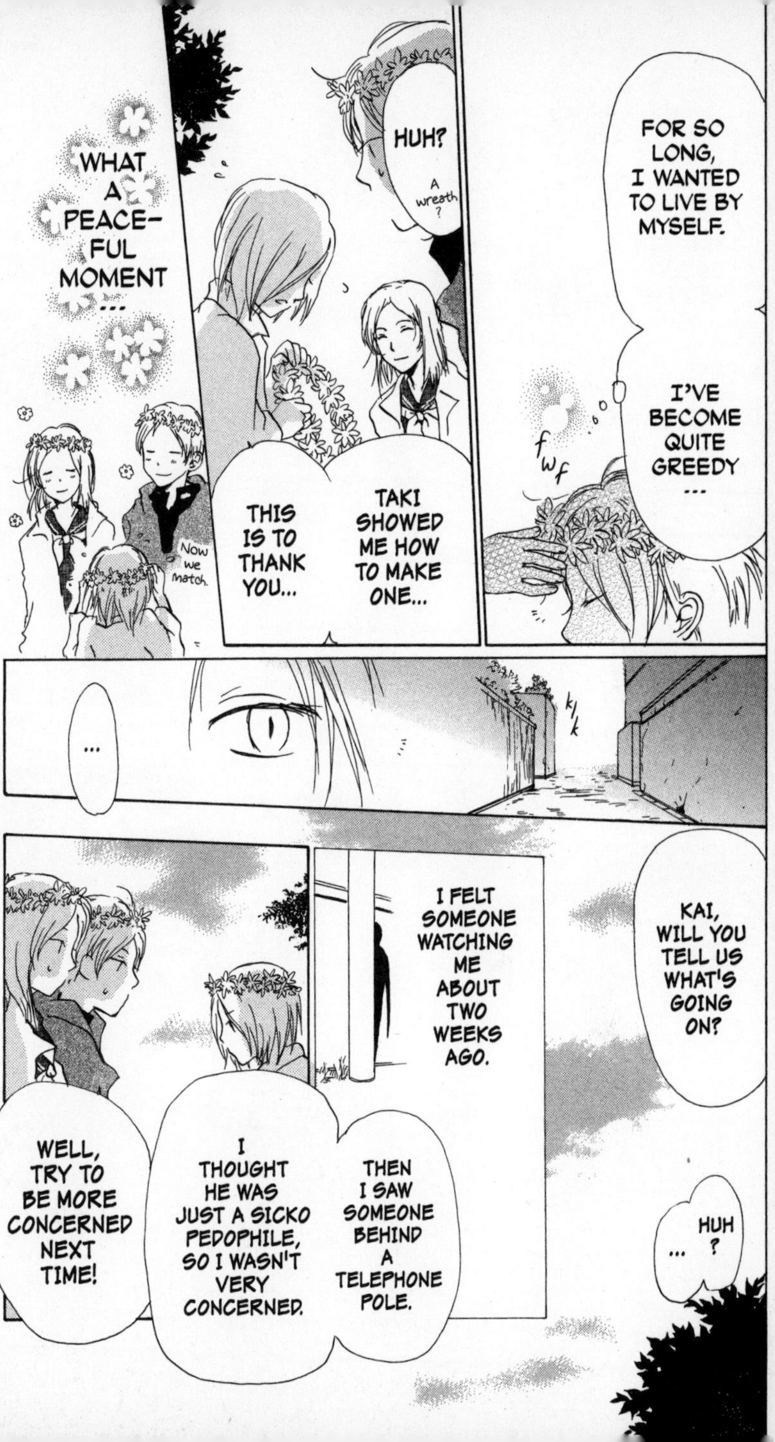
FOR SO LONG, I WANTED TO LIVE BY MYSELF.
I'VE BECOME QUITE GREEDY...
fwf
HUH?
A wreath?
TAKI SHOWED ME HOW TO MAKE ONE...
THIS IS TO THANK YOU...
WHAT A PEACE-FUL MOMENT...
Now we match.
klk
...
KAI, WILL YOU TELL US WHAT'S GOING ON?
...HUH?
I FELT SOMEONE WATCHING ME ABOUT TWO WEEKS AGO.
THEN I SAW SOMEONE BEHIND A TELEPHONE POLE.
I THOUGHT HE WAS JUST A SICKO PEDOPHILE, SO I WASN'T VERY CONCERNED.
WELL, TRY TO BE MORE CONCERNED NEXT TIME!

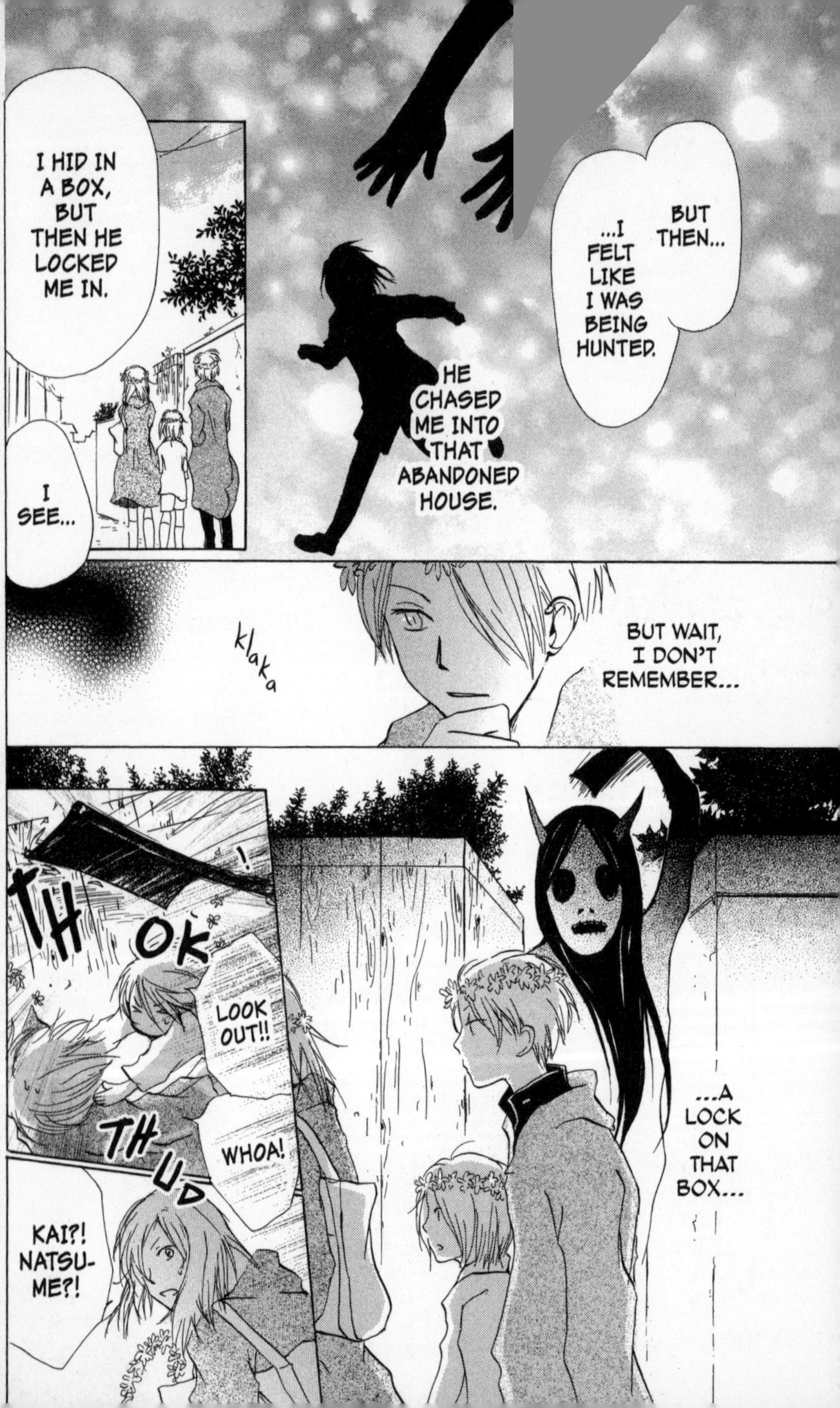
BUT THEN... ...I FELT LIKE I WAS BEING HUNTED.
HE CHASED ME INTO THAT ABANDONED HOUSE.
I HID IN A BOX, BUT THEN HE LOCKED ME IN.
I SEE...
BUT WAIT, I DON'T REMEMBER...
klaka
...A LOCK ON THAT BOX...
!
THOK
LOOK OUT!!
THUD
WHOA!
KAI?! NATSUME?!

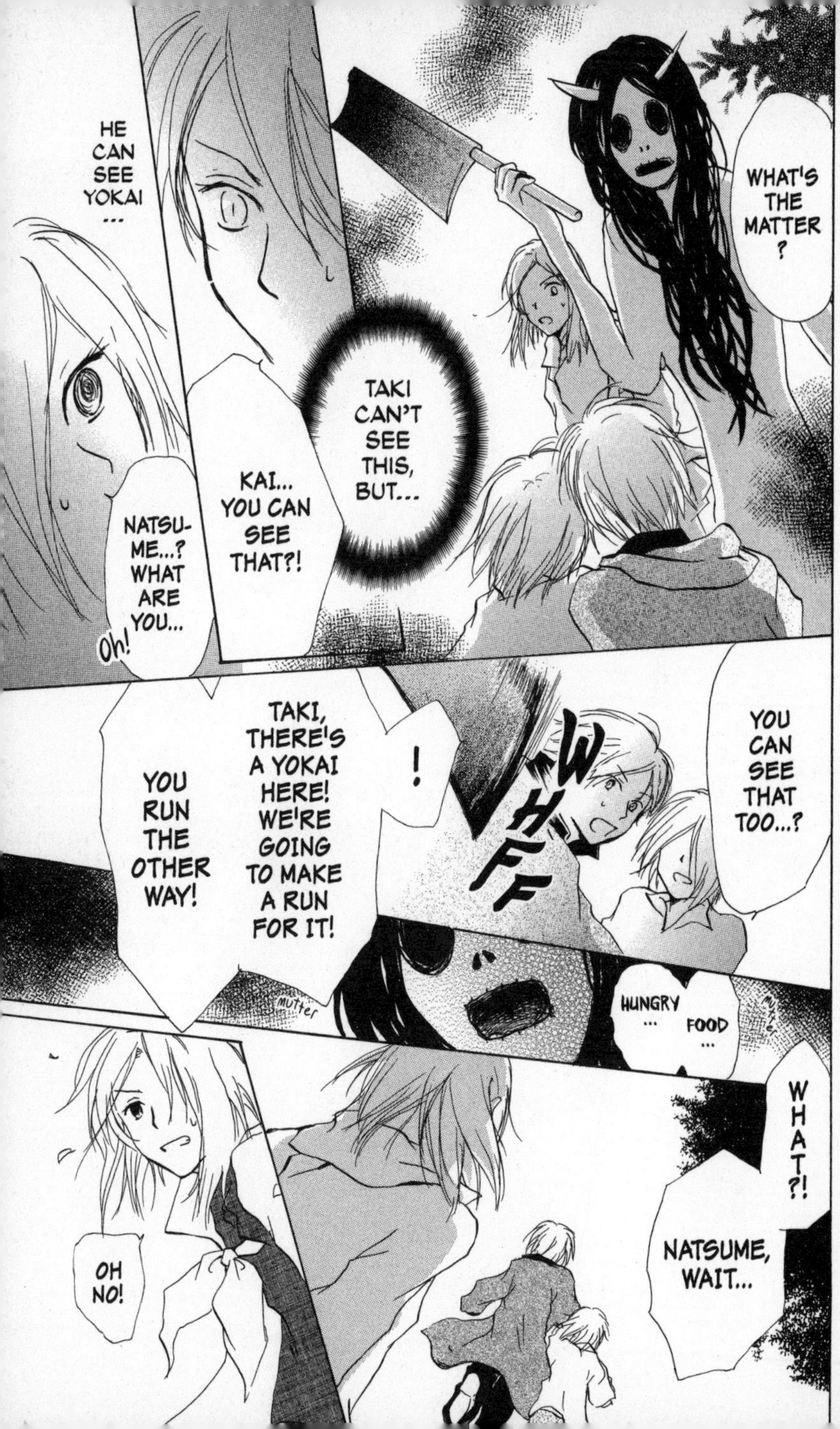
WHAT'S THE MATTER?
TAKI CAN'T SEE THIS, BUT...
HE CAN SEE YOKAI...
KAI... YOU CAN SEE THAT?!
NATSUME...? WHAT ARE YOU...
Oh!
YOU CAN SEE THAT TOO...?
WHFF
!
TAKI, THERE'S A YOKAI HERE! WE'RE GOING TO MAKE A RUN FOR IT!
YOU RUN THE OTHER WAY!
mutter
HUNGRY...
FOOD...
mutter
WHAT?!
NATSUME, WAIT...
OH NO!

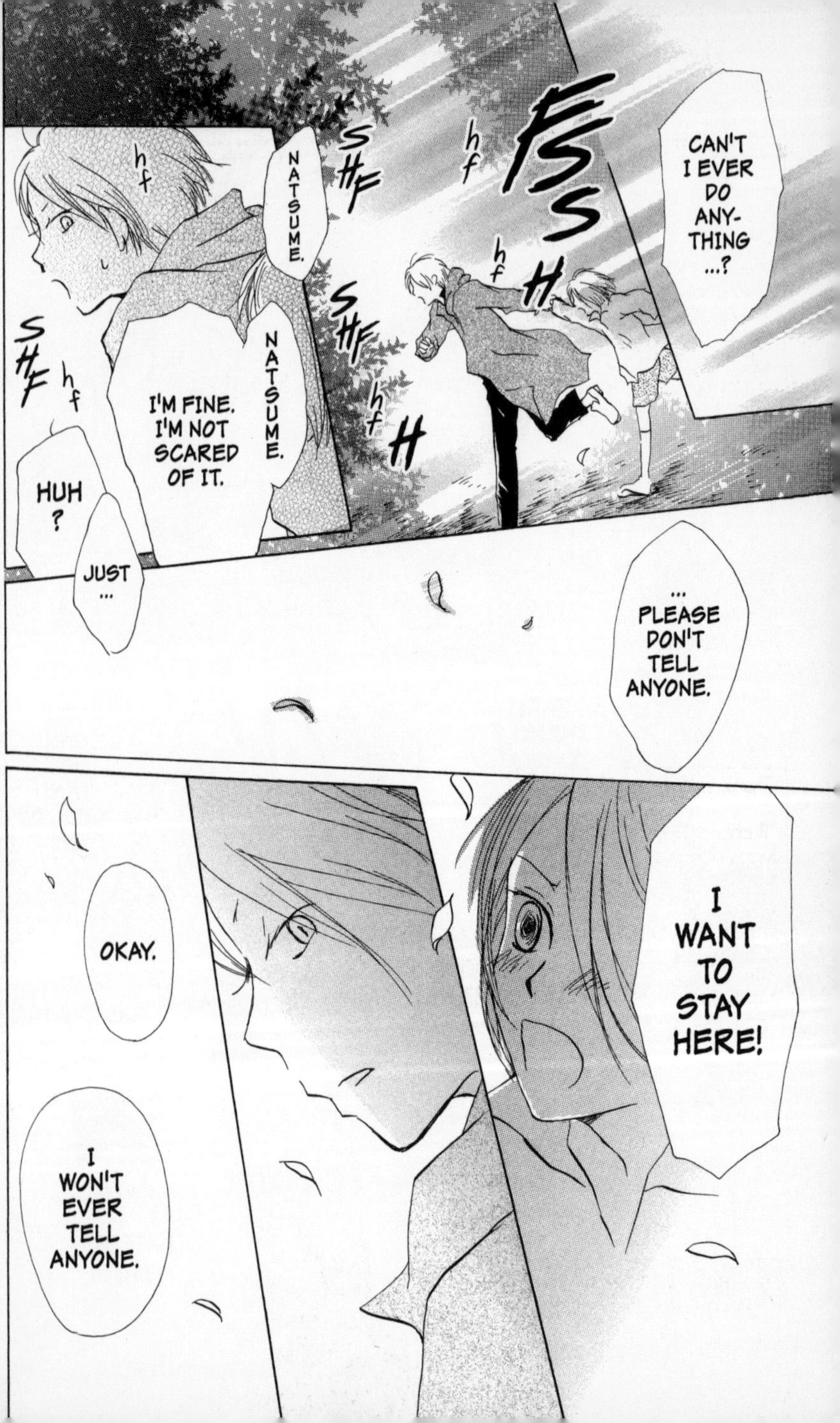
CAN'T I EVER DO ANY-THING...?
FSSH
hf
hf
SHF
NATSUME.
SHF
hf
H
NATSUME.
I'M FINE. I'M NOT SCARED OF IT.
hf
SHF
hf
HUH?
JUST...
...PLEASE DON'T TELL ANYONE.
I WANT TO STAY HERE!
OKAY.
I WON'T EVER TELL ANYONE.

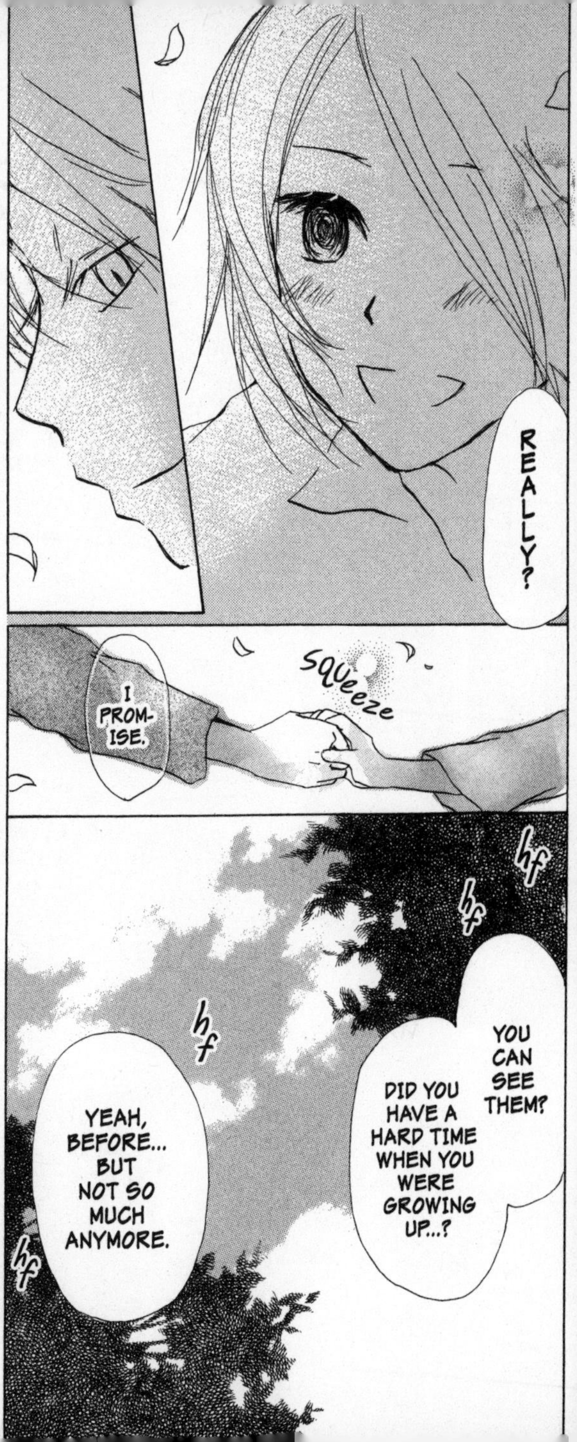
REALLY?
SQUEEZE
I PROMISE.
hf
hf
YOU CAN SEE THEM?
DID YOU HAVE A HARD TIME WHEN YOU WERE GROWING UP...?
hf
YEAH, BEFORE... BUT NOT SO MUCH ANYMORE.
hf

01

Hello, I'm Midorikawa. This is my 14th ever graphic novel, and the sixth for Natsume. I would like to thank the readers who are picking this up for the first time, as well as those who have been with me from the beginning.

I get nervous every time that I personally address the readers in this space. But I also get so happy, I start grinning like a fool. I'm so grateful about this sixth volume. Thank you so much!

There isn't very much new, never-published material in this volume, so I have to apologize to the people who read this first in the magazine, but I hope you enjoy it nevertheless.

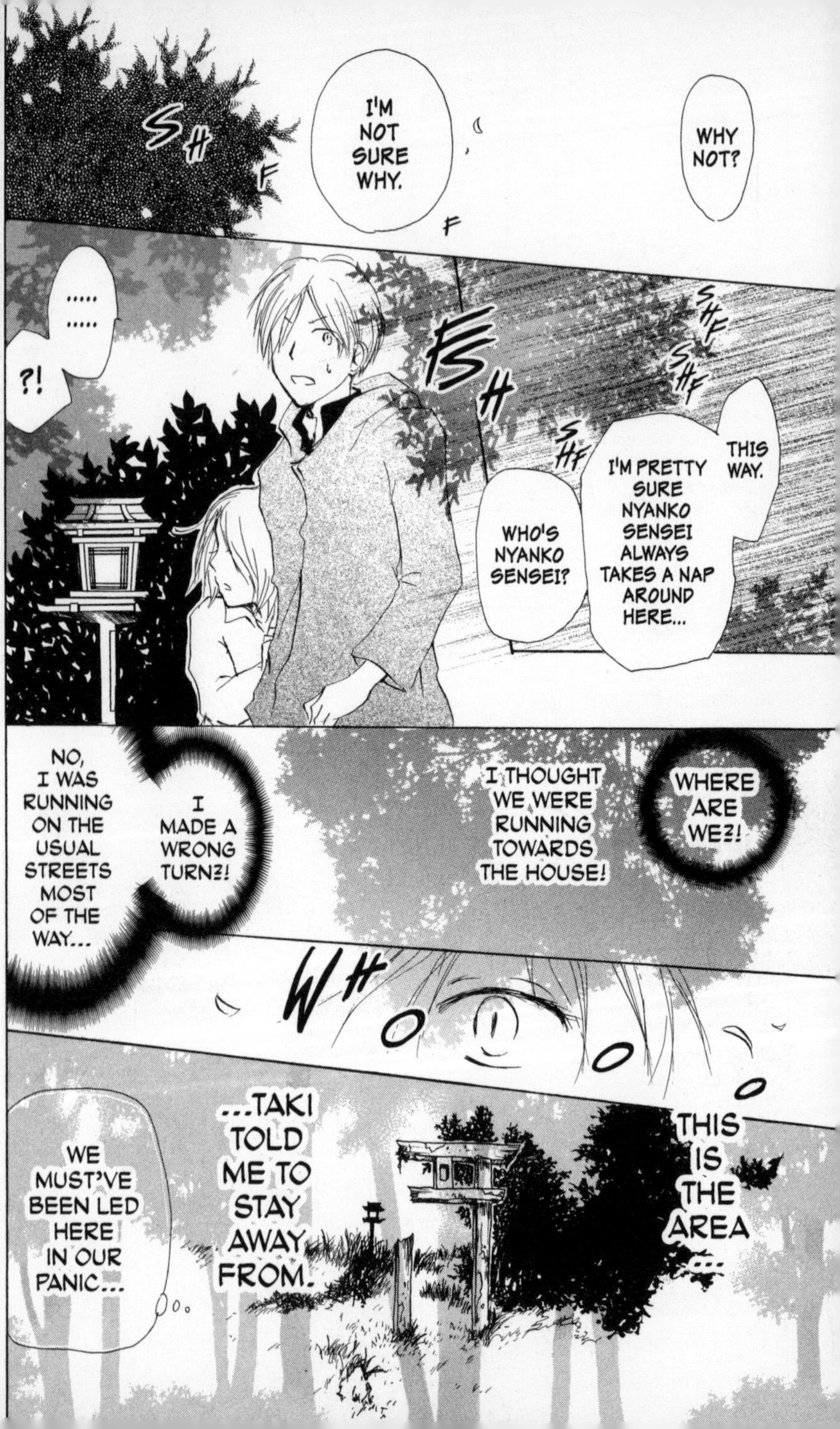
WHY NOT?
I'M NOT SURE WHY.
SHF
F
SHF SHF
THIS WAY.
I'M PRETTY SURE NYANKO SENSEI ALWAYS TAKES A NAP AROUND HERE...
SHF
WHO'S NYANKO SENSEI?
FSH
....
?!
WHERE ARE WE?!
I THOUGHT WE WERE RUNNING TOWARDS THE HOUSE!
I MADE A WRONG TURN?!
NO, I WAS RUNNING ON THE USUAL STREETS MOST OF THE WAY...
WH
THIS IS THE AREA...
...TAKI TOLD ME TO STAY AWAY FROM.
WE MUST'VE BEEN LED HERE IN OUR PANIC...

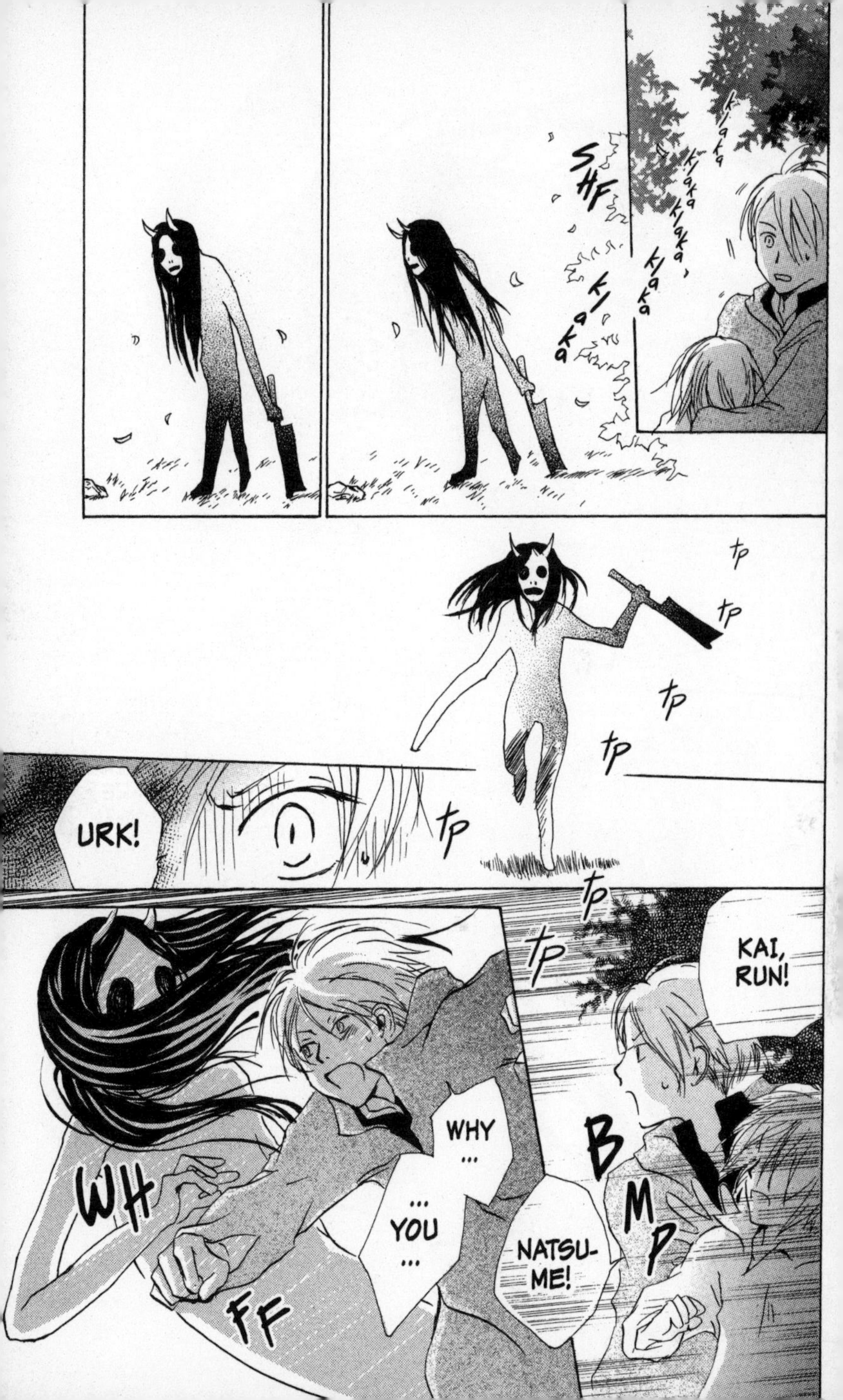
klaka
klaka klaka,
klaka
SHF
klaka
tp
tp
tp
tp
tp
URK!
tp
tp
KAI, RUN!
BMP
NATSU-ME!
WHY ...
... YOU ...
WHFF

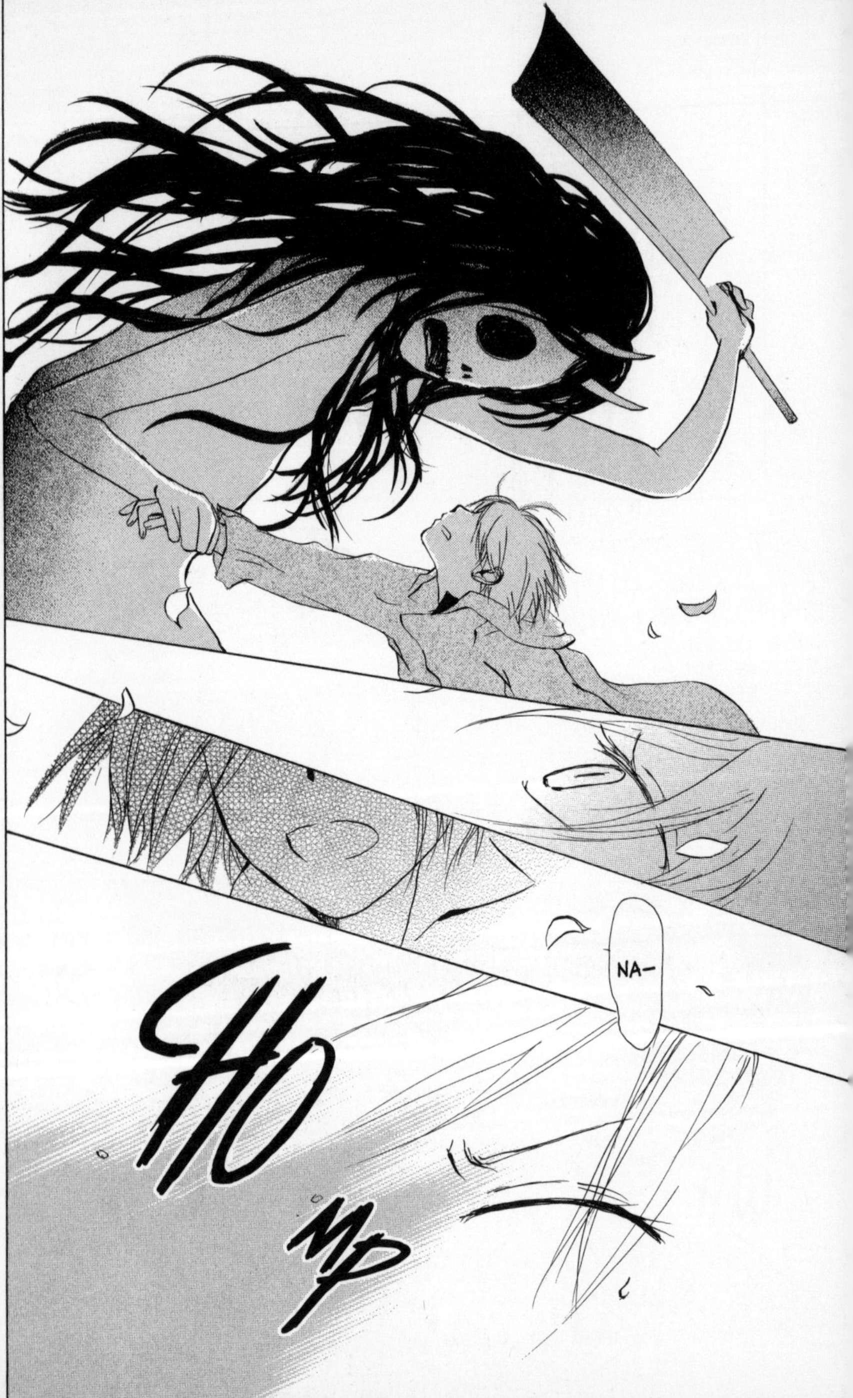
NA–
CHOMP

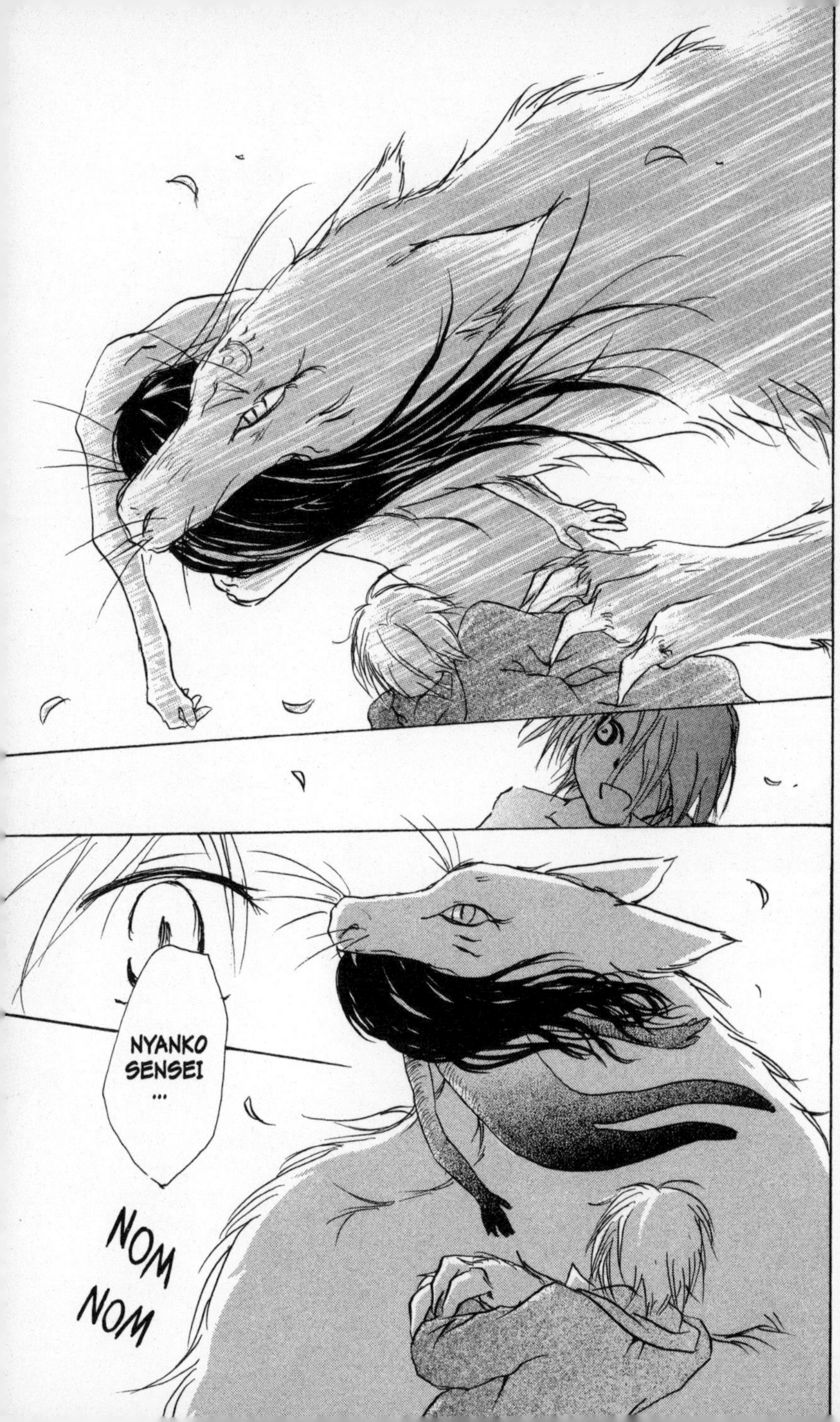
NYANKO SENSEI ...
NOM NOM

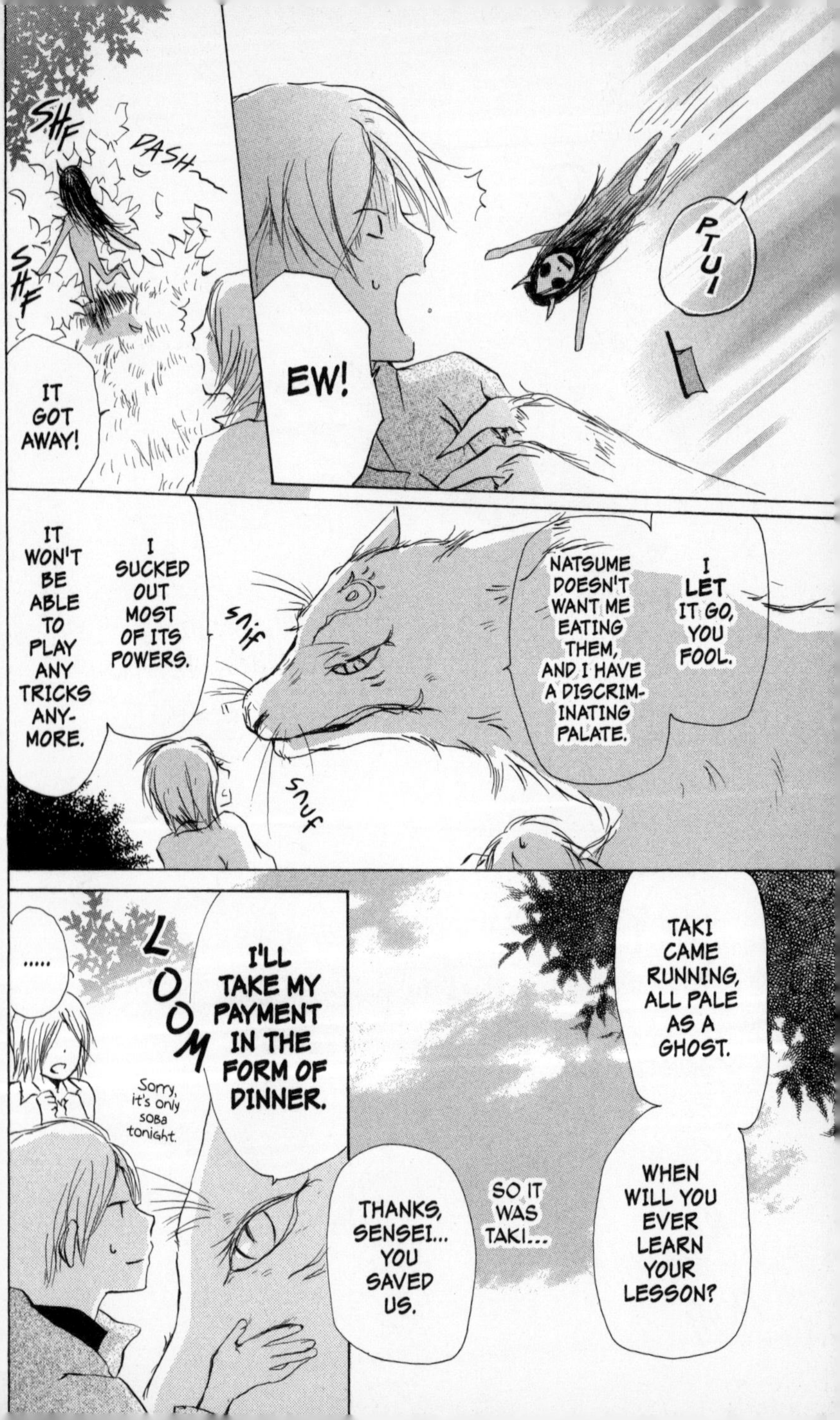
PTUI
EW!
SHF
DASH
SHF
IT GOT AWAY!
I LET IT GO, YOU FOOL.
NATSUME DOESN'T WANT ME EATING THEM, AND I HAVE A DISCRIMINATING PALATE.
sniff
I SUCKED OUT MOST OF ITS POWERS.
IT WON'T BE ABLE TO PLAY ANY TRICKS ANYMORE.
snuf
TAKI CAME RUNNING, ALL PALE AS A GHOST.
WHEN WILL YOU EVER LEARN YOUR LESSON?
SO IT WAS TAKI...
THANKS, SENSEI... YOU SAVED US.
I'LL TAKE MY PAYMENT IN THE FORM OF DINNER.
LOOM
.....
Sorry, it's only soba tonight.

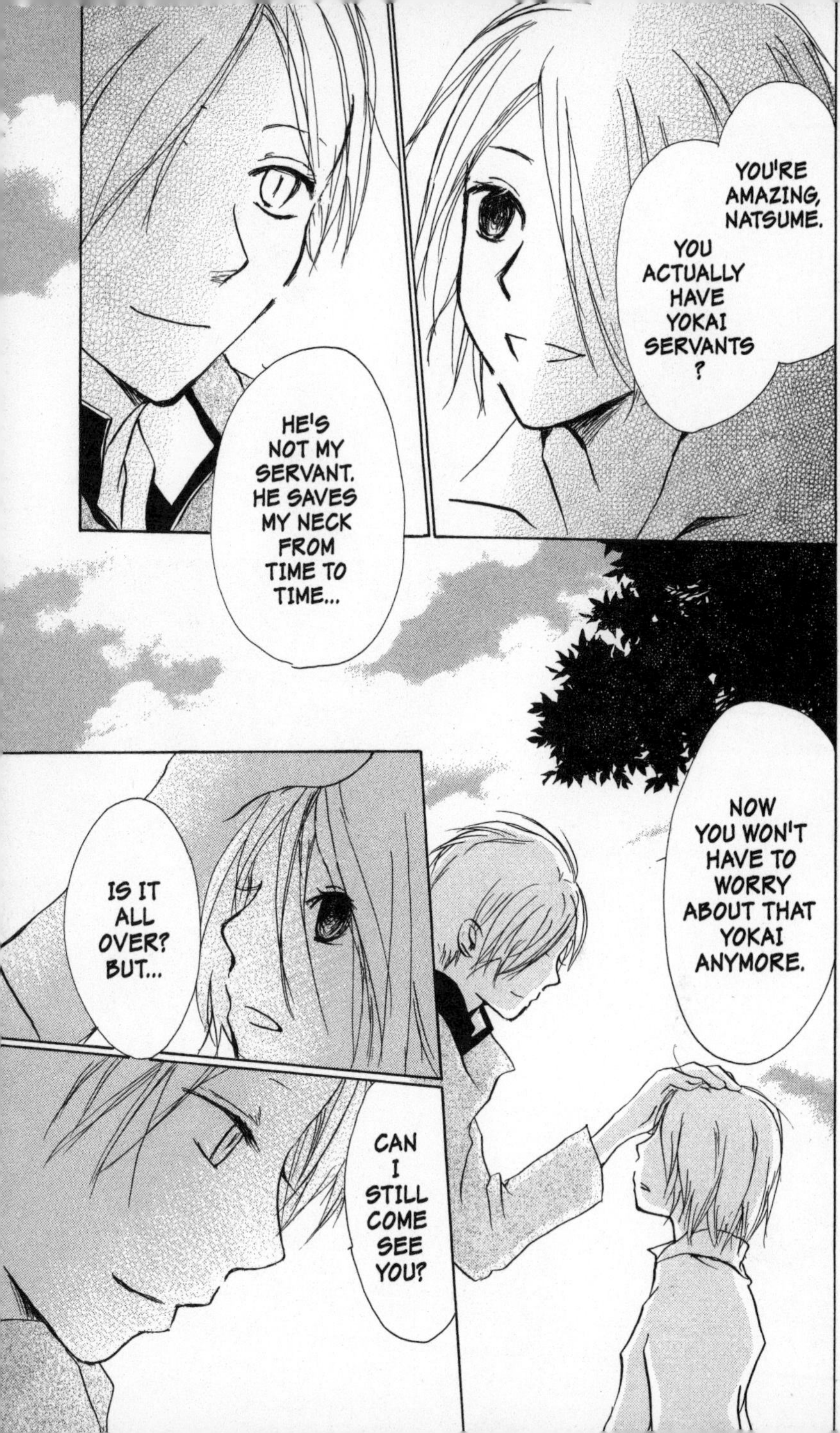
YOU'RE AMAZING, NATSUME.
YOU ACTUALLY HAVE YOKAI SERVANTS?
HE'S NOT MY SERVANT. HE SAVES MY NECK FROM TIME TO TIME...
NOW YOU WON'T HAVE TO WORRY ABOUT THAT YOKAI ANYMORE.
IS IT ALL OVER? BUT...
CAN I STILL COME SEE YOU?

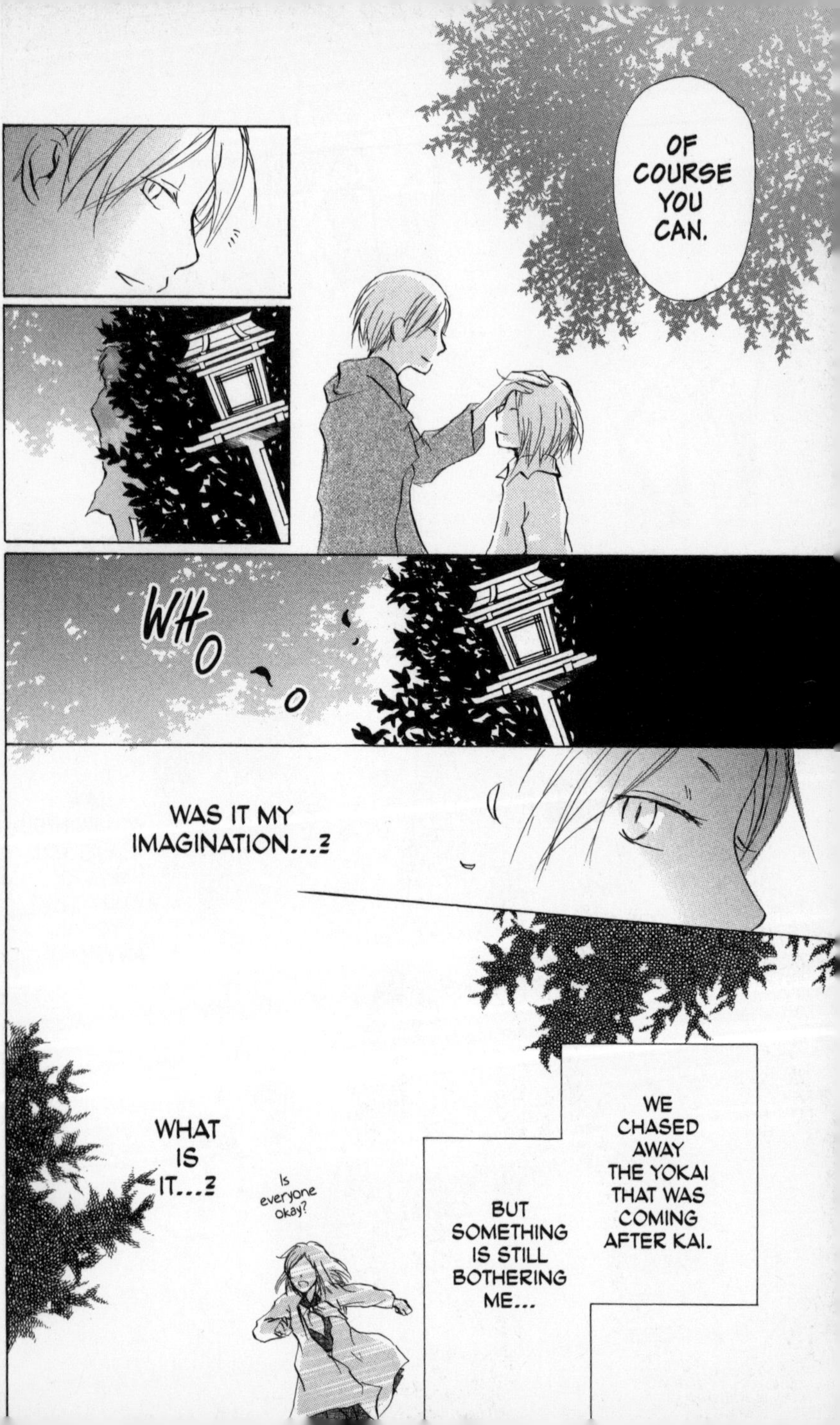
OF COURSE YOU CAN.
WHOOO
WAS IT MY IMAGINATION...?
WE CHASED AWAY THE YOKAI THAT WAS COMING AFTER KAI.
BUT SOMETHING IS STILL BOTHERING ME...
Is everyone okay?
WHAT IS IT...?

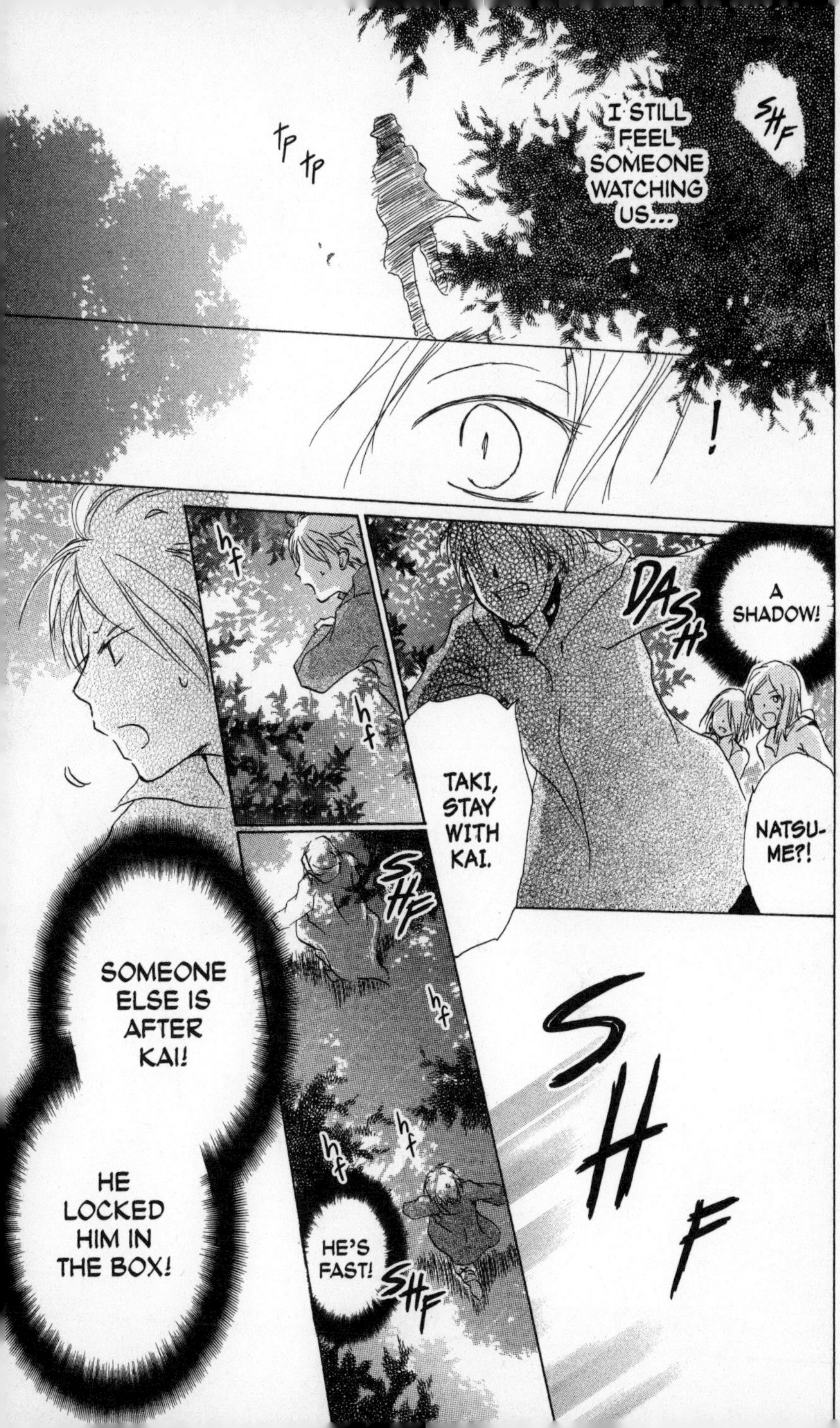
SHF
I STILL FEEL SOMEONE WATCHING US...
tp tp
!
A SHADOW!
DASH
NATSU-ME?!
TAKI, STAY WITH KAI.
hf
hf
SHF
SHF
hf
hf
hf
HE'S FAST!
SHF
SOMEONE ELSE IS AFTER KAI!
HE LOCKED HIM IN THE BOX!

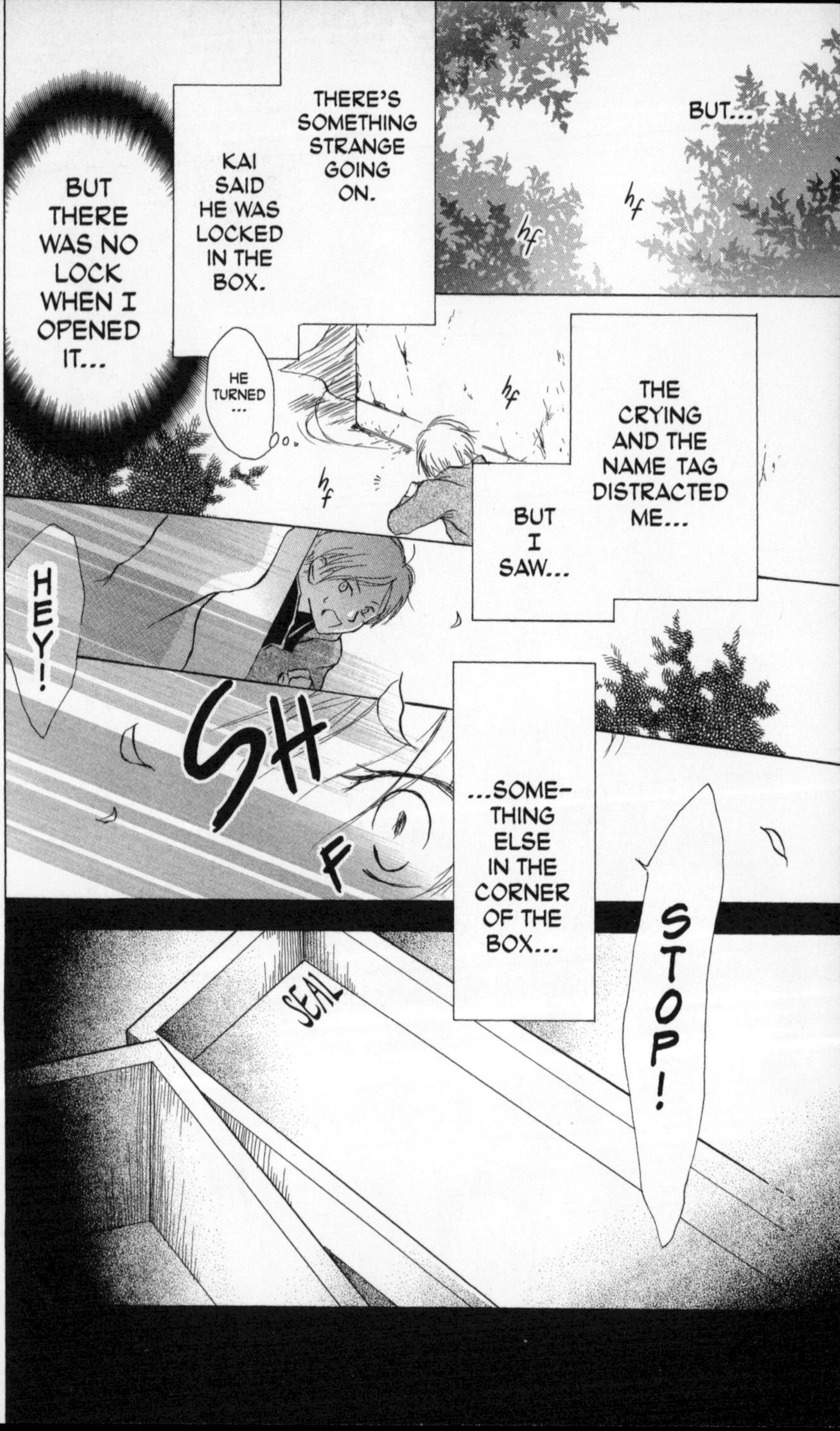
BUT...
hf
hf
THERE'S SOMETHING STRANGE GOING ON.
KAI SAID HE WAS LOCKED IN THE BOX.
BUT THERE WAS NO LOCK WHEN I OPENED IT...
THE CRYING AND THE NAME TAG DISTRACTED ME...
BUT I SAW...
hf
HE TURNED...
hf
HEY!
SHF
...SOME-THING ELSE IN THE CORNER OF THE BOX...
STOP!
SEAL

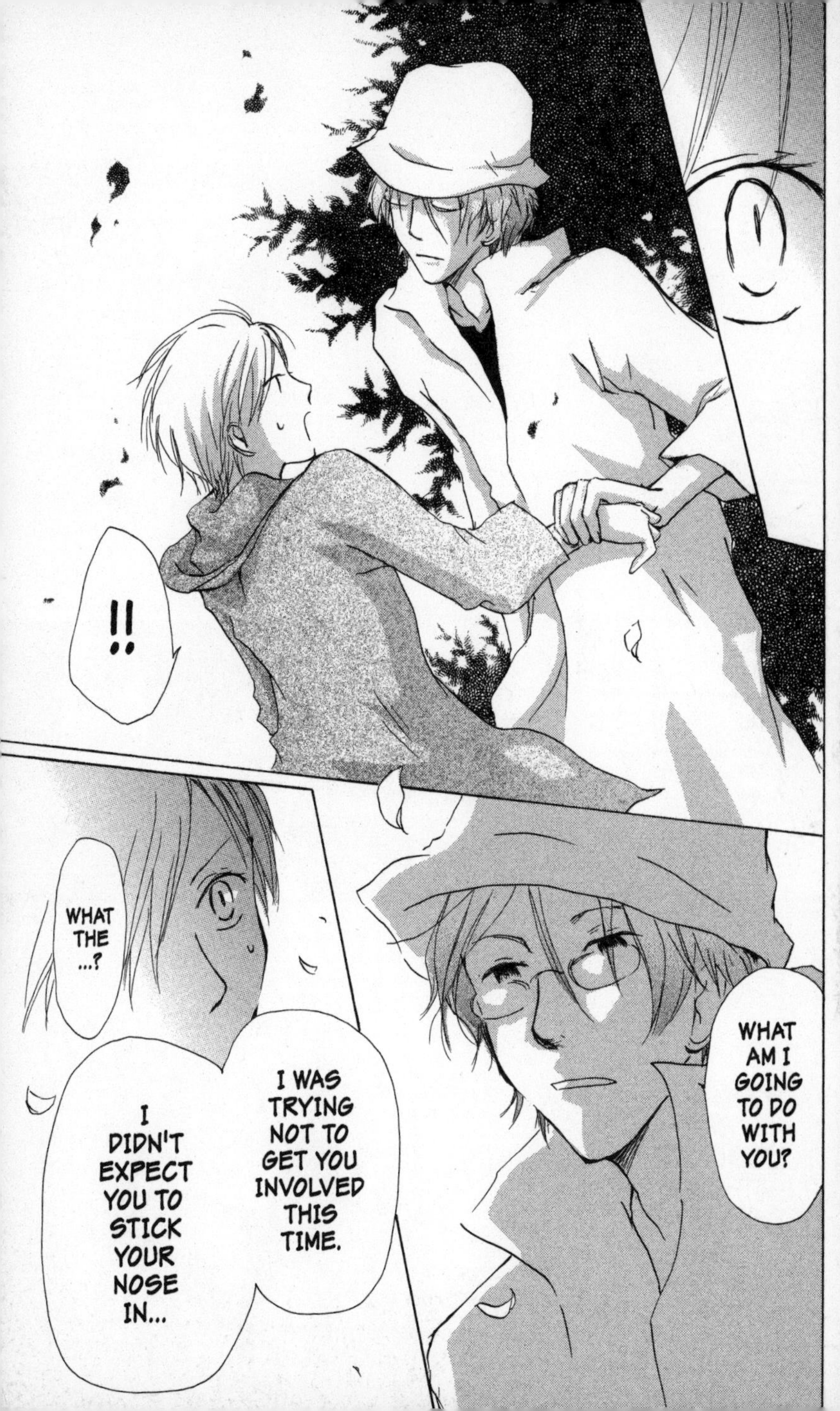
!!
WHAT AM I GOING TO DO WITH YOU?
I WAS TRYING NOT TO GET YOU INVOLVED THIS TIME.
I DIDN'T EXPECT YOU TO STICK YOUR NOSE IN...
WHAT THE ...?

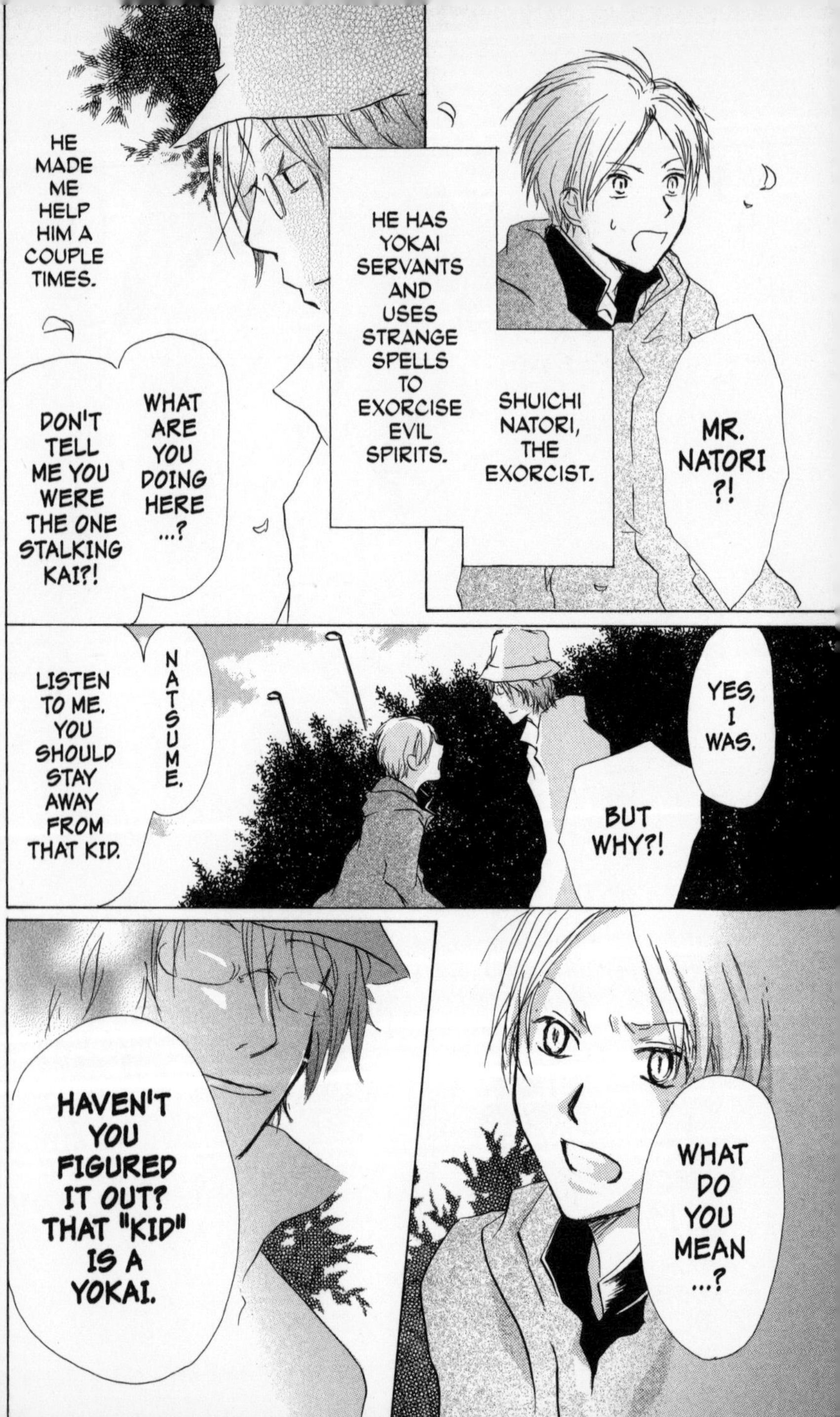
MR. NATORI ?!
SHUICHI NATORI, THE EXORCIST.
HE HAS YOKAI SERVANTS AND USES STRANGE SPELLS TO EXORCISE EVIL SPIRITS.
HE MADE ME HELP HIM A COUPLE TIMES.
WHAT ARE YOU DOING HERE ...?
DON'T TELL ME YOU WERE THE ONE STALKING KAI?!
YES, I WAS.
BUT WHY?!
NATSUME.
LISTEN TO ME. YOU SHOULD STAY AWAY FROM THAT KID.
WHAT DO YOU MEAN ...?
HAVEN'T YOU FIGURED IT OUT? THAT "KID" IS A YOKAI.

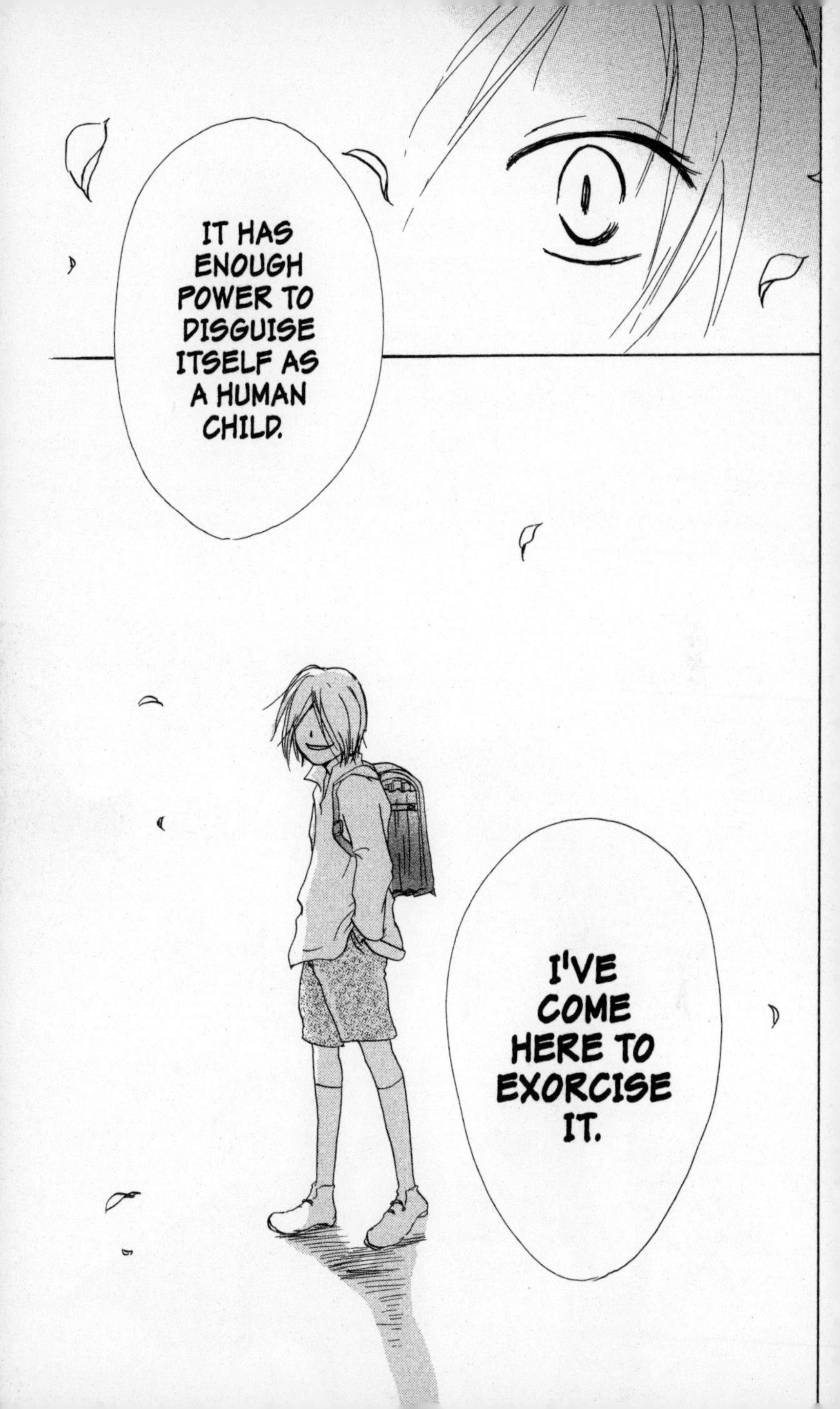
IT HAS ENOUGH POWER TO DISGUISE ITSELF AS A HUMAN CHILD.
I'VE COME HERE TO EXORCISE IT.

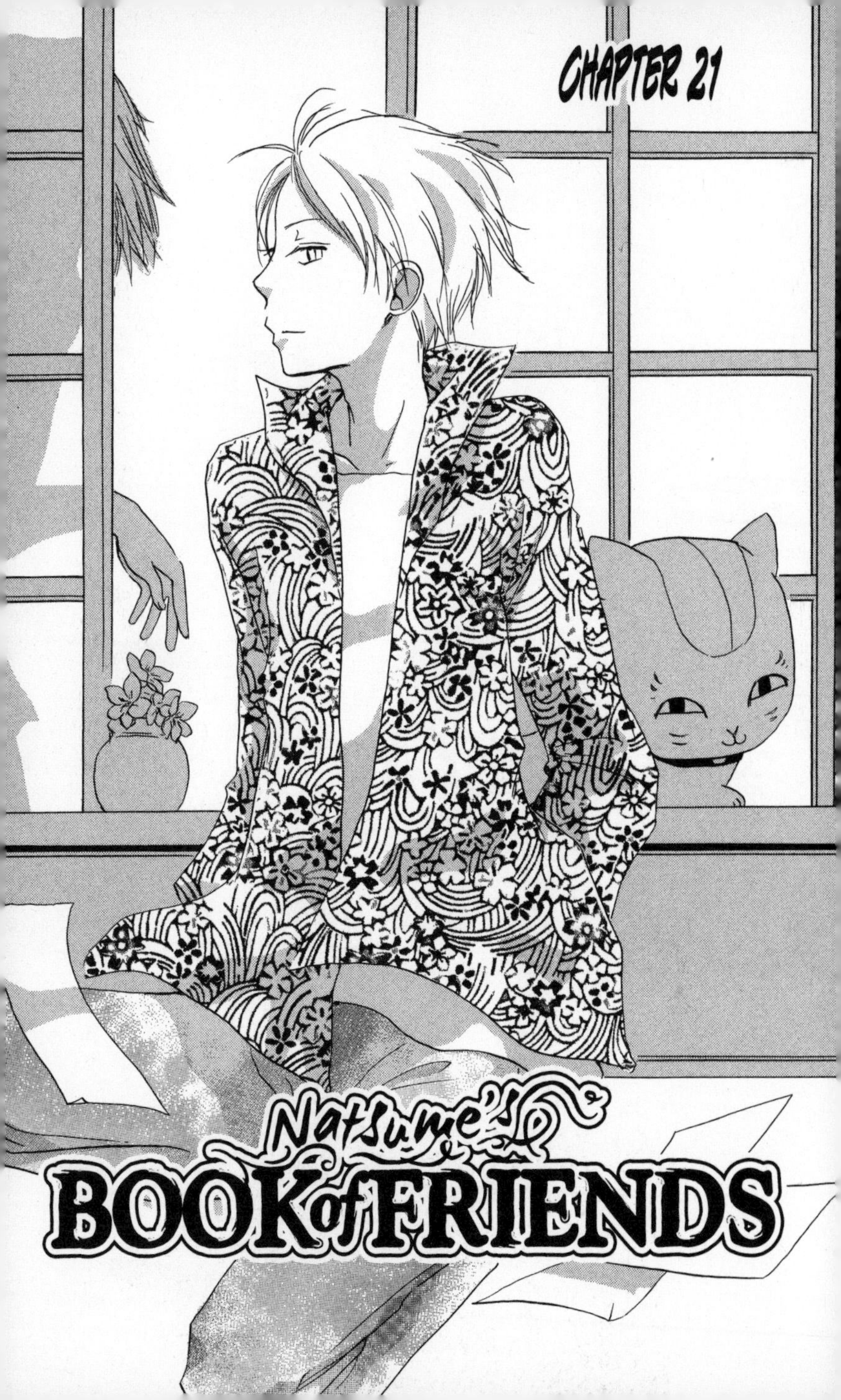
CHAPTER 21
Natsume's
BOOK of FRIENDS

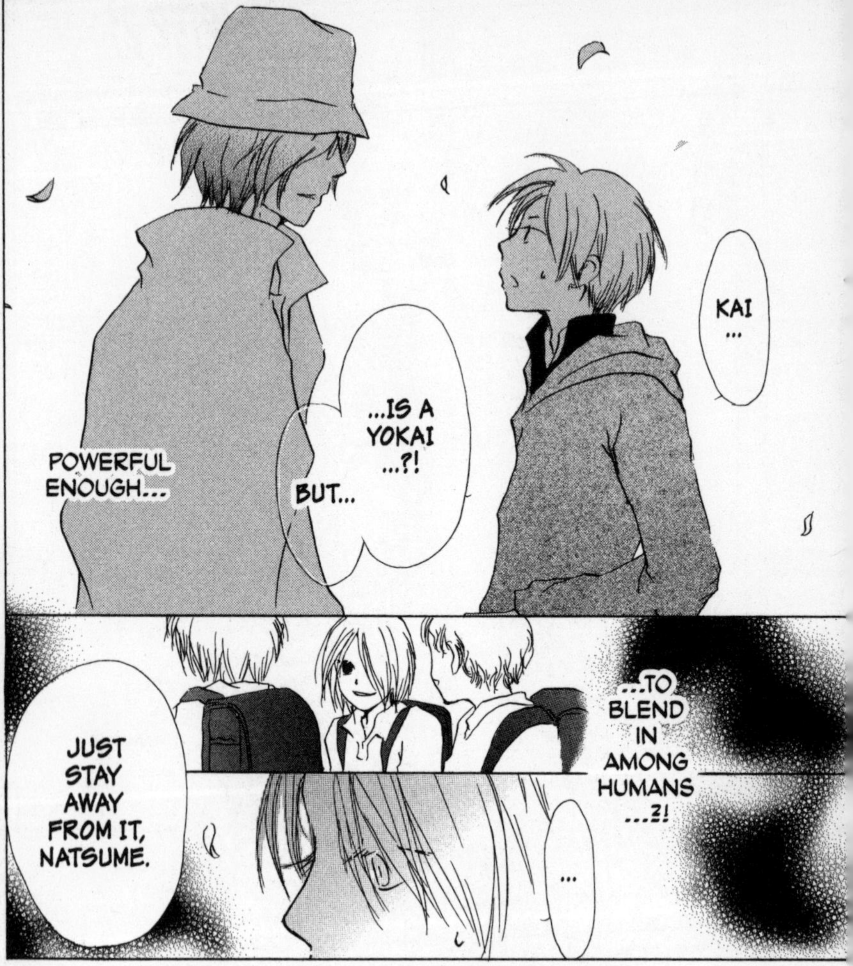
KAI ...
...IS A YOKAI ...?!
BUT...
POWERFUL ENOUGH...
...TO BLEND IN AMONG HUMANS ...?!
...
JUST STAY AWAY FROM IT, NATSUME.

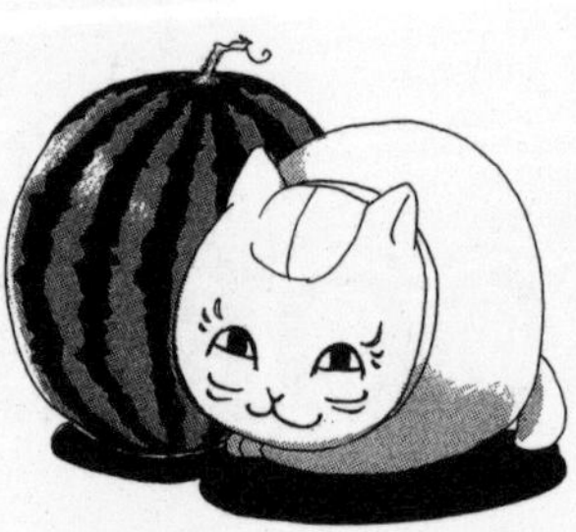

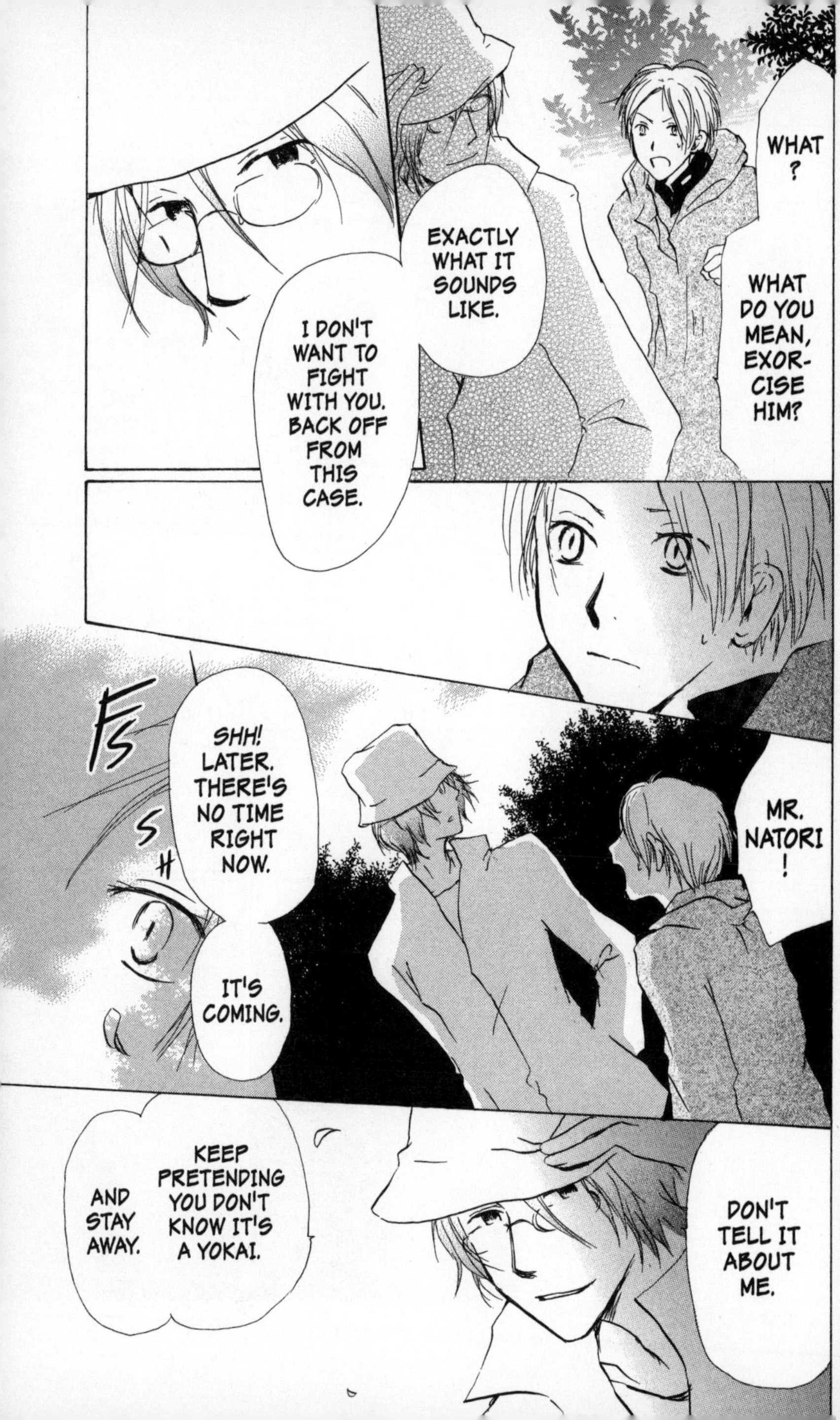
WHAT?
WHAT DO YOU MEAN, EXORCISE HIM?
EXACTLY WHAT IT SOUNDS LIKE.
I DON'T WANT TO FIGHT WITH YOU. BACK OFF FROM THIS CASE.
MR. NATORI!
SHH! LATER. THERE'S NO TIME RIGHT NOW.
FS
SH
IT'S COMING.
DON'T TELL IT ABOUT ME.
KEEP PRETENDING YOU DON'T KNOW IT'S A YOKAI.
AND STAY AWAY.

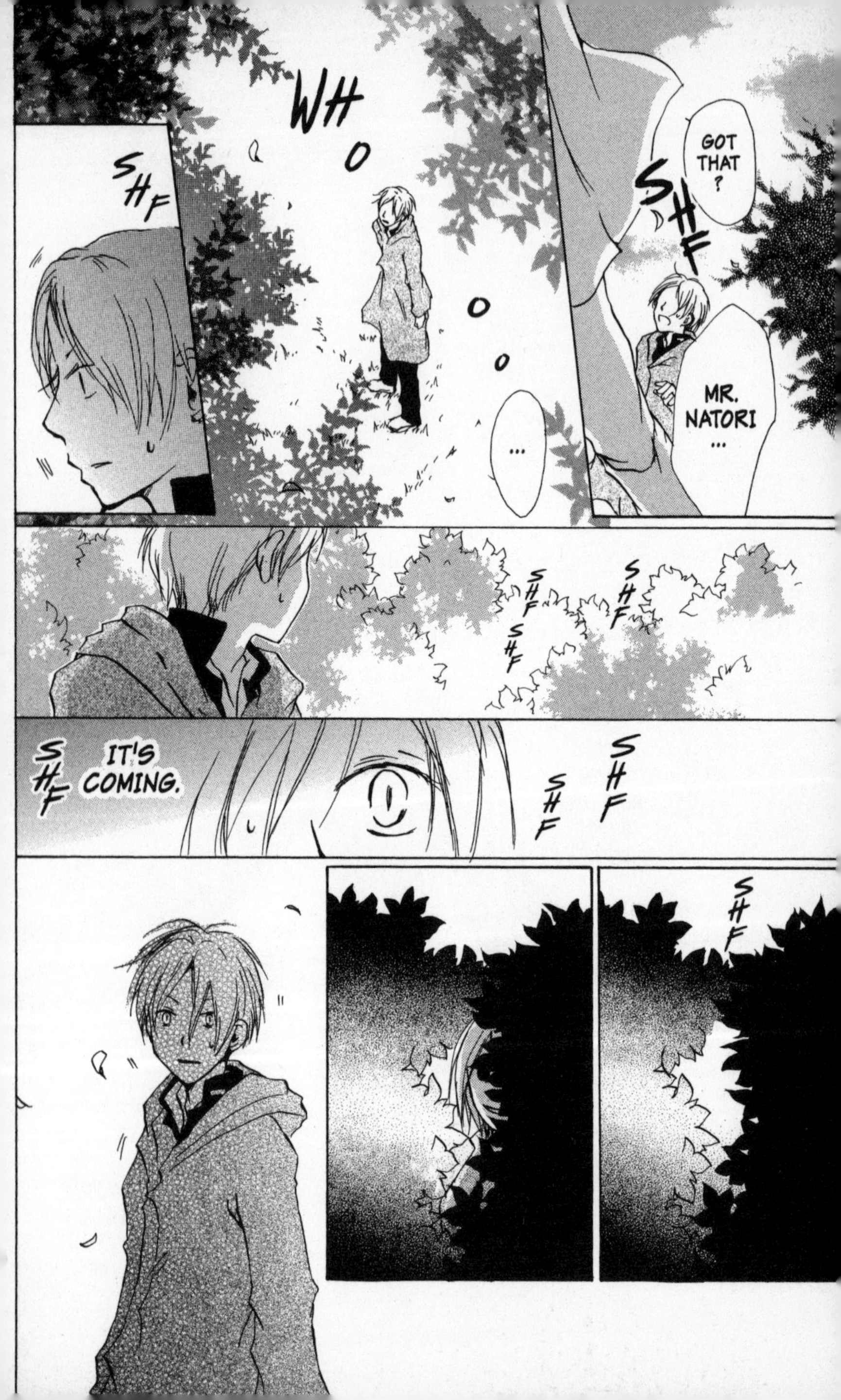
GOT THAT?
SHF
MR. NATORI...
WHOOO
...
SHF
SHF
SHF
SHF
SHF
SHF
IT'S COMING.
SHF
SHF

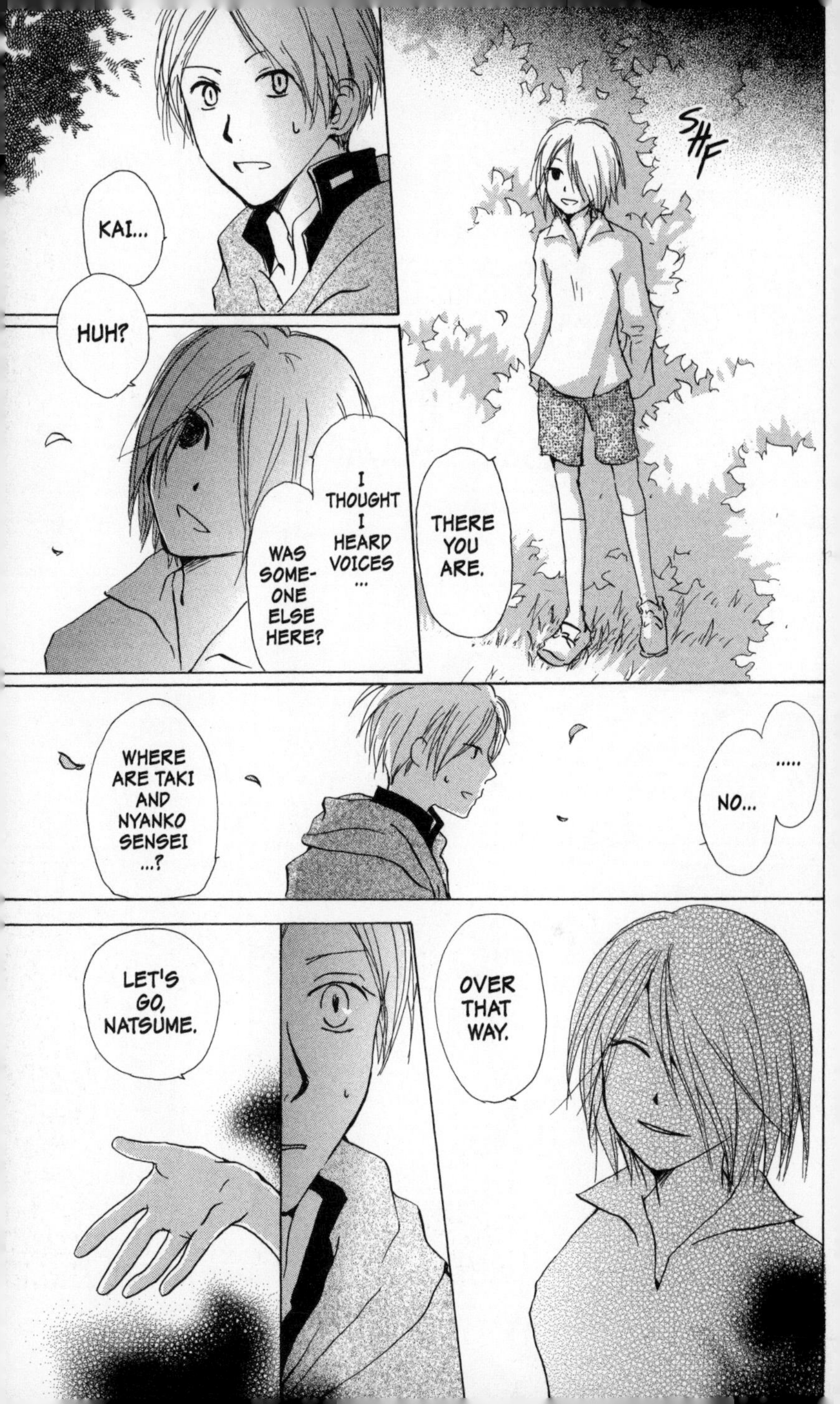
SHF
THERE YOU ARE.
KAI...
HUH?
I THOUGHT I HEARD VOICES ...
WAS SOME-ONE ELSE HERE?
..... NO...
WHERE ARE TAKI AND NYANKO SENSEI ...?
OVER THAT WAY.
LET'S GO, NATSUME.

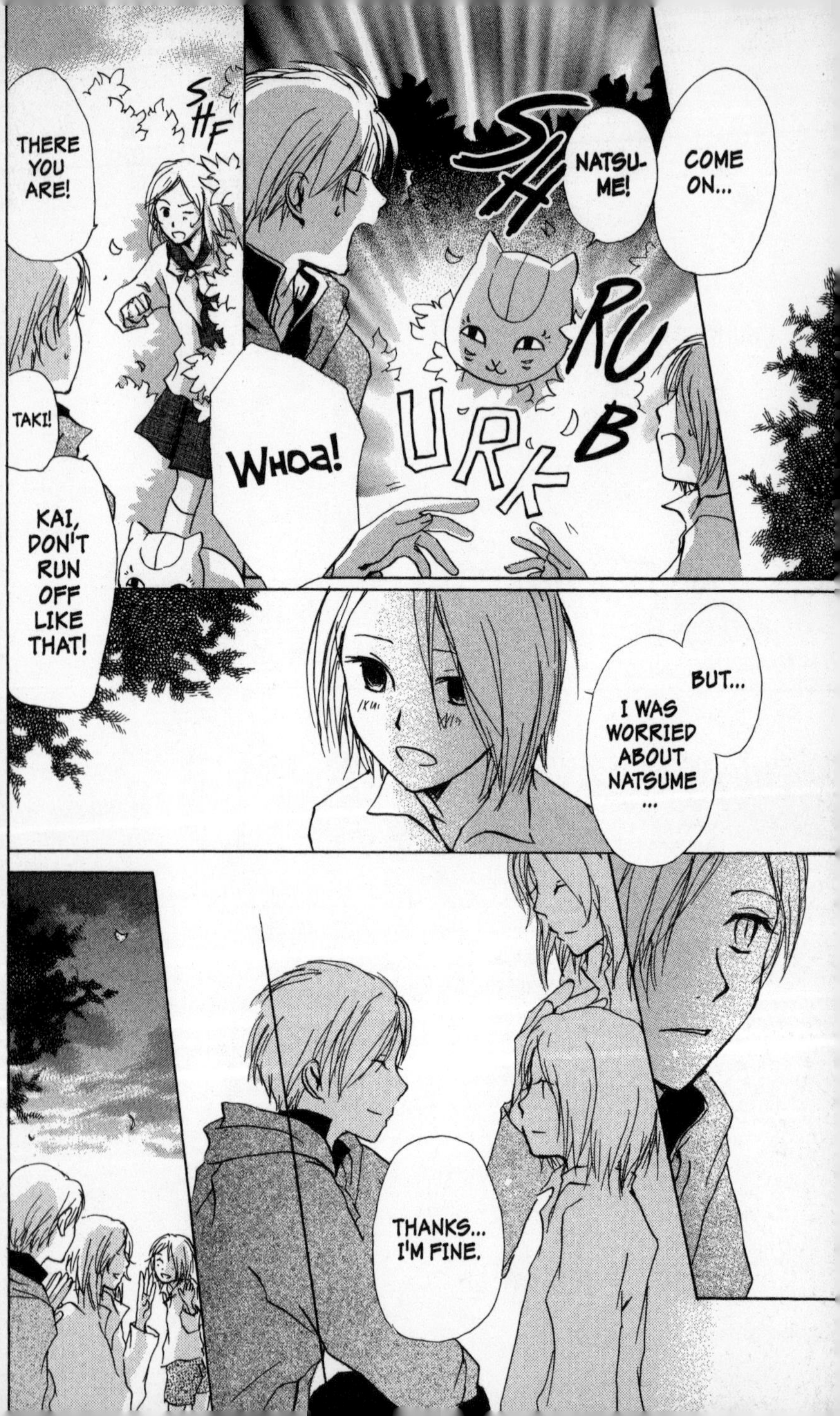
COME ON...
NATSU-ME!
SHRUB
URK
WHOA!
SHF
THERE YOU ARE!
TAKI!
KAI, DON'T RUN OFF LIKE THAT!
BUT... I WAS WORRIED ABOUT NATSUME ...
THANKS... I'M FINE.

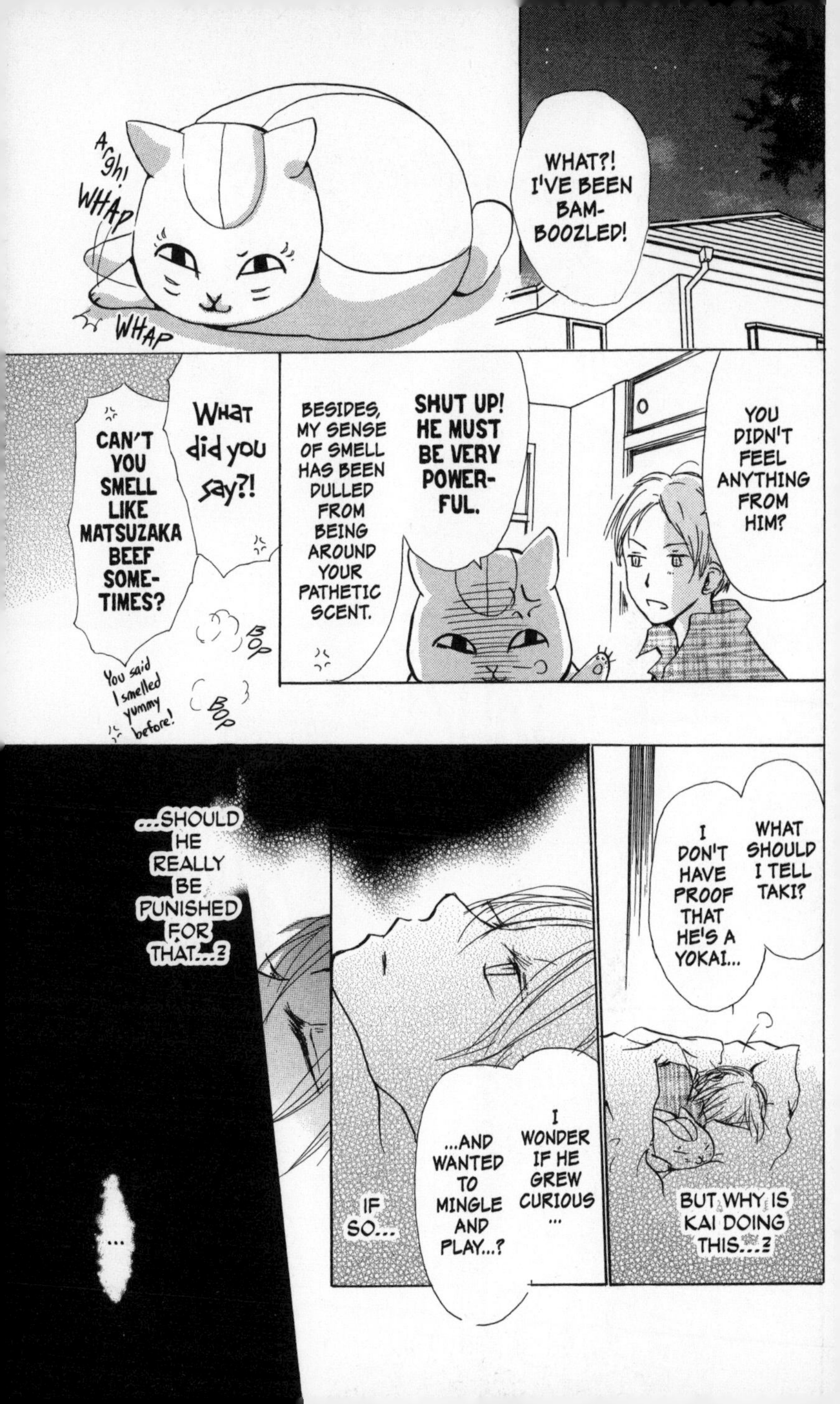
WHAT?! I'VE BEEN BAM-BOOZLED!
Argh!
WHAP
WHAP
YOU DIDN'T FEEL ANYTHING FROM HIM?
SHUT UP! HE MUST BE VERY POWER-FUL.
BESIDES, MY SENSE OF SMELL HAS BEEN DULLED FROM BEING AROUND YOUR PATHETIC SCENT.
What did you say?!
CAN'T YOU SMELL LIKE MATSUZAKA BEEF SOME-TIMES?
BOP
BOP
You said I smelled yummy before!
WHAT SHOULD I TELL TAKI?
I DON'T HAVE PROOF THAT HE'S A YOKAI...
BUT WHY IS KAI DOING THIS...?
I WONDER IF HE GREW CURIOUS...
...AND WANTED TO MINGLE AND PLAY...?
IF SO...
...SHOULD HE REALLY BE PUNISHED FOR THAT...?
...

OPEN.

COME HERE.

KAI, HOLD ON... I'LL BE RIGHT THERE.

COME HERE.

COME.

OPEN THIS FOR ME.

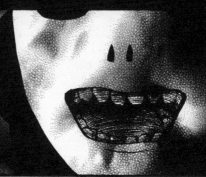

OH... IT WAS A DREAM.

BONK

GASP

WHOA!

WMP

SIGH.

tweet tweet

Morning!

Good morning.

WHAT A VIVID DREAM...

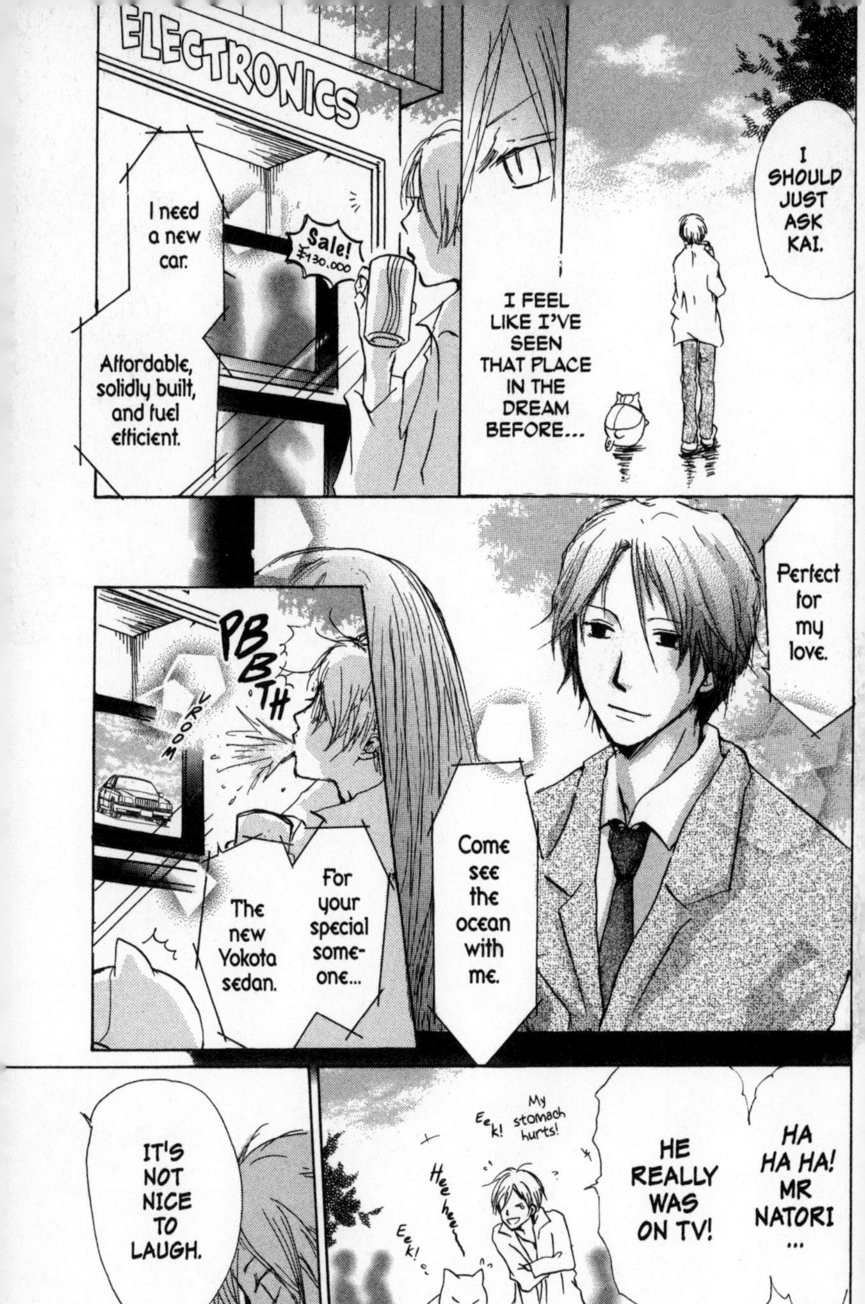
I SHOULD JUST ASK KAI.
I FEEL LIKE I'VE SEEN THAT PLACE IN THE DREAM BEFORE...
ELECTRONICS
I need a new car.
Sale! ¥130,000
Affordable, solidly built, and fuel efficient.
Perfect for my love.
Come see the ocean with me.
PBBTH
VROOOM
For your special some-one...
The new Yokota sedan.
HA HA HA! MR NATORI...
HE REALLY WAS ON TV!
My stomach hurts!
Eek!
Hee hee
Eek!
IT'S NOT NICE TO LAUGH.

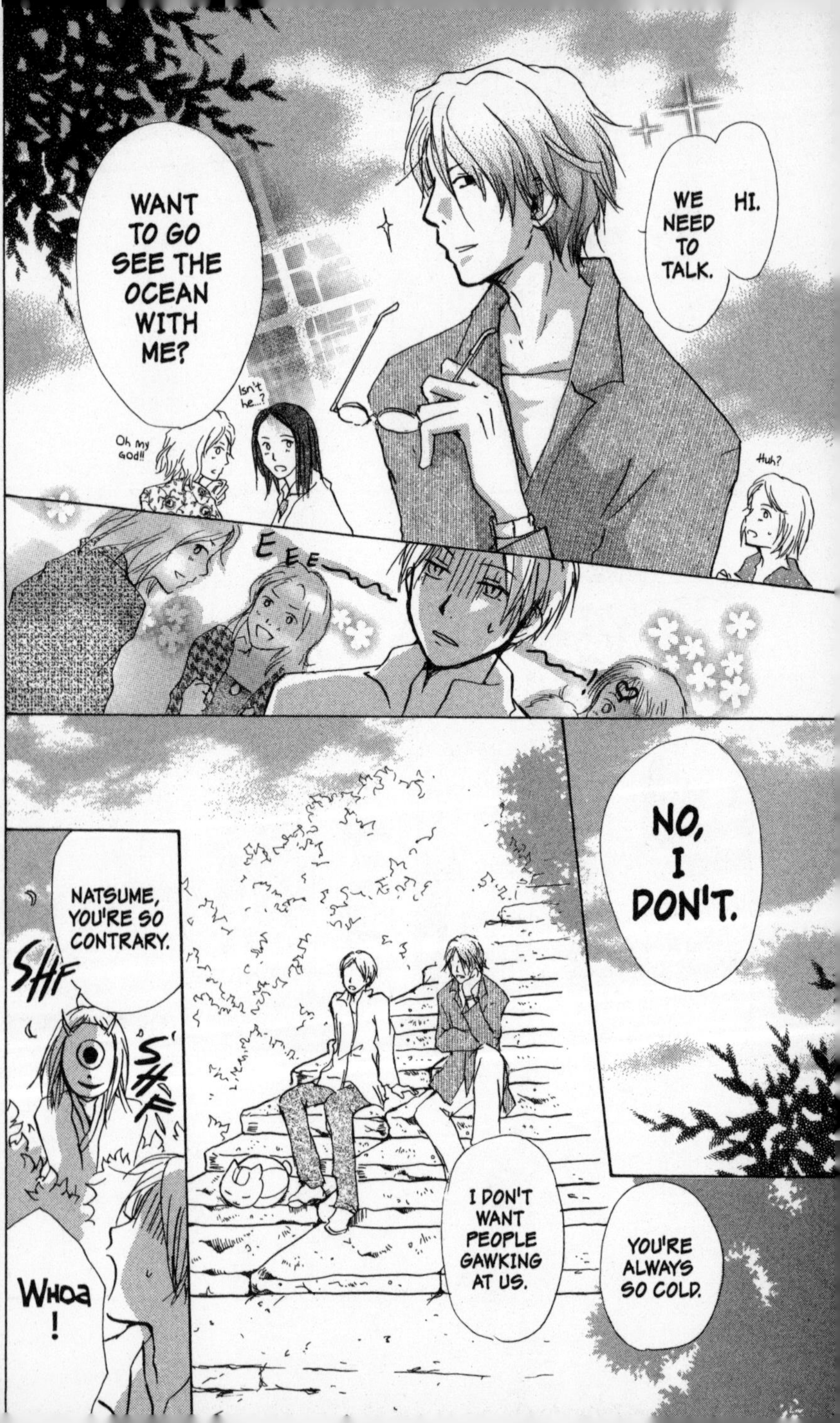
HI.
WE NEED TO TALK.
WANT TO GO SEE THE OCEAN WITH ME?
Huh?
Isn't he...?
Oh my god!!
EEE
NO, I DON'T.
YOU'RE ALWAYS SO COLD.
I DON'T WANT PEOPLE GAWKING AT US.
NATSUME, YOU'RE SO CONTRARY.
SHF
SHF
Whoa!

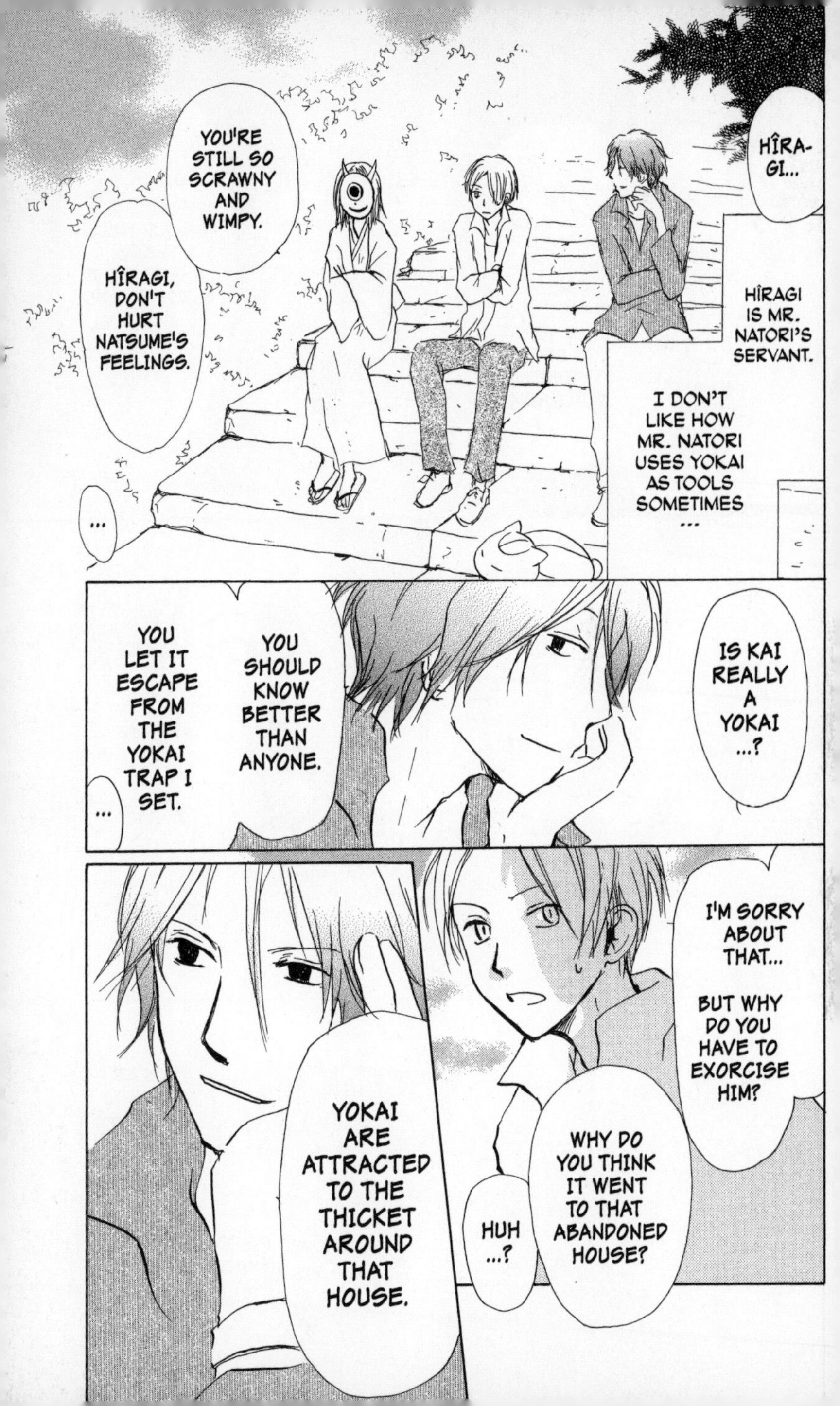
HÎRAGI...
HÎRAGI IS MR. NATORI'S SERVANT.
I DON'T LIKE HOW MR. NATORI USES YOKAI AS TOOLS SOMETIMES...
YOU'RE STILL SO SCRAWNY AND WIMPY.
HÎRAGI, DON'T HURT NATSUME'S FEELINGS.
...
IS KAI REALLY A YOKAI...?
YOU SHOULD KNOW BETTER THAN ANYONE.
YOU LET IT ESCAPE FROM THE YOKAI TRAP I SET.
...
I'M SORRY ABOUT THAT...
BUT WHY DO YOU HAVE TO EXORCISE HIM?
WHY DO YOU THINK IT WENT TO THAT ABANDONED HOUSE?
HUH...?
YOKAI ARE ATTRACTED TO THE THICKET AROUND THAT HOUSE.

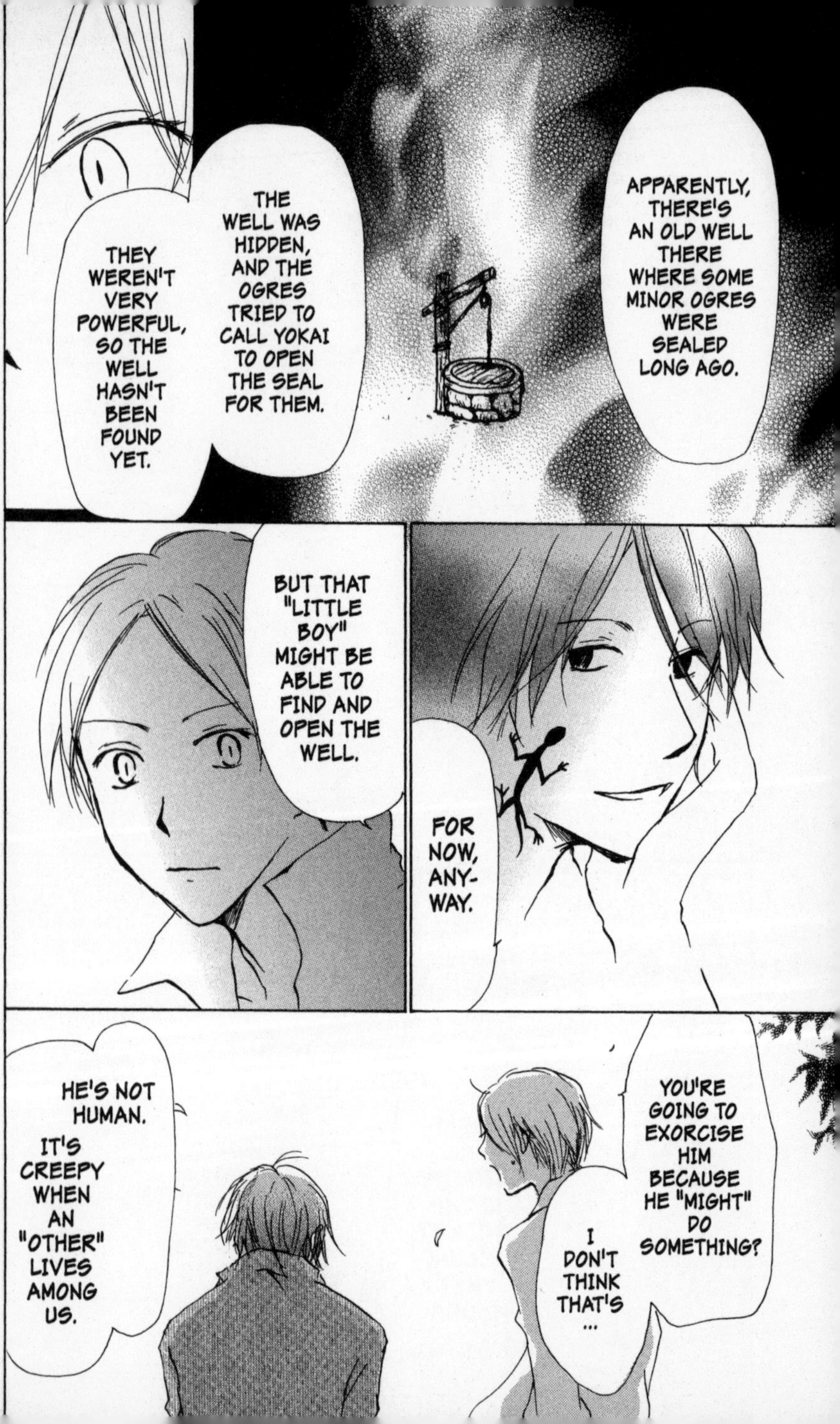
APPARENTLY, THERE'S AN OLD WELL THERE WHERE SOME MINOR OGRES WERE SEALED LONG AGO.
THE WELL WAS HIDDEN, AND THE OGRES TRIED TO CALL YOKAI TO OPEN THE SEAL FOR THEM.
THEY WEREN'T VERY POWERFUL, SO THE WELL HASN'T BEEN FOUND YET.
FOR NOW, ANY-WAY.
BUT THAT "LITTLE BOY" MIGHT BE ABLE TO FIND AND OPEN THE WELL.
YOU'RE GOING TO EXORCISE HIM BECAUSE HE "MIGHT" DO SOMETHING?
I DON'T THINK THAT'S ...
HE'S NOT HUMAN.
IT'S CREEPY WHEN AN "OTHER" LIVES AMONG US.

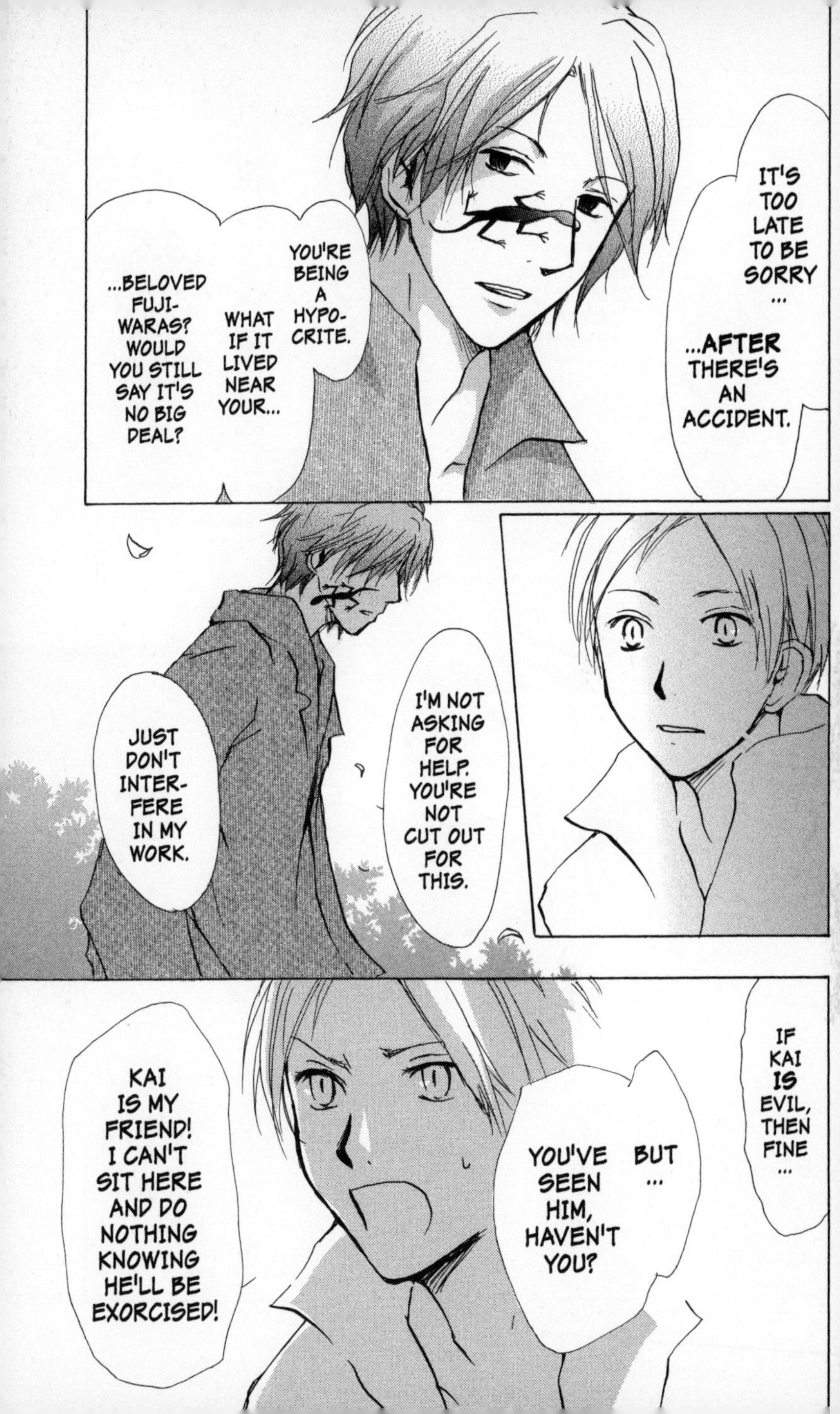
IT'S TOO LATE TO BE SORRY...
...AFTER THERE'S AN ACCIDENT.
YOU'RE BEING A HYPO-CRITE.
WHAT IF IT LIVED NEAR YOUR...
...BELOVED FUJI-WARAS? WOULD YOU STILL SAY IT'S NO BIG DEAL?
I'M NOT ASKING FOR HELP. YOU'RE NOT CUT OUT FOR THIS.
JUST DON'T INTER-FERE IN MY WORK.
IF KAI IS EVIL, THEN FINE...
BUT...
YOU'VE SEEN HIM, HAVEN'T YOU?
KAI IS MY FRIEND! I CAN'T SIT HERE AND DO NOTHING KNOWING HE'LL BE EXORCISED!

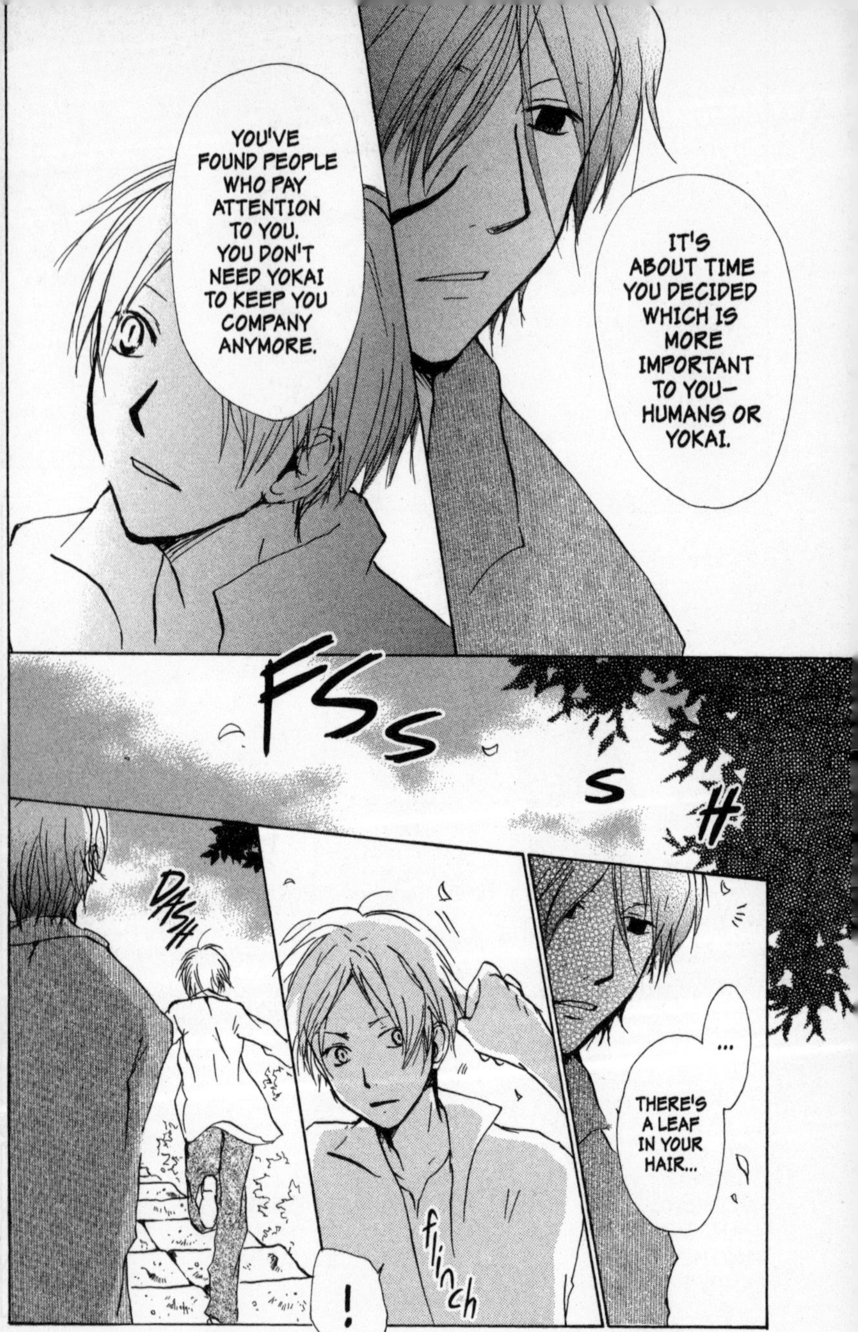
IT'S ABOUT TIME YOU DECIDED WHICH IS MORE IMPORTANT TO YOU—HUMANS OR YOKAI.
YOU'VE FOUND PEOPLE WHO PAY ATTENTION TO YOU. YOU DON'T NEED YOKAI TO KEEP YOU COMPANY ANYMORE.
FSSSSH
...
THERE'S A LEAF IN YOUR HAIR...
flinch
!
DASH

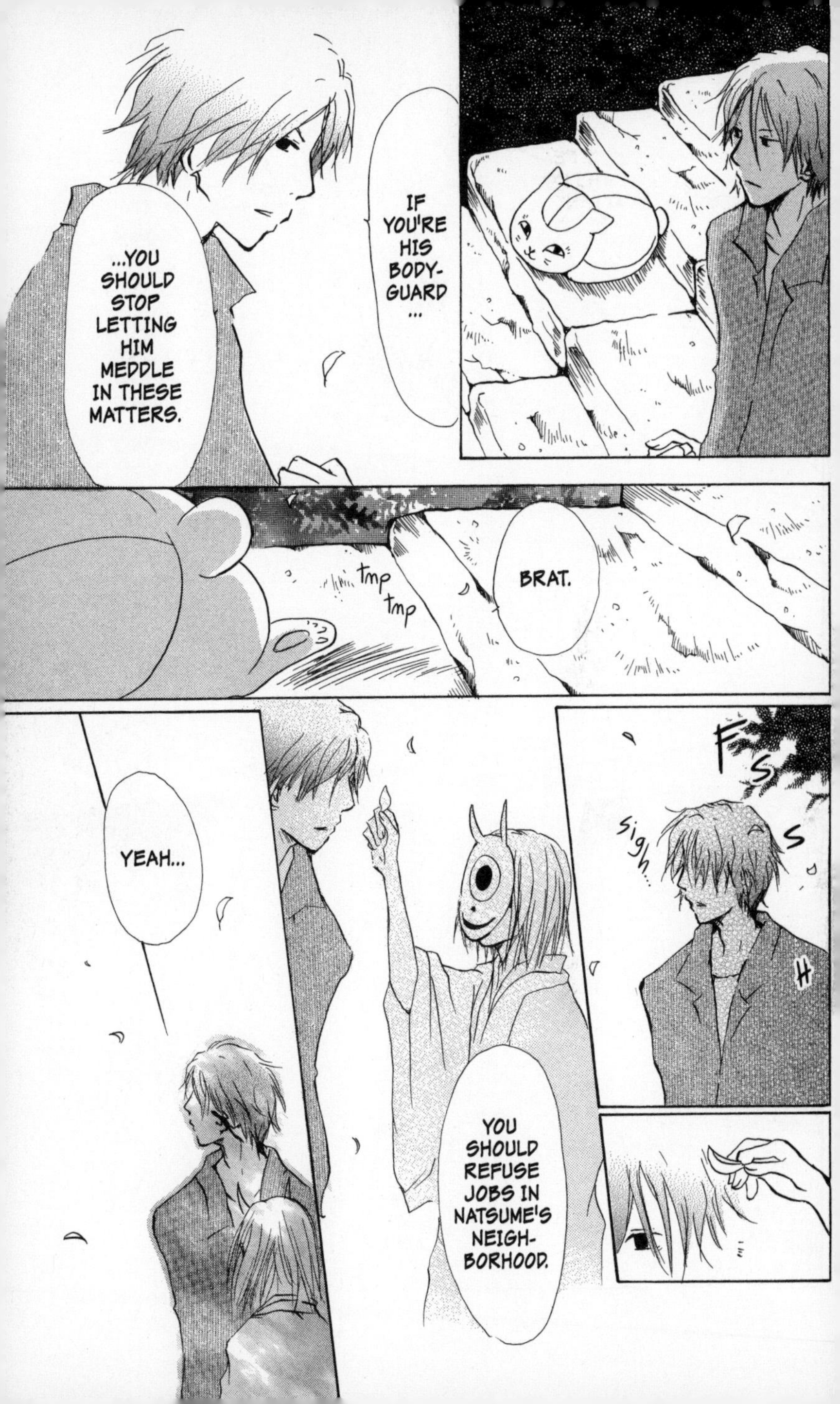
IF YOU'RE HIS BODY-GUARD ...
...YOU SHOULD STOP LETTING HIM MEDDLE IN THESE MATTERS.
BRAT.
tmp tmp
FSS
sigh...
H
YOU SHOULD REFUSE JOBS IN NATSUME'S NEIGH-BORHOOD.
YEAH...

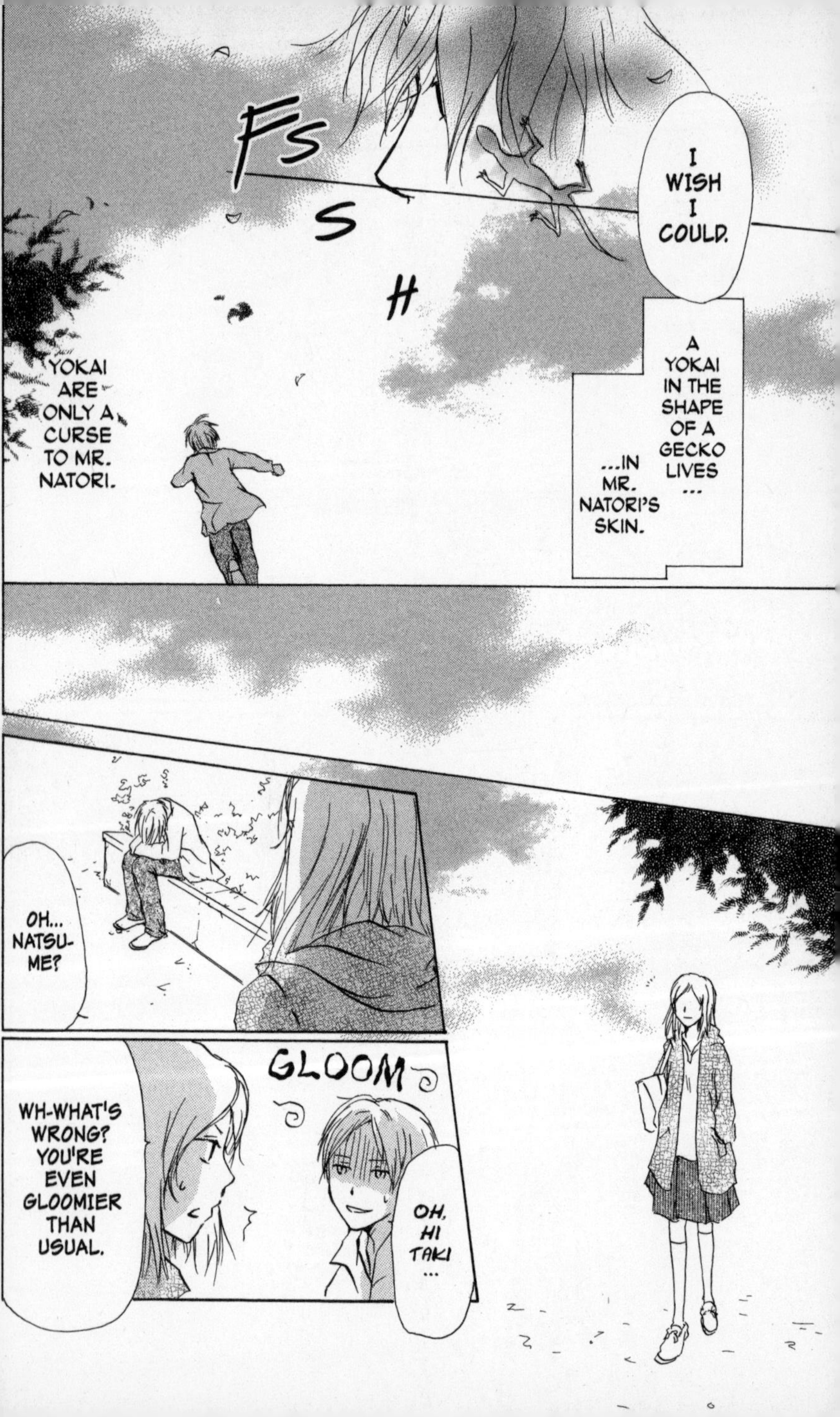
I WISH I COULD.
FSSH
A YOKAI IN THE SHAPE OF A GECKO LIVES ...
...IN MR. NATORI'S SKIN.
YOKAI ARE ONLY A CURSE TO MR. NATORI.
OH... NATSU-ME?
GLOOM
OH, HI TAKI ...
WH-WHAT'S WRONG? YOU'RE EVEN GLOOMIER THAN USUAL.

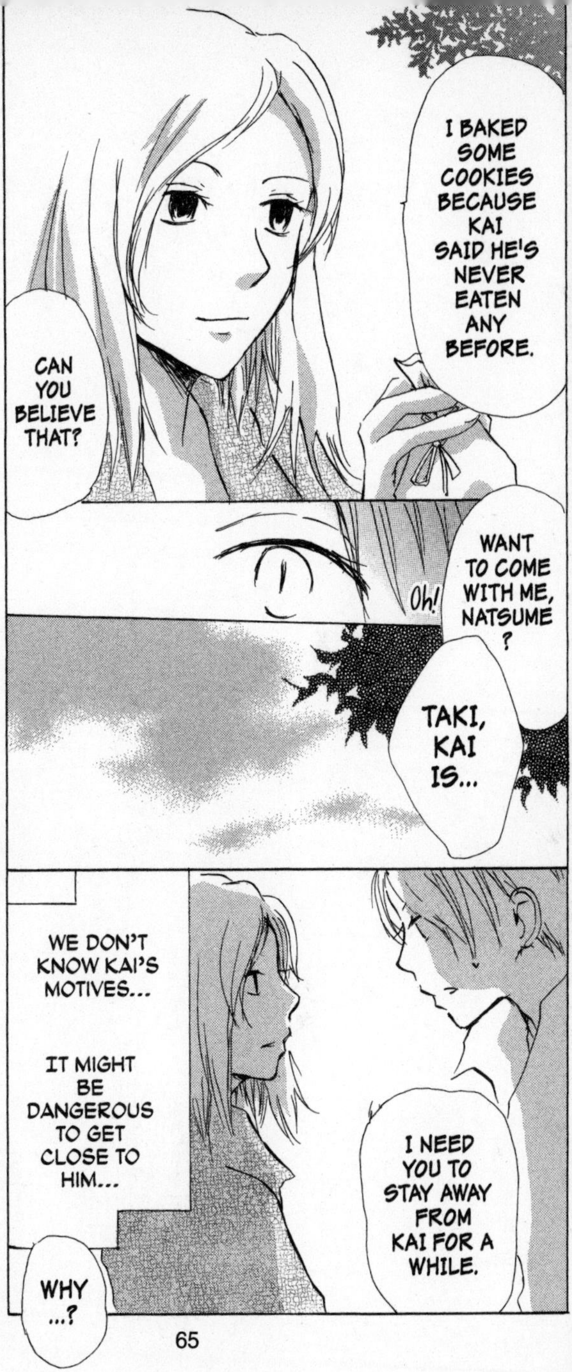

I BAKED SOME COOKIES BECAUSE KAI SAID HE'S NEVER EATEN ANY BEFORE.
CAN YOU BELIEVE THAT?
WANT TO COME WITH ME, NATSUME?
Oh!
TAKI, KAI IS...
WE DON'T KNOW KAI'S MOTIVES...
IT MIGHT BE DANGEROUS TO GET CLOSE TO HIM...
I NEED YOU TO STAY AWAY FROM KAI FOR A WHILE.
WHY ...?

02

❋My second autograph session: part 1

Incredibly, they held a second autograph session for me. My signature looks like an elementary school kid wrote it, so it's a little embarrassing, but I was so happy because it's an opportunity to meet my readers. I'm not a good speaker either, so I was eager to go out of my comfort zone and develop my meet-and-greet skills. So I was off to Hachioji where it was held. I had never been there before, and I was excited to see so many shops around the train station. One of those shops, Kumazawa Books, was the site of the session. So many books on each floor! I was so excited and nervous. It was within the Tokyo metropolitan area, so my very first editor and the editor in charge of the pocket edition of my series *Akaku Saku Koe* were able to come, which was a big relief.

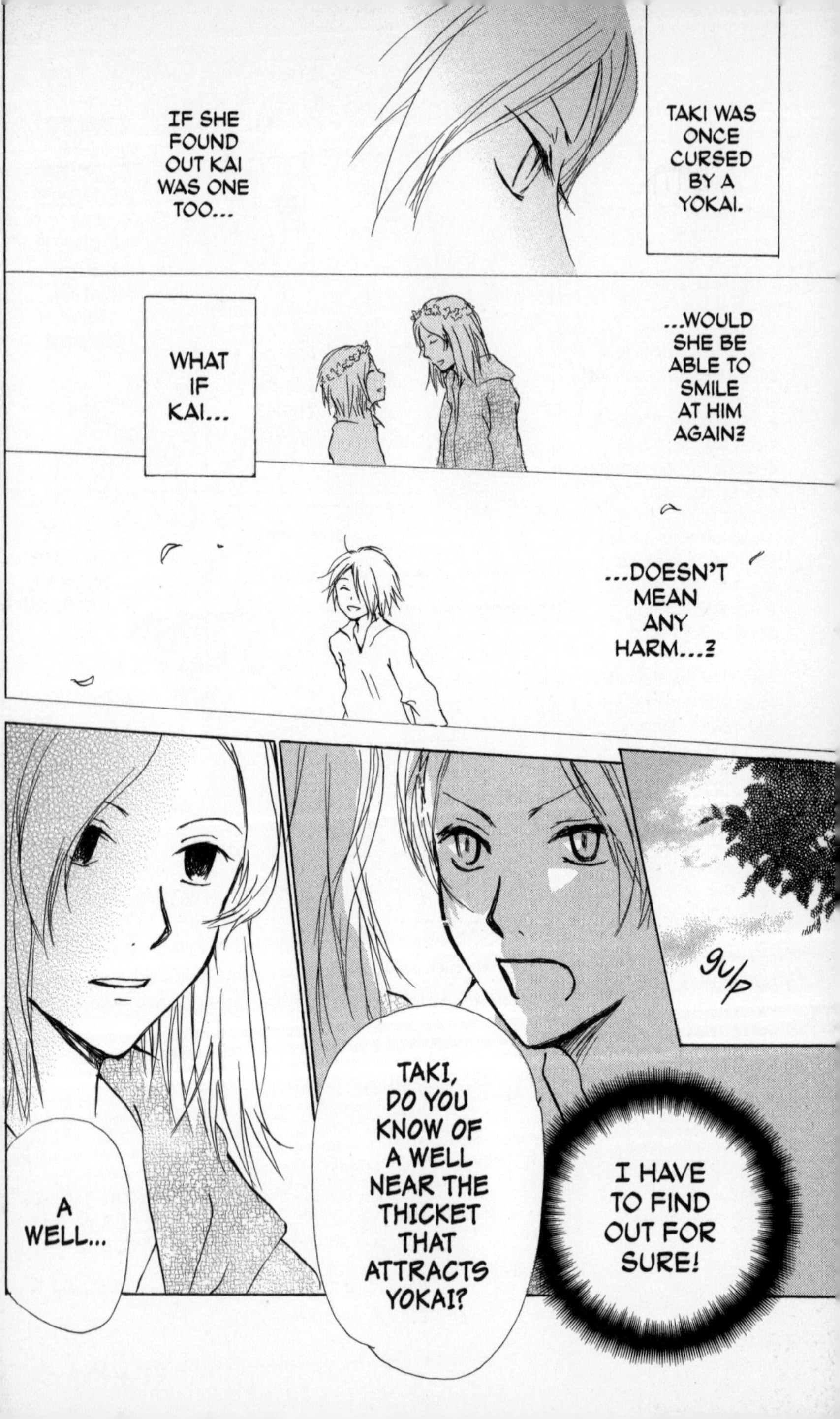
TAKI WAS ONCE CURSED BY A YOKAI.
IF SHE FOUND OUT KAI WAS ONE TOO...
...WOULD SHE BE ABLE TO SMILE AT HIM AGAIN?
WHAT IF KAI...
...DOESN'T MEAN ANY HARM...?
gulp
I HAVE TO FIND OUT FOR SURE!
TAKI, DO YOU KNOW OF A WELL NEAR THE THICKET THAT ATTRACTS YOKAI?
A WELL...

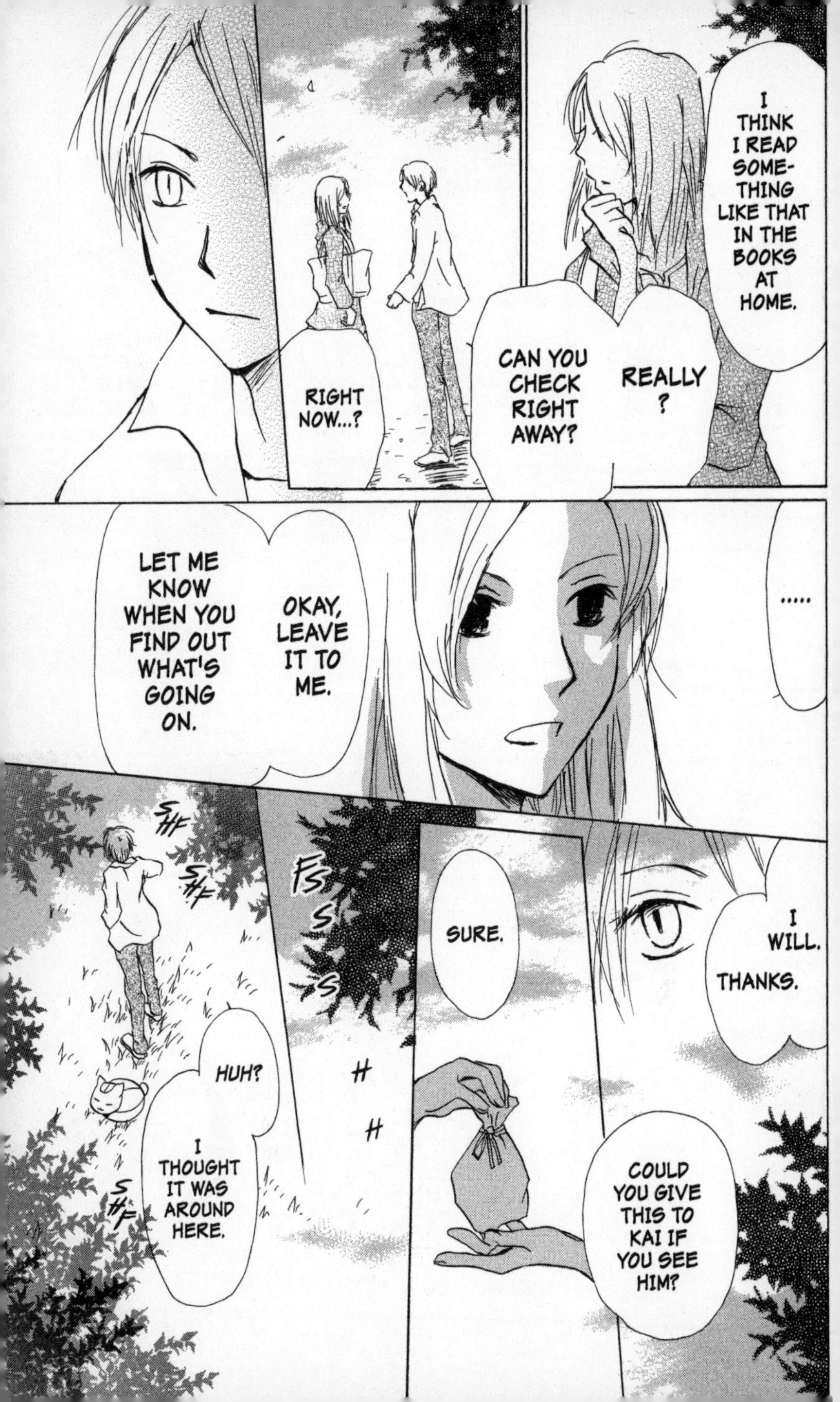
I THINK I READ SOMETHING LIKE THAT IN THE BOOKS AT HOME.
REALLY?
CAN YOU CHECK RIGHT AWAY?
RIGHT NOW...?
.....
OKAY, LEAVE IT TO ME.
LET ME KNOW WHEN YOU FIND OUT WHAT'S GOING ON.
I WILL.
THANKS.
SURE.
COULD YOU GIVE THIS TO KAI IF YOU SEE HIM?
FSSS
HH
SHF
SHF
HUH?
I THOUGHT IT WAS AROUND HERE.
SHF

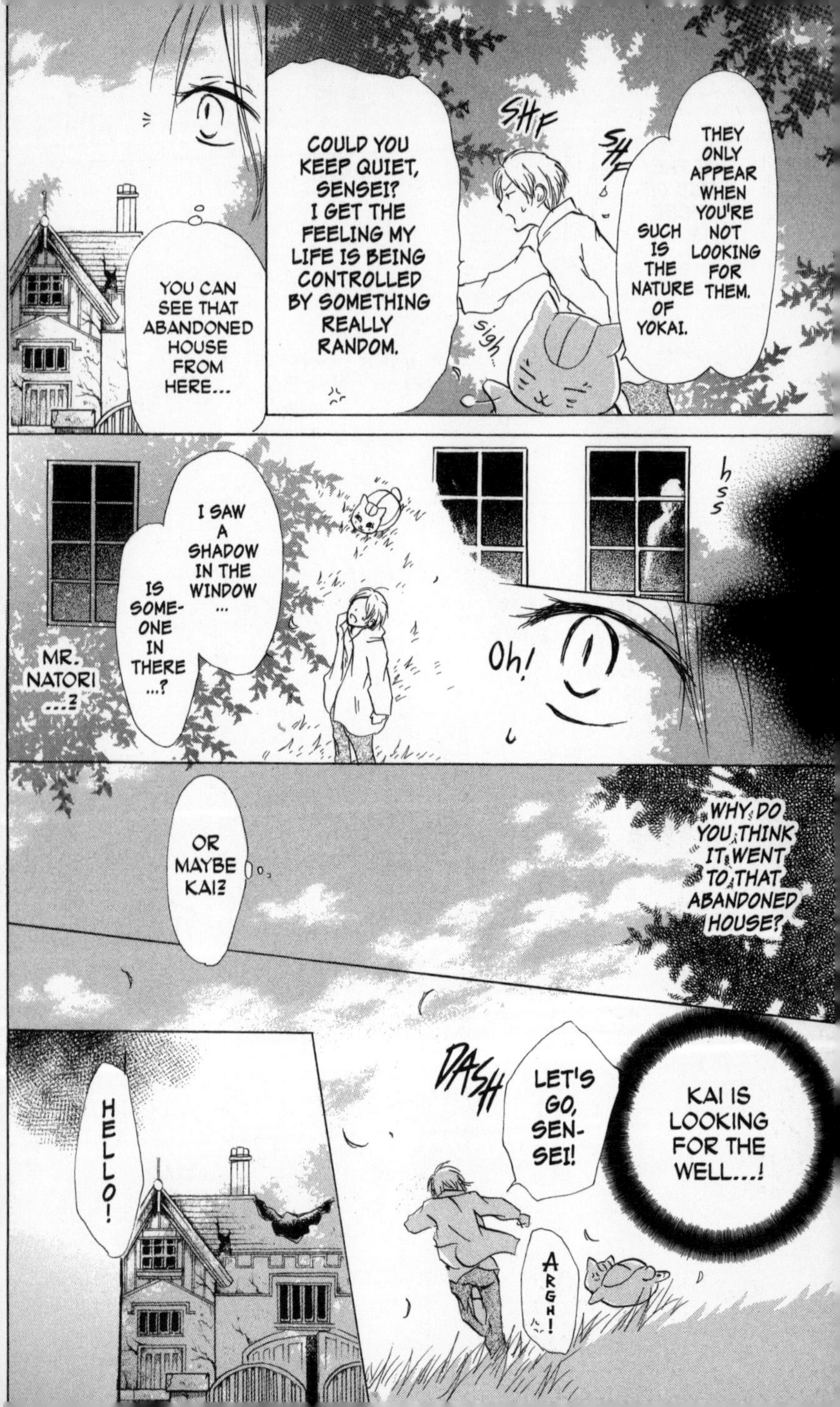
THEY ONLY APPEAR WHEN YOU'RE NOT LOOKING FOR THEM.
SUCH IS THE NATURE OF YOKAI.
SHF
SHF
sigh...
COULD YOU KEEP QUIET, SENSEI? I GET THE FEELING MY LIFE IS BEING CONTROLLED BY SOMETHING REALLY RANDOM.
YOU CAN SEE THAT ABANDONED HOUSE FROM HERE...
hss
Oh!
I SAW A SHADOW IN THE WINDOW...
IS SOME-ONE IN THERE...?
MR. NATORI...?
WHY DO YOU THINK IT WENT TO THAT ABANDONED HOUSE?
OR MAYBE KAI?
KAI IS LOOKING FOR THE WELL...!
LET'S GO, SEN-SEI!
DASH
ARGH!
HELLO!

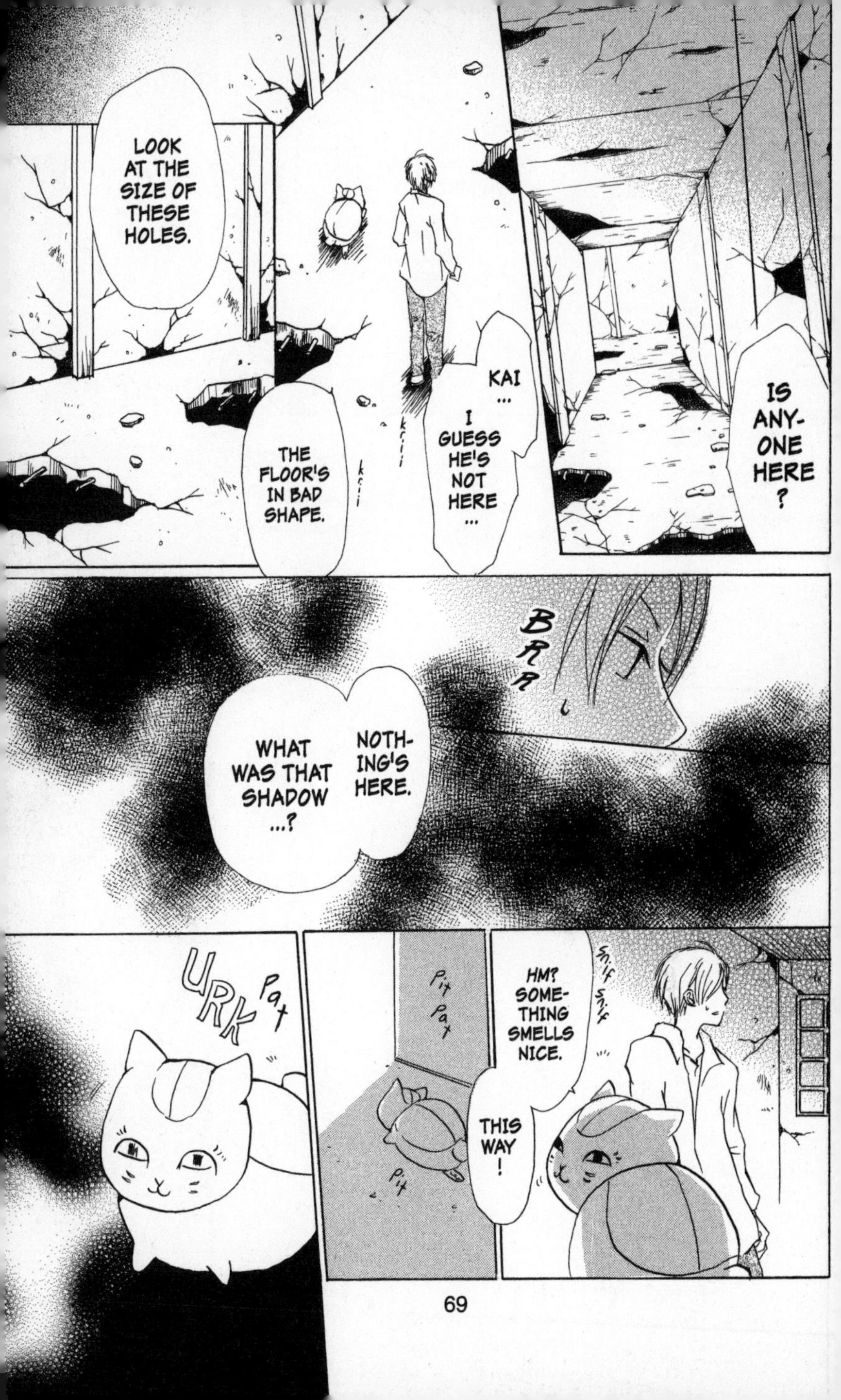
IS ANY-ONE HERE?
KAI... I GUESS HE'S NOT HERE...
kri kri
THE FLOOR'S IN BAD SHAPE.
LOOK AT THE SIZE OF THESE HOLES.
BRR
NOTH-ING'S HERE.
WHAT WAS THAT SHADOW...?
snif snif
HM? SOME-THING SMELLS NICE.
THIS WAY!
Pit Pat
Pit
URK
Pat

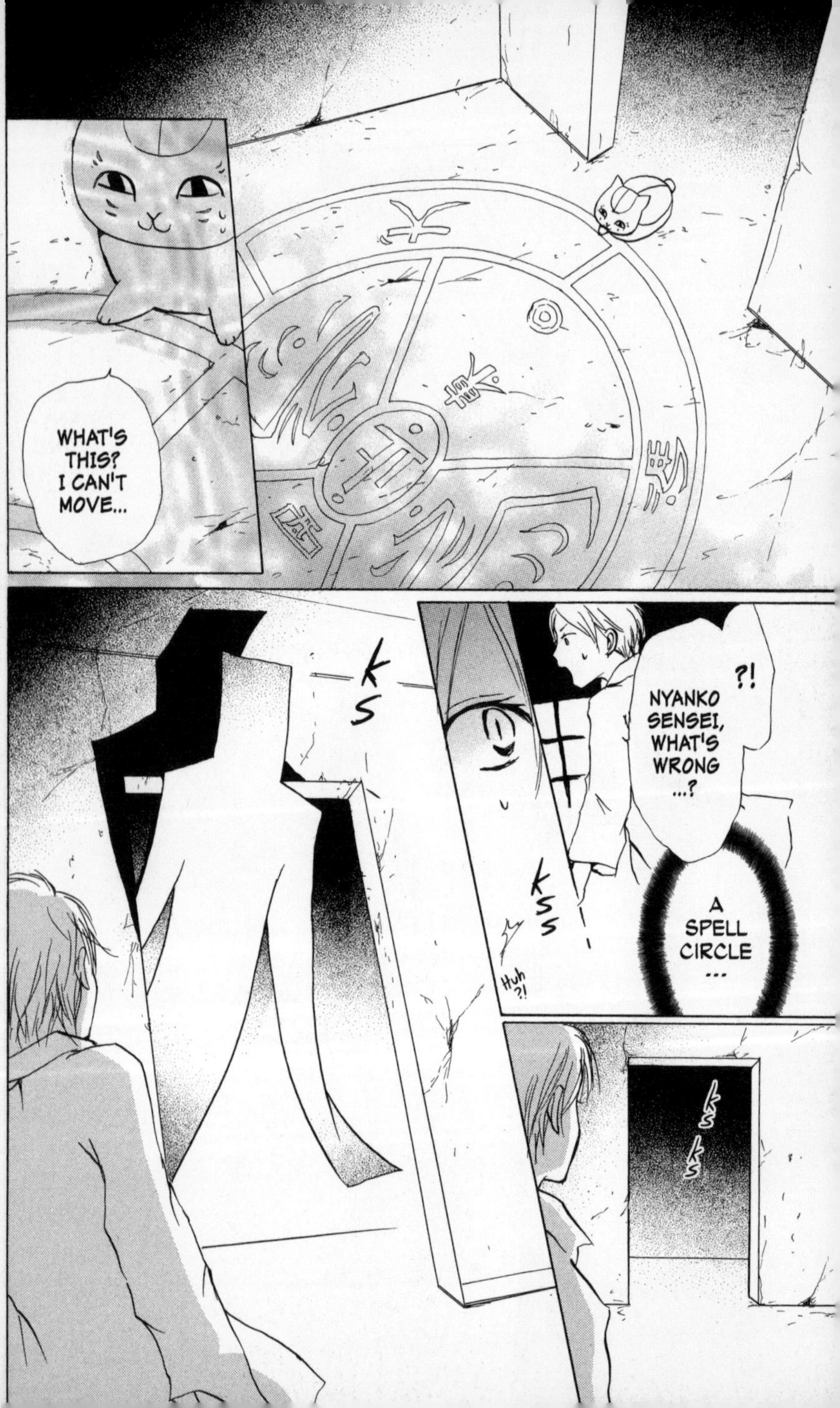
WHAT'S THIS? I CAN'T MOVE...
?!
NYANKO SENSEI, WHAT'S WRONG ...?
A SPELL CIRCLE ...
KSS
Huh ?!
ks ks
KS

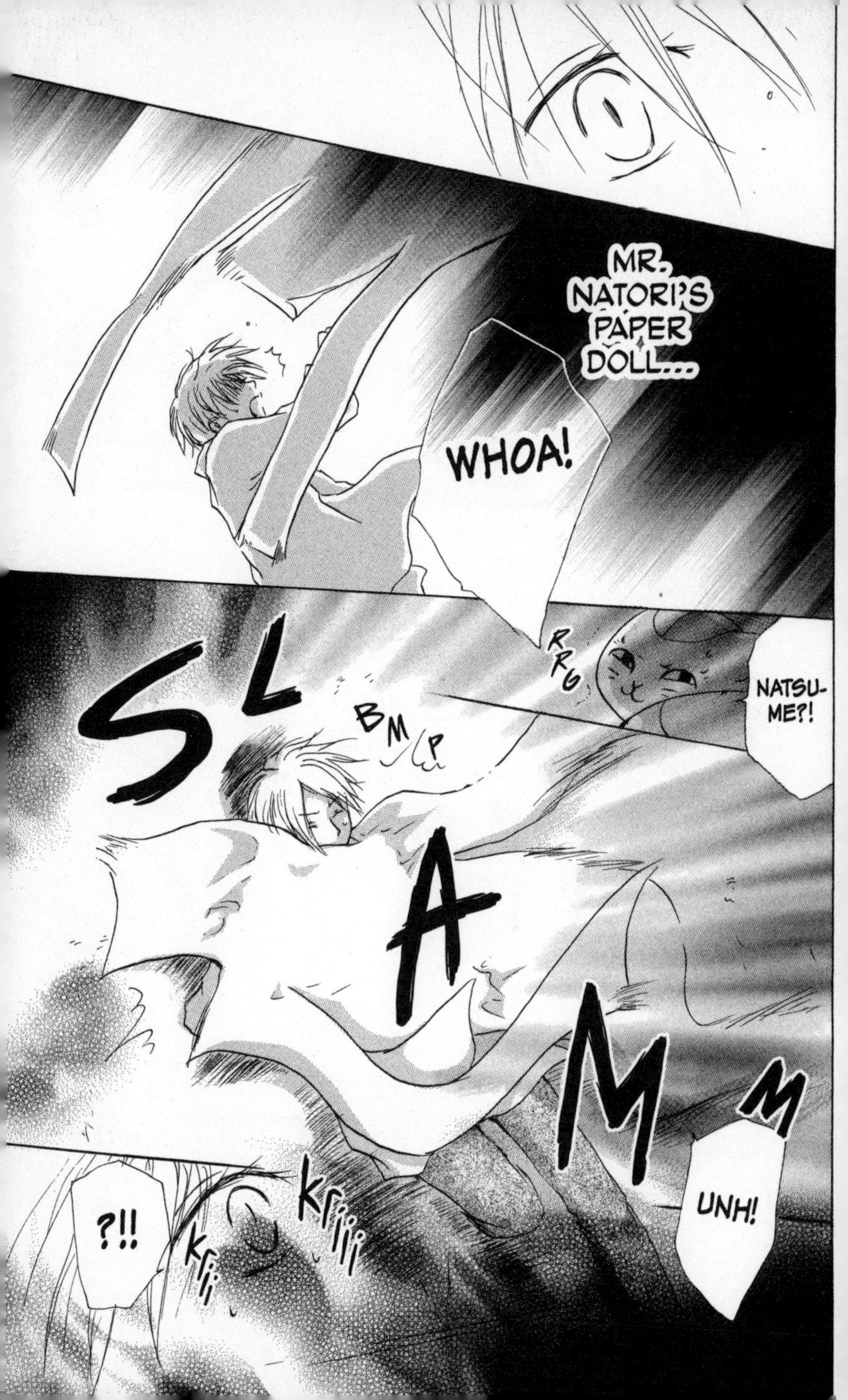
MR. NATORI'S PAPER DOLL...
WHOA!
NATSU-ME?!
RRG
BMP
SLAMM
UNH!
Kriii
Krii
?!!

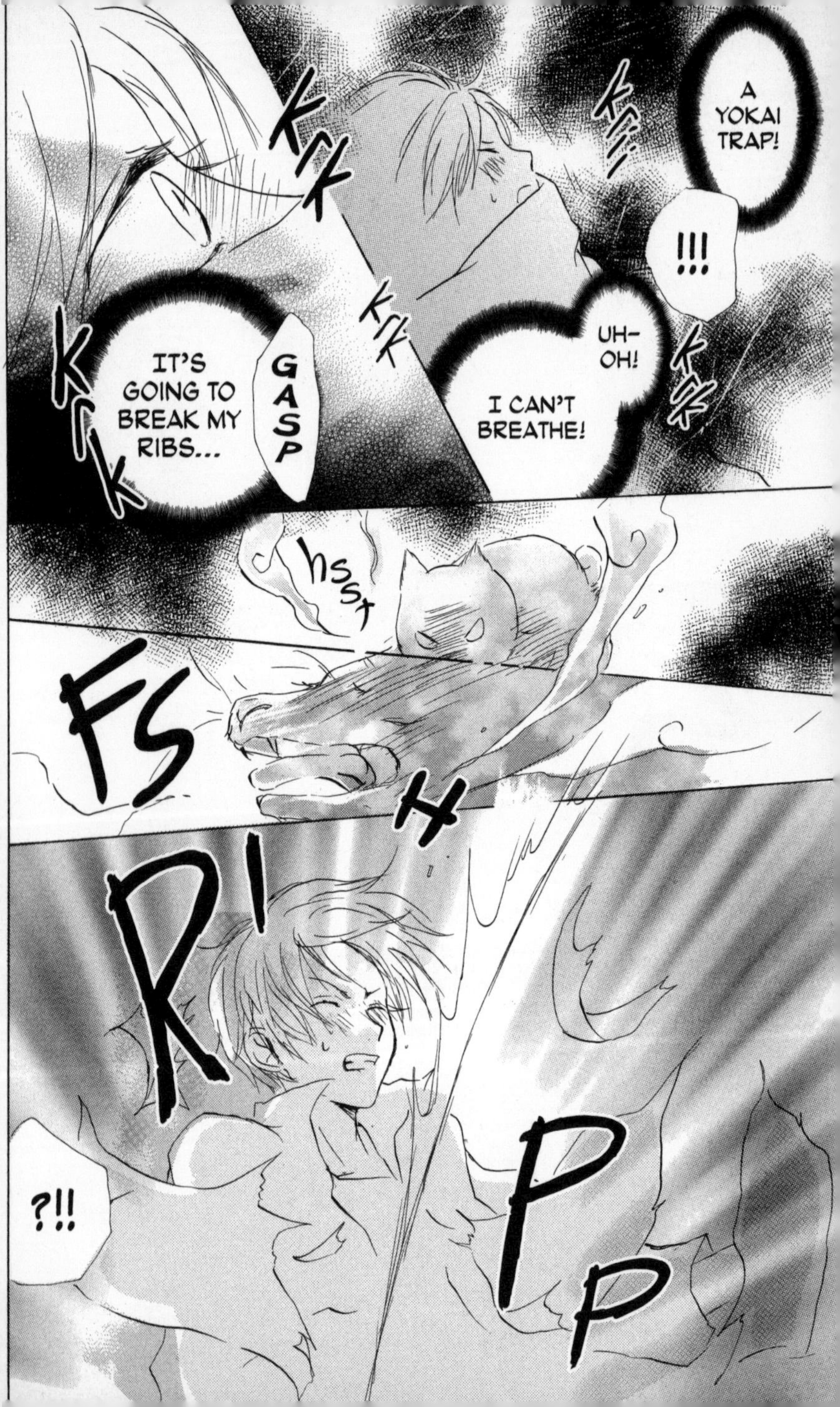
A YOKAI TRAP!
!!!
UH-OH!
I CAN'T BREATHE!
KRKK
KRK
GASP
IT'S GOING TO BREAK MY RIBS...
KRKK
HSSK
FSH
RIPP
?!!

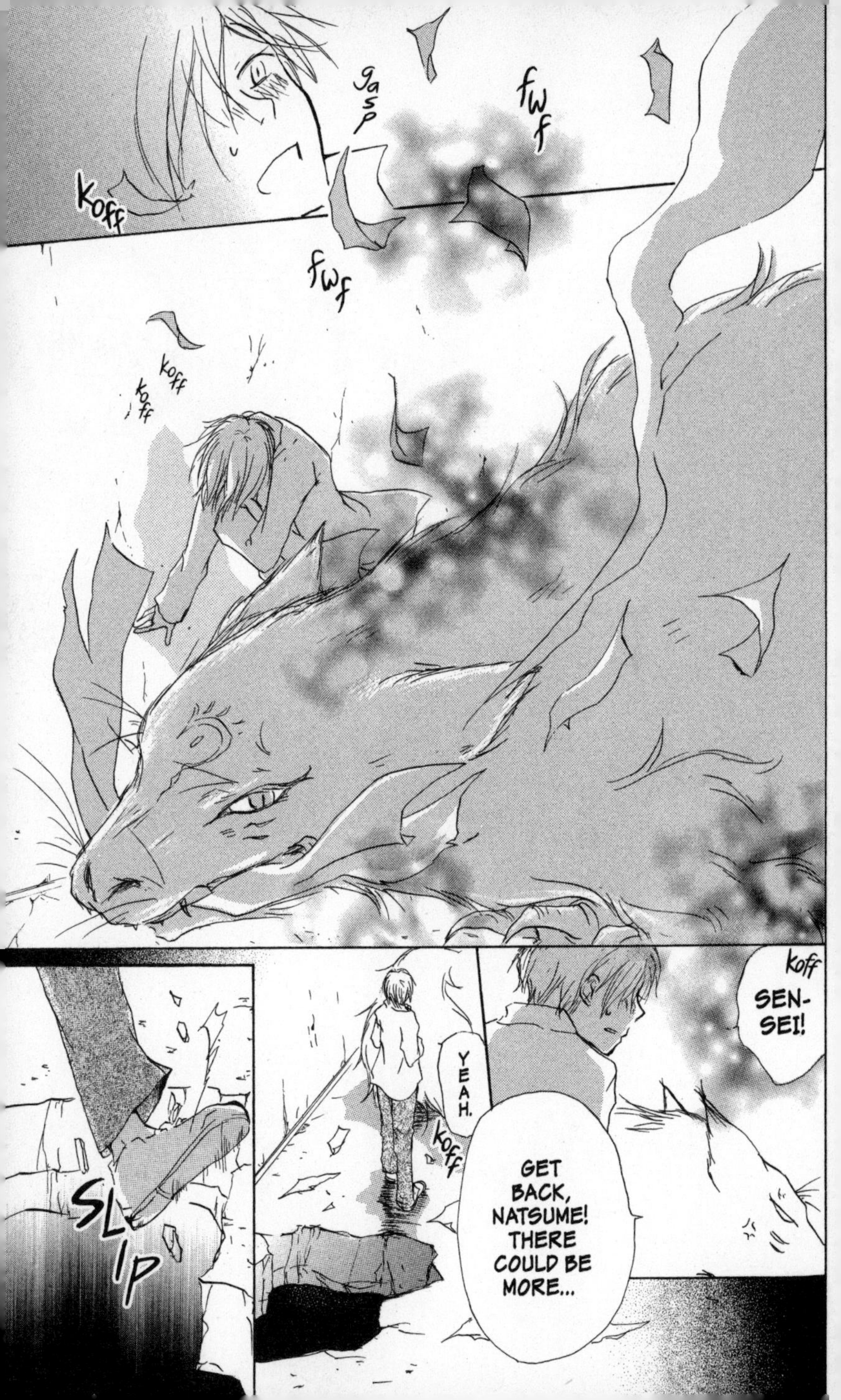
fwf
gasp
fwf
koff
koff
koff
koff
SEN-SEI!
GET BACK, NATSUME! THERE COULD BE MORE...
YEAH.
koff
SLIP

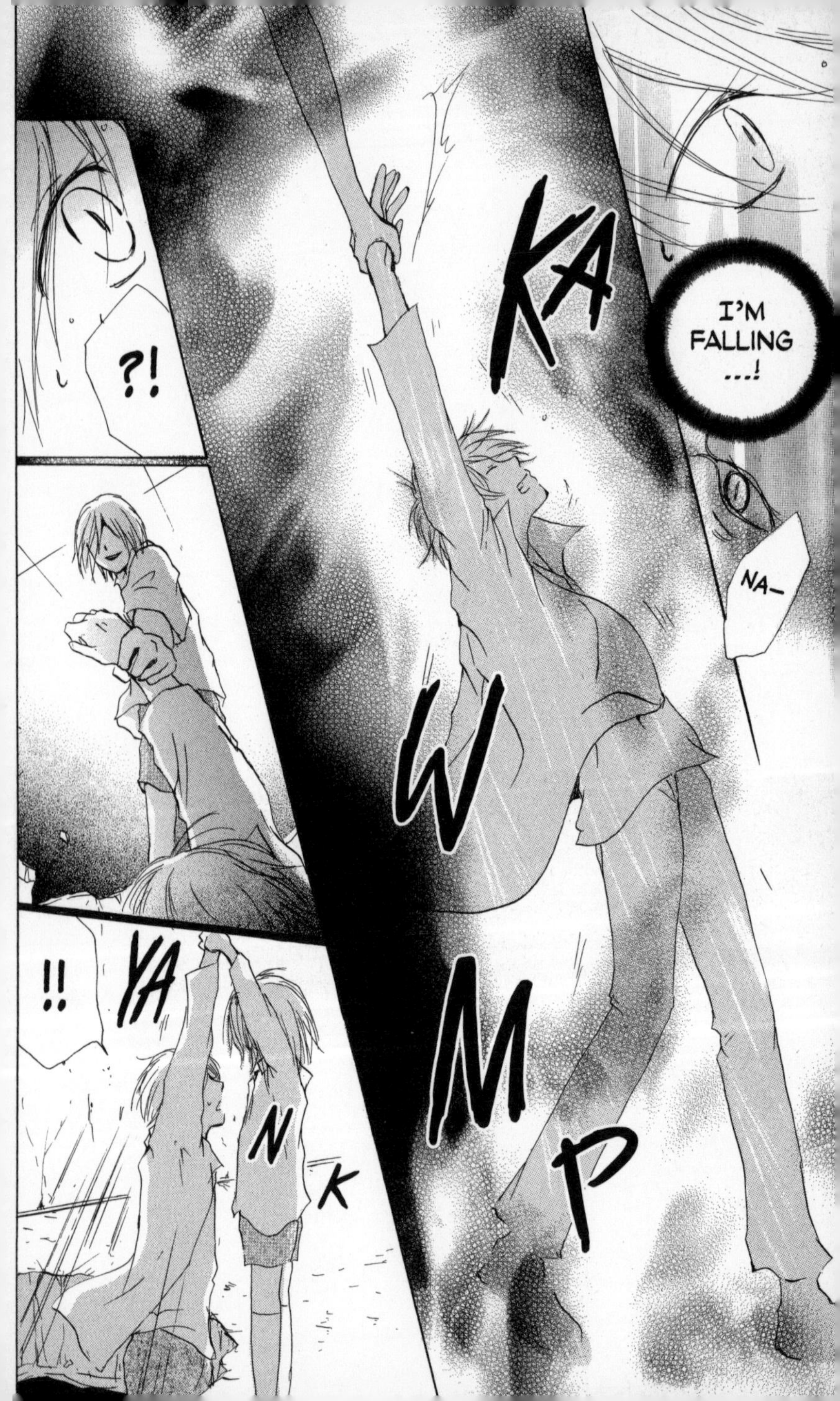
I'M FALLING ...!
NA—
KA
WUMP
?!
!!
YANK

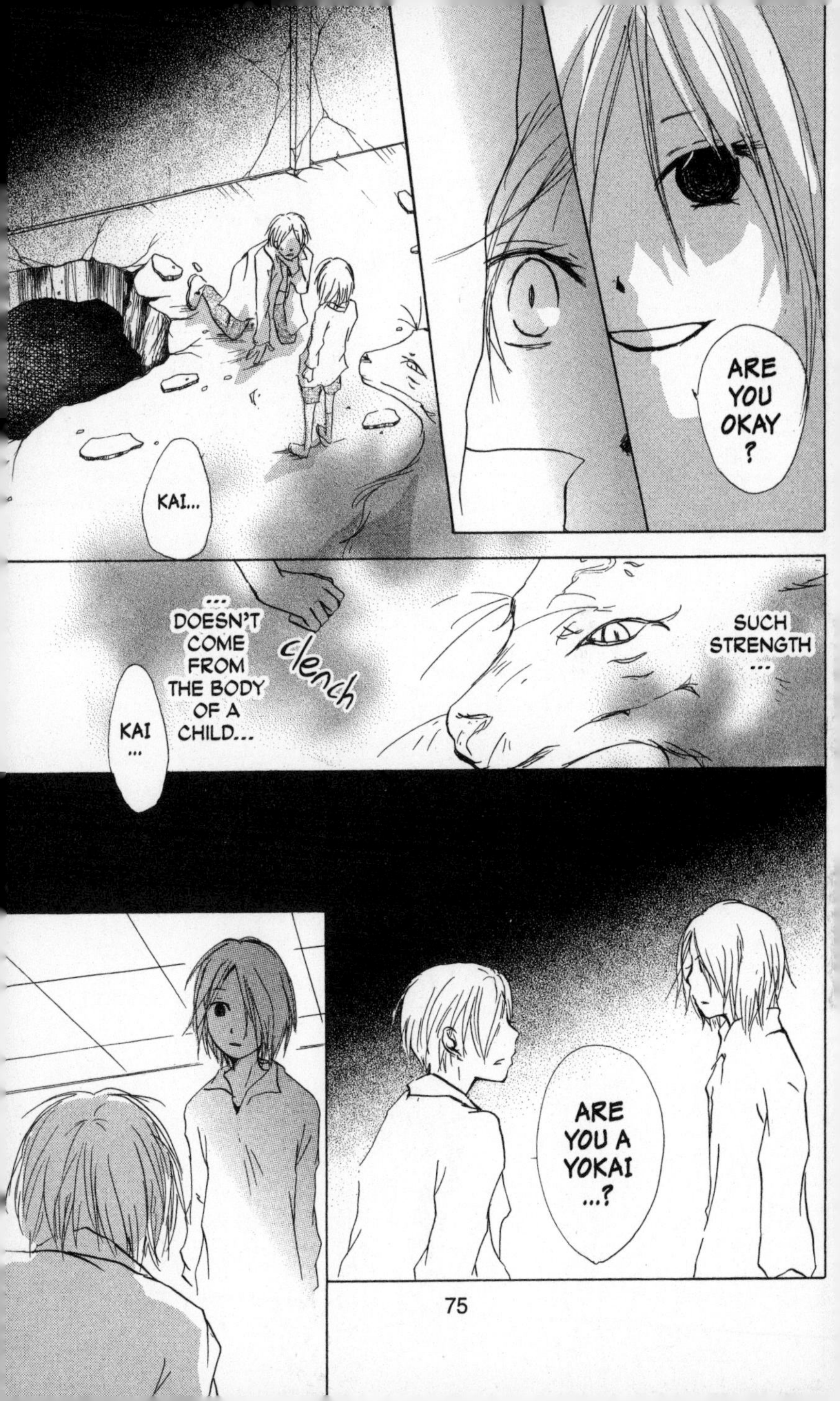
ARE YOU OKAY?
KAI...
SUCH STRENGTH...
...DOESN'T COME FROM THE BODY OF A CHILD...
clench
KAI...
ARE YOU A YOKAI...?

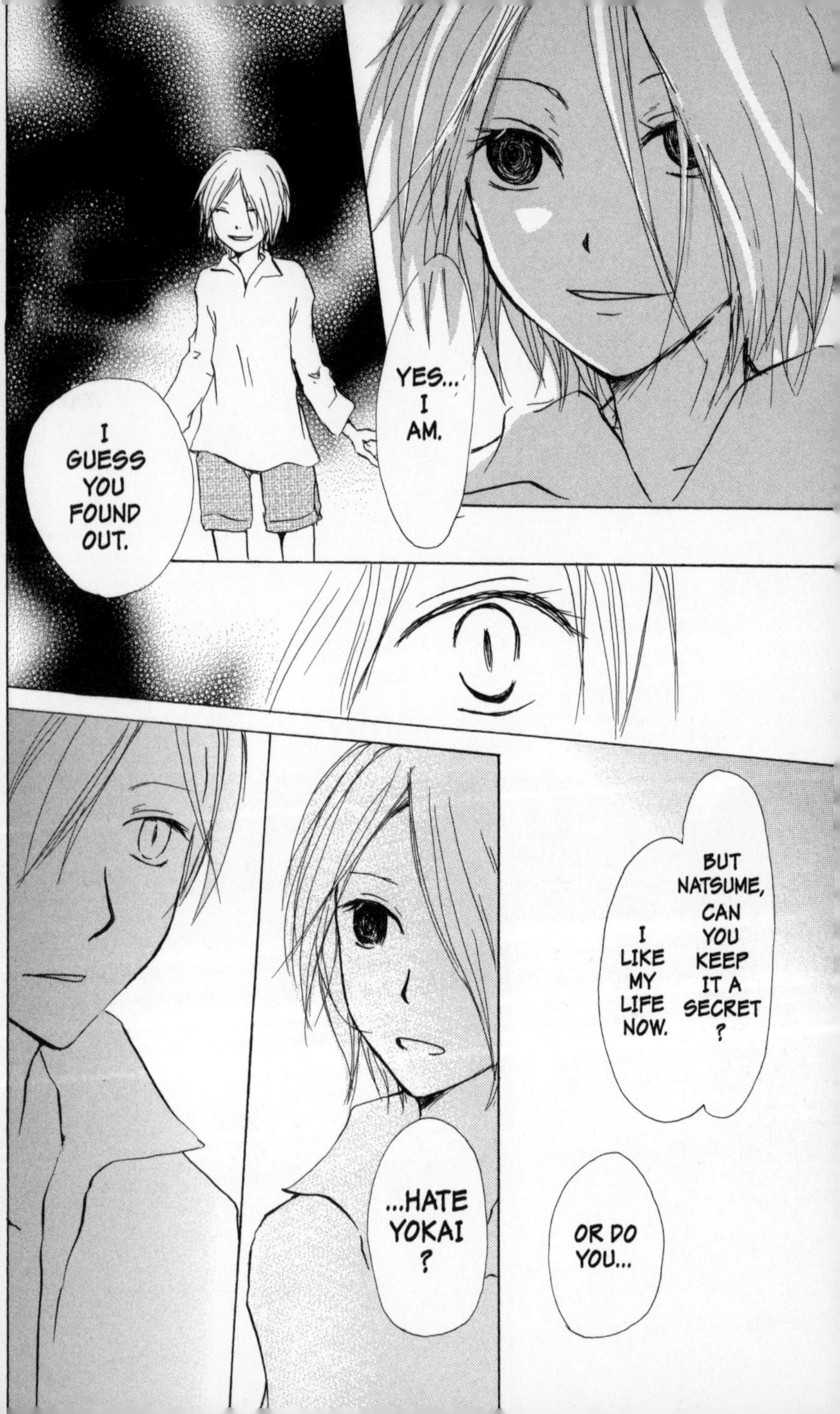
YES... I AM.
I GUESS YOU FOUND OUT.
I LIKE MY LIFE NOW. BUT NATSUME, CAN YOU KEEP IT A SECRET?
OR DO YOU...
...HATE YOKAI?

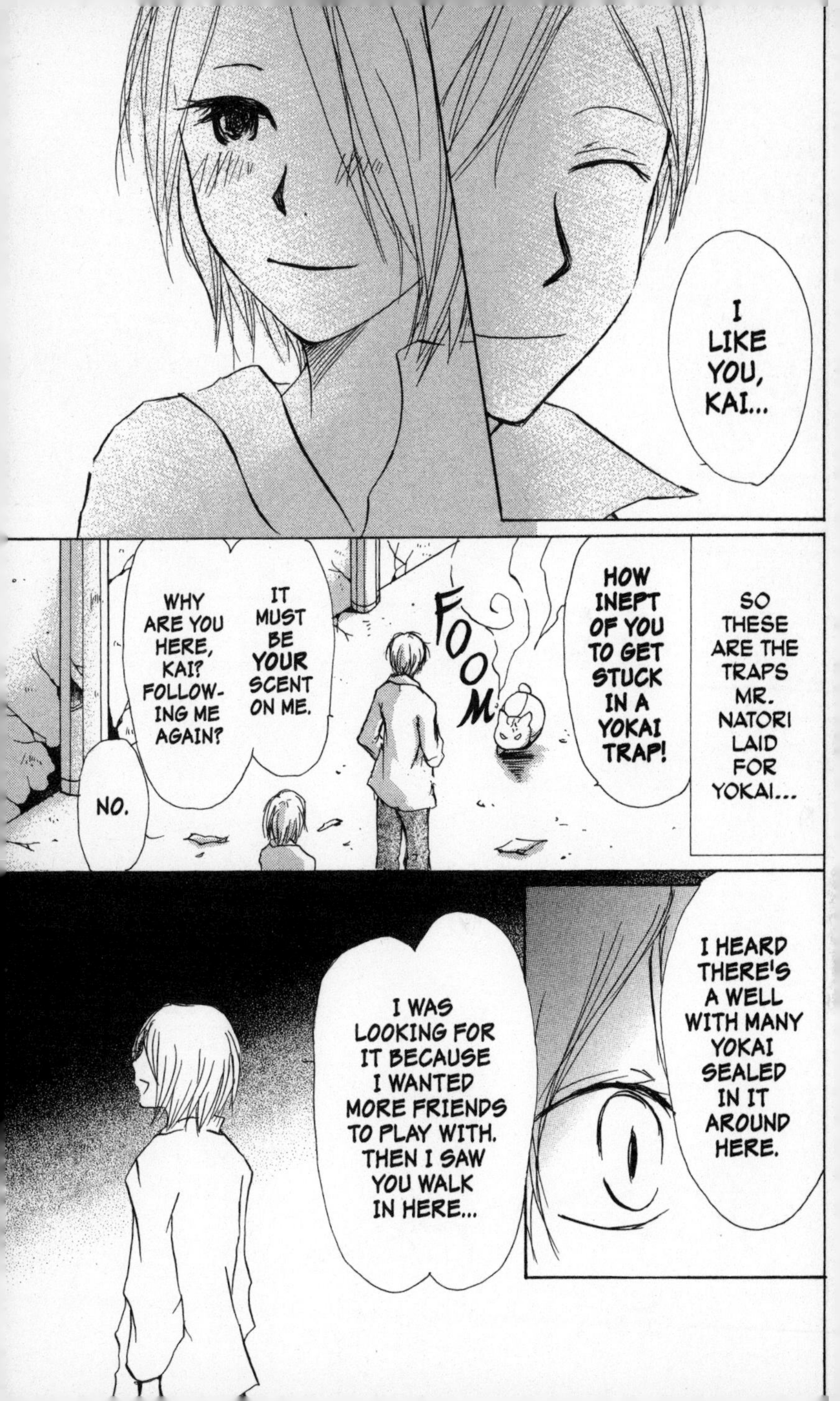
I LIKE YOU, KAI...
SO THESE ARE THE TRAPS MR. NATORI LAID FOR YOKAI...
HOW INEPT OF YOU TO GET STUCK IN A YOKAI TRAP!
FOOM
IT MUST BE YOUR SCENT ON ME.
WHY ARE YOU HERE, KAI? FOLLOW-ING ME AGAIN?
NO.
I HEARD THERE'S A WELL WITH MANY YOKAI SEALED IN IT AROUND HERE.
I WAS LOOKING FOR IT BECAUSE I WANTED MORE FRIENDS TO PLAY WITH. THEN I SAW YOU WALK IN HERE...

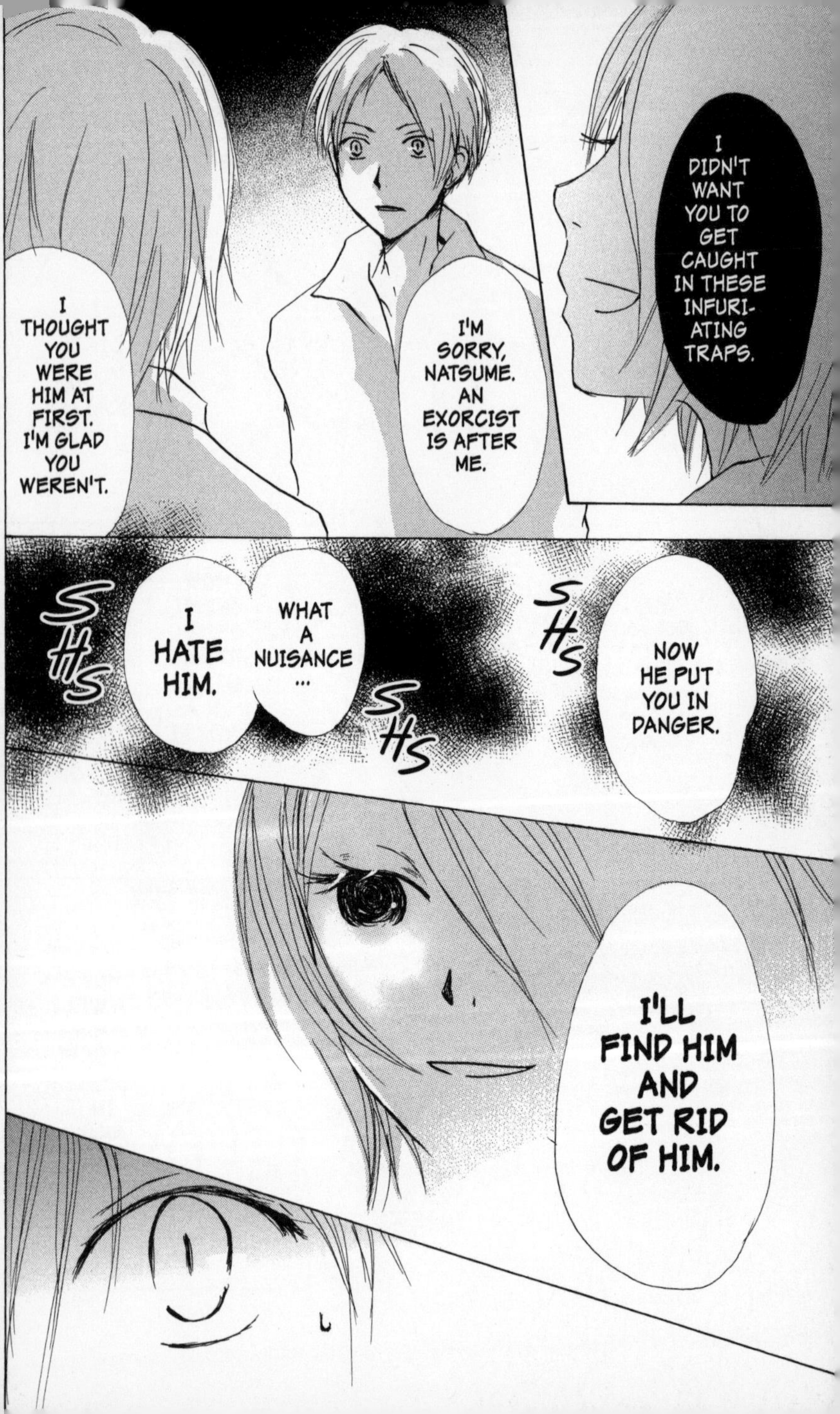
I DIDN'T WANT YOU TO GET CAUGHT IN THESE INFURIATING TRAPS.
I'M SORRY, NATSUME. AN EXORCIST IS AFTER ME.
I THOUGHT YOU WERE HIM AT FIRST. I'M GLAD YOU WEREN'T.
NOW HE PUT YOU IN DANGER.
SHS
SHS
WHAT A NUISANCE...
I HATE HIM.
SHS
I'LL FIND HIM AND GET RID OF HIM.

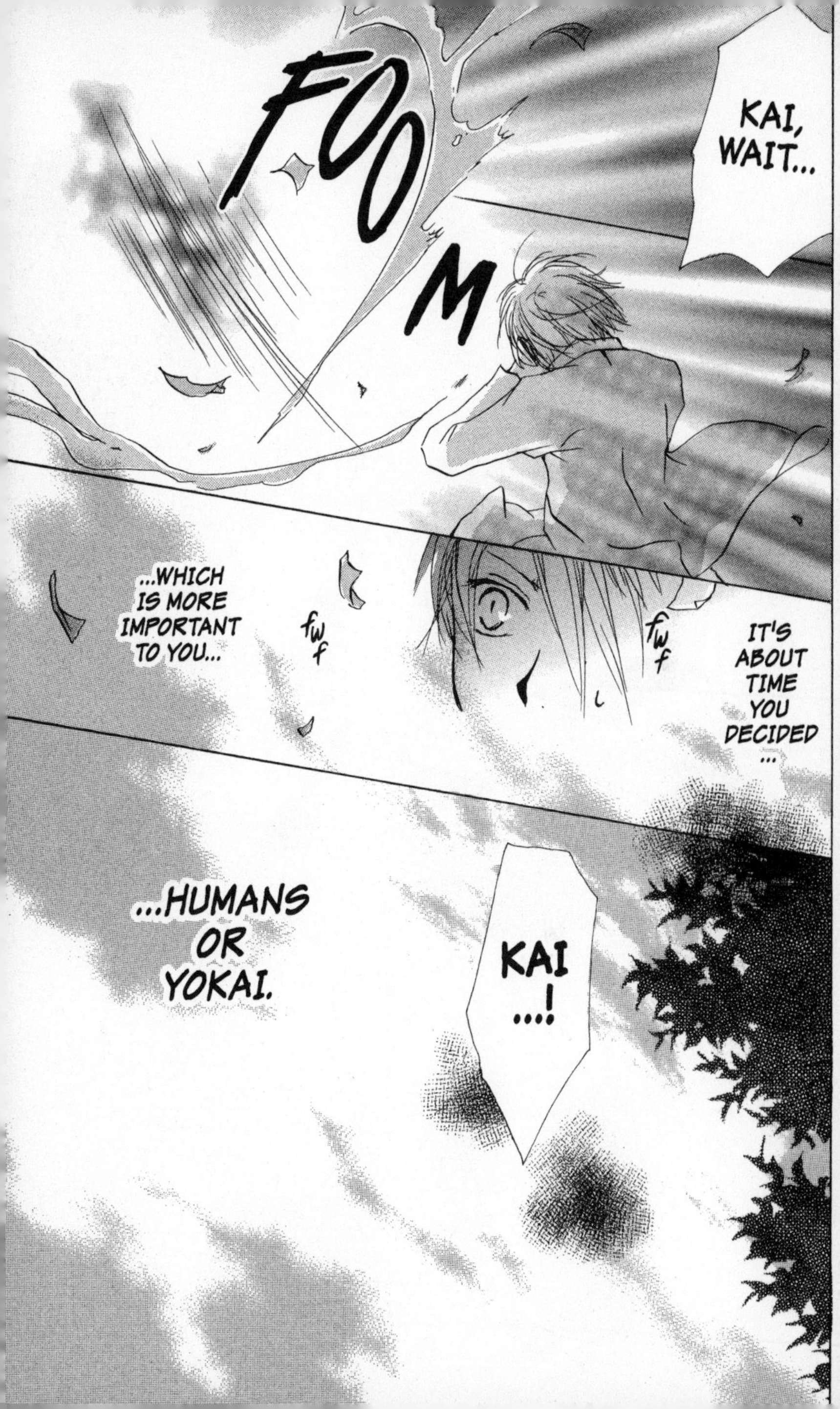
KAI, WAIT...
FOOM
IT'S ABOUT TIME YOU DECIDED...
fwf
fwf
...WHICH IS MORE IMPORTANT TO YOU...
KAI...!
...HUMANS OR YOKAI.

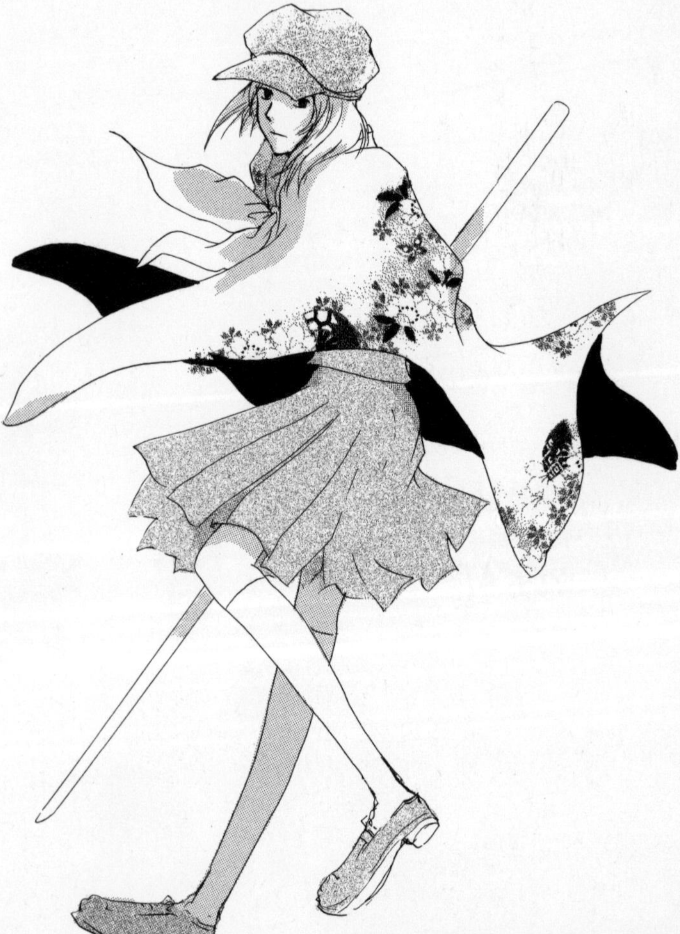

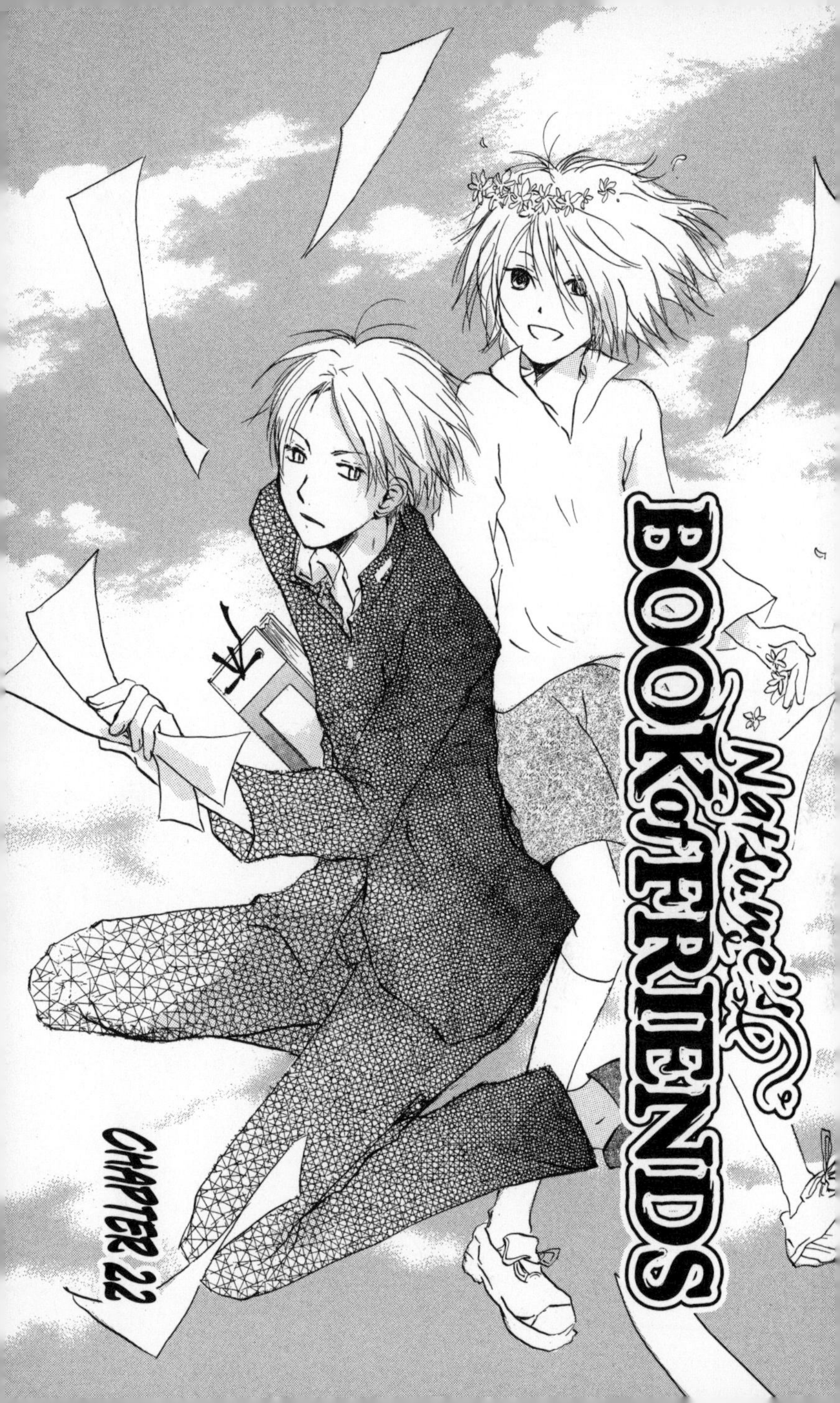
Natsume's BOOK of FRIENDS
CHAPTER 22

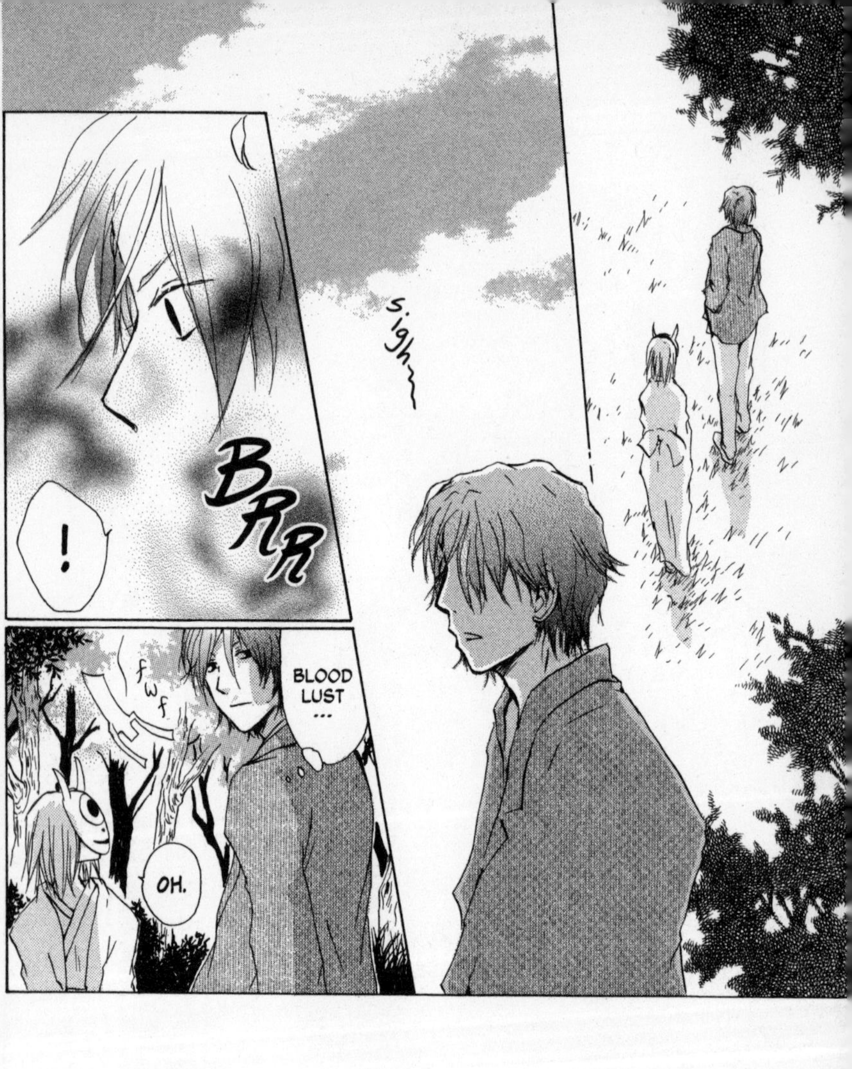
sigh~
BRR
!
fwf
BLOOD LUST ...
OH.

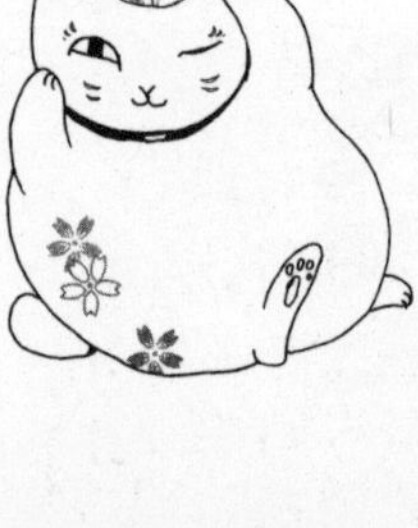

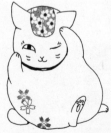

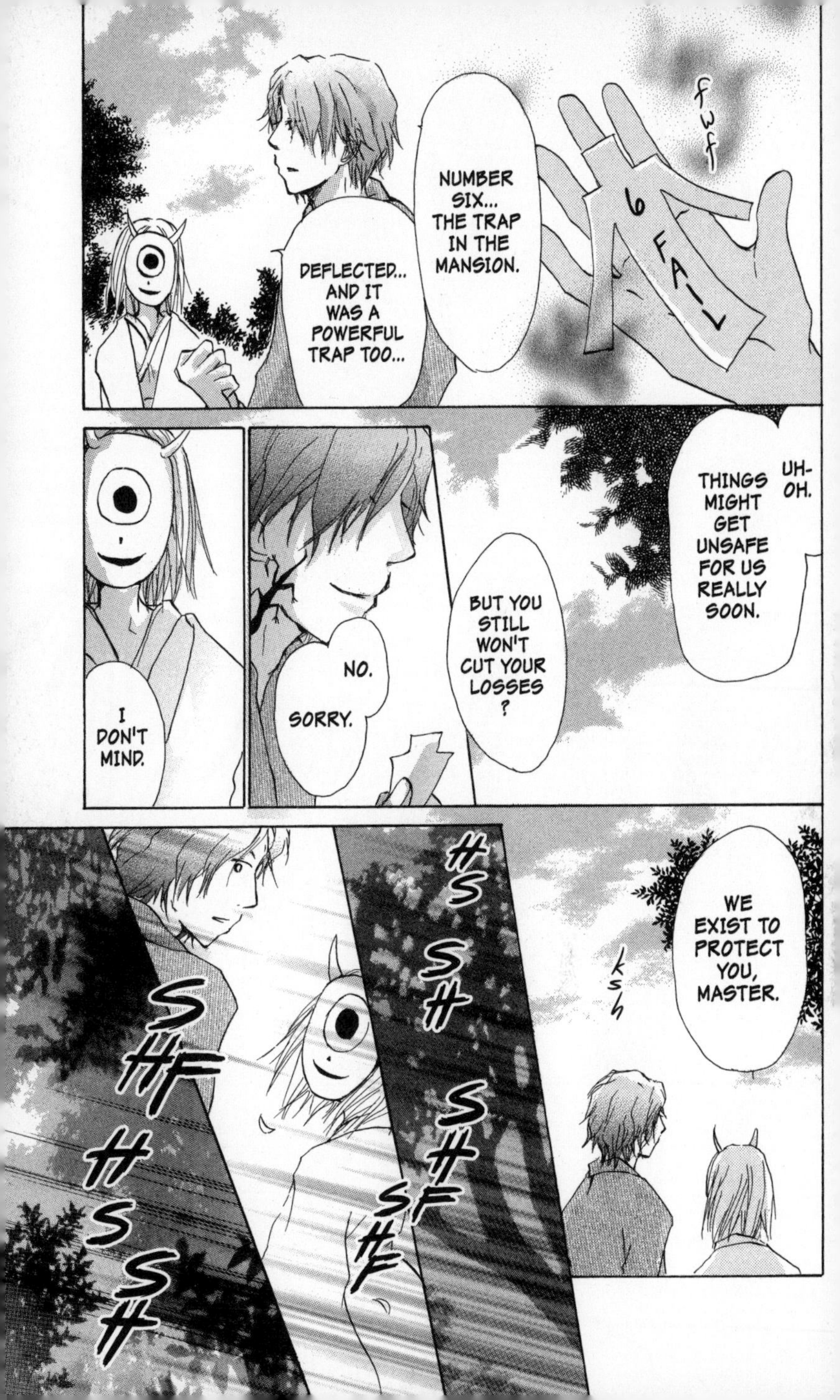
fwf
6
FAIL
NUMBER SIX... THE TRAP IN THE MANSION.
DEFLECTED... AND IT WAS A POWERFUL TRAP TOO...
UH-OH.
THINGS MIGHT GET UNSAFE FOR US REALLY SOON.
BUT YOU STILL WON'T CUT YOUR LOSSES?
NO.
SORRY.
I DON'T MIND.
WE EXIST TO PROTECT YOU, MASTER.
ksh
HS
SH
SHF
SF
SHF
SHF
HS
SH

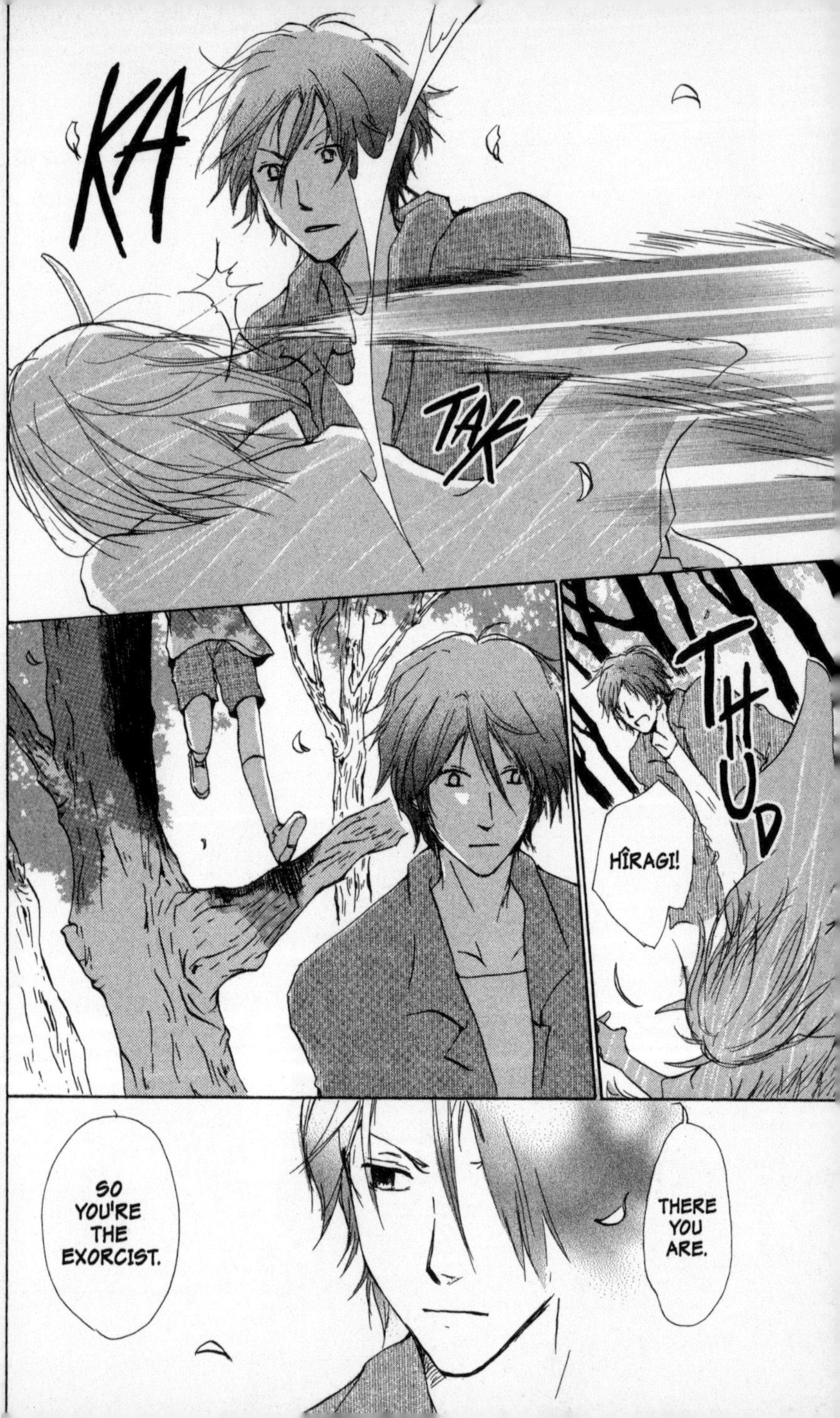
KA
TAK
THUD
HÎRAGI!
THERE YOU ARE.
SO YOU'RE THE EXORCIST.

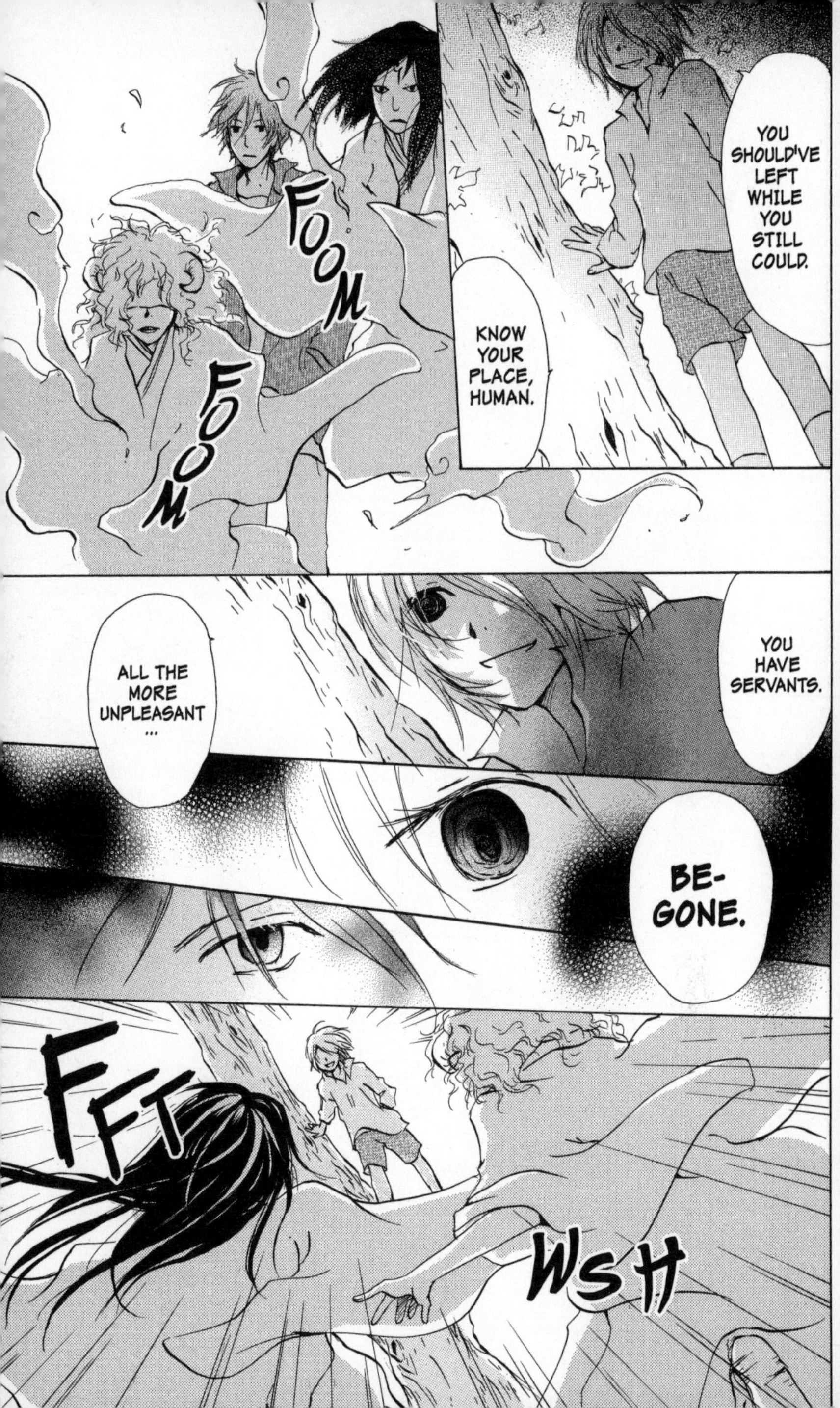
YOU SHOULD'VE LEFT WHILE YOU STILL COULD.
KNOW YOUR PLACE, HUMAN.
FOOM
FOOM
YOU HAVE SERVANTS.
ALL THE MORE UNPLEASANT ...
BE-GONE.
FFT
WSH

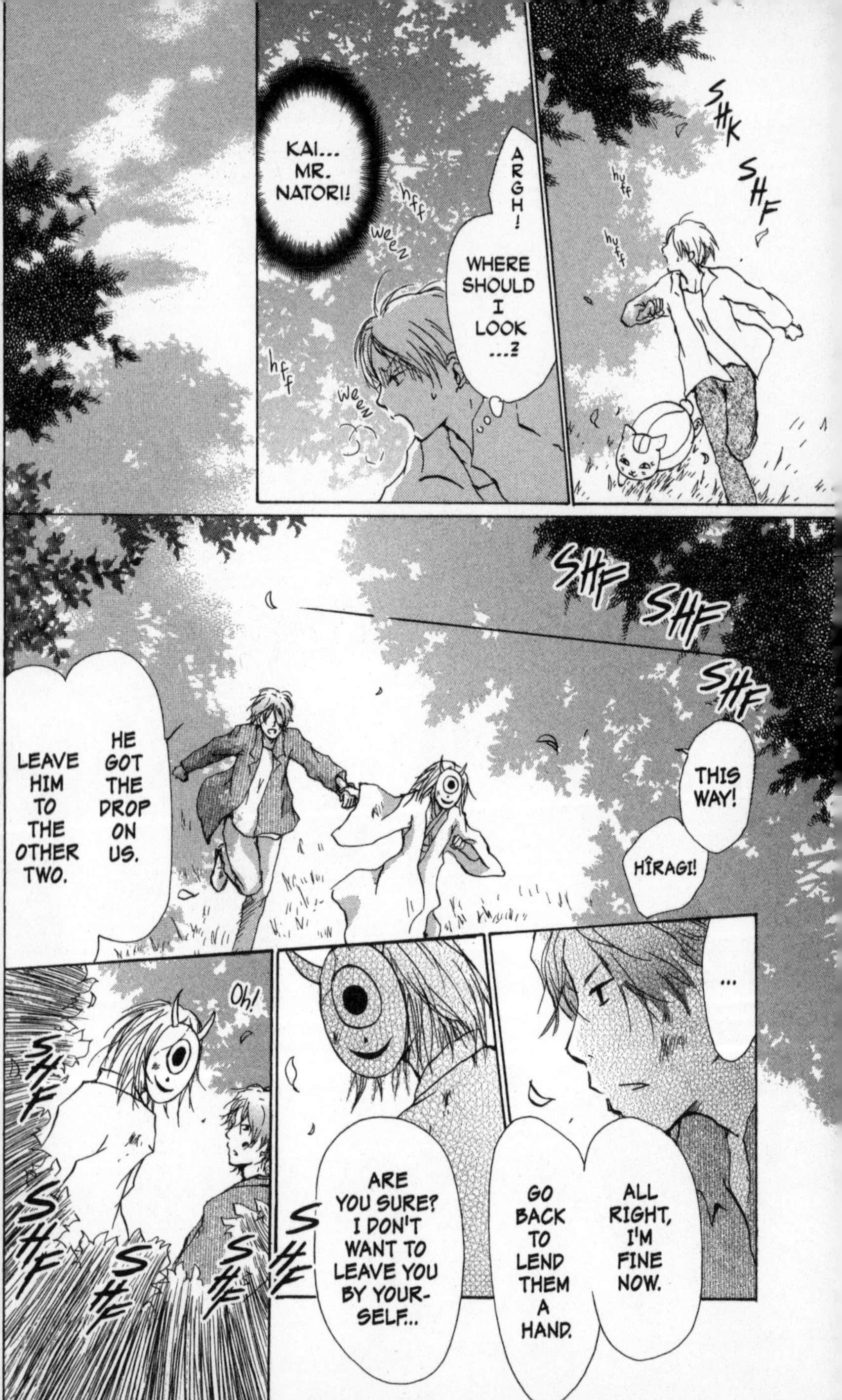
SHK
SHF
huff
huff
ARGH!
WHERE SHOULD I LOOK ...?
hff
weez
hff
ween
KAI... MR. NATORI!
SHF
SHF
SHF
THIS WAY!
HÎRAGI!
HE GOT THE DROP ON US.
LEAVE HIM TO THE OTHER TWO.
...
ALL RIGHT, I'M FINE NOW.
GO BACK TO LEND THEM A HAND.
ARE YOU SURE? I DON'T WANT TO LEAVE YOU BY YOURSELF...
SHF
Oh!
SHF
SHF
SHF
SHF

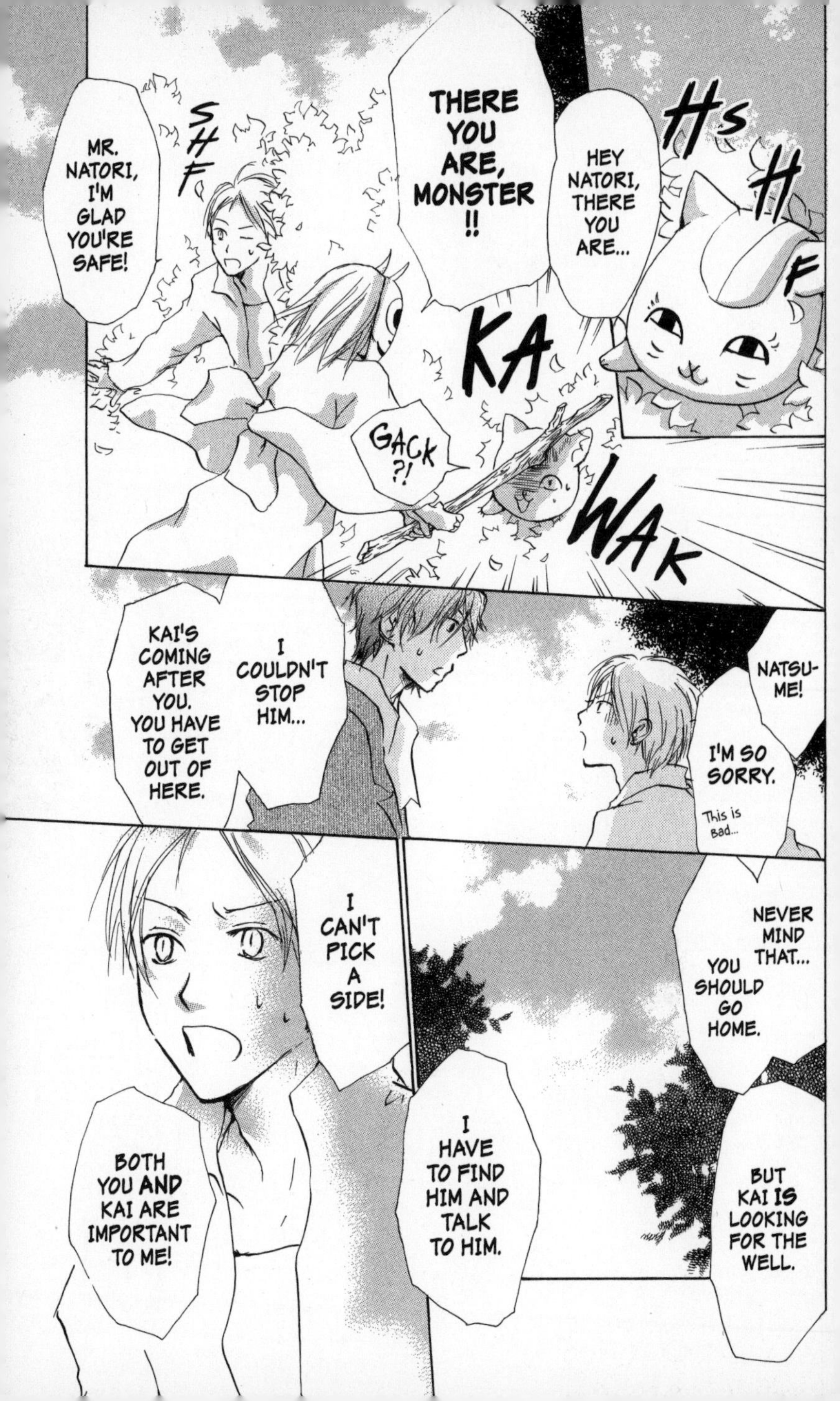
HS H F
HEY NATORI, THERE YOU ARE...
THERE YOU ARE, MONSTER!!
KA
WAK
GACK ?!
SHF
MR. NATORI, I'M GLAD YOU'RE SAFE!
NATSU-ME!
I'M SO SORRY.
This is bad...
I COULDN'T STOP HIM...
KAI'S COMING AFTER YOU. YOU HAVE TO GET OUT OF HERE.
NEVER MIND THAT...
YOU SHOULD GO HOME.
BUT KAI IS LOOKING FOR THE WELL.
I HAVE TO FIND HIM AND TALK TO HIM.
I CAN'T PICK A SIDE!
BOTH YOU AND KAI ARE IMPORTANT TO ME!

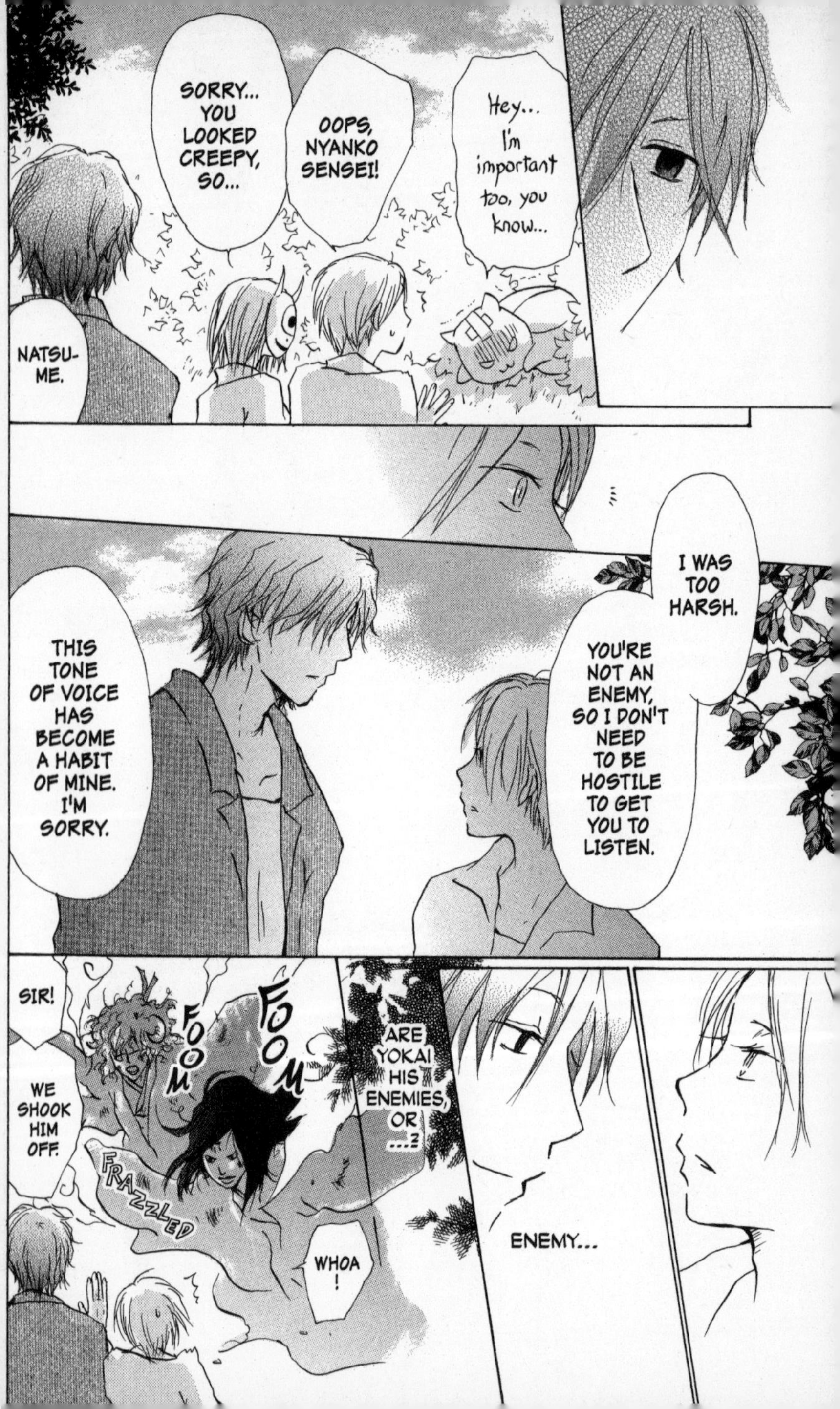
Hey... I'm important too, you know...
OOPS, NYANKO SENSEI!
SORRY... YOU LOOKED CREEPY, SO...
NATSU-ME.
I WAS TOO HARSH.
YOU'RE NOT AN ENEMY, SO I DON'T NEED TO BE HOSTILE TO GET YOU TO LISTEN.
THIS TONE OF VOICE HAS BECOME A HABIT OF MINE. I'M SORRY.
ENEMY...
ARE YOKAI HIS ENEMIES, OR ...?
FOOM
FOOM
SIR!
WE SHOOK HIM OFF.
FRAZZLED
WHOA!

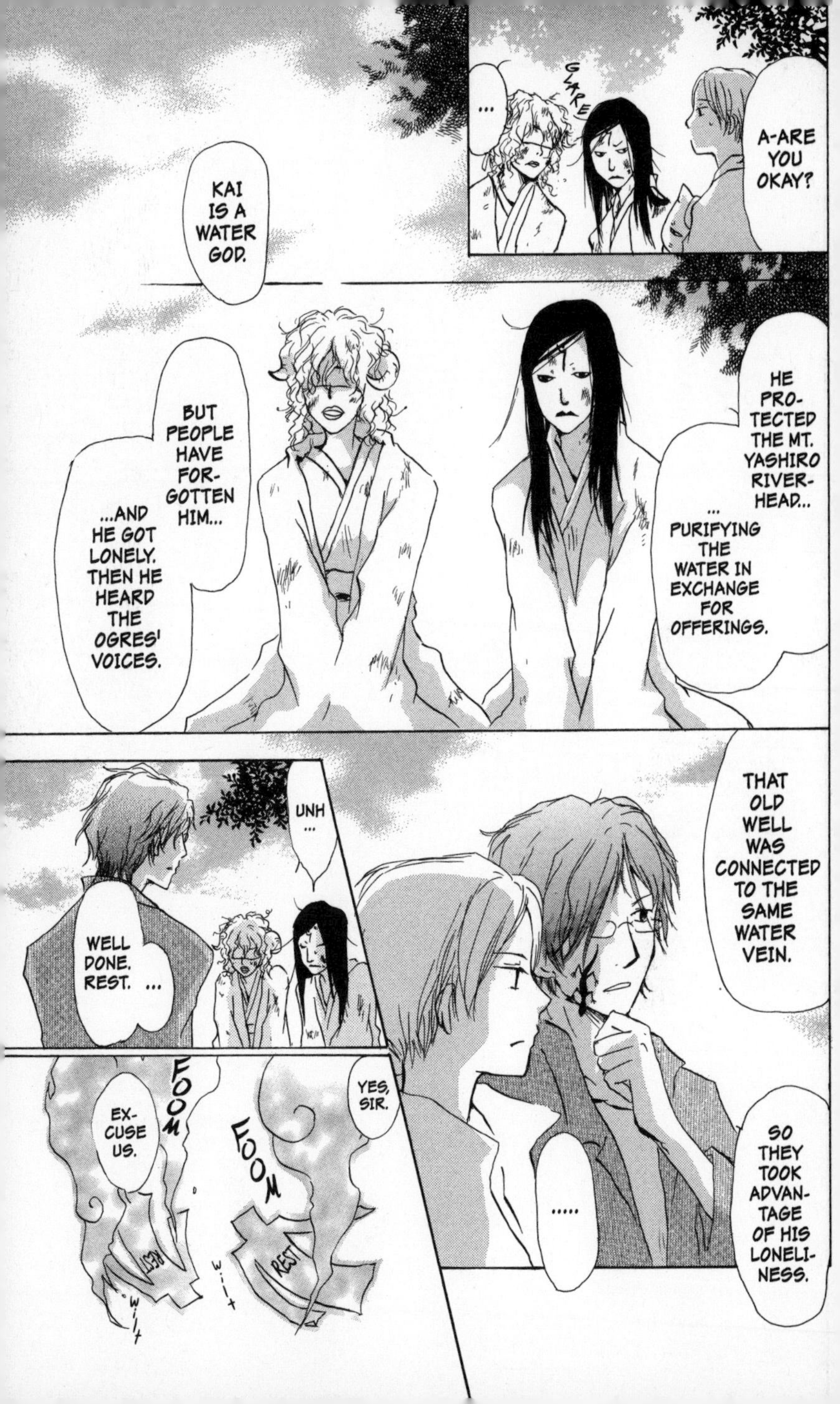
A-ARE YOU OKAY?
GLARE
...
KAI IS A WATER GOD.
HE PROTECTED THE MT. YASHIRO RIVER-HEAD...
... PURIFYING THE WATER IN EXCHANGE FOR OFFERINGS.
BUT PEOPLE HAVE FOR-GOTTEN HIM...
...AND HE GOT LONELY. THEN HE HEARD THE OGRES' VOICES.
THAT OLD WELL WAS CONNECTED TO THE SAME WATER VEIN.
SO THEY TOOK ADVAN-TAGE OF HIS LONELI-NESS.
.....
UNH ...
WELL DONE. REST. ...
YES, SIR.
EX-CUSE US.
FOOM
FOOM
REST
REST
wilt
wilt

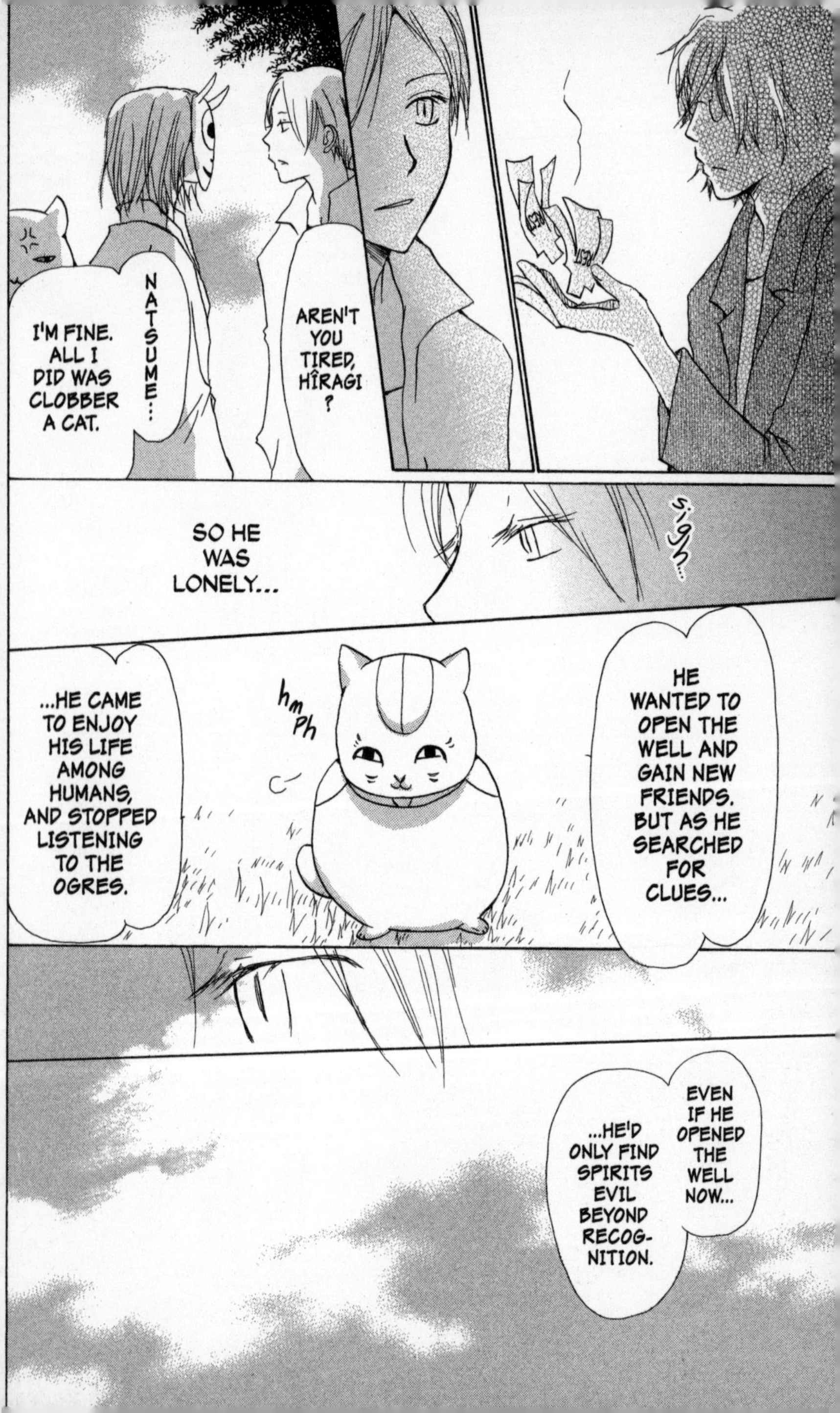
AREN'T YOU TIRED, HÎRAGI?
NATSUME...
I'M FINE. ALL I DID WAS CLOBBER A CAT.
sigh...
SO HE WAS LONELY...
HE WANTED TO OPEN THE WELL AND GAIN NEW FRIENDS. BUT AS HE SEARCHED FOR CLUES...
hmph
...HE CAME TO ENJOY HIS LIFE AMONG HUMANS, AND STOPPED LISTENING TO THE OGRES.
EVEN IF HE OPENED THE WELL NOW...
...HE'D ONLY FIND SPIRITS EVIL BEYOND RECOG-NITION.

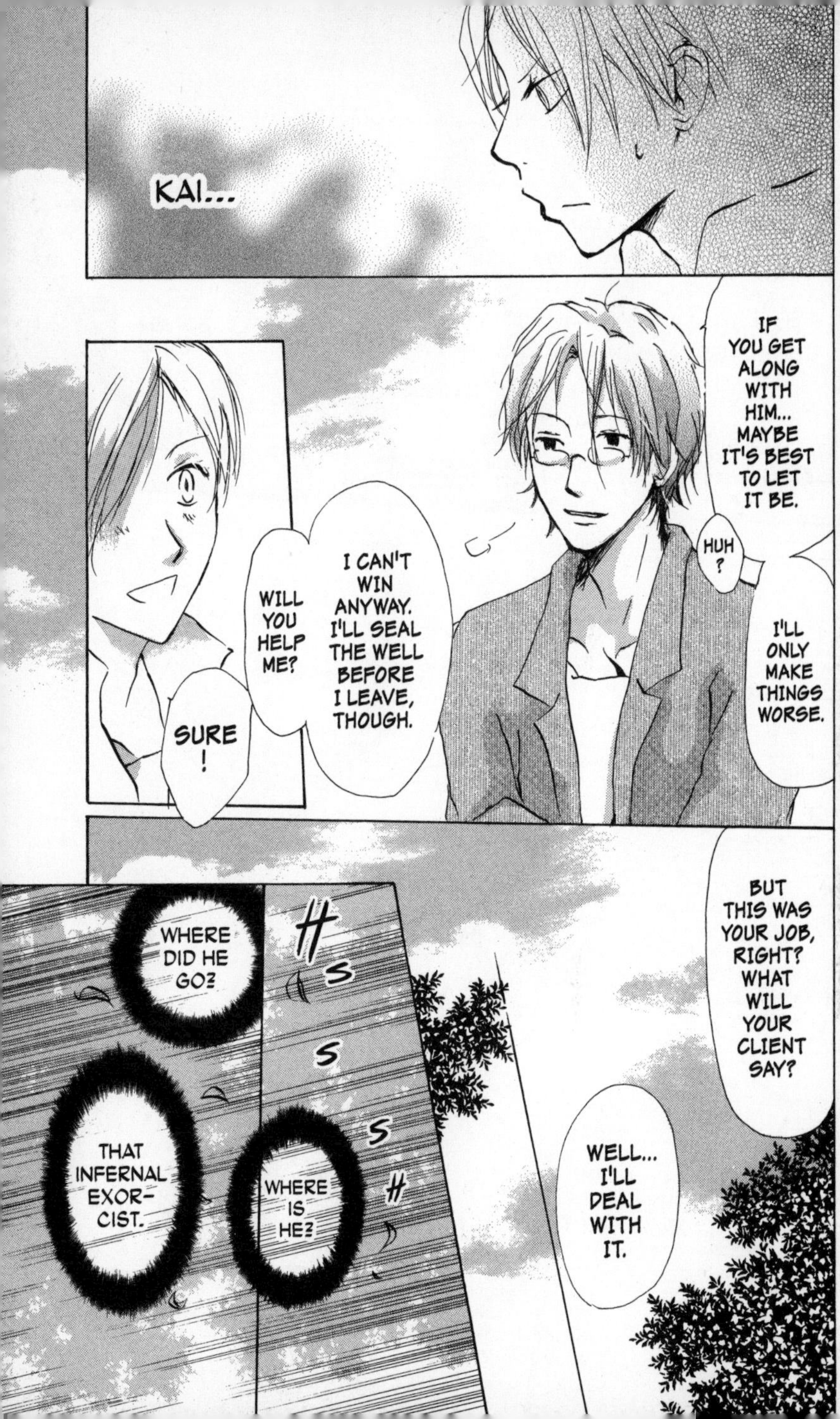
KAI...
IF YOU GET ALONG WITH HIM... MAYBE IT'S BEST TO LET IT BE.
HUH?
I'LL ONLY MAKE THINGS WORSE.
I CAN'T WIN ANYWAY. I'LL SEAL THE WELL BEFORE I LEAVE, THOUGH.
WILL YOU HELP ME?
SURE!
BUT THIS WAS YOUR JOB, RIGHT? WHAT WILL YOUR CLIENT SAY?
WELL... I'LL DEAL WITH IT.
HSSSH
WHERE IS HE?
WHERE DID HE GO?
THAT INFERNAL EXORCIST.

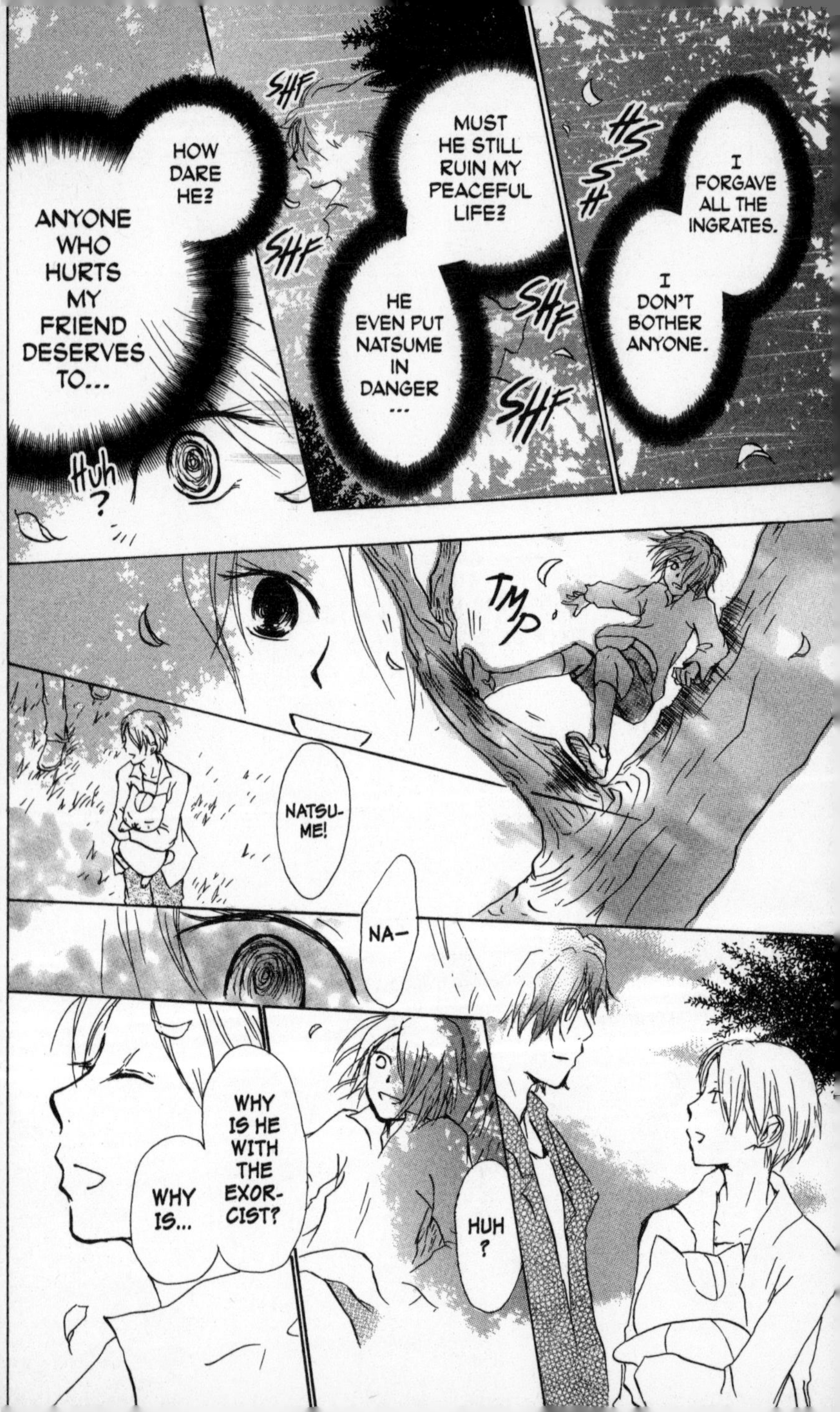
HSSH
I FORGAVE ALL THE INGRATES.
I DON'T BOTHER ANYONE.
SHF SHF SHF SHF
MUST HE STILL RUIN MY PEACEFUL LIFE?
HE EVEN PUT NATSUME IN DANGER...
HOW DARE HE?
ANYONE WHO HURTS MY FRIEND DESERVES TO...
Huh?
TMP
NATSU-ME!
NA—
HUH?
WHY IS HE WITH THE EXORCIST?
WHY IS...

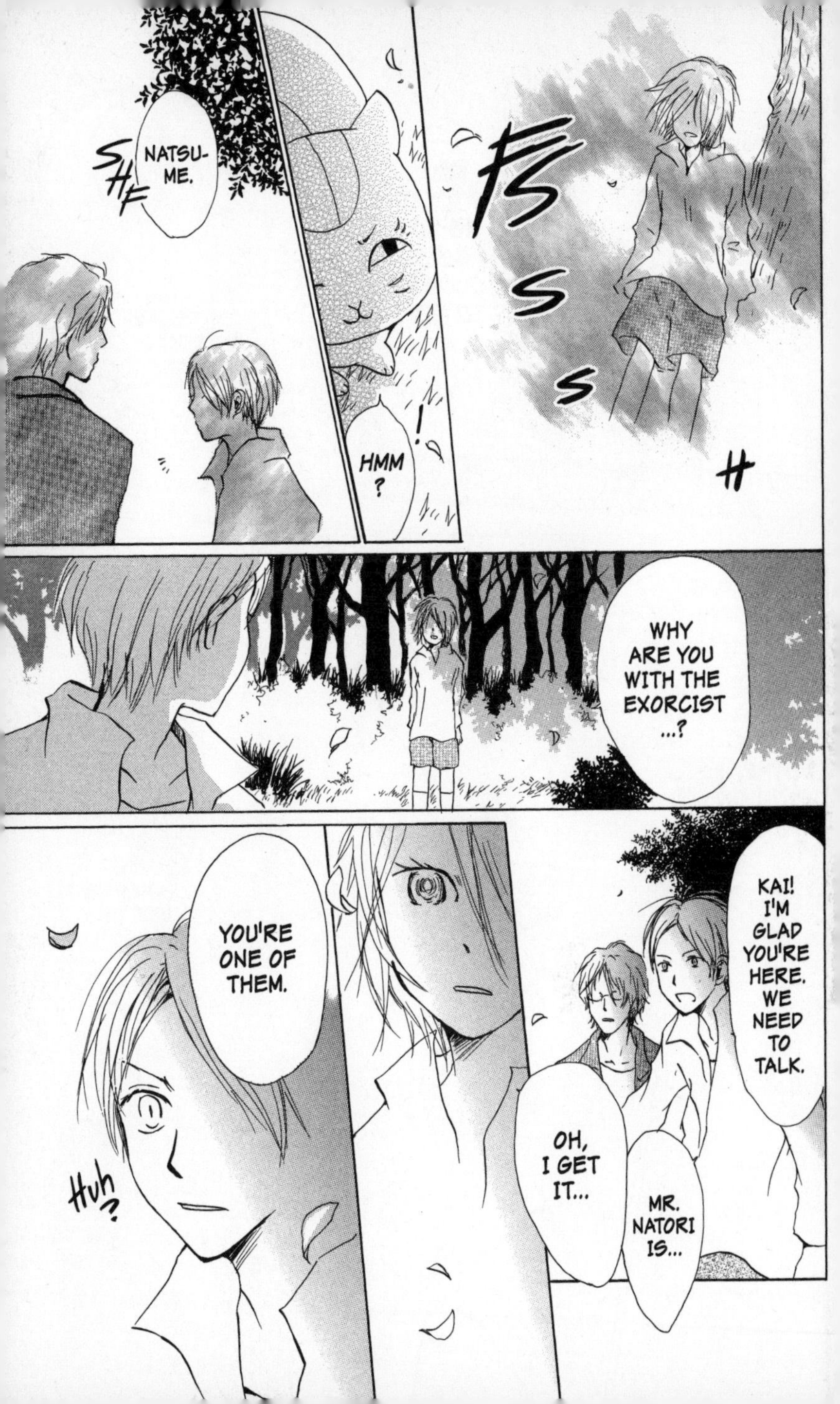
FS
S
S
H
!
HMM ?
NATSU-ME.
SHF
WHY ARE YOU WITH THE EXORCIST ...?
KAI! I'M GLAD YOU'RE HERE. WE NEED TO TALK.
OH, I GET IT...
MR. NATORI IS...
YOU'RE ONE OF THEM.
Huh?

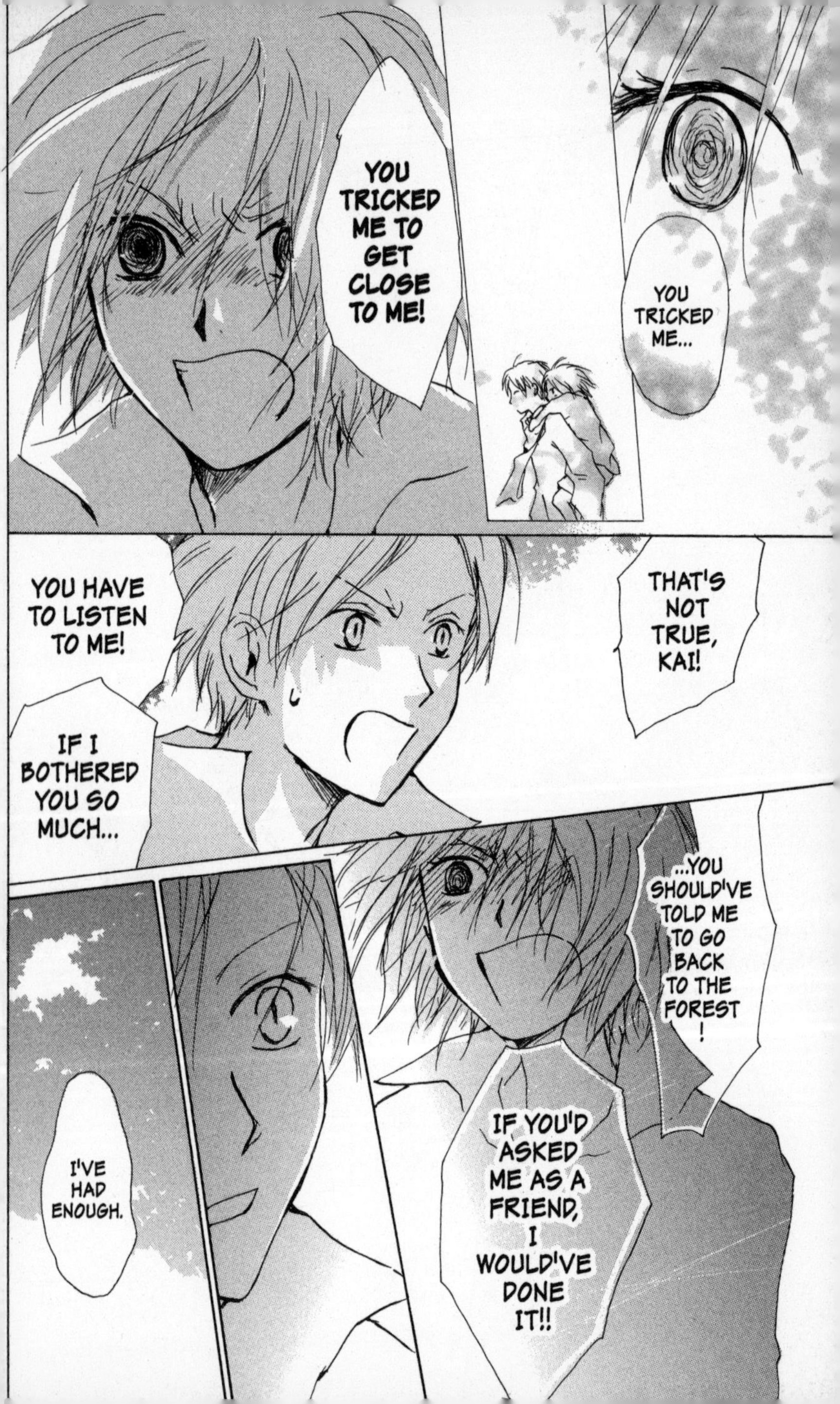
YOU TRICKED ME...
YOU TRICKED ME TO GET CLOSE TO ME!
THAT'S NOT TRUE, KAI!
YOU HAVE TO LISTEN TO ME!
IF I BOTHERED YOU SO MUCH...
...YOU SHOULD'VE TOLD ME TO GO BACK TO THE FOREST!
IF YOU'D ASKED ME AS A FRIEND, I WOULD'VE DONE IT!!
I'VE HAD ENOUGH.

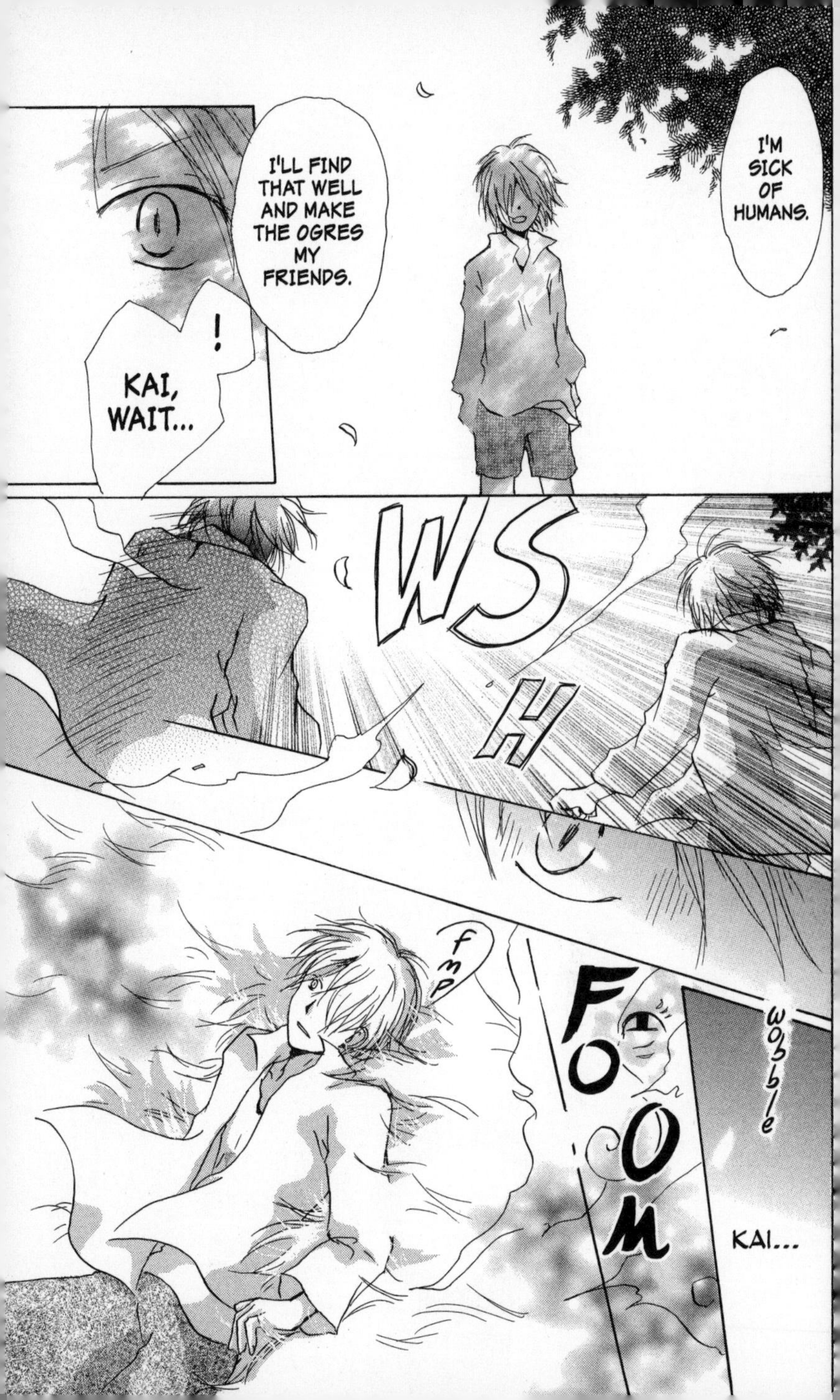

I'M SICK OF HUMANS.
I'LL FIND THAT WELL AND MAKE THE OGRES MY FRIENDS.
!
KAI, WAIT...
WSH
wobble
FOOM
fmp
KAI...

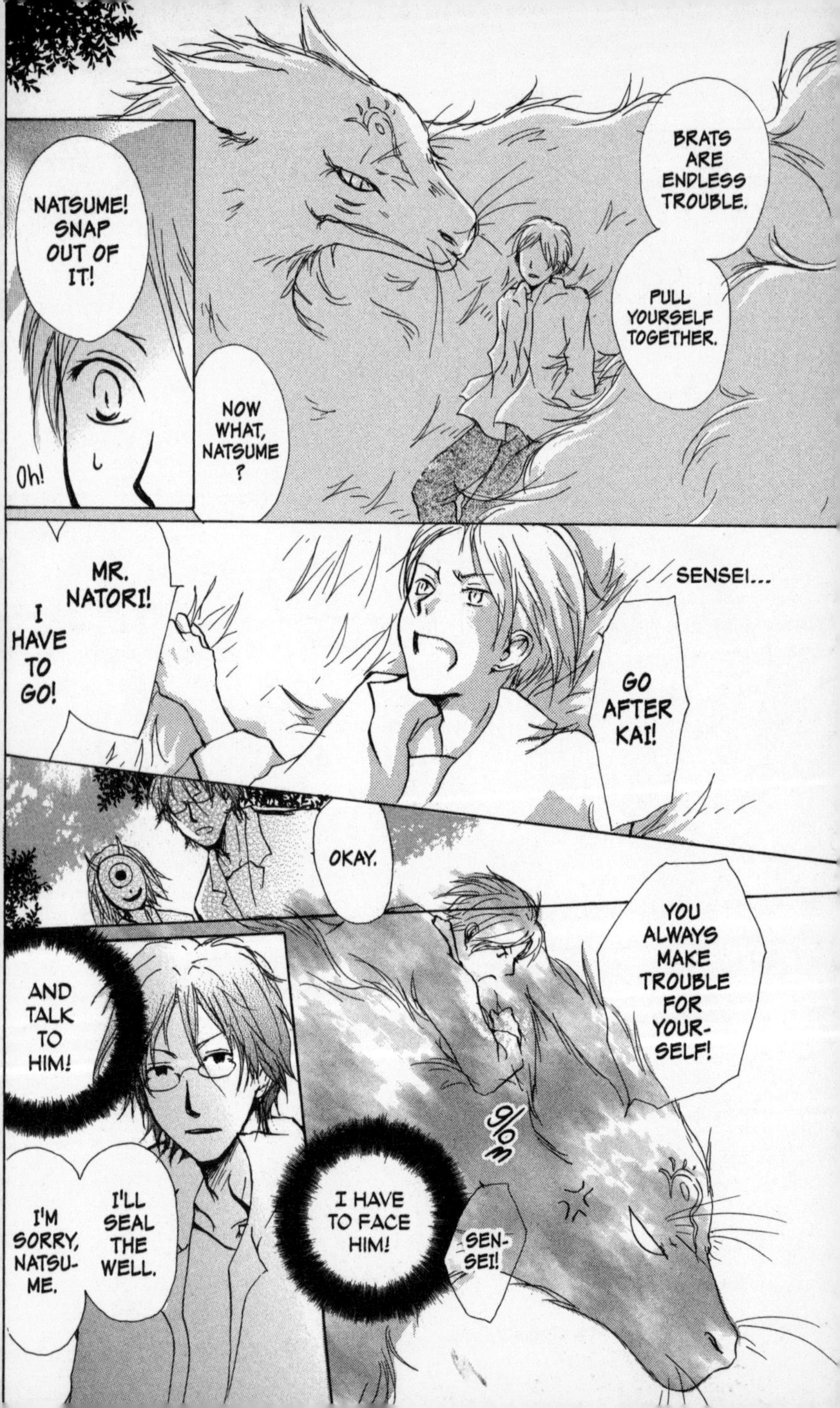
BRATS ARE ENDLESS TROUBLE.
PULL YOURSELF TOGETHER.
NOW WHAT, NATSUME?
NATSUME! SNAP OUT OF IT!
Oh!
SENSEI...
GO AFTER KAI!
MR. NATORI!
I HAVE TO GO!
OKAY.
YOU ALWAYS MAKE TROUBLE FOR YOUR-SELF!
SEN-SEI!
I HAVE TO FACE HIM!
AND TALK TO HIM!
I'LL SEAL THE WELL.
I'M SORRY, NATSU-ME.

03

❋ My second autograph session: part 2

They made a cute, traditional Japanese-themed space in a corner of the bookstore. Round paper lanterns and Japanese patterned cloth were beautifully arranged. I had to hold myself back from prancing around snapping tons of pictures.

Thankfully, a lot of people came, and as usual, I was really nervous and speechless with joy. But their enthusiasm was really contagious. It hit home that I can't make anything that would disappoint them. I promise to keep working harder. I was so happy to have met my fans. Thank you for the letters, flowers, and gifts— I'll cherish them.

I would also like to thank my editors who helped, along with Kumazawa Bookstore.

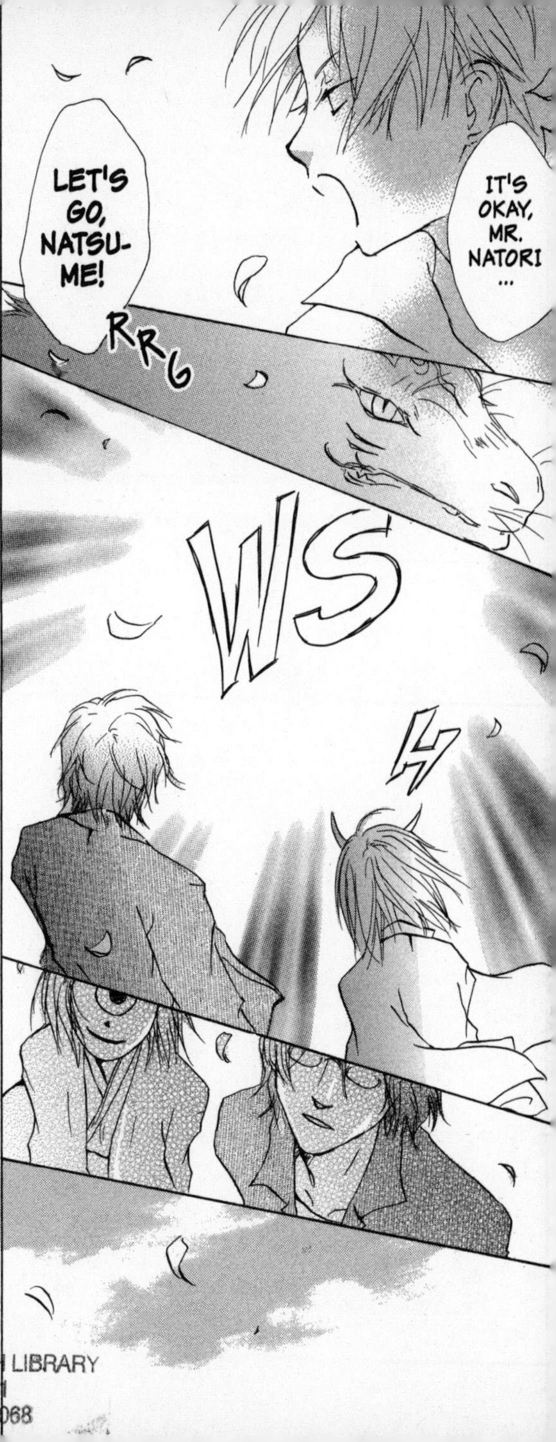
IT'S OKAY, MR. NATORI ...
LET'S GO, NATSUME!
RRG
WS
H

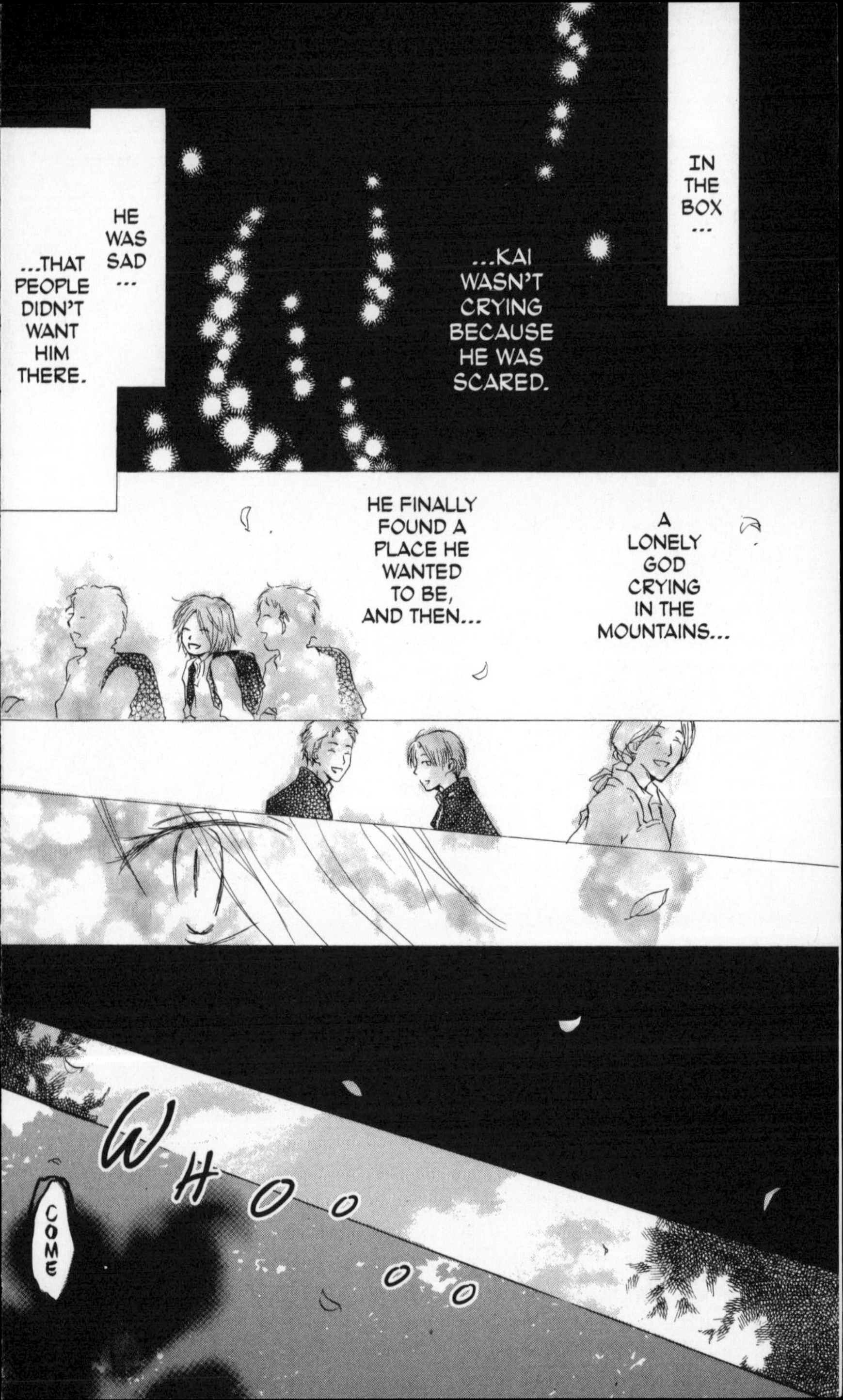
IN THE BOX ...
...KAI WASN'T CRYING BECAUSE HE WAS SCARED.
HE WAS SAD ...
...THAT PEOPLE DIDN'T WANT HIM THERE.
A LONELY GOD CRYING IN THE MOUNTAINS...
HE FINALLY FOUND A PLACE HE WANTED TO BE, AND THEN...
WHOOOOO
COME

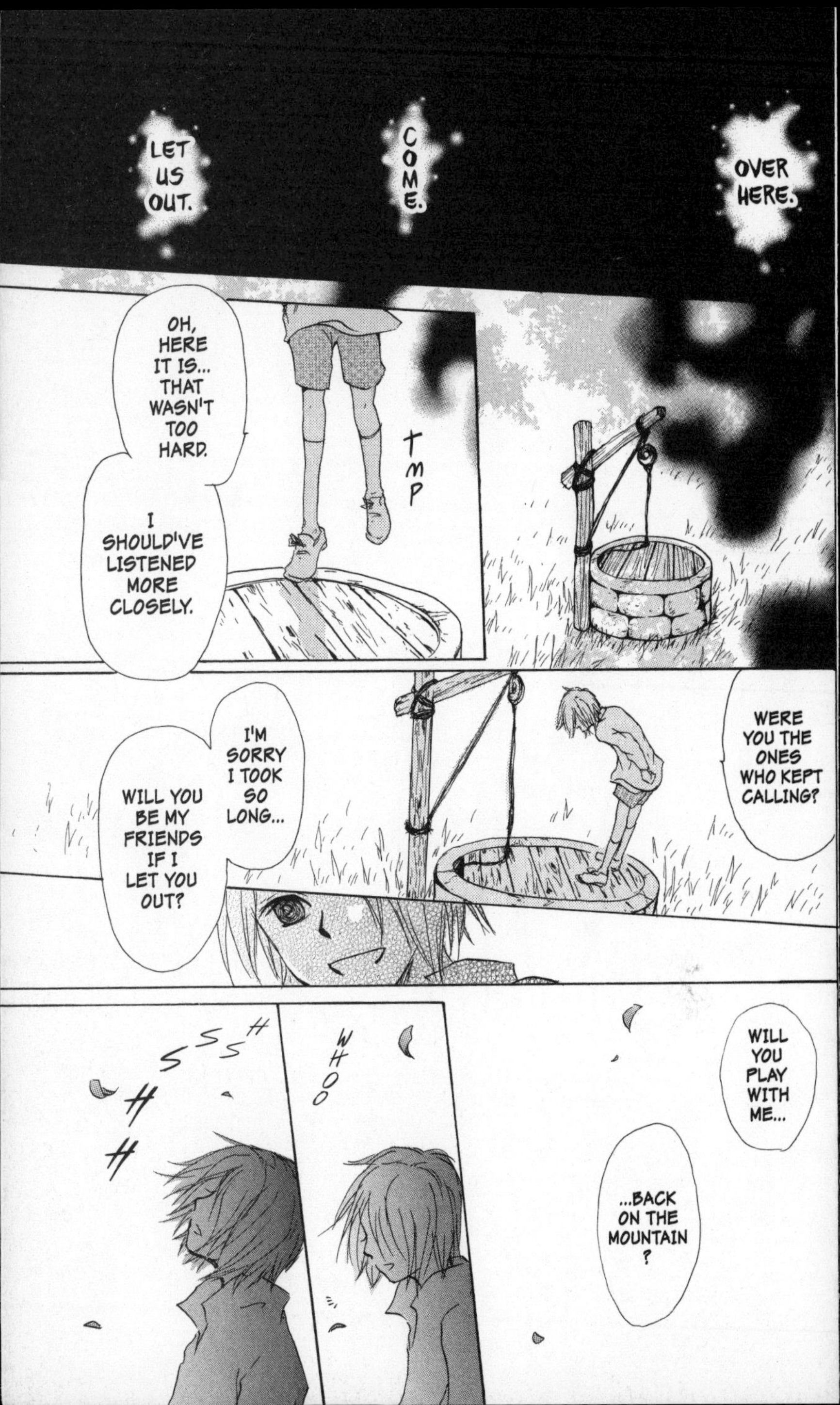
OVER HERE.
COME.
LET US OUT.
TMP
OH, HERE IT IS... THAT WASN'T TOO HARD.
I SHOULD'VE LISTENED MORE CLOSELY.
WERE YOU THE ONES WHO KEPT CALLING?
I'M SORRY I TOOK SO LONG...
WILL YOU BE MY FRIENDS IF I LET YOU OUT?
WILL YOU PLAY WITH ME...
...BACK ON THE MOUNTAIN ?
WHOO
SSSHHH

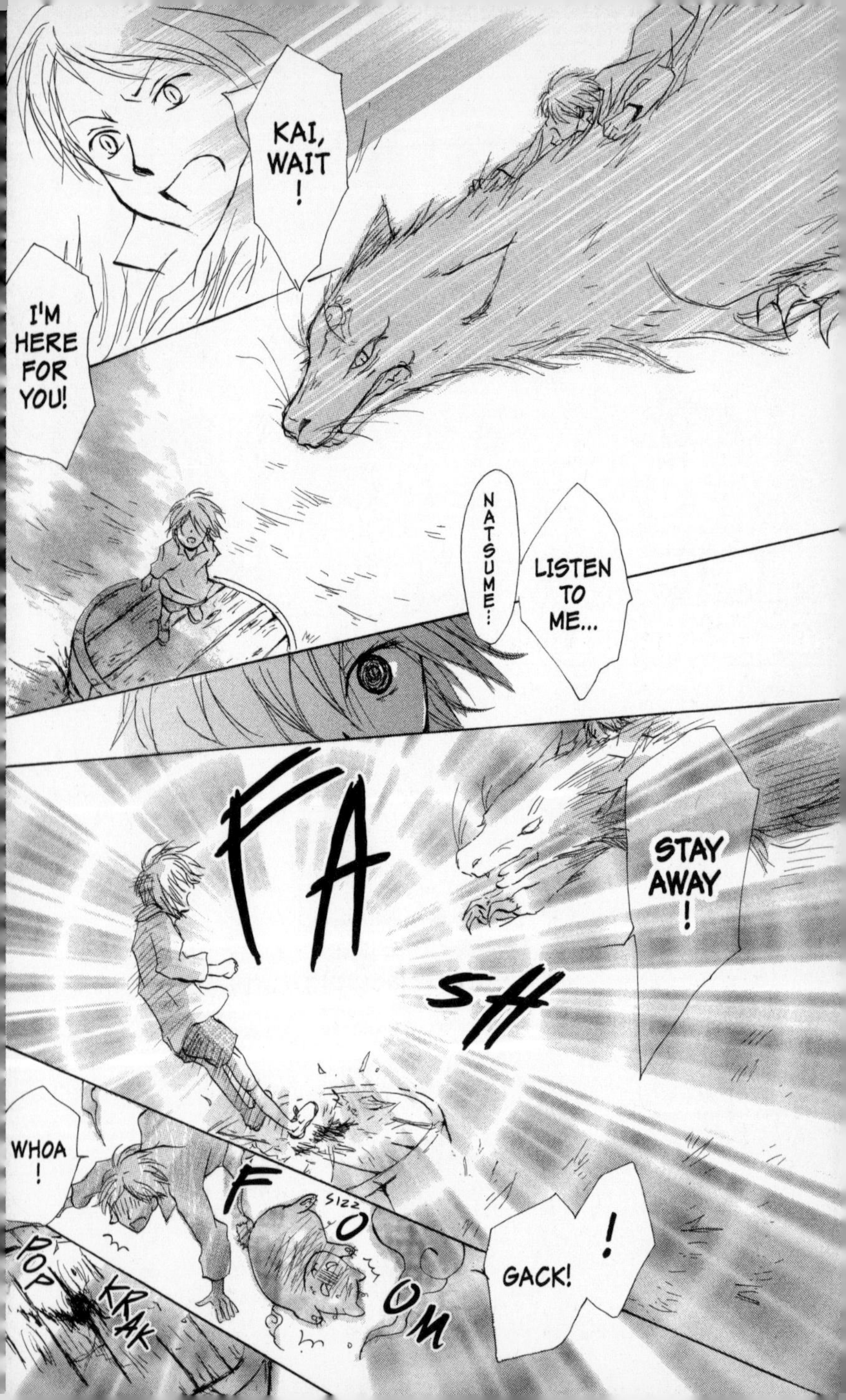
KAI, WAIT!
I'M HERE FOR YOU!
LISTEN TO ME...
NATSUME...
STAY AWAY!
FASH
!
GACK!
FOOM
SIZZ
KRAK
POP
WHOA!

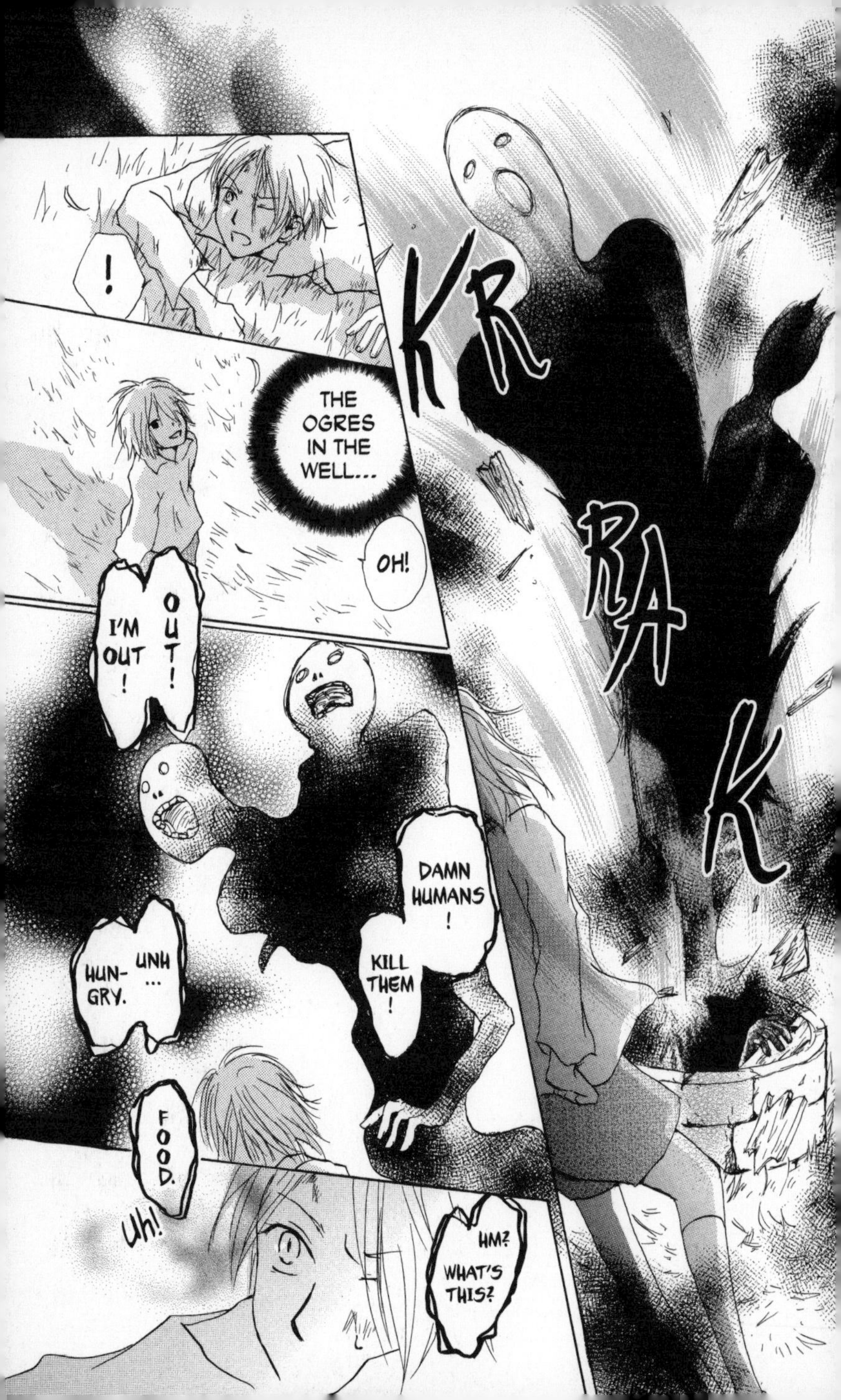

KRRAK
!
THE OGRES IN THE WELL...
OH!
OUT!
I'M OUT!
DAMN HUMANS!
KILL THEM!
UNH... HUNGRY.
FOOD.
HM? WHAT'S THIS?
Uh!

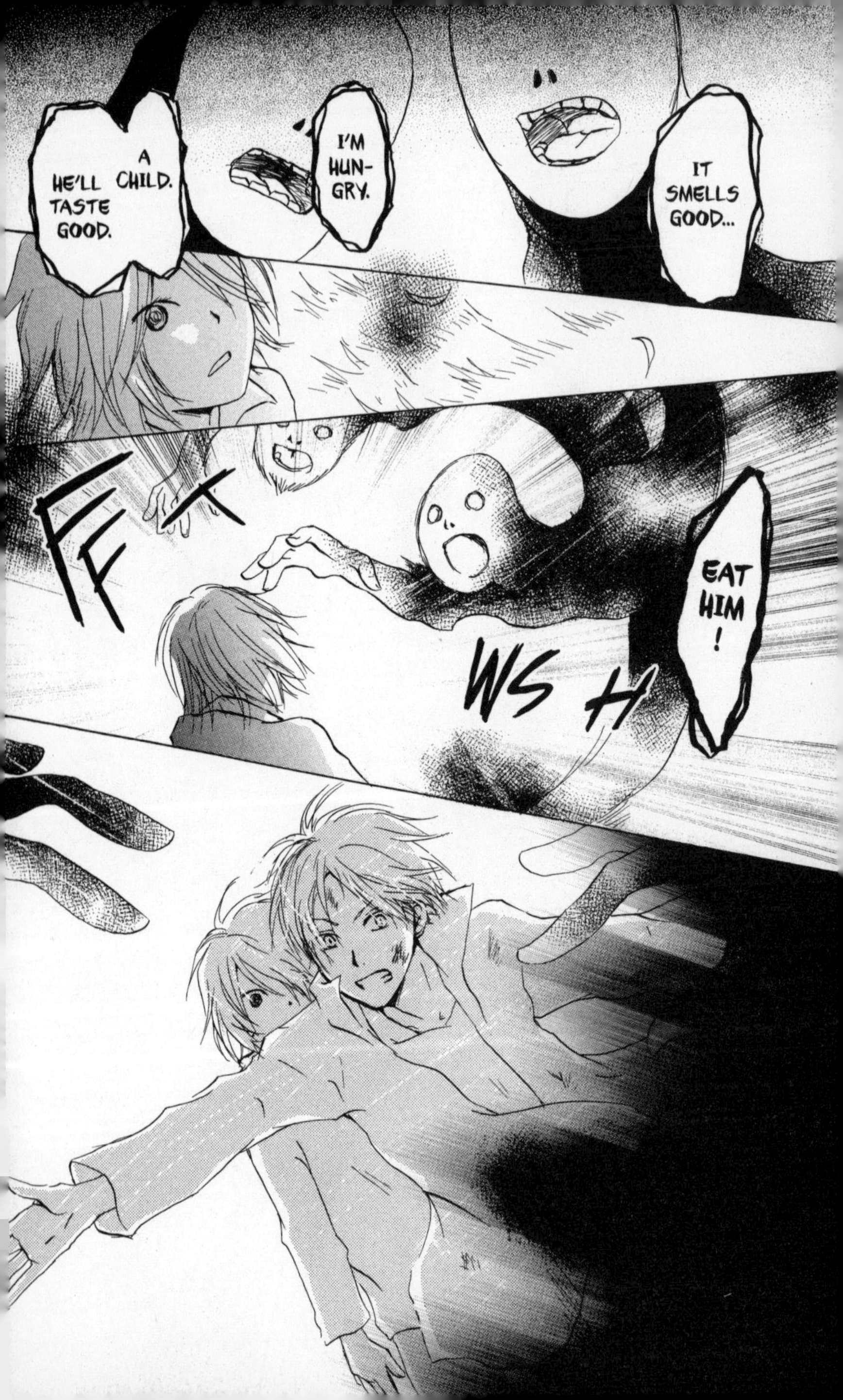
IT SMELLS GOOD...
I'M HUN-GRY.
A CHILD. HE'LL TASTE GOOD.
EAT HIM!
FF
WSH

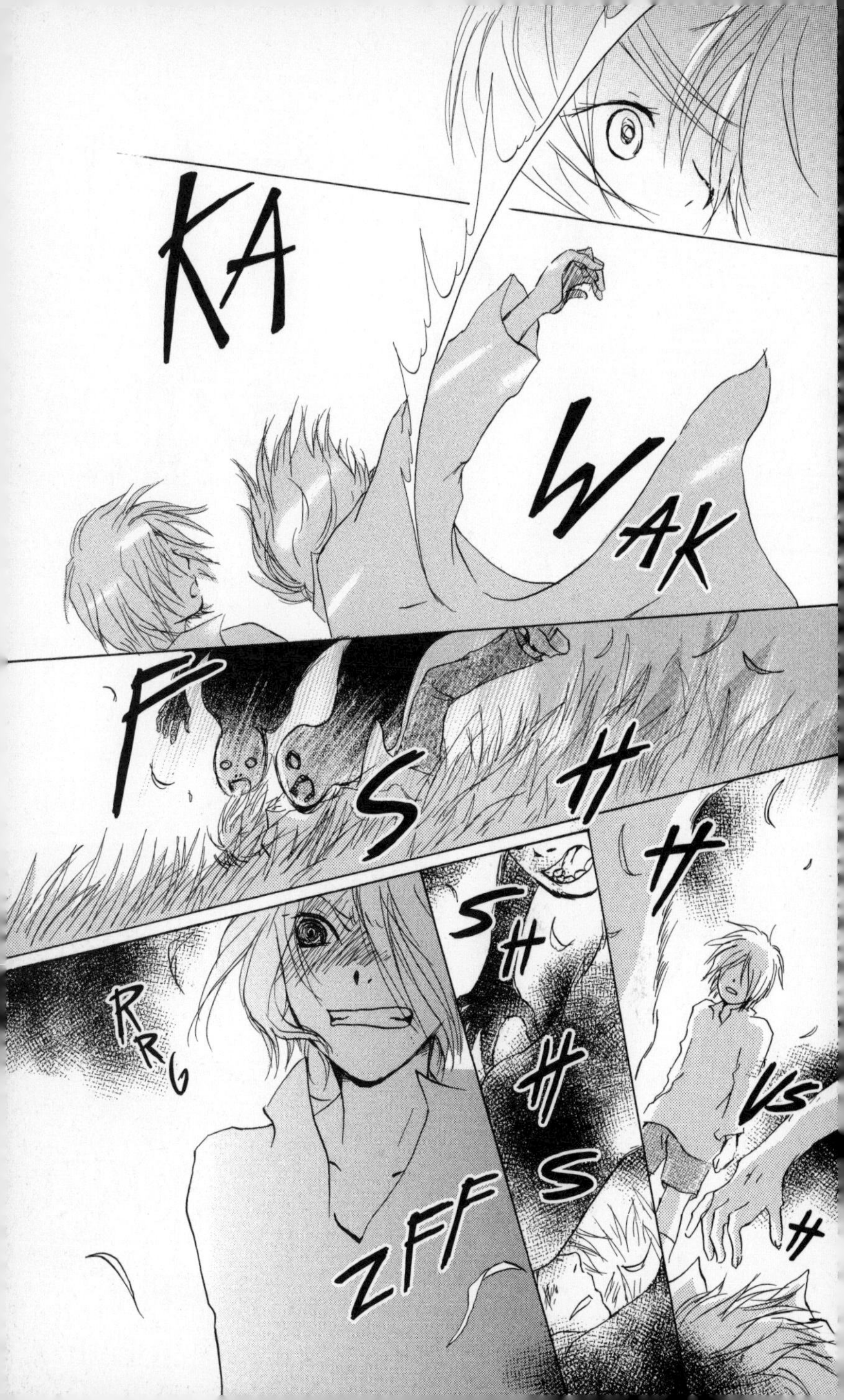
KA
WAK
FSHH
VSH
SHHS
RRG
ZFF

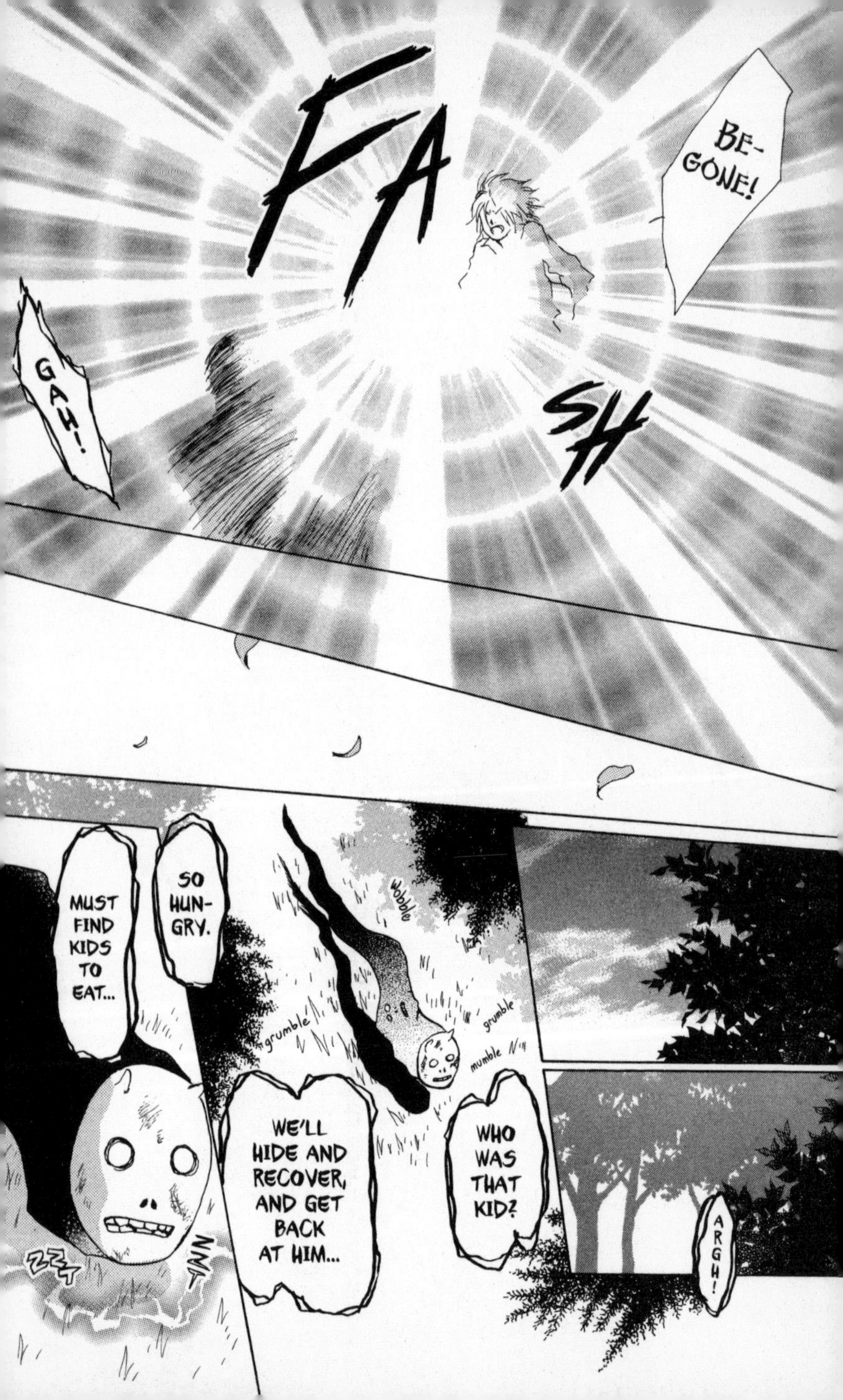
BE-GONE!
FA
SH
GAH!
ARGH!
wobble
grumble
mumble
grumble
WHO WAS THAT KID?
WE'LL HIDE AND RECOVER, AND GET BACK AT HIM...
SO HUN-GRY.
MUST FIND KIDS TO EAT...
NNT
ZZZT

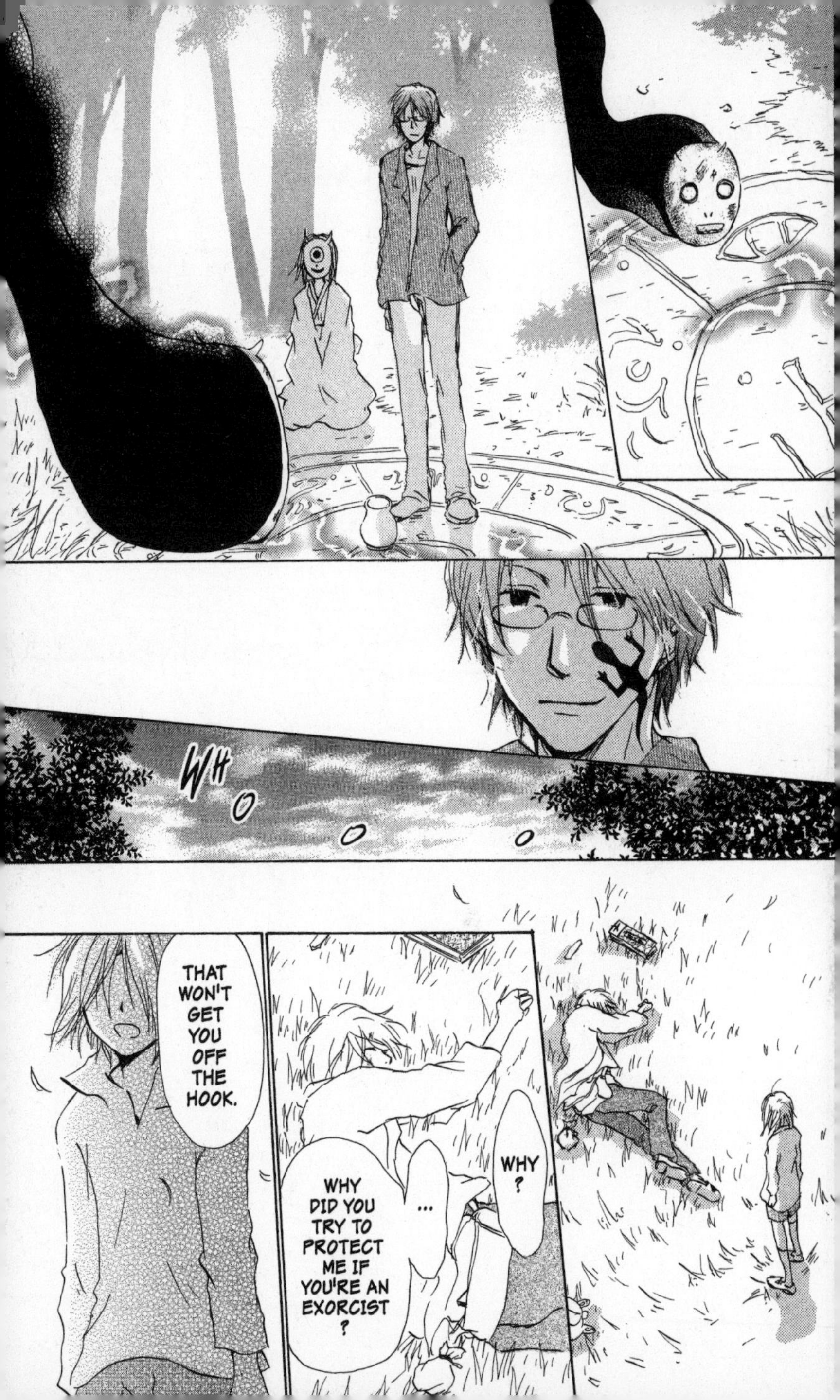
WHOOO
WHY?
...
WHY DID YOU TRY TO PROTECT ME IF YOU'RE AN EXORCIST?
THAT WON'T GET YOU OFF THE HOOK.

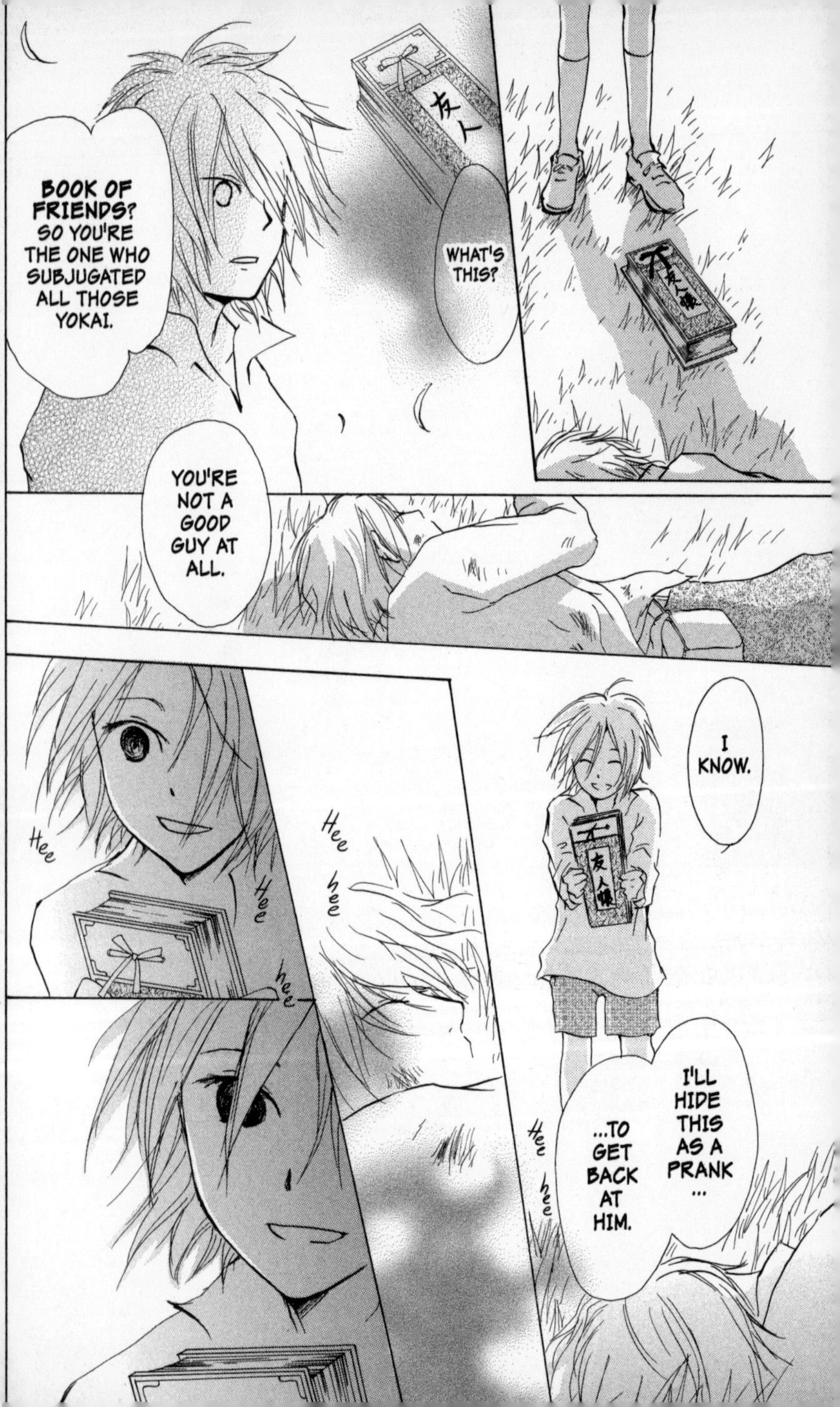
友人帳
WHAT'S THIS?
BOOK OF FRIENDS? SO YOU'RE THE ONE WHO SUBJUGATED ALL THOSE YOKAI.
YOU'RE NOT A GOOD GUY AT ALL.
I KNOW.
友人帳
I'LL HIDE THIS AS A PRANK...
...TO GET BACK AT HIM.
Hee hee
Hee
Hee hee
Hee hee hee

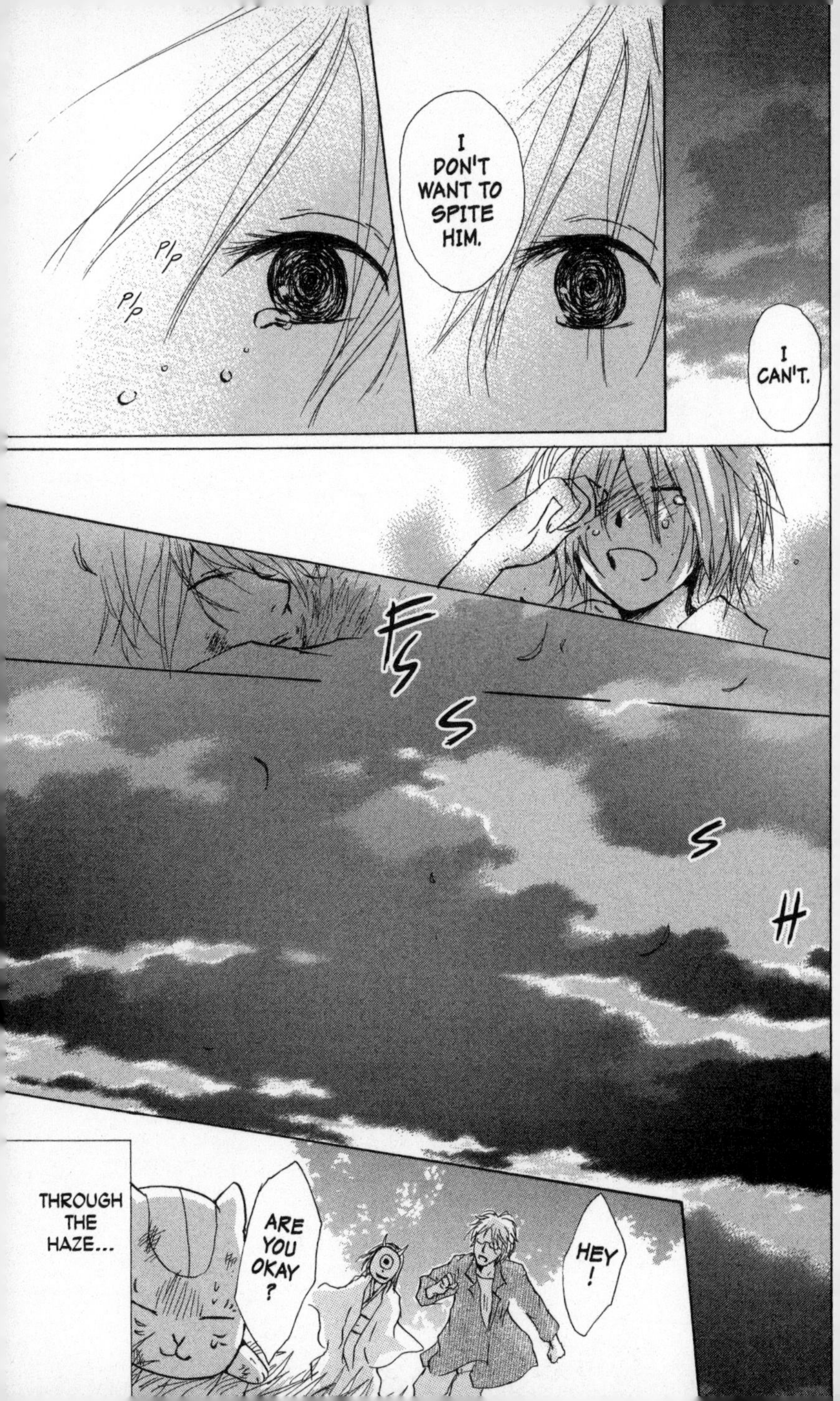
I CAN'T.
I DON'T WANT TO SPITE HIM.
P/P
P/P
FSSSH
HEY!
ARE YOU OKAY?
THROUGH THE HAZE...

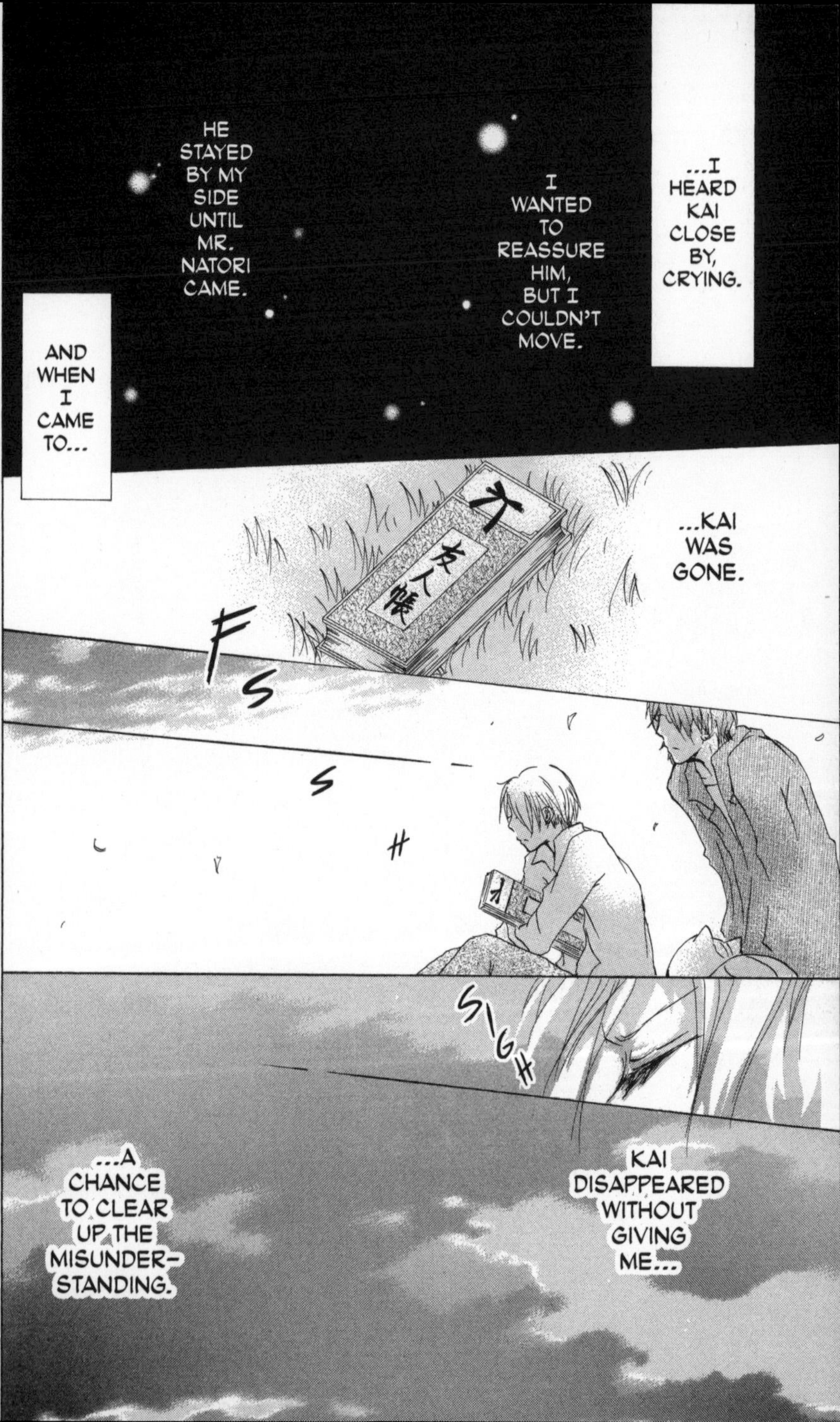
...I HEARD KAI CLOSE BY, CRYING.
I WANTED TO REASSURE HIM, BUT I COULDN'T MOVE.
HE STAYED BY MY SIDE UNTIL MR. NATORI CAME.
AND WHEN I CAME TO...
友人帳
...KAI WAS GONE.
FS
S
H
SIGH
KAI DISAPPEARED WITHOUT GIVING ME...
...A CHANCE TO CLEAR UP THE MISUNDER-STANDING.

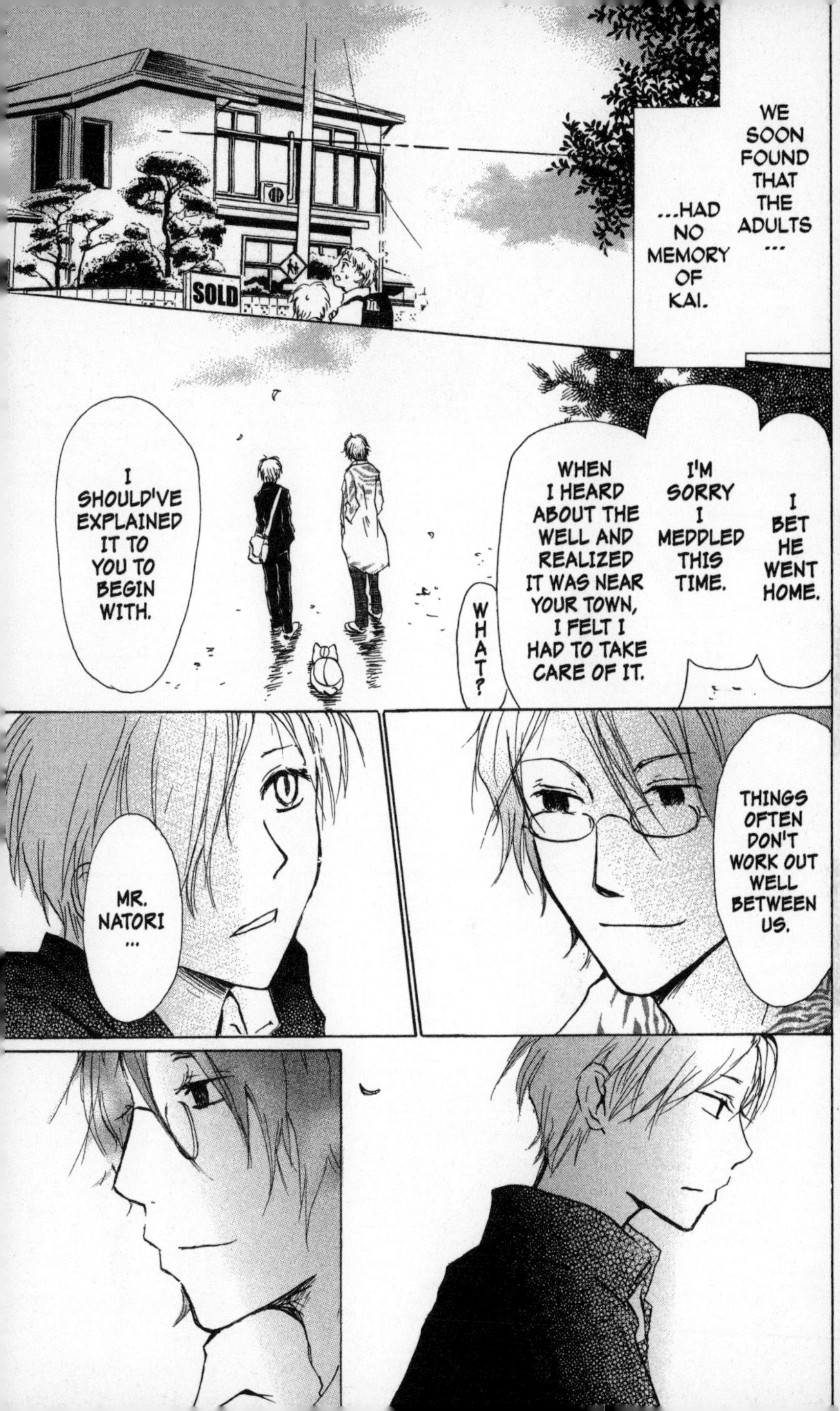
WE SOON FOUND THAT THE ADULTS...
...HAD NO MEMORY OF KAI.
SOLD
I BET HE WENT HOME.
I'M SORRY I MEDDLED THIS TIME.
WHEN I HEARD ABOUT THE WELL AND REALIZED IT WAS NEAR YOUR TOWN, I FELT I HAD TO TAKE CARE OF IT.
WHAT?
I SHOULD'VE EXPLAINED IT TO YOU TO BEGIN WITH.
THINGS OFTEN DON'T WORK OUT WELL BETWEEN US.
MR. NATORI...

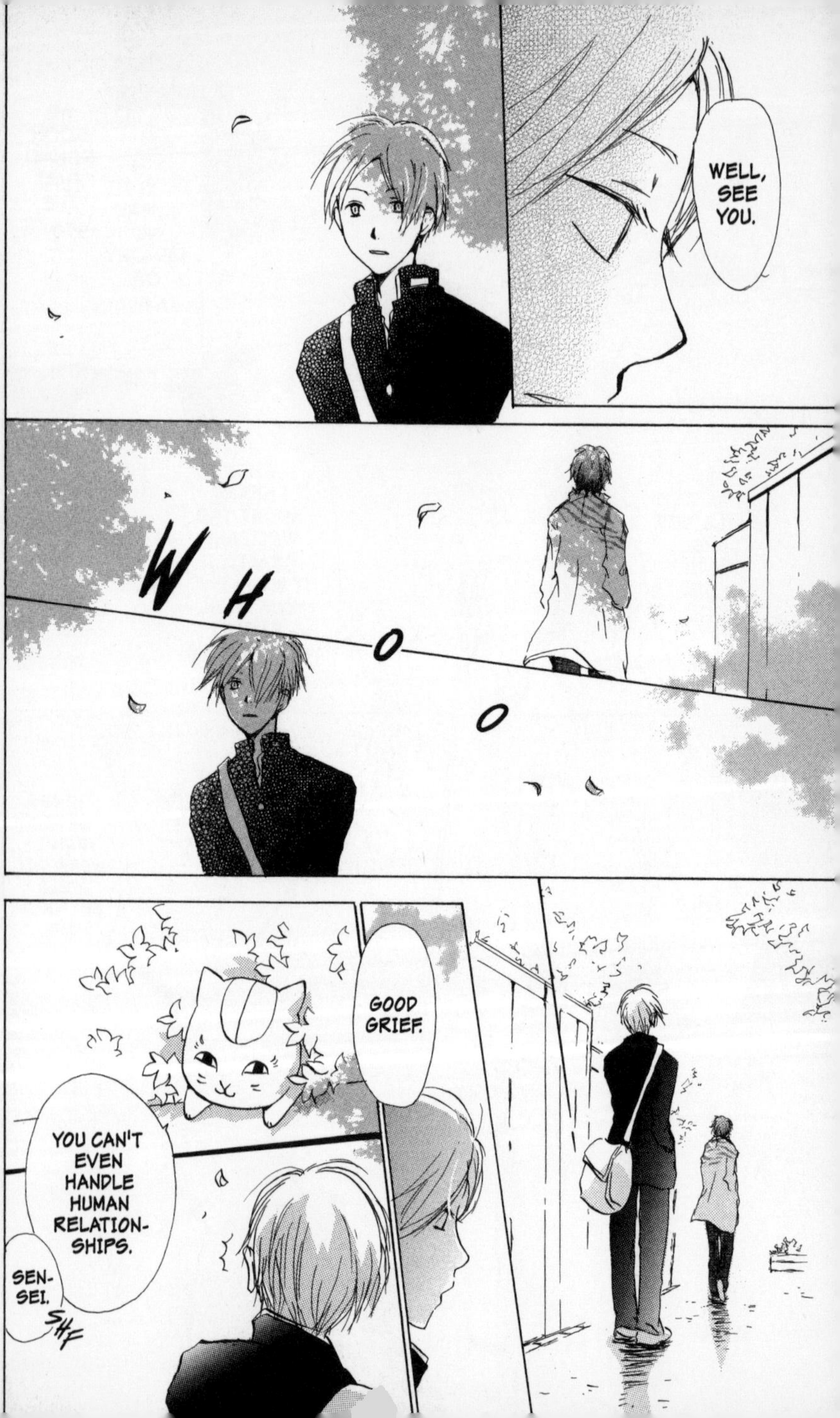
WELL, SEE YOU.
WHOOO
GOOD GRIEF.
YOU CAN'T EVEN HANDLE HUMAN RELATION-SHIPS.
SEN-SEI.
SHF

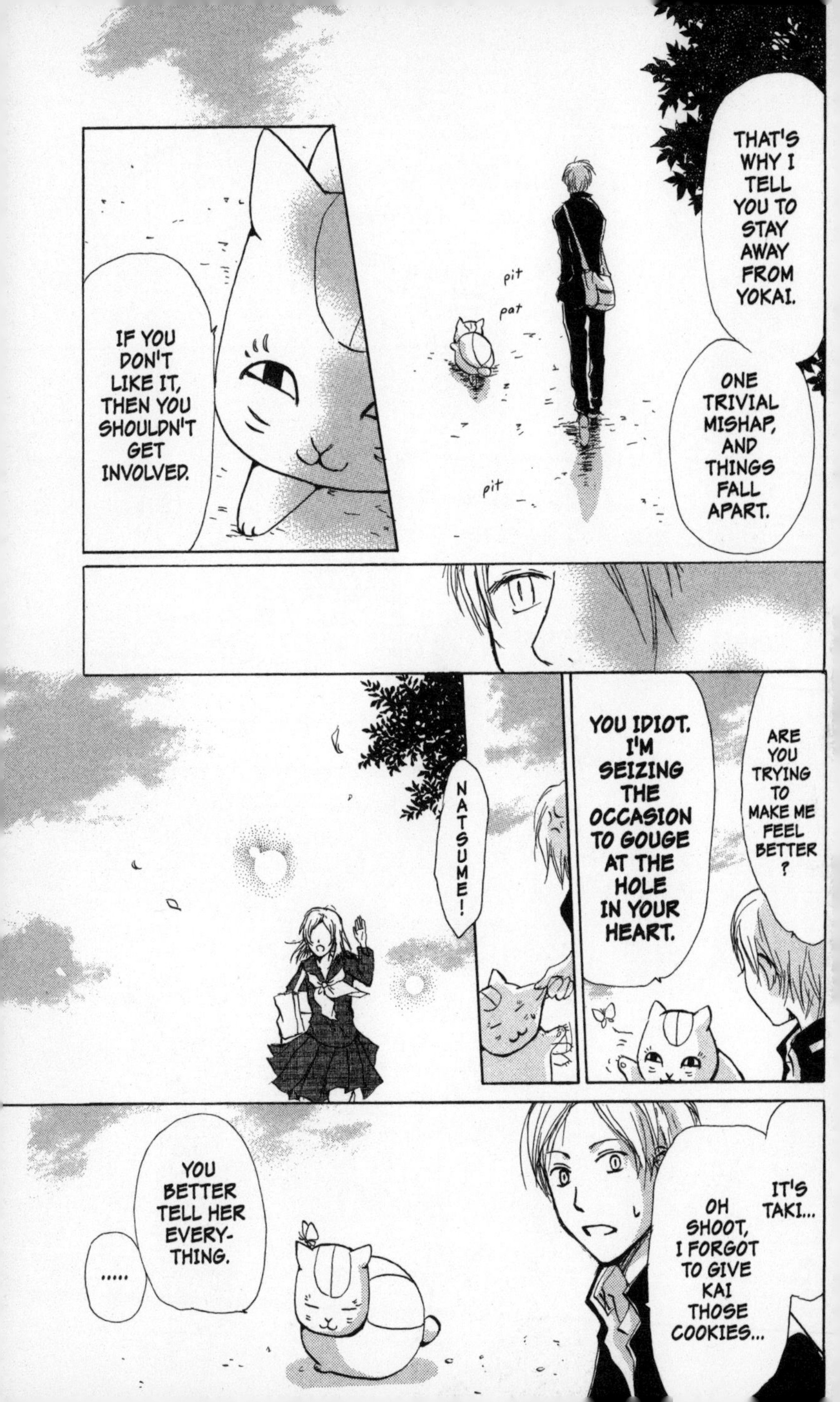
THAT'S WHY I TELL YOU TO STAY AWAY FROM YOKAI.
ONE TRIVIAL MISHAP, AND THINGS FALL APART.
pit
pat
pit
IF YOU DON'T LIKE IT, THEN YOU SHOULDN'T GET INVOLVED.
ARE YOU TRYING TO MAKE ME FEEL BETTER?
YOU IDIOT. I'M SEIZING THE OCCASION TO GOUGE AT THE HOLE IN YOUR HEART.
NATSUME!
IT'S TAKI...
OH SHOOT, I FORGOT TO GIVE KAI THOSE COOKIES...
YOU BETTER TELL HER EVERYTHING.
.....

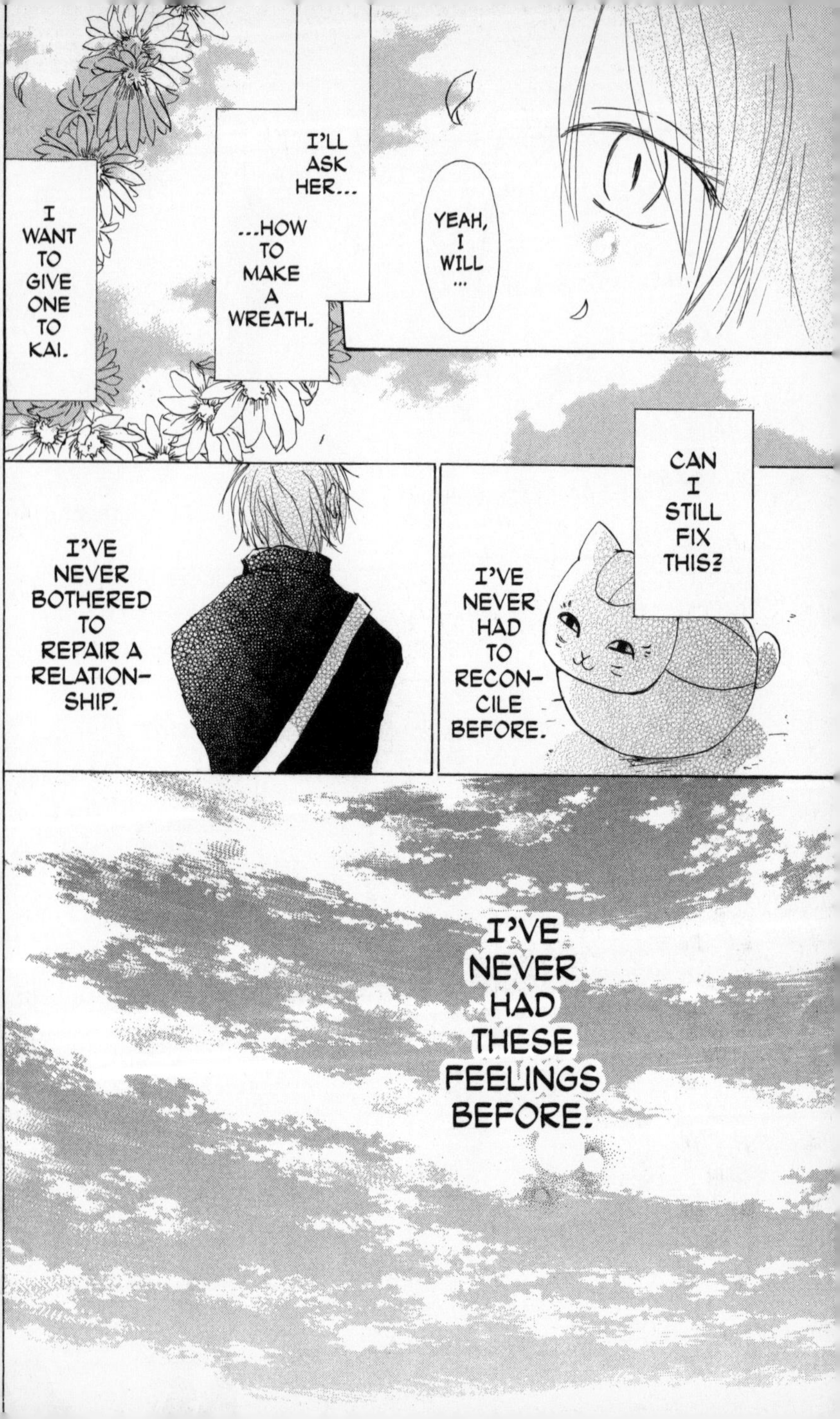
YEAH, I WILL...
I'LL ASK HER...
...HOW TO MAKE A WREATH.
I WANT TO GIVE ONE TO KAI.
CAN I STILL FIX THIS?
I'VE NEVER HAD TO RECONCILE BEFORE.
I'VE NEVER BOTHERED TO REPAIR A RELATIONSHIP.
I'VE NEVER HAD THESE FEELINGS BEFORE.

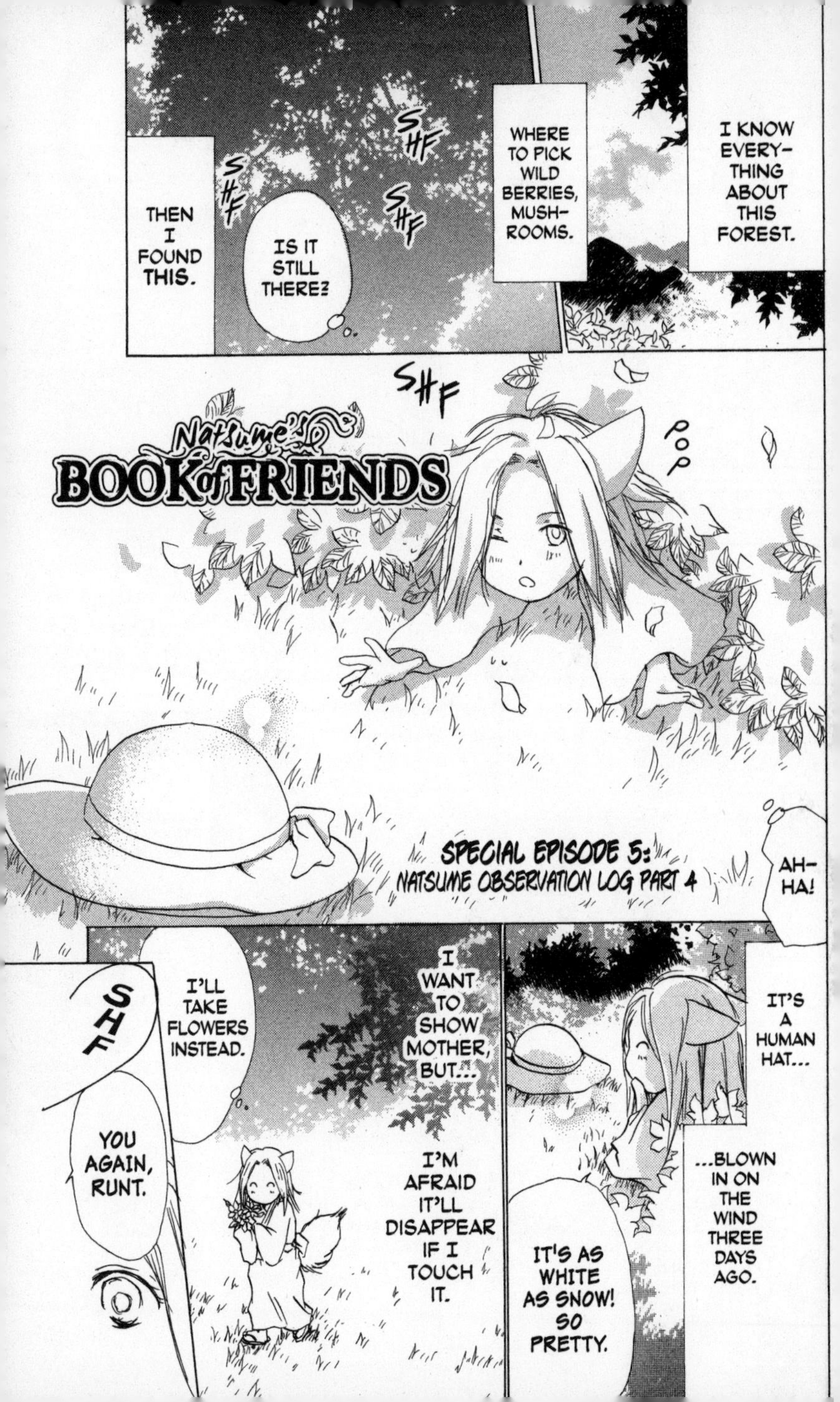
I KNOW EVERY-THING ABOUT THIS FOREST.
WHERE TO PICK WILD BERRIES, MUSH-ROOMS.
SHF
SHF
SHF
IS IT STILL THERE?
THEN I FOUND THIS.
SHF
POP
Natsume's BOOK of FRIENDS
AH-HA!
SPECIAL EPISODE 5:
NATSUME OBSERVATION LOG PART 4
IT'S A HUMAN HAT...
...BLOWN IN ON THE WIND THREE DAYS AGO.
IT'S AS WHITE AS SNOW! SO PRETTY.
I WANT TO SHOW MOTHER, BUT...
I'M AFRAID IT'LL DISAPPEAR IF I TOUCH IT.
I'LL TAKE FLOWERS INSTEAD.
SHF
YOU AGAIN, RUNT.

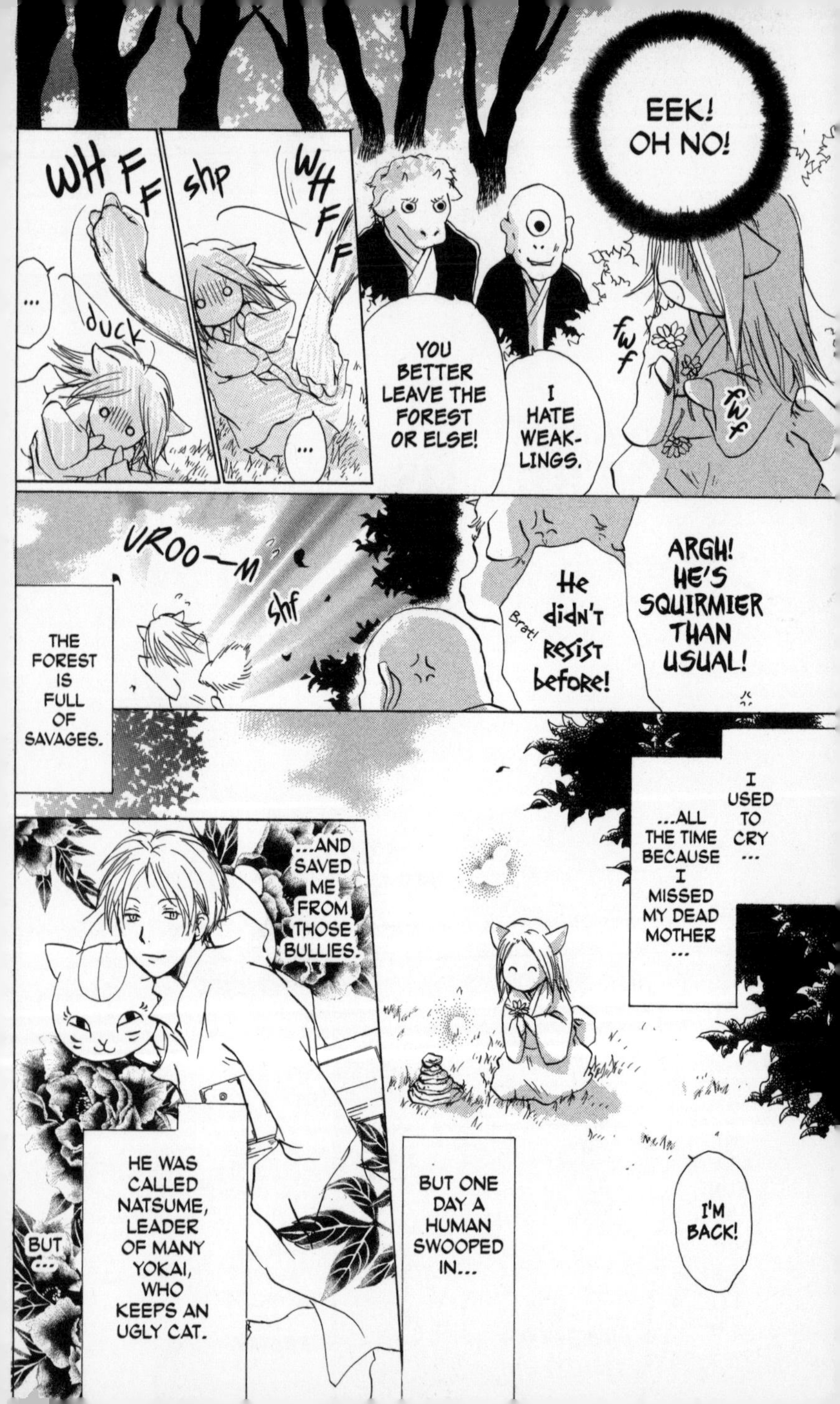
EEK! OH NO!
fwf
fwf
I HATE WEAK-LINGS.
YOU BETTER LEAVE THE FOREST OR ELSE!
WHFF
shp
...
WHFF
...
duck
ARGH! HE'S SQUIRMIER THAN USUAL!
He didn't resist before!
Brat!
VROO—M
shf
THE FOREST IS FULL OF SAVAGES.
I USED TO CRY...
...ALL THE TIME BECAUSE I MISSED MY DEAD MOTHER...
I'M BACK!
BUT ONE DAY A HUMAN SWOOPED IN...
...AND SAVED ME FROM THOSE BULLIES.
HE WAS CALLED NATSUME, LEADER OF MANY YOKAI, WHO KEEPS AN UGLY CAT.
BUT...

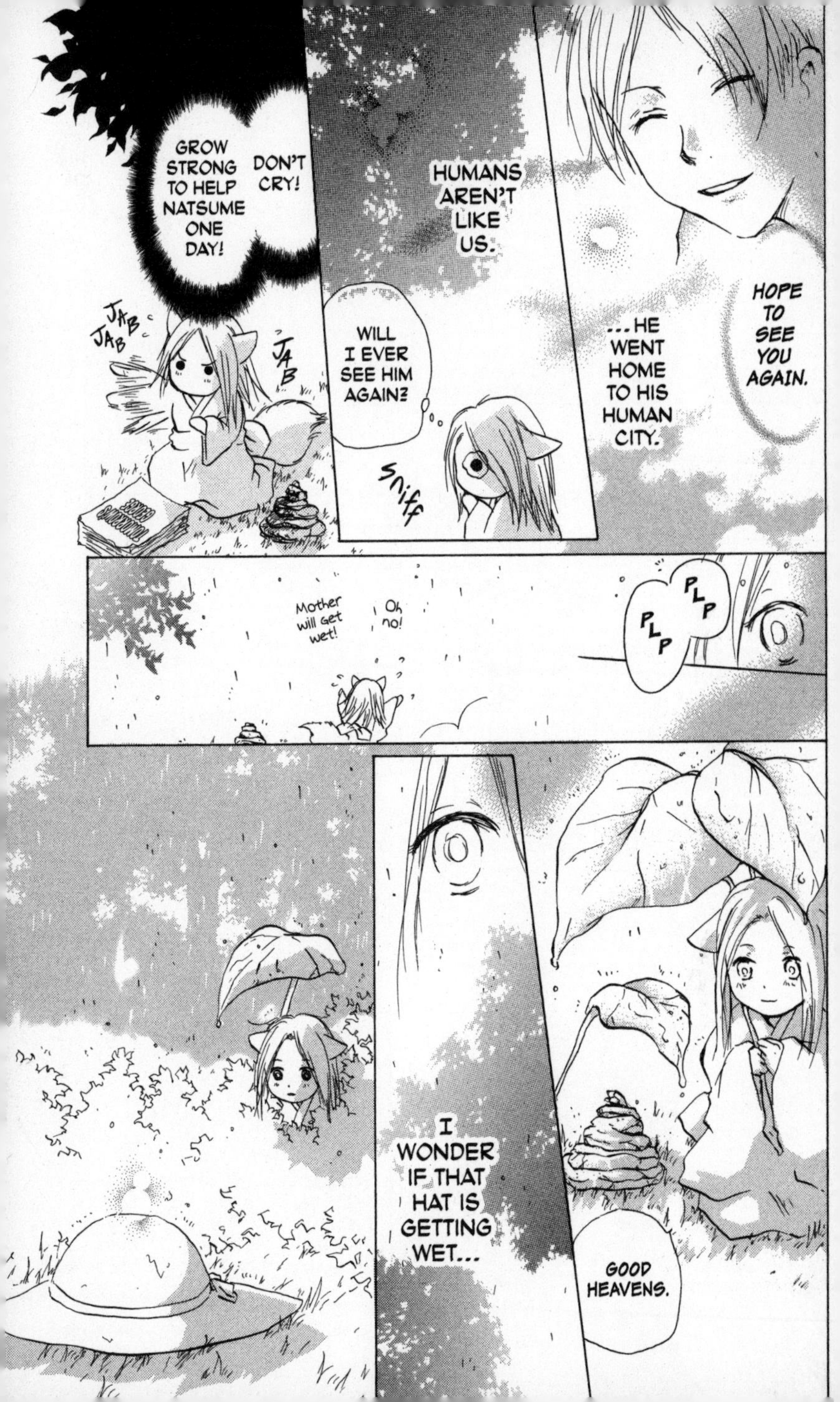
HOPE TO SEE YOU AGAIN.
...HE WENT HOME TO HIS HUMAN CITY.
HUMANS AREN'T LIKE US.
WILL I EVER SEE HIM AGAIN?
Sniff
DON'T CRY!
GROW STRONG TO HELP NATSUME ONE DAY!
JAB JAB
JAB
PLP
PLP
Oh no!
Mother will get wet!
GOOD HEAVENS.
I WONDER IF THAT HAT IS GETTING WET...

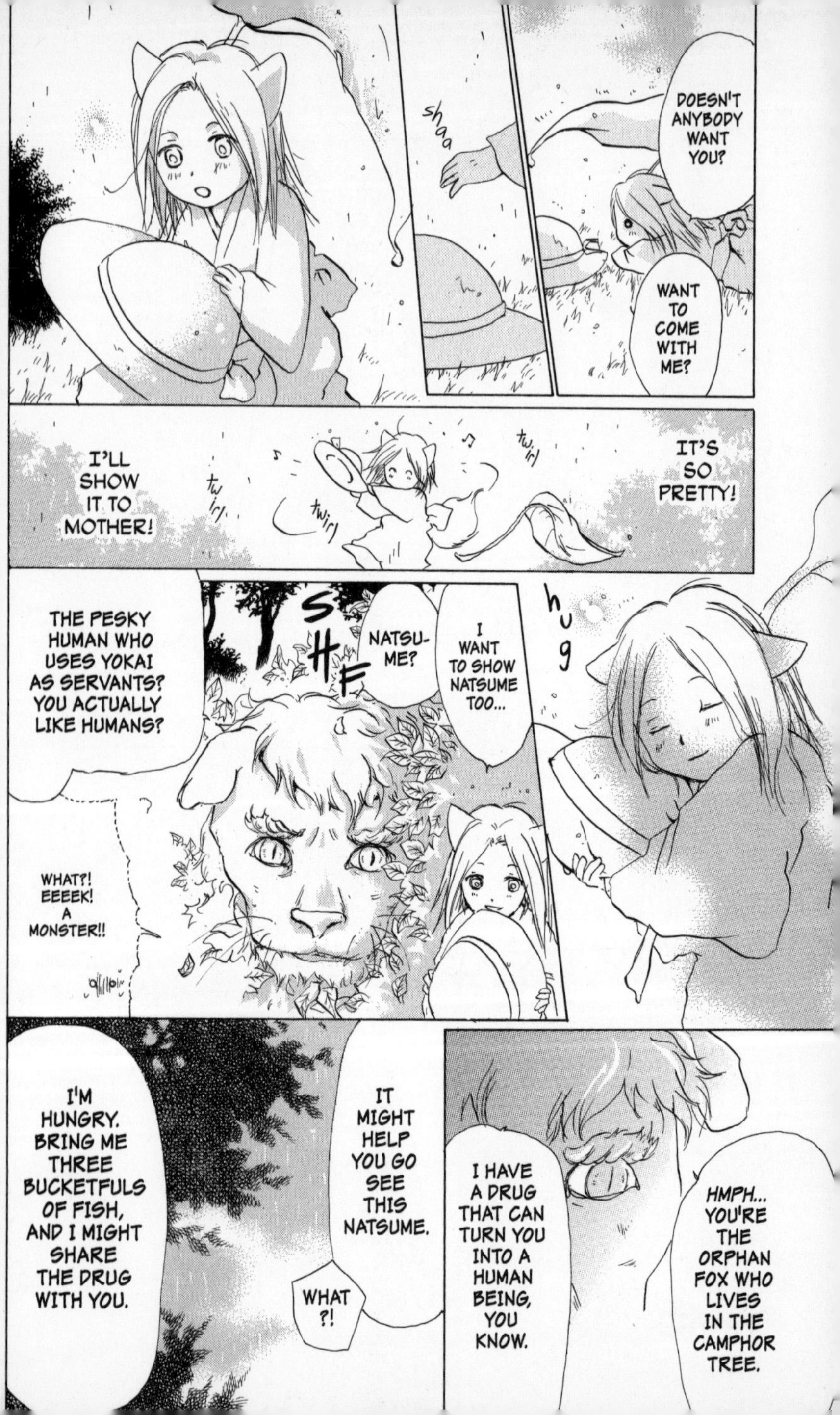
DOESN'T ANYBODY WANT YOU?
WANT TO COME WITH ME?
shaa
IT'S SO PRETTY!
twirl
twirl
twirl
I'LL SHOW IT TO MOTHER!
hug
I WANT TO SHOW NATSUME TOO...
NATSUME?
SHF
THE PESKY HUMAN WHO USES YOKAI AS SERVANTS? YOU ACTUALLY LIKE HUMANS?
WHAT?! EEEEK! A MONSTER!!
HMPH... YOU'RE THE ORPHAN FOX WHO LIVES IN THE CAMPHOR TREE.
I HAVE A DRUG THAT CAN TURN YOU INTO A HUMAN BEING, YOU KNOW.
IT MIGHT HELP YOU GO SEE THIS NATSUME.
WHAT?!
I'M HUNGRY. BRING ME THREE BUCKETFULS OF FISH, AND I MIGHT SHARE THE DRUG WITH YOU.

04

❀ Anime: part 1

As I mentioned in the previous volume, Natsume is going to be an animated series. When they first brought up the offer, the manga hadn't sold as many copies yet. I really wanted to jump with joy, but it didn't quite feel real to me. When I thought about my work actually being animated, my face would melt into a smile. But I was terrified of the possibility that the plans might fall through. It was an uncanny period of happiness, you see. But it also gave me a lot of motivation. At the time, I was a little bit lost over where to take the manga next, but this helped me focus on Natsume a lot more.

Then I also heard that the director and some other staff members were coming to Kumamoto for location shoots, and I was finally able to jump with joy. Getting animated was exciting enough; now they were coming to visit for location shoots? I wept tears of pure happiness.

I'm so grateful to everyone.

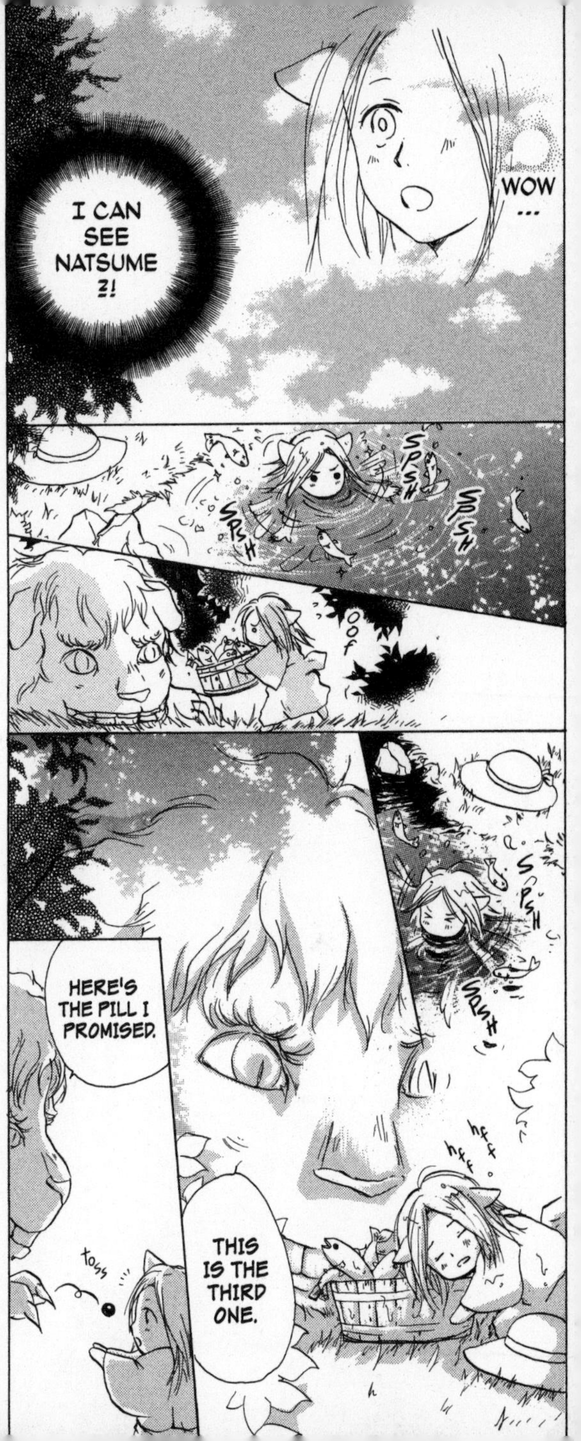
WOW ...
I CAN SEE NATSUME ?!
SPSH
SPSH
SPSH
OOF
SPSH
SPSH
HERE'S THE PILL I PROMISED.
hff
hff
toss
THIS IS THE THIRD ONE.

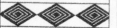

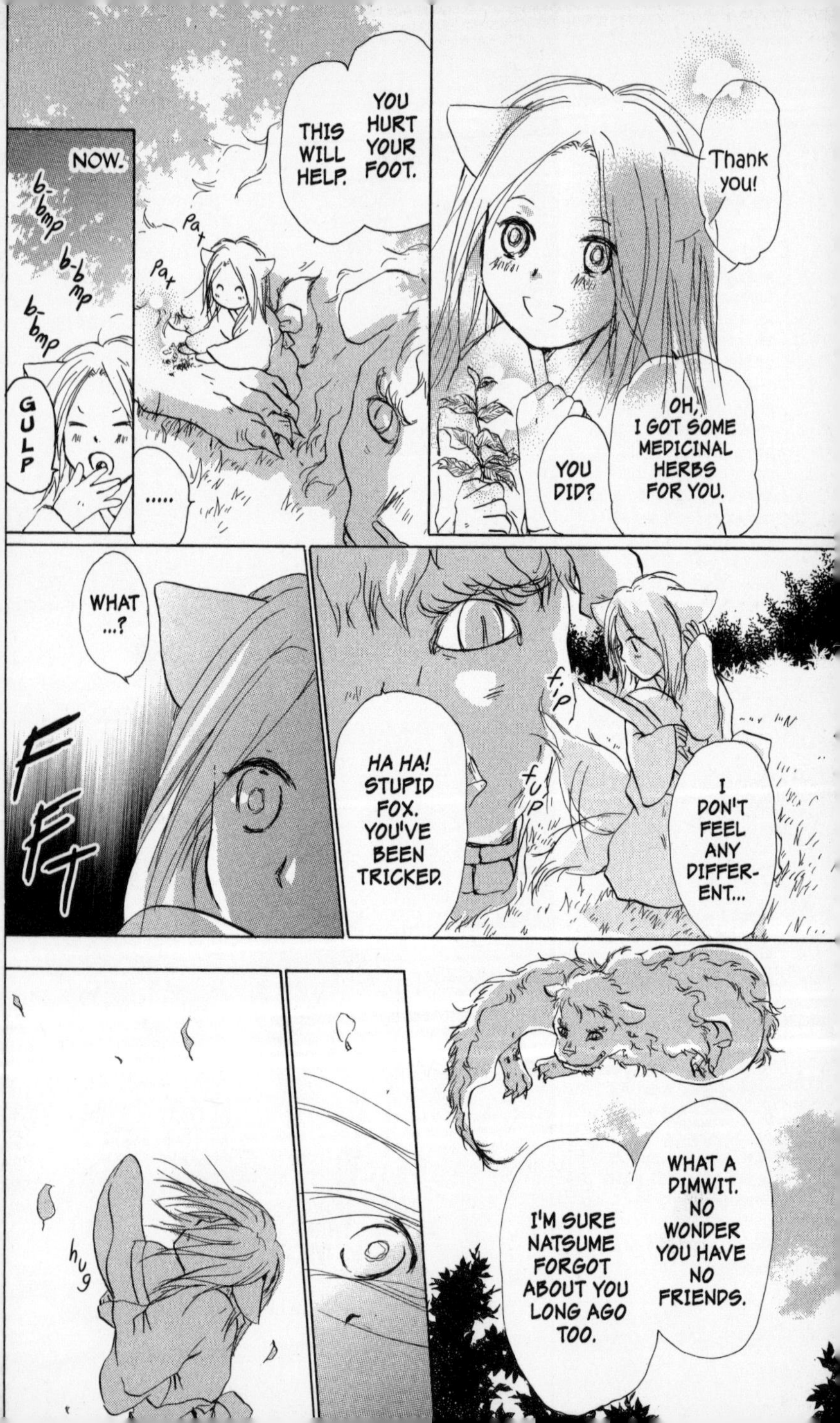
Thank you!
OH, I GOT SOME MEDICINAL HERBS FOR YOU.
YOU DID?
YOU HURT YOUR FOOT.
THIS WILL HELP.
pat
pat
.....
NOW.
b-bmp
b-bmp
b-bmp
GULP
I DON'T FEEL ANY DIFFER-ENT...
fup
HA HA! STUPID FOX. YOU'VE BEEN TRICKED.
WHAT ...?
FFT
WHAT A DIMWIT. NO WONDER YOU HAVE NO FRIENDS.
I'M SURE NATSUME FORGOT ABOUT YOU LONG AGO TOO.
hug

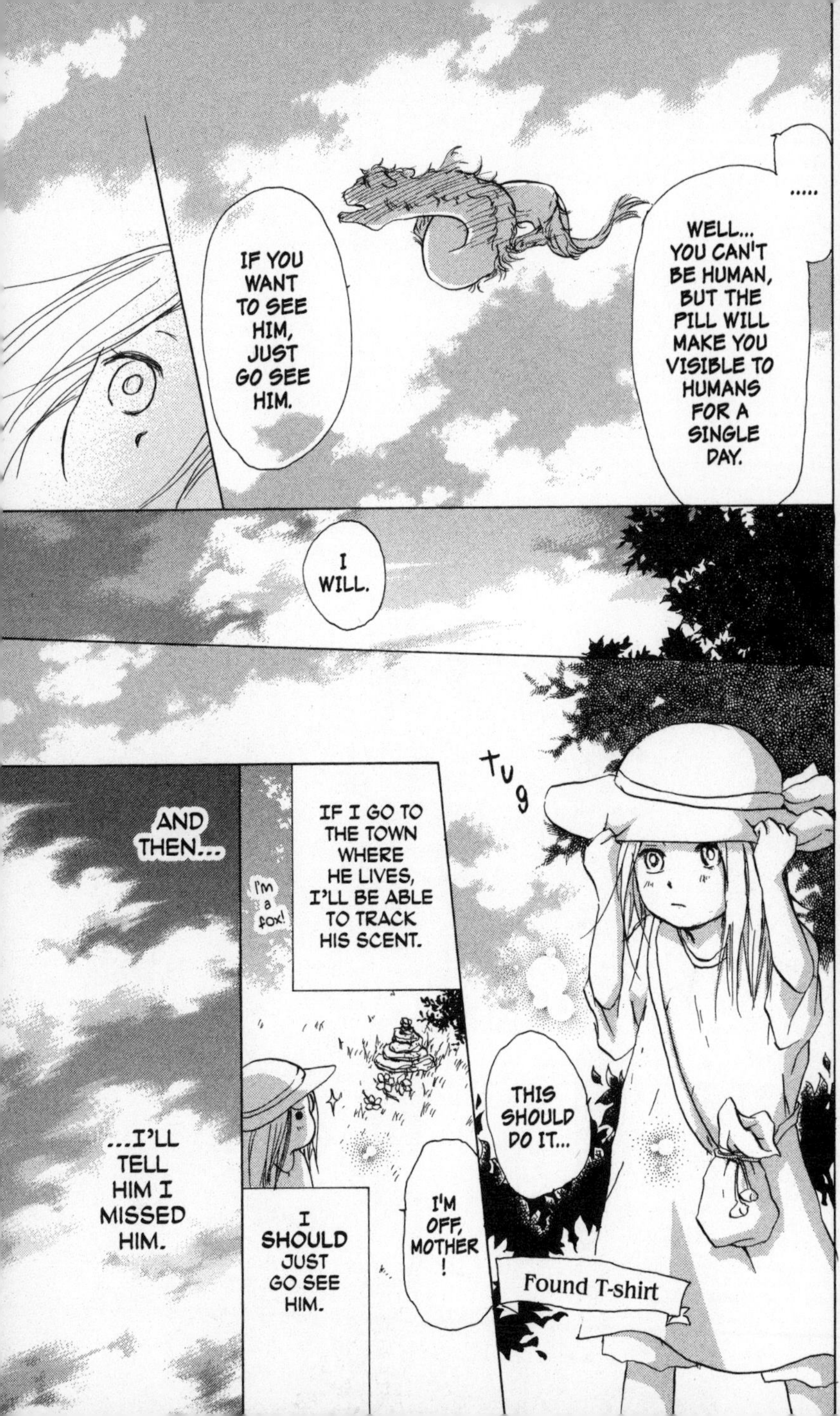
.....
WELL... YOU CAN'T BE HUMAN, BUT THE PILL WILL MAKE YOU VISIBLE TO HUMANS FOR A SINGLE DAY.
IF YOU WANT TO SEE HIM, JUST GO SEE HIM.
I WILL.
TUG
THIS SHOULD DO IT...
Found T-shirt
IF I GO TO THE TOWN WHERE HE LIVES, I'LL BE ABLE TO TRACK HIS SCENT.
I'm a fox!
I'M OFF, MOTHER!
I SHOULD JUST GO SEE HIM.
AND THEN...
...I'LL TELL HIM I MISSED HIM.

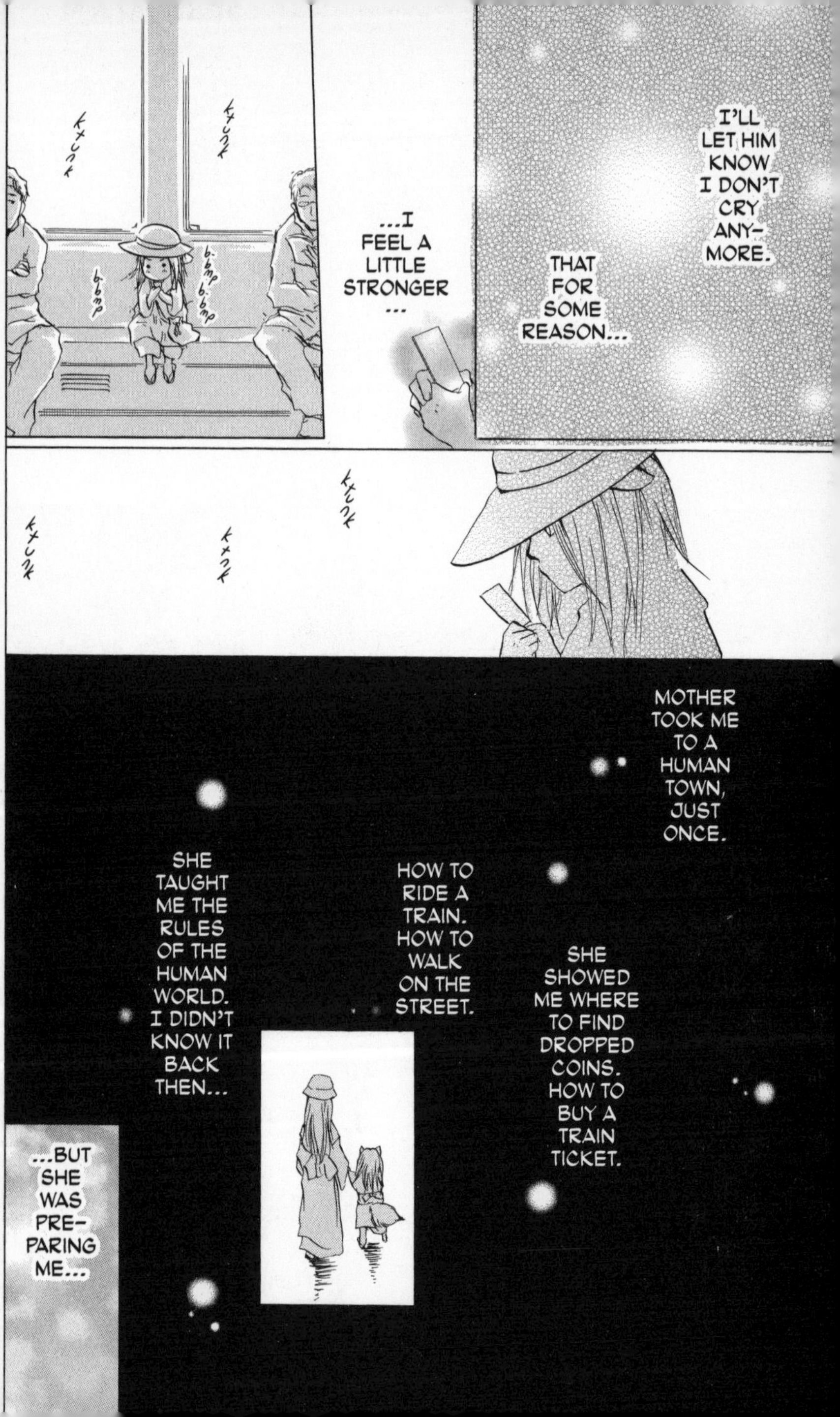
I'LL LET HIM KNOW I DON'T CRY ANYMORE.
THAT FOR SOME REASON...
...I FEEL A LITTLE STRONGER...
MOTHER TOOK ME TO A HUMAN TOWN, JUST ONCE.
SHE SHOWED ME WHERE TO FIND DROPPED COINS. HOW TO BUY A TRAIN TICKET.
HOW TO RIDE A TRAIN. HOW TO WALK ON THE STREET.
SHE TAUGHT ME THE RULES OF THE HUMAN WORLD. I DIDN'T KNOW IT BACK THEN...
...BUT SHE WAS PREPARING ME...

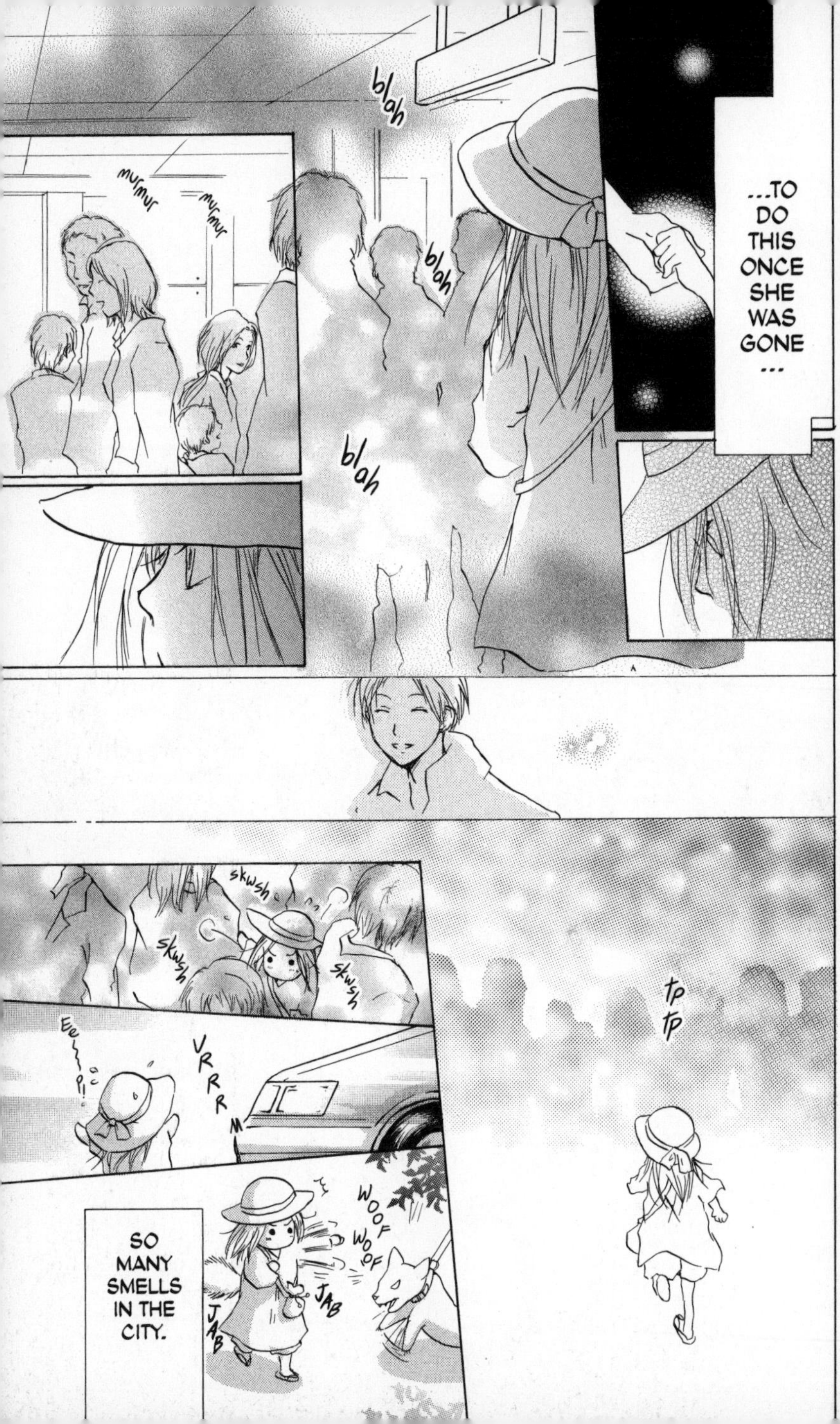

...TO DO THIS ONCE SHE WAS GONE...
blah
blah
blah
murmur
murmur
tp tp
skwsh
skwsh
skwsh
Eep!!
VRRRM
WOOF WOOF
JAB
JAB
SO MANY SMELLS IN THE CITY.

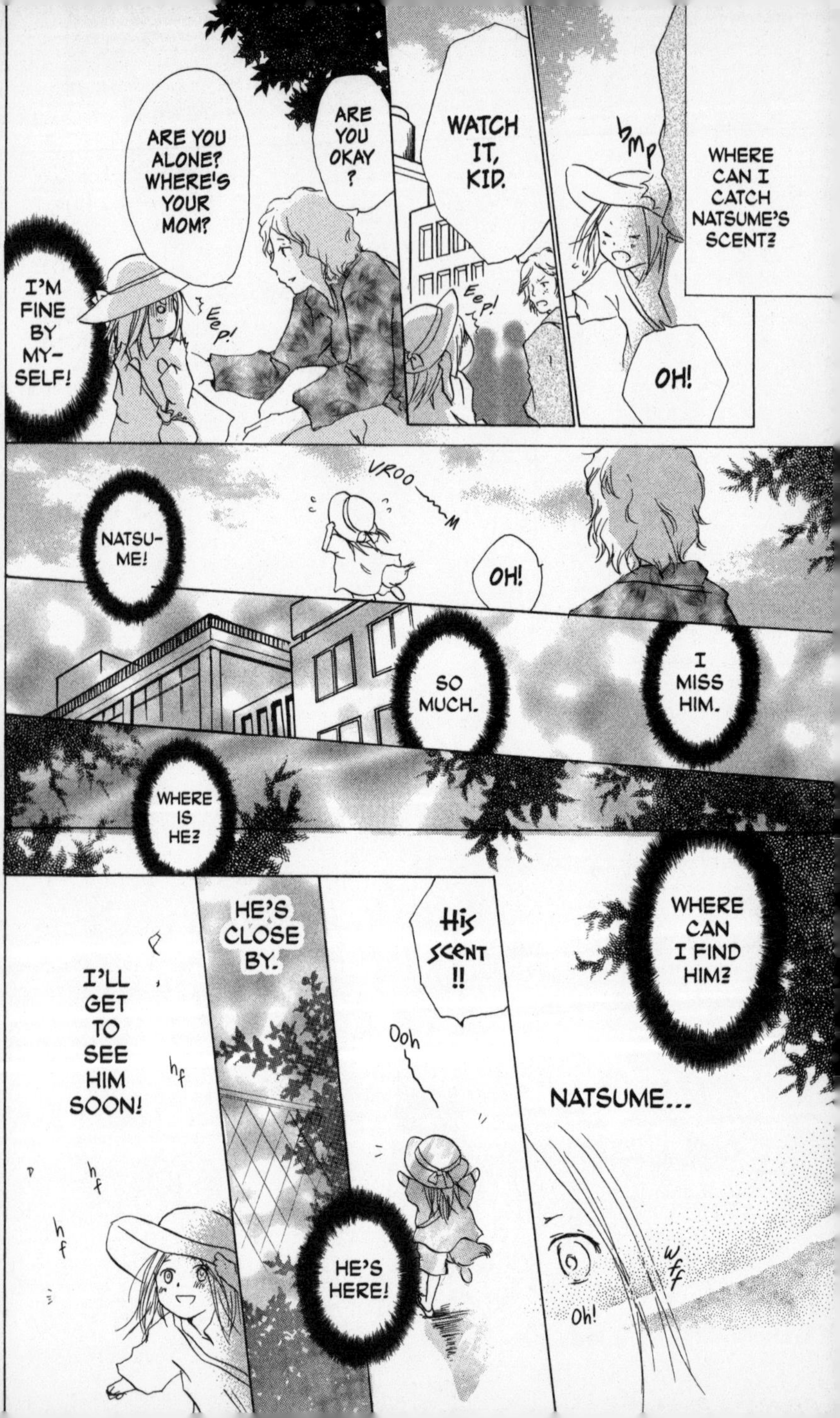
WHERE CAN I CATCH NATSUME'S SCENT?
bmp
OH!
WATCH IT, KID.
Eep!
ARE YOU OKAY?
ARE YOU ALONE? WHERE'S YOUR MOM?
Eep!
I'M FINE BY MY-SELF!
OH!
VROOOM
NATSU-ME!
I MISS HIM.
SO MUCH.
WHERE IS HE?
WHERE CAN I FIND HIM?
NATSUME...
wff
Oh!
His scent!!
Ooh
HE'S HERE!
HE'S CLOSE BY.
I'LL GET TO SEE HIM SOON!
hf
hf
hf

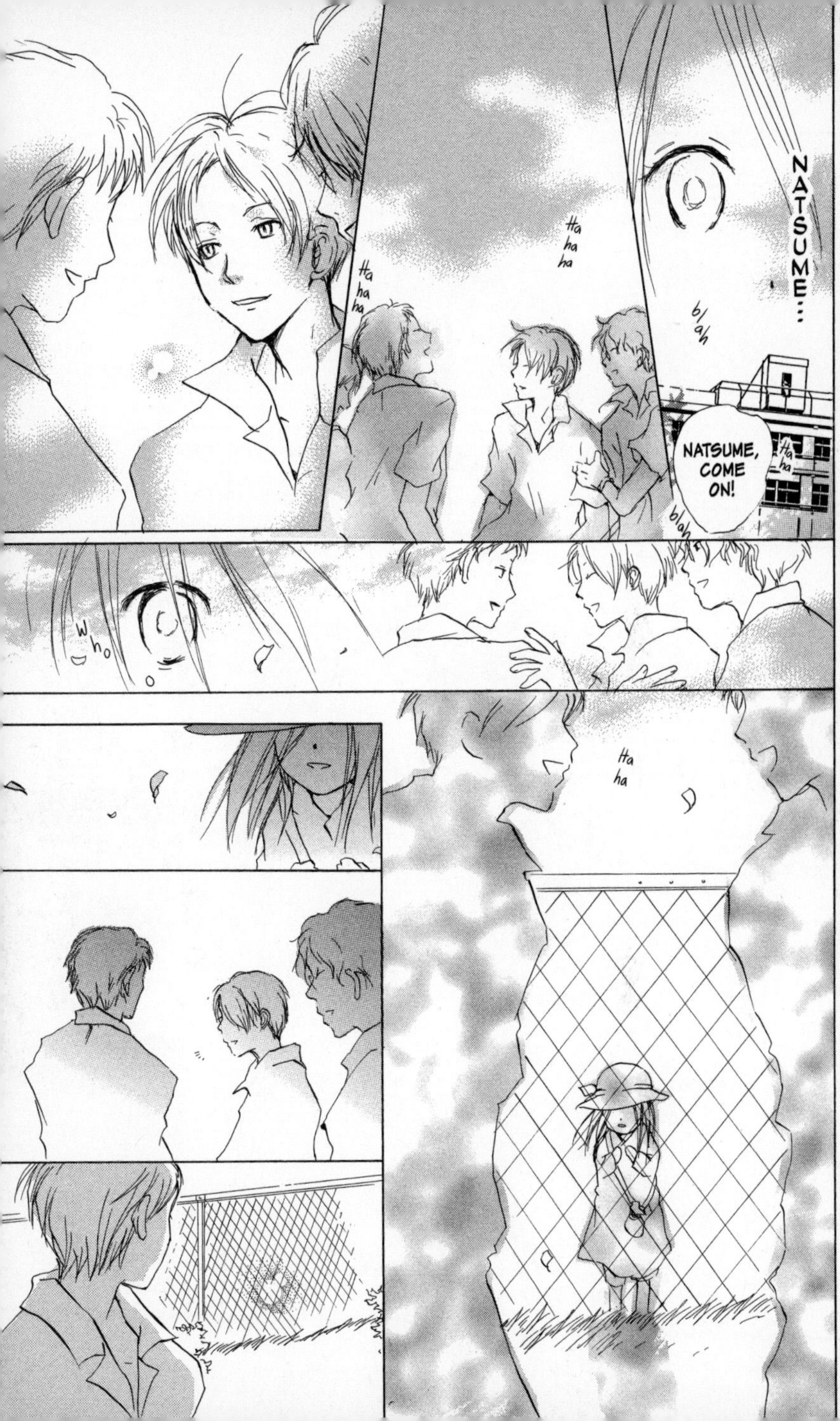
NATSUME...
blah
NATSUME, COME ON!
Ha ha
blah
Ha ha ha
Ha ha ha
Who
Ha ha

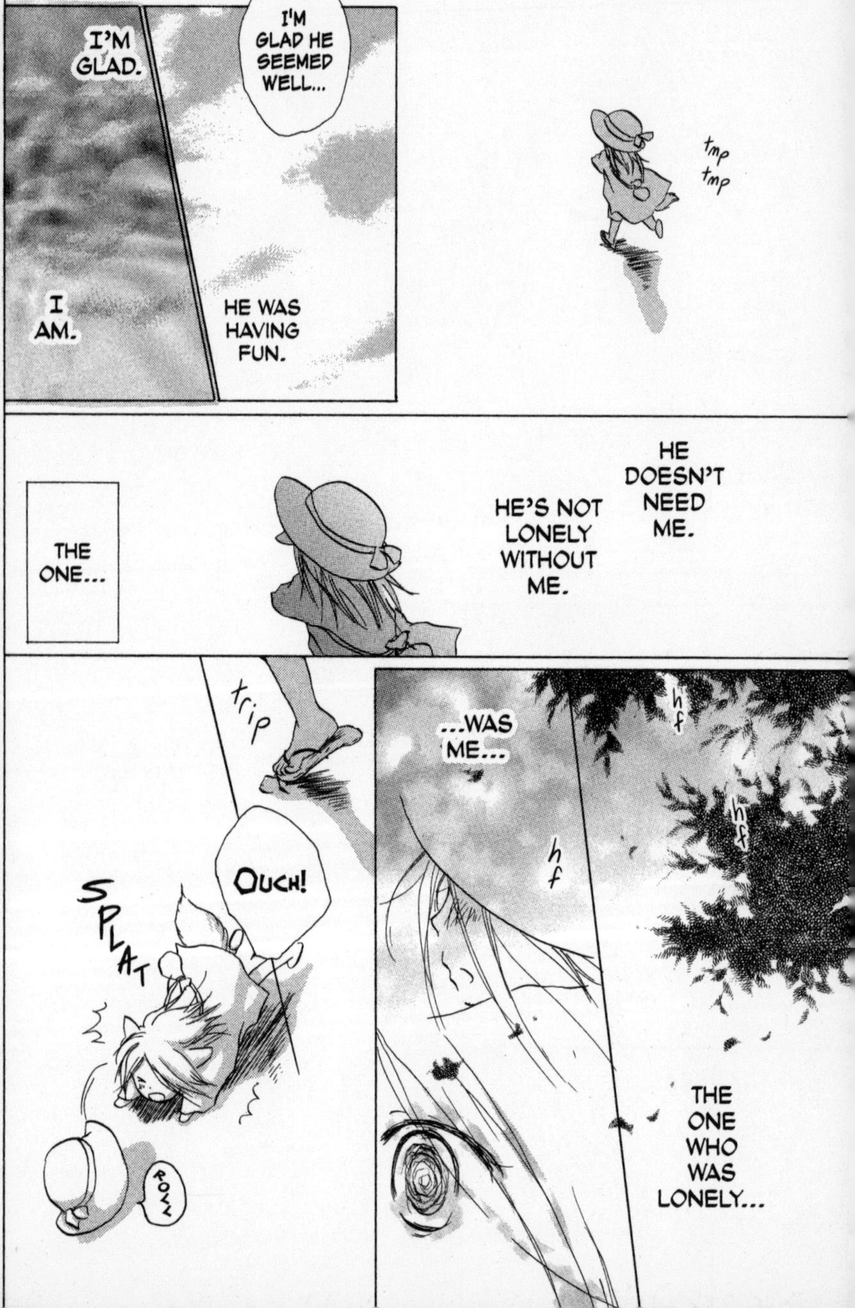
tmp
tmp
I'M GLAD HE SEEMED WELL...
HE WAS HAVING FUN.
I'M GLAD.
I AM.
HE DOESN'T NEED ME.
HE'S NOT LONELY WITHOUT ME.
THE ONE...
hf
hf
THE ONE WHO WAS LONELY...
...WAS ME...
hf
trip
OUCH!
SPLAT
roll

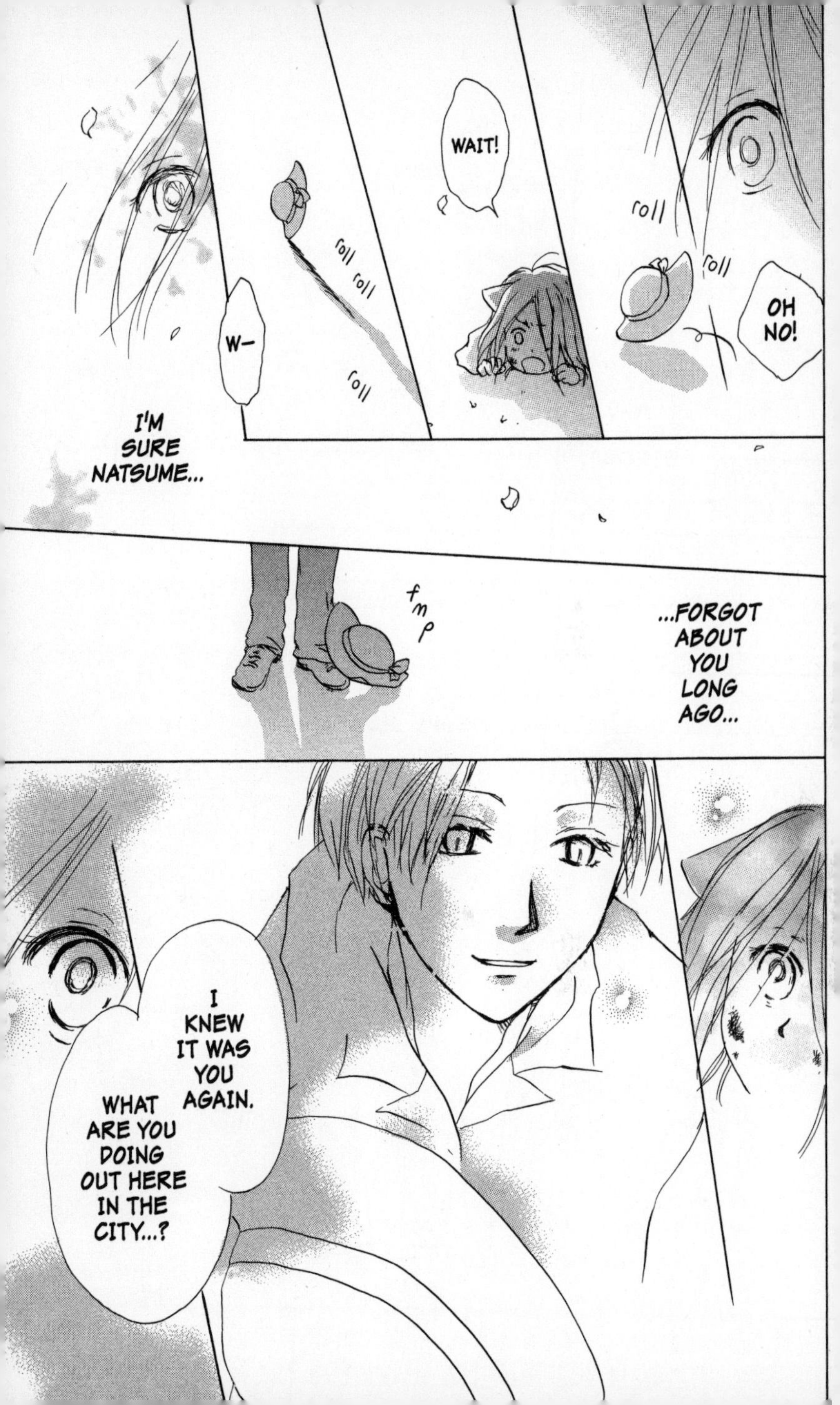
roll
roll
OH NO!
WAIT!
roll
roll
roll
W-
I'M SURE NATSUME...
...FORGOT ABOUT YOU LONG AGO...
fmp
I KNEW IT WAS YOU AGAIN.
WHAT ARE YOU DOING OUT HERE IN THE CITY...?

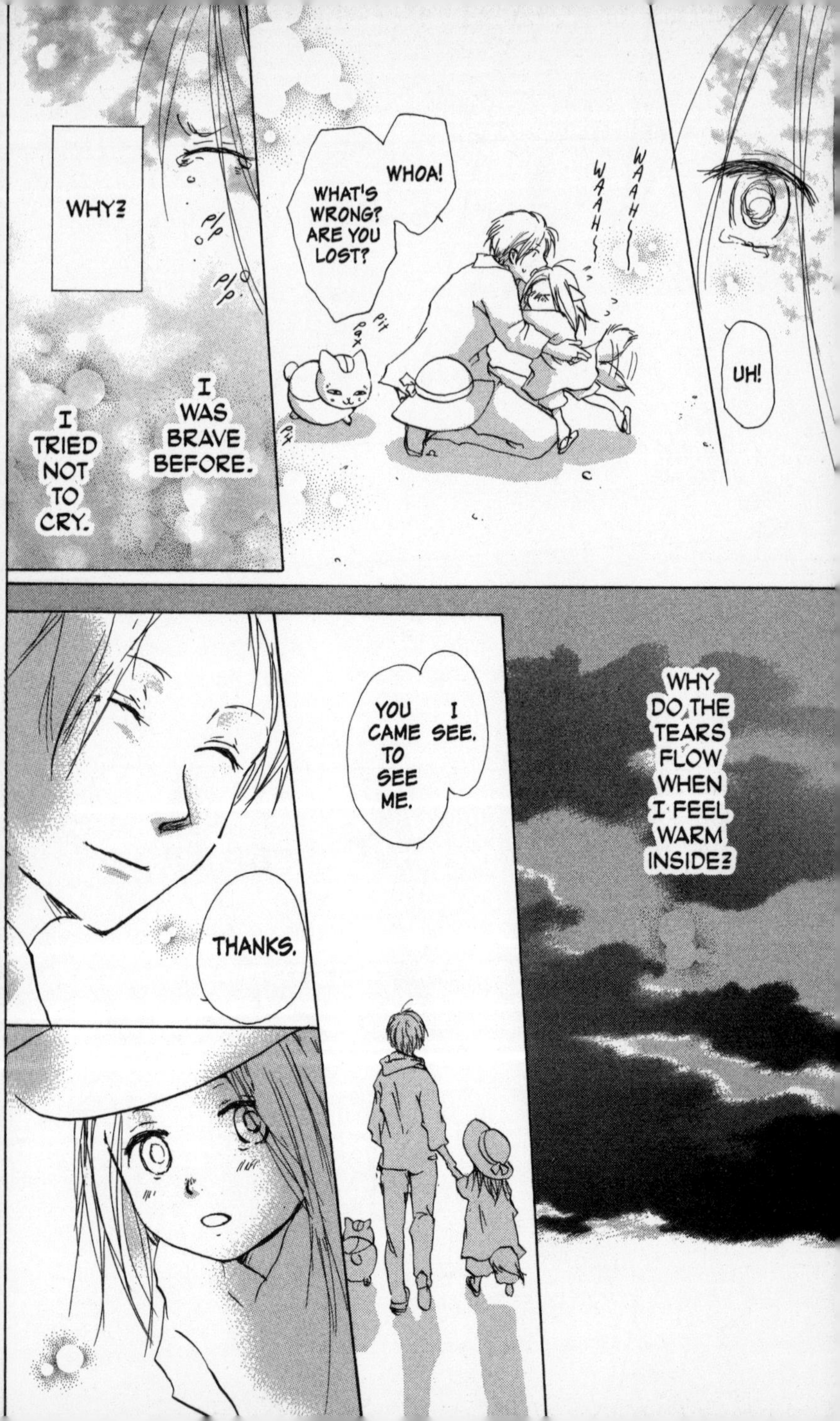

UH!
WAAAH~
WAAAH~
WHOA!
WHAT'S WRONG? ARE YOU LOST?
pit pat
pit
WHY?
I WAS BRAVE BEFORE.
I TRIED NOT TO CRY.
WHY DO THE TEARS FLOW WHEN I FEEL WARM INSIDE?
I SEE.
YOU CAME TO SEE ME.
THANKS.

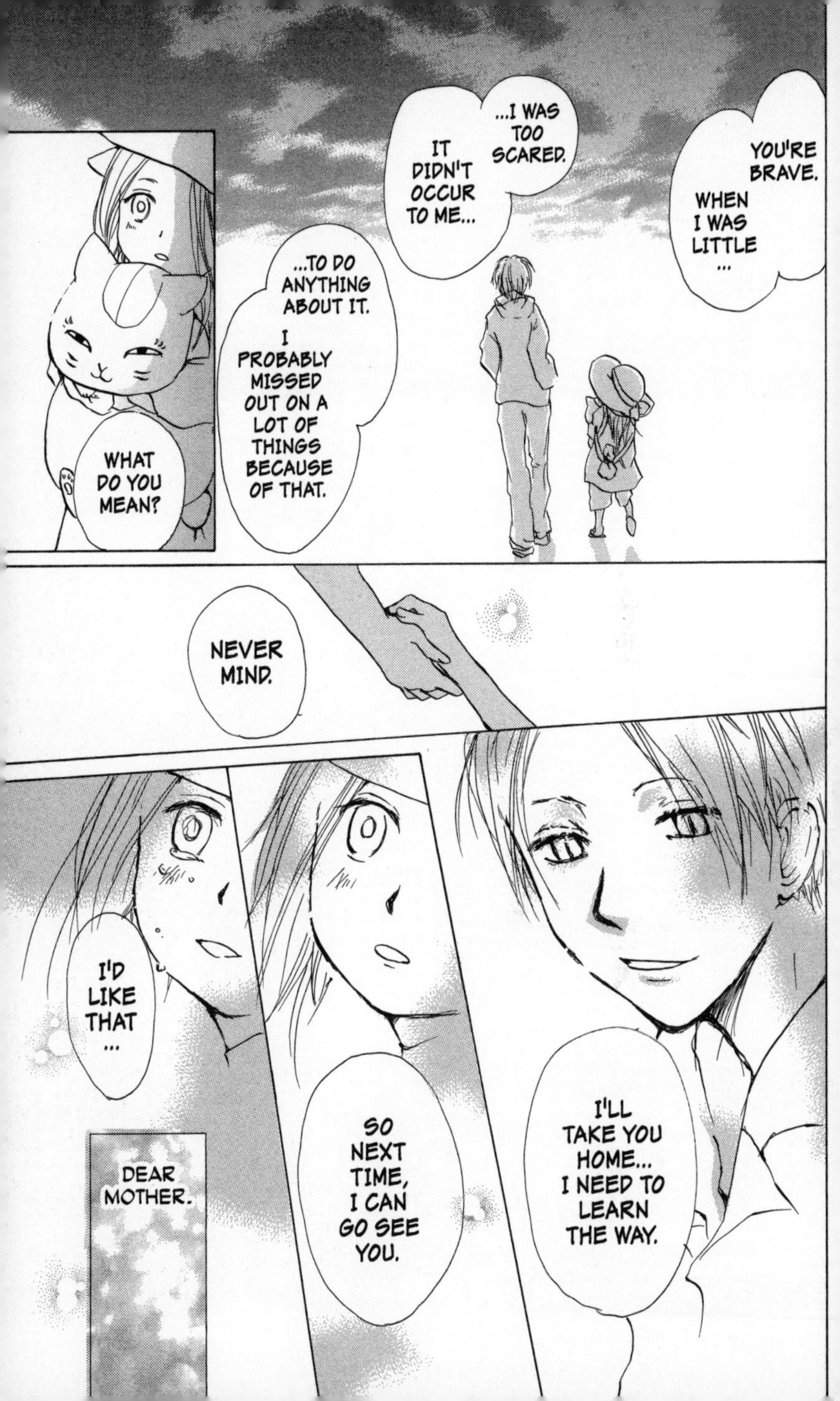
YOU'RE BRAVE.
WHEN I WAS LITTLE ...
...I WAS TOO SCARED.
IT DIDN'T OCCUR TO ME...
...TO DO ANYTHING ABOUT IT.
I PROBABLY MISSED OUT ON A LOT OF THINGS BECAUSE OF THAT.
WHAT DO YOU MEAN?
NEVER MIND.
I'LL TAKE YOU HOME... I NEED TO LEARN THE WAY.
SO NEXT TIME, I CAN GO SEE YOU.
I'D LIKE THAT ...
DEAR MOTHER.

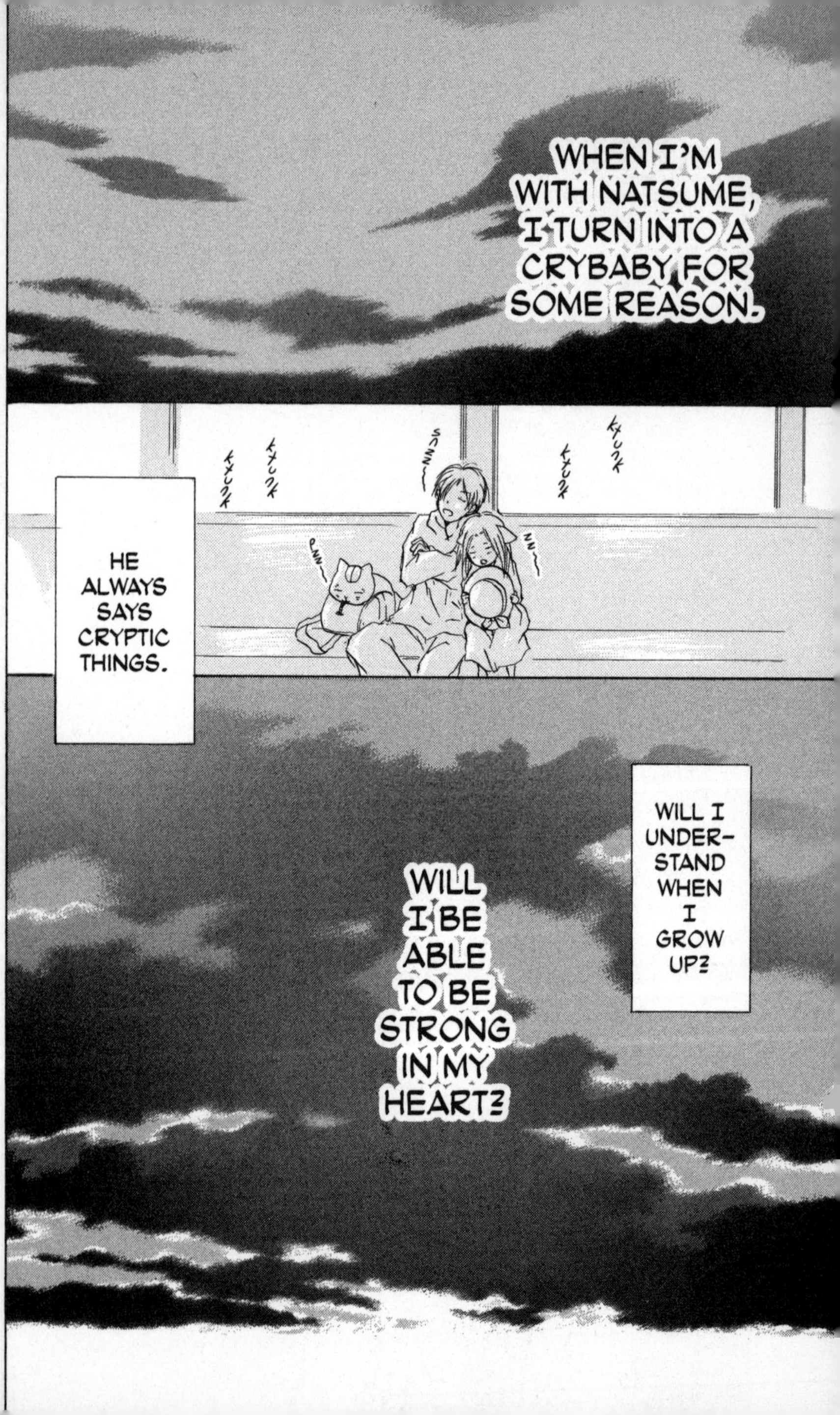

WHEN I'M WITH NATSUME, I TURN INTO A CRYBABY FOR SOME REASON.
HE ALWAYS SAYS CRYPTIC THINGS.
WILL I UNDER-STAND WHEN I GROW UP?
WILL I BE ABLE TO BE STRONG IN MY HEART?

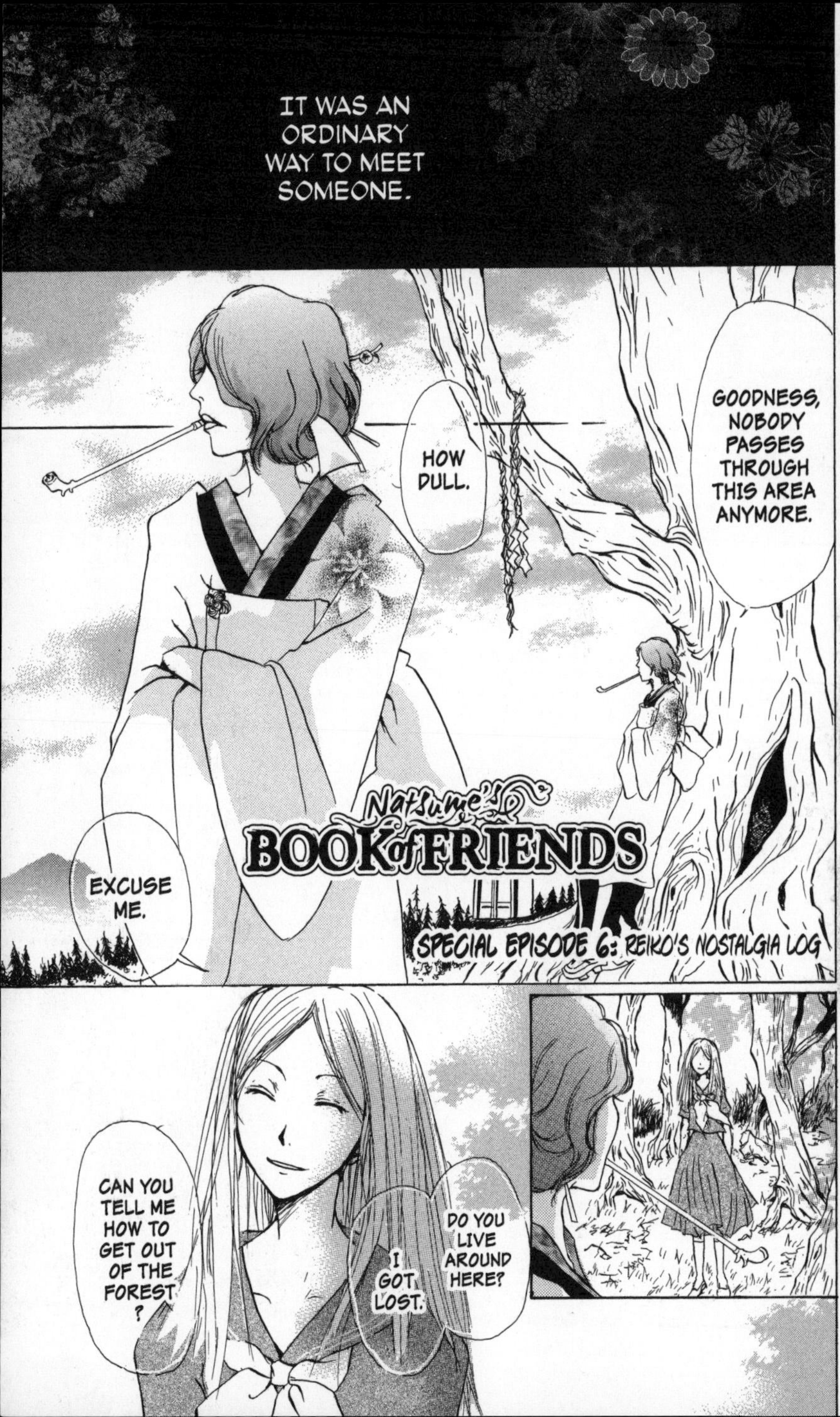
IT WAS AN ORDINARY WAY TO MEET SOMEONE.
GOODNESS, NOBODY PASSES THROUGH THIS AREA ANYMORE.
HOW DULL.
Natsume's BOOK of FRIENDS
SPECIAL EPISODE 6: REIKO'S NOSTALGIA LOG
EXCUSE ME.
DO YOU LIVE AROUND HERE?
I GOT LOST.
CAN YOU TELL ME HOW TO GET OUT OF THE FOREST?

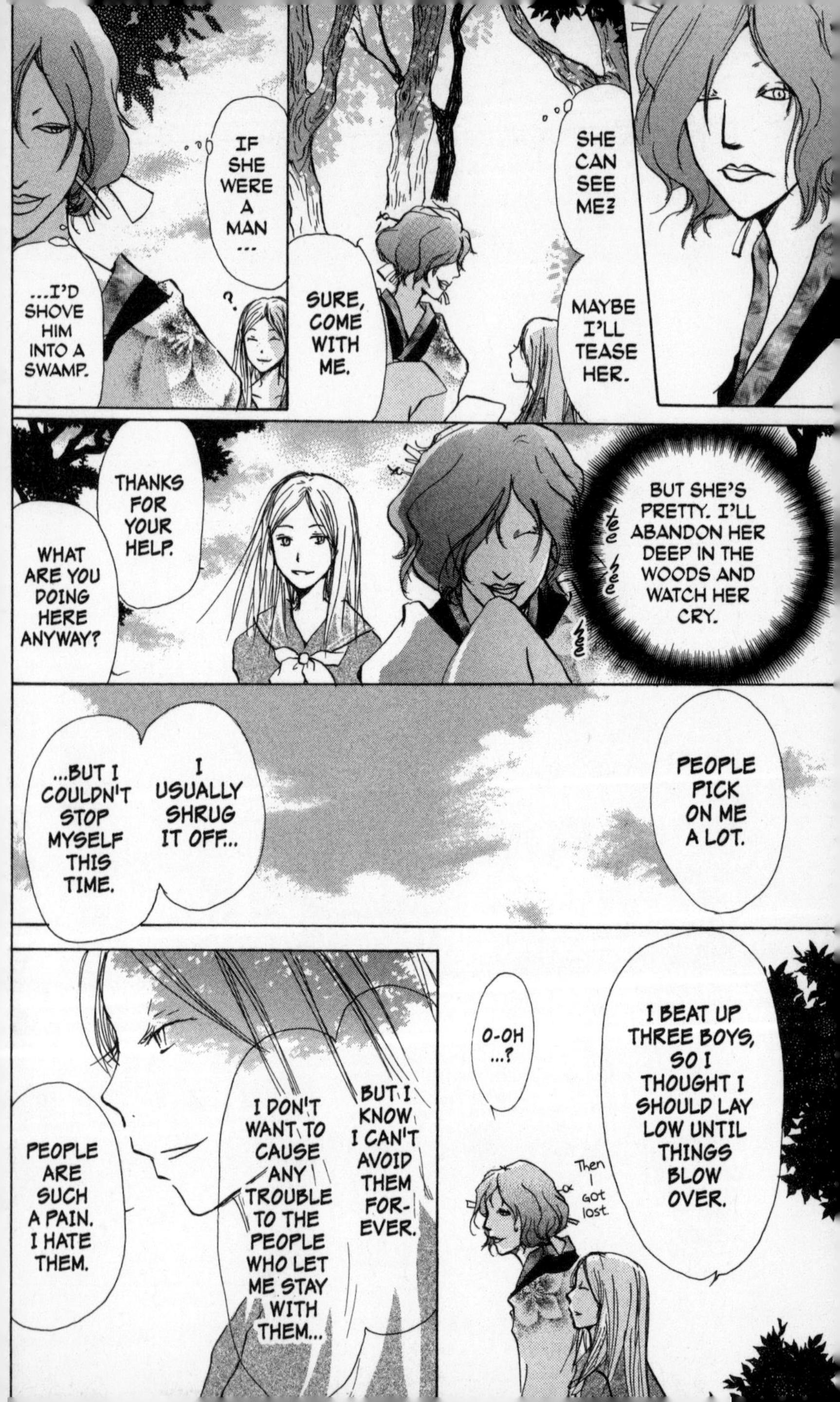
SHE CAN SEE ME?
MAYBE I'LL TEASE HER.
SURE, COME WITH ME.
IF SHE WERE A MAN...
...I'D SHOVE HIM INTO A SWAMP.
BUT SHE'S PRETTY. I'LL ABANDON HER DEEP IN THE WOODS AND WATCH HER CRY.
tee hee hee
THANKS FOR YOUR HELP.
WHAT ARE YOU DOING HERE ANYWAY?
PEOPLE PICK ON ME A LOT.
I USUALLY SHRUG IT OFF...
...BUT I COULDN'T STOP MYSELF THIS TIME.
I BEAT UP THREE BOYS, SO I THOUGHT I SHOULD LAY LOW UNTIL THINGS BLOW OVER.
Then I got lost.
O-OH...?
BUT I KNOW I CAN'T AVOID THEM FOREVER.
I DON'T WANT TO CAUSE ANY TROUBLE TO THE PEOPLE WHO LET ME STAY WITH THEM...
PEOPLE ARE SUCH A PAIN. I HATE THEM.

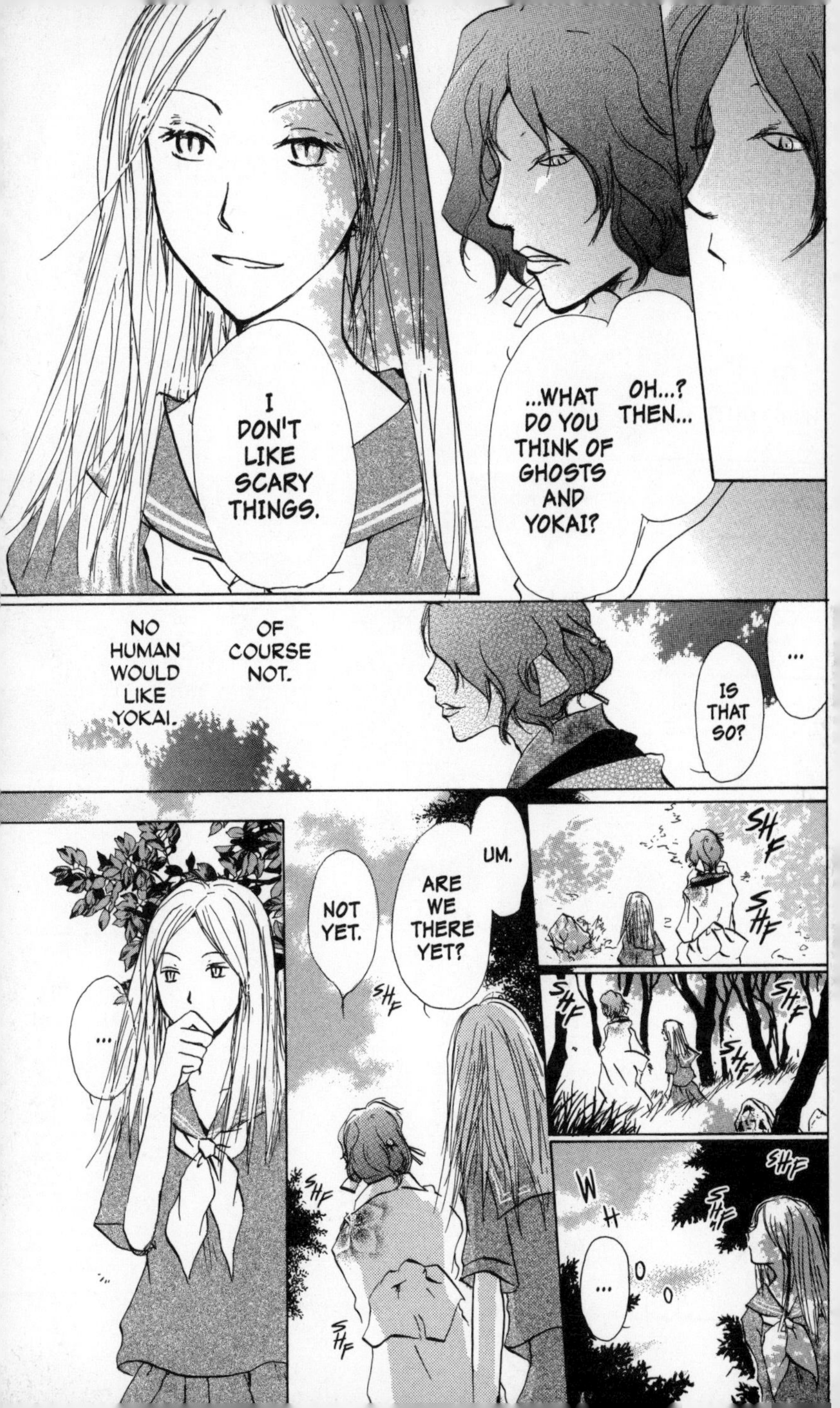
OH...? THEN...
...WHAT DO YOU THINK OF GHOSTS AND YOKAI?
I DON'T LIKE SCARY THINGS.
...
IS THAT SO?
OF COURSE NOT.
NO HUMAN WOULD LIKE YOKAI.
SHF
SHF
SHF
SHF
SHF
SHF
SHF
WHOO
...
UM.
ARE WE THERE YET?
NOT YET.
SHF
SHF
SHF
...

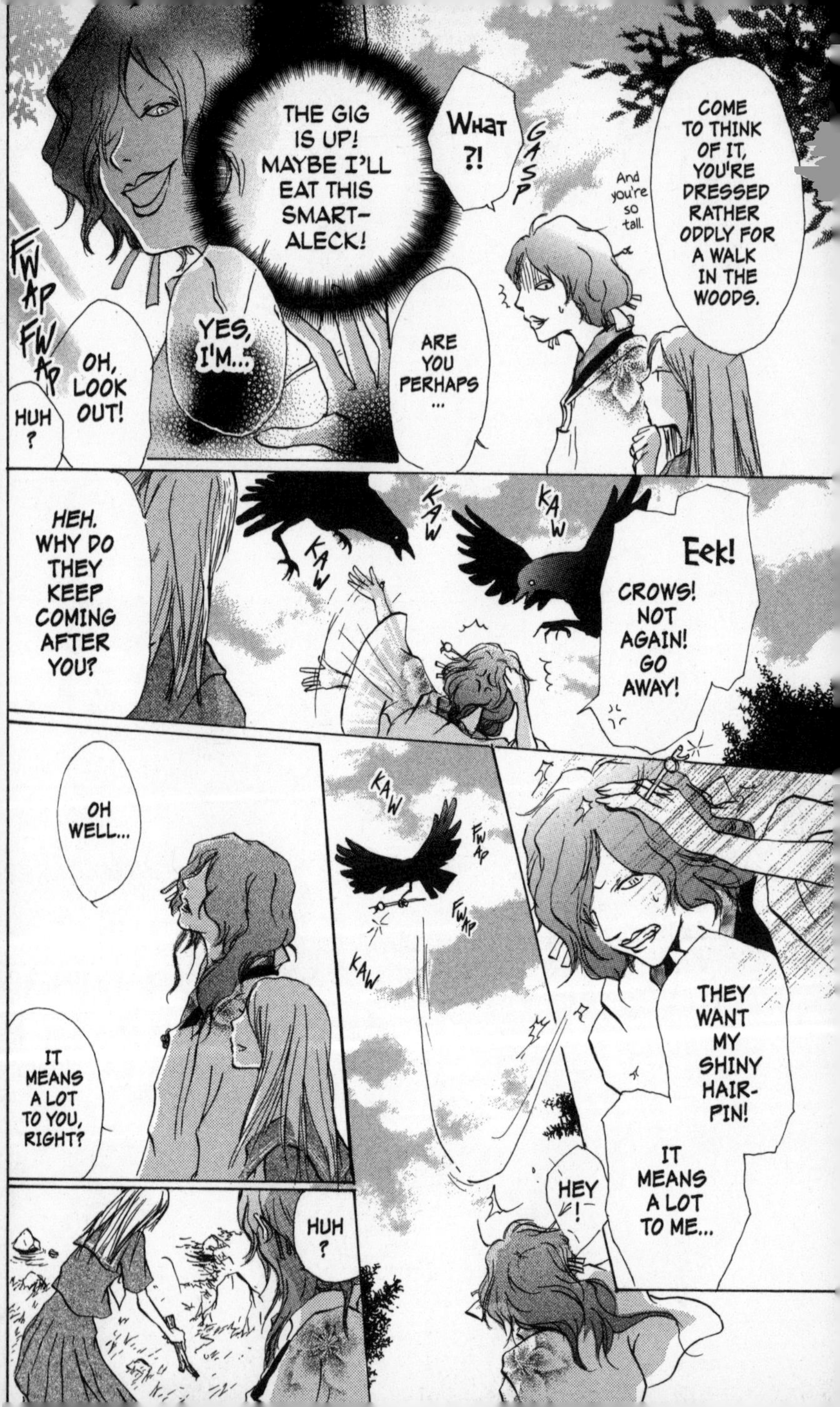
COME TO THINK OF IT, YOU'RE DRESSED RATHER ODDLY FOR A WALK IN THE WOODS.
And you're so tall.
GASP
WHAT?!
THE GIG IS UP! MAYBE I'LL EAT THIS SMART-ALECK!
ARE YOU PERHAPS ...
YES, I'M...
FWAP FWAP
OH, LOOK OUT!
HUH?
Eek!
CROWS! NOT AGAIN! GO AWAY!
KAW
KAW
KAW
HEH. WHY DO THEY KEEP COMING AFTER YOU?
THEY WANT MY SHINY HAIR-PIN!
IT MEANS A LOT TO ME...
HEY!
KAW
FWAP
FWAP
KAW
OH WELL...
IT MEANS A LOT TO YOU, RIGHT?
HUH?

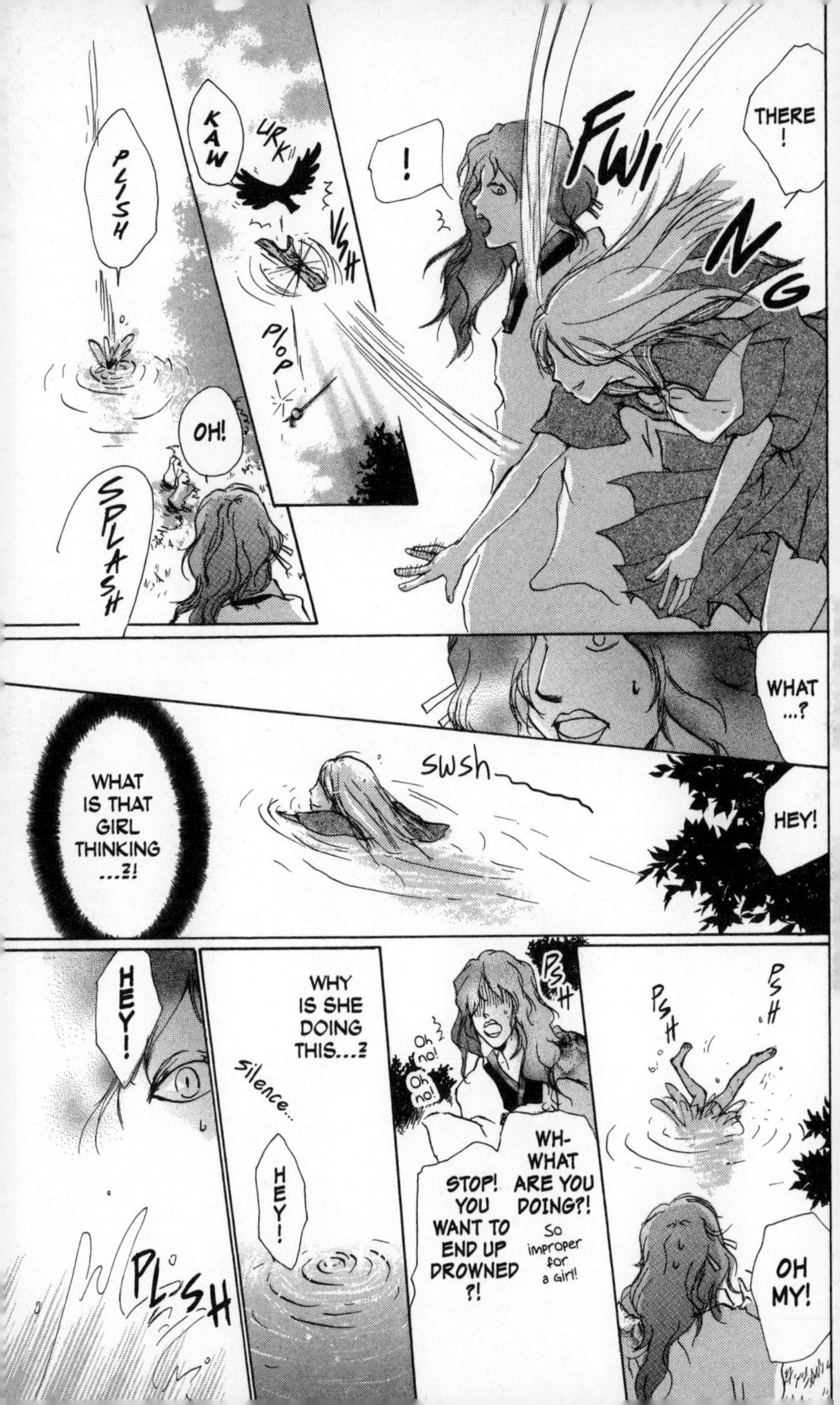
THERE!
FWING
!
KAW
URK
VSSH
PLOP
PLISH
OH!
SPLASH
WHAT...?
HEY!
SWSH
WHAT IS THAT GIRL THINKING...?!
PSH
PSH
OH MY!
PSH
Oh no!
Oh no!
WH-WHAT ARE YOU DOING?!
So improper for a girl!
STOP! YOU WANT TO END UP DROWNED?!
WHY IS SHE DOING THIS...?
silence...
HEY!
HEY!
PLSH

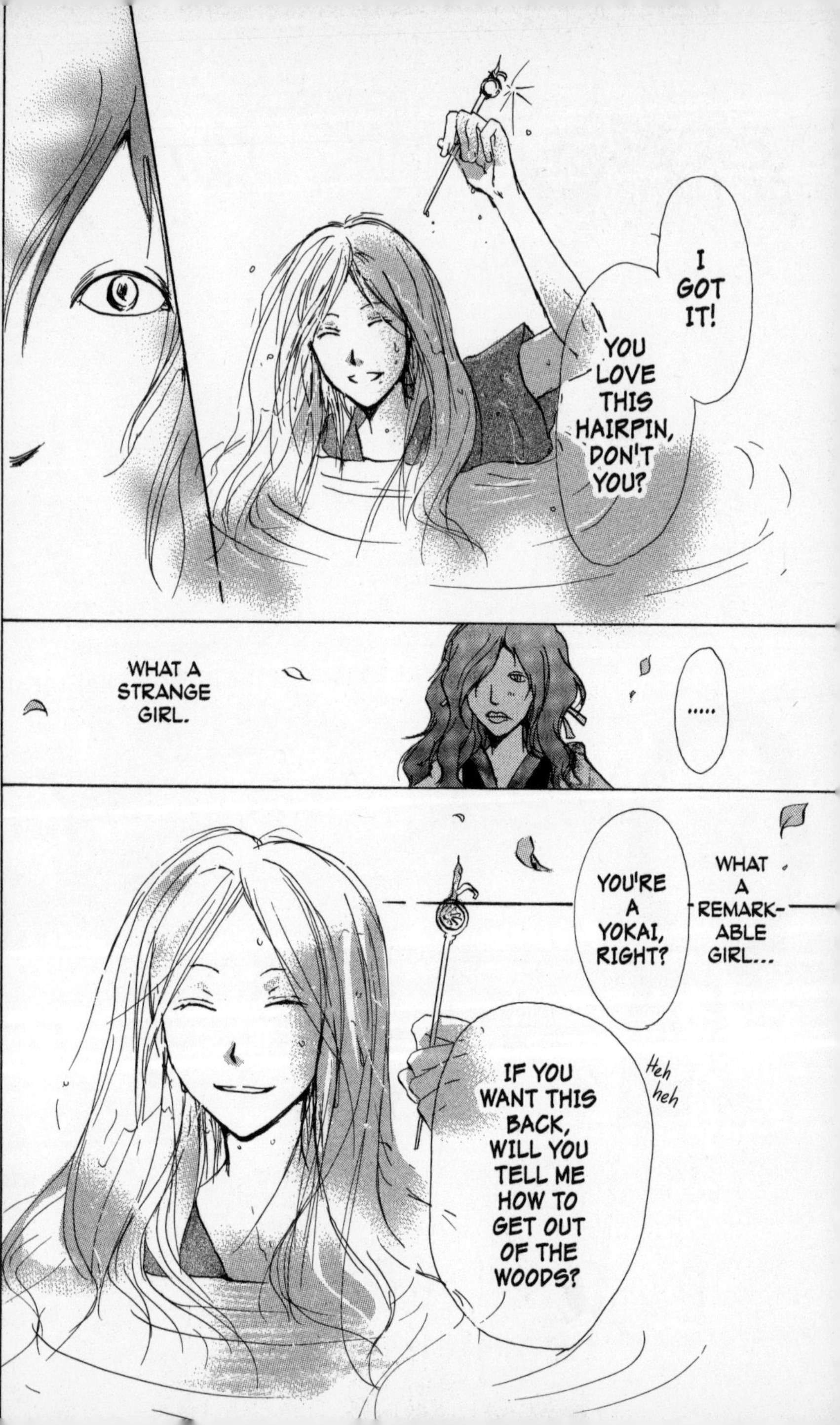
I GOT IT!
YOU LOVE THIS HAIRPIN, DON'T YOU?
.....
WHAT A STRANGE GIRL.
WHAT A REMARKABLE GIRL...
YOU'RE A YOKAI, RIGHT?
Heh heh
IF YOU WANT THIS BACK, WILL YOU TELL ME HOW TO GET OUT OF THE WOODS?

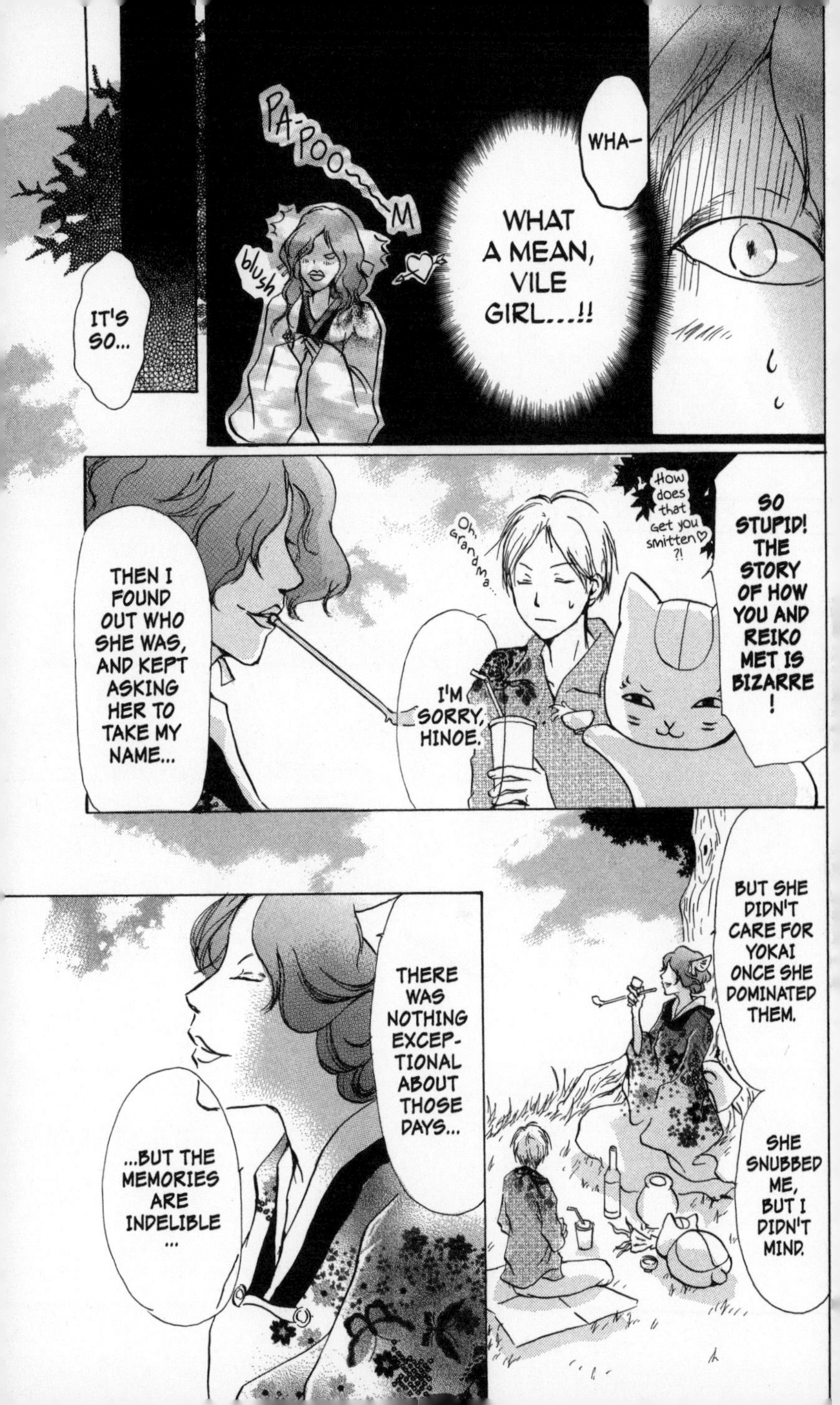
WHA–
WHAT A MEAN, VILE GIRL...!!
PA-POO~~M
blush
IT'S SO...
SO STUPID! THE STORY OF HOW YOU AND REIKO MET IS BIZARRE!
How does that get you smitten♡?!
Oh, Grandma...
I'M SORRY, HINOE.
THEN I FOUND OUT WHO SHE WAS, AND KEPT ASKING HER TO TAKE MY NAME...
BUT SHE DIDN'T CARE FOR YOKAI ONCE SHE DOMINATED THEM.
SHE SNUBBED ME, BUT I DIDN'T MIND.
THERE WAS NOTHING EXCEP-TIONAL ABOUT THOSE DAYS...
...BUT THE MEMORIES ARE INDELIBLE...

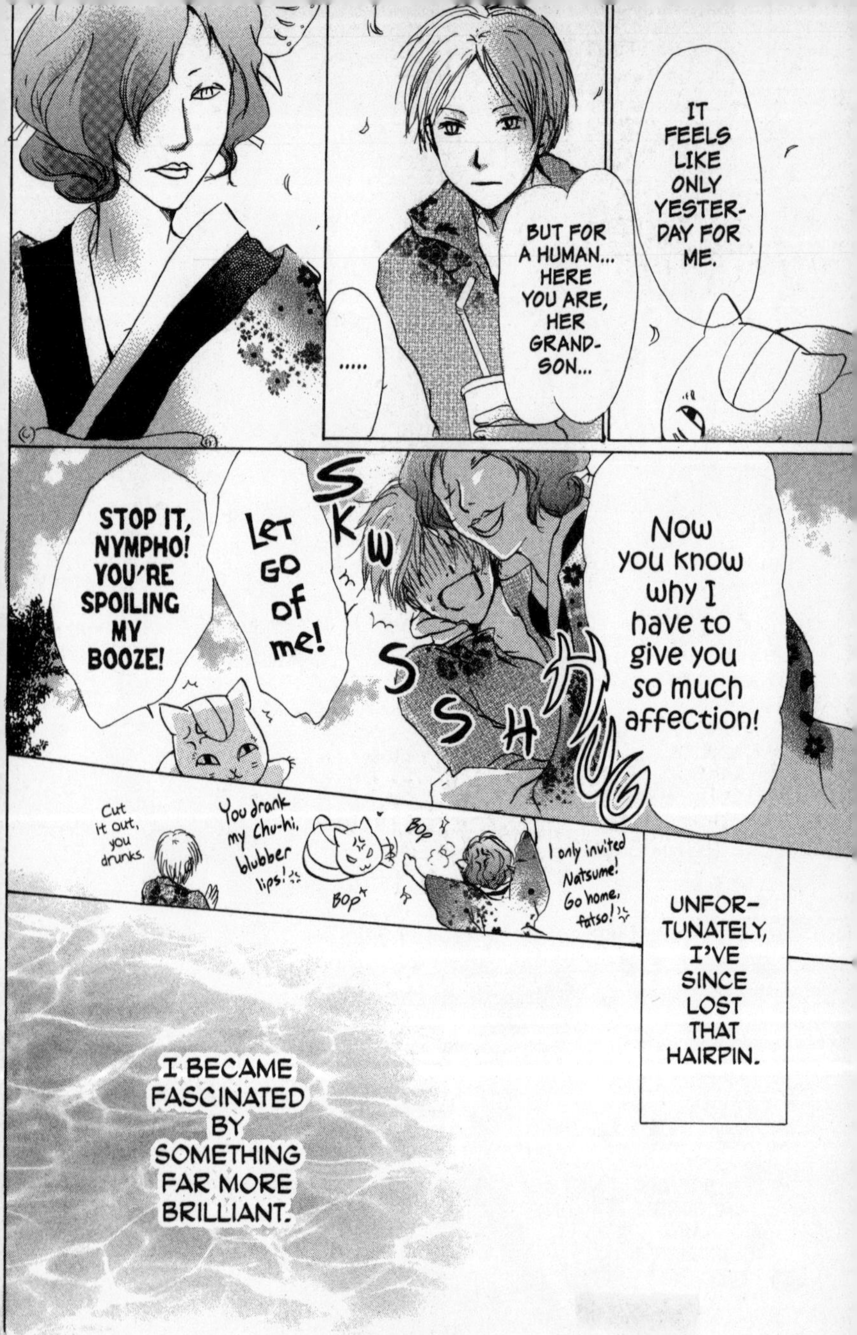

IT FEELS LIKE ONLY YESTER-DAY FOR ME.
BUT FOR A HUMAN... HERE YOU ARE, HER GRAND-SON...
.....
Now you know why I have to give you so much affection!
HUG
SKWSSH
Let go of me!
STOP IT, NYMPHO! YOU'RE SPOILING MY BOOZE!
I only invited Natsume! Go home, fatso!
Bop
Bop
You drank my Chu-hi, blubber lips!
Cut it out, you drunks.
UNFOR-TUNATELY, I'VE SINCE LOST THAT HAIRPIN.
I BECAME FASCINATED BY SOMETHING FAR MORE BRILLIANT.

NATSUME'S BOOK OF FRIENDS, VOL. 6: END

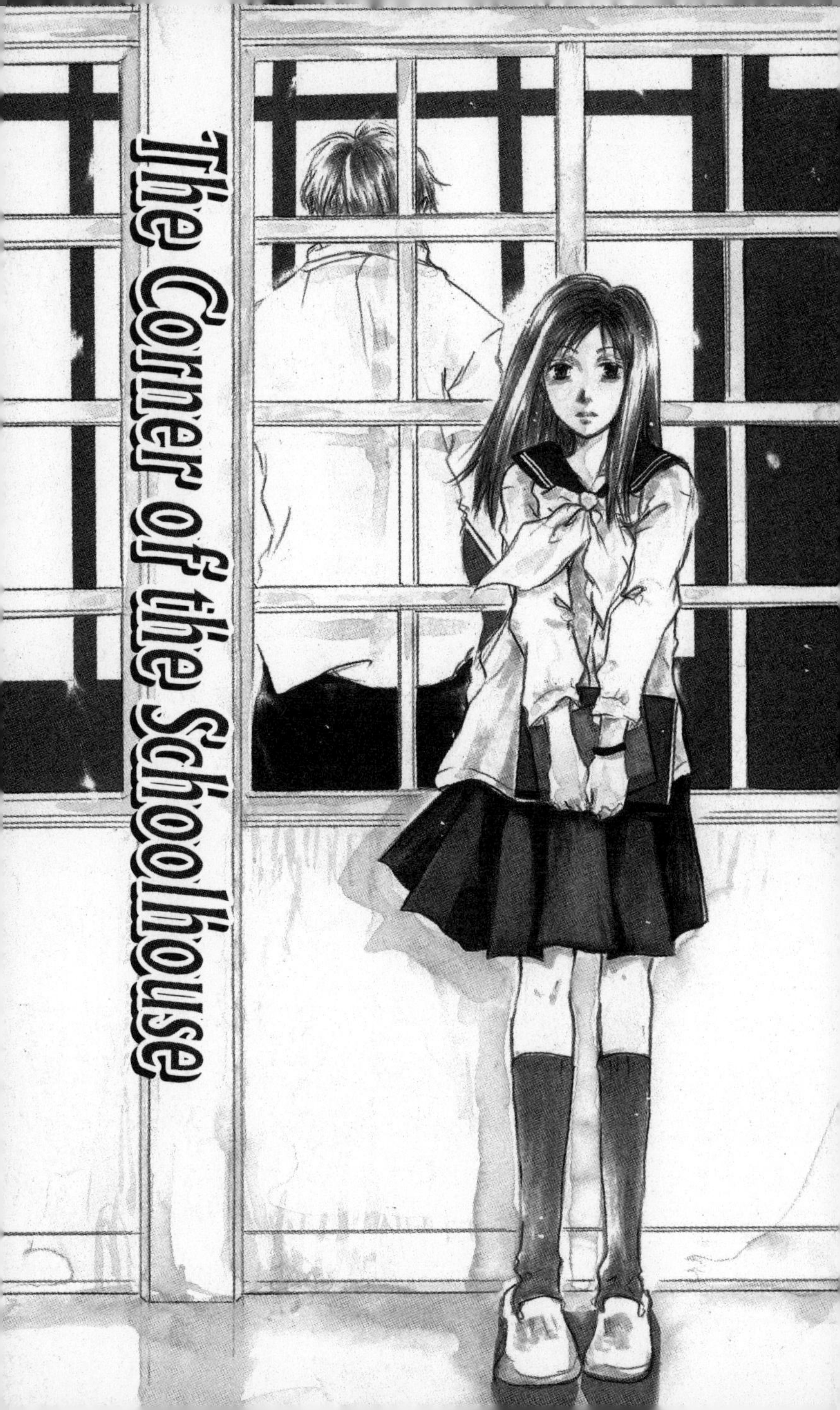
The Corner of the Schoolhouse

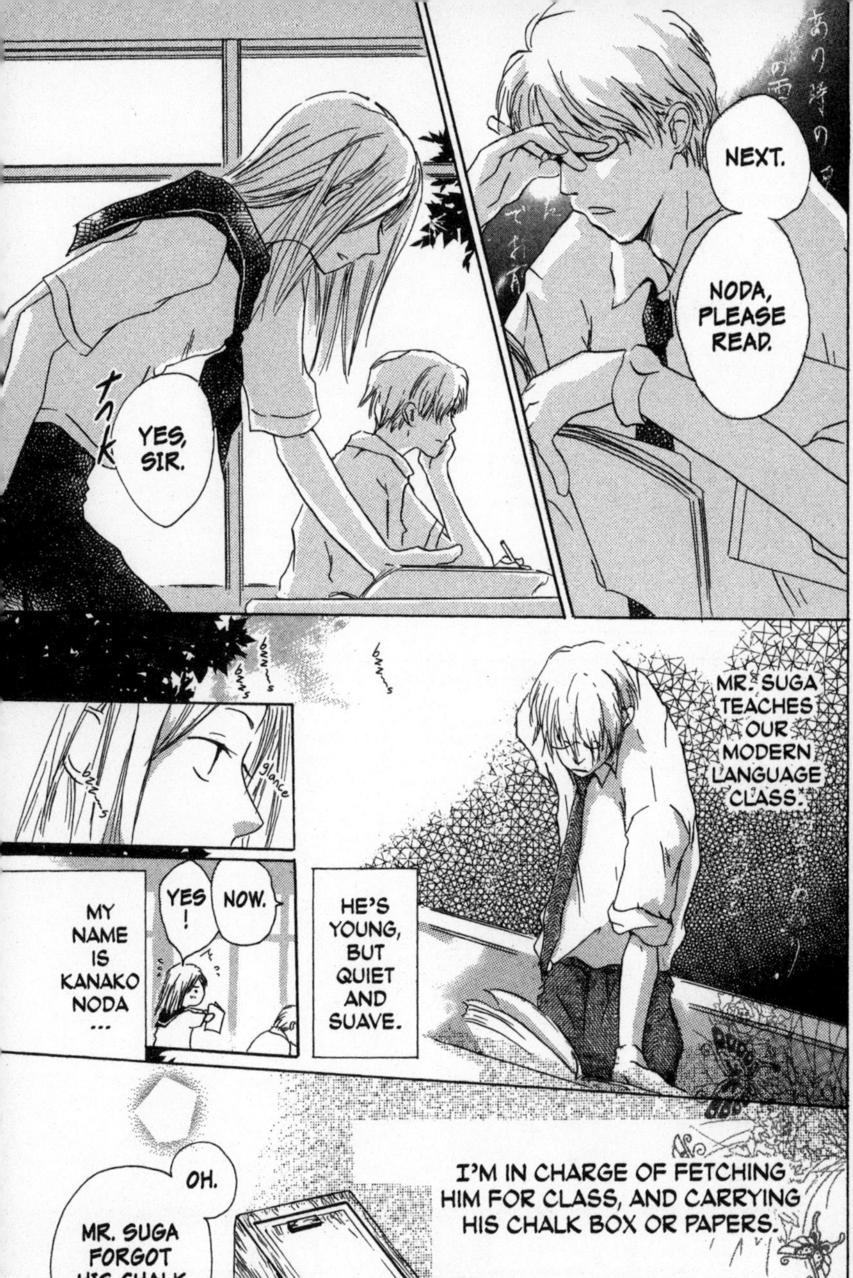
NEXT.
NODA, PLEASE READ.
YES, SIR.
MR. SUGA TEACHES OUR MODERN LANGUAGE CLASS.
bzzz
glance
HE'S YOUNG, BUT QUIET AND SUAVE.
NOW.
YES!
MY NAME IS KANAKO NODA...
I'M IN CHARGE OF FETCHING HIM FOR CLASS, AND CARRYING HIS CHALK BOX OR PAPERS.
OH.
MR. SUGA FORGOT HIS CHALK BOX.

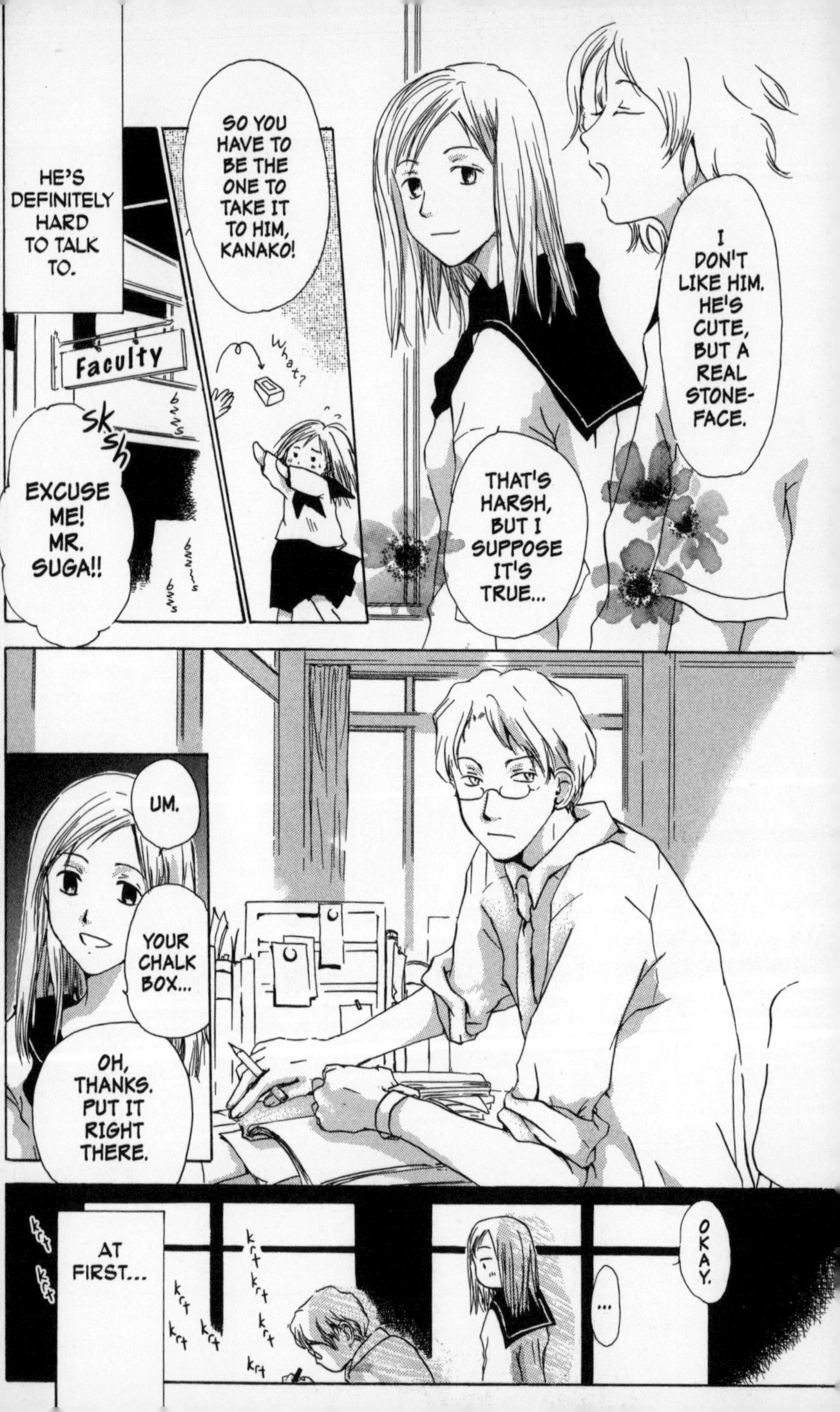
I DON'T LIKE HIM. HE'S CUTE, BUT A REAL STONE-FACE.
THAT'S HARSH, BUT I SUPPOSE IT'S TRUE...
SO YOU HAVE TO BE THE ONE TO TAKE IT TO HIM, KANAKO!
What?
HE'S DEFINITELY HARD TO TALK TO.
Faculty
bzzs
SK SH
EXCUSE ME! MR. SUGA!!
bzzs
bzzs
UM.
YOUR CHALK BOX...
OH, THANKS. PUT IT RIGHT THERE.
OKAY.
...
krt krt krt krt
krt krt krt krt
AT FIRST...
krt krt

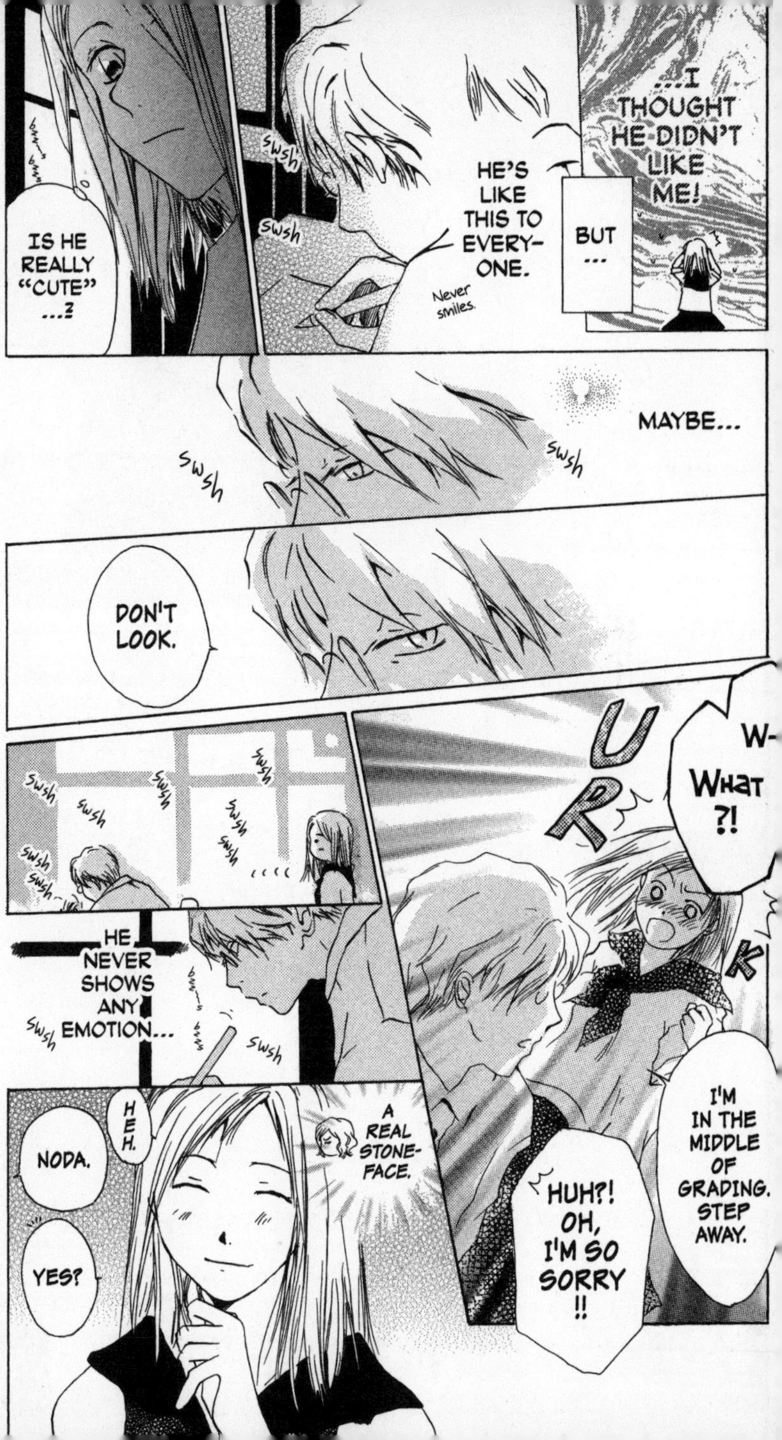
...I THOUGHT HE DIDN'T LIKE ME!
BUT...
HE'S LIKE THIS TO EVERYONE.
Never smiles.
swsh
swsh
bzzz bzzz
IS HE REALLY "CUTE"...?
MAYBE...
swsh
swsh
DON'T LOOK.
URK
W-WHAT?!
I'M IN THE MIDDLE OF GRADING. STEP AWAY.
HUH?! OH, I'M SO SORRY!!
swsh
swsh
swsh
swsh
swsh
swsh
swsh
HE NEVER SHOWS ANY EMOTION...
bzzz bzzz
swsh
swsh
A REAL STONE-FACE.
HEH.
NODA.
YES?

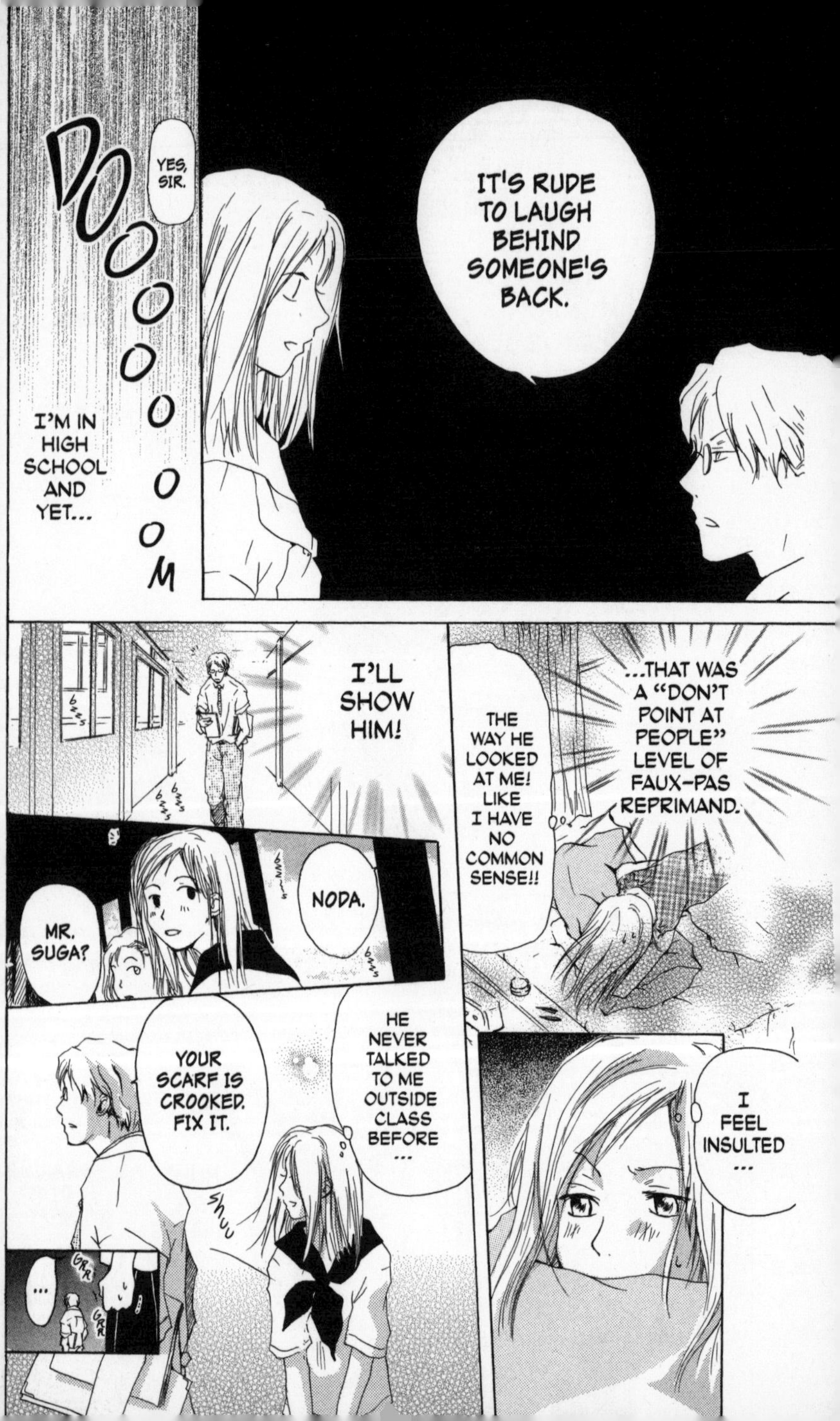
IT'S RUDE TO LAUGH BEHIND SOMEONE'S BACK.
YES, SIR.
DOOOOOOOOM
I'M IN HIGH SCHOOL AND YET...
...THAT WAS A "DON'T POINT AT PEOPLE" LEVEL OF FAUX-PAS REPRIMAND.
THE WAY HE LOOKED AT ME! LIKE I HAVE NO COMMON SENSE!!
I'LL SHOW HIM!
NODA.
MR. SUGA?
I FEEL INSULTED...
HE NEVER TALKED TO ME OUTSIDE CLASS BEFORE...
YOUR SCARF IS CROOKED. FIX IT.
SHUU
...
GRR
GRR

05

❋Anime: part 2

As a privilege of being the manga artist, they let me see the rough drafts of the character designs. Natsume had such presence, and the yokai looked so lively. Looking at them almost made me swoon. When things surpass your expectations, I found that you're left speechless. Still in a trance, I opened my mouth to try to convey my enthusiasm. But I blurted out something incomprehensible and rude like, "I-I can't wait to see the girls." I wanted to prostrate myself in apology like they do in manga. Later, they sent me a design sketch of Reiko, who was showing a bit of her midriff. Was it a shot for my benefit?! (It's probably to show whether or not she was wearing a shirt underneath.) As I took a look at the other characters, yokai, and background art they sent me, I got emotional. I couldn't wait for everyone everywhere to see it.

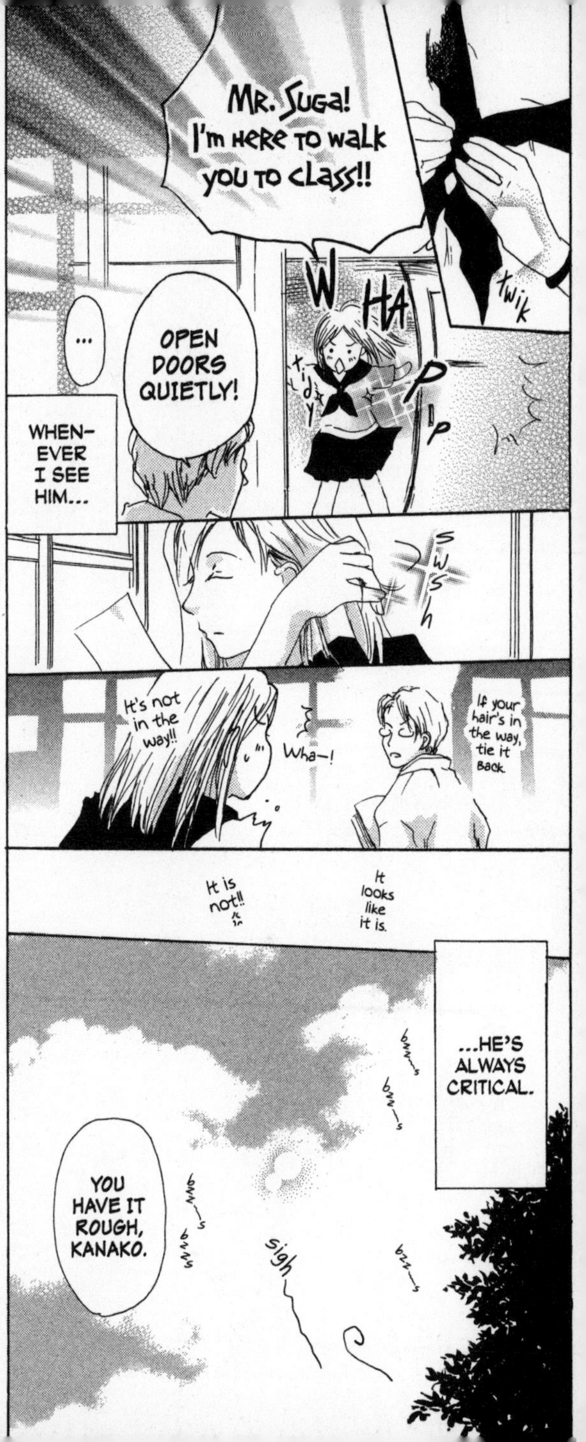
MR. SUGA! I'M HERE TO WALK YOU TO CLASS!!
twik
WHAP
tidy
...
OPEN DOORS QUIETLY!
WHEN-EVER I SEE HIM...
swish
If your hair's in the way, tie it back.
Wha-!
It's not in the way!!
It looks like it is.
It is not!!
...HE'S ALWAYS CRITICAL.
bzzz
bzzz
bzzz
bzzz
sigh
bzzz
YOU HAVE IT ROUGH, KANAKO.

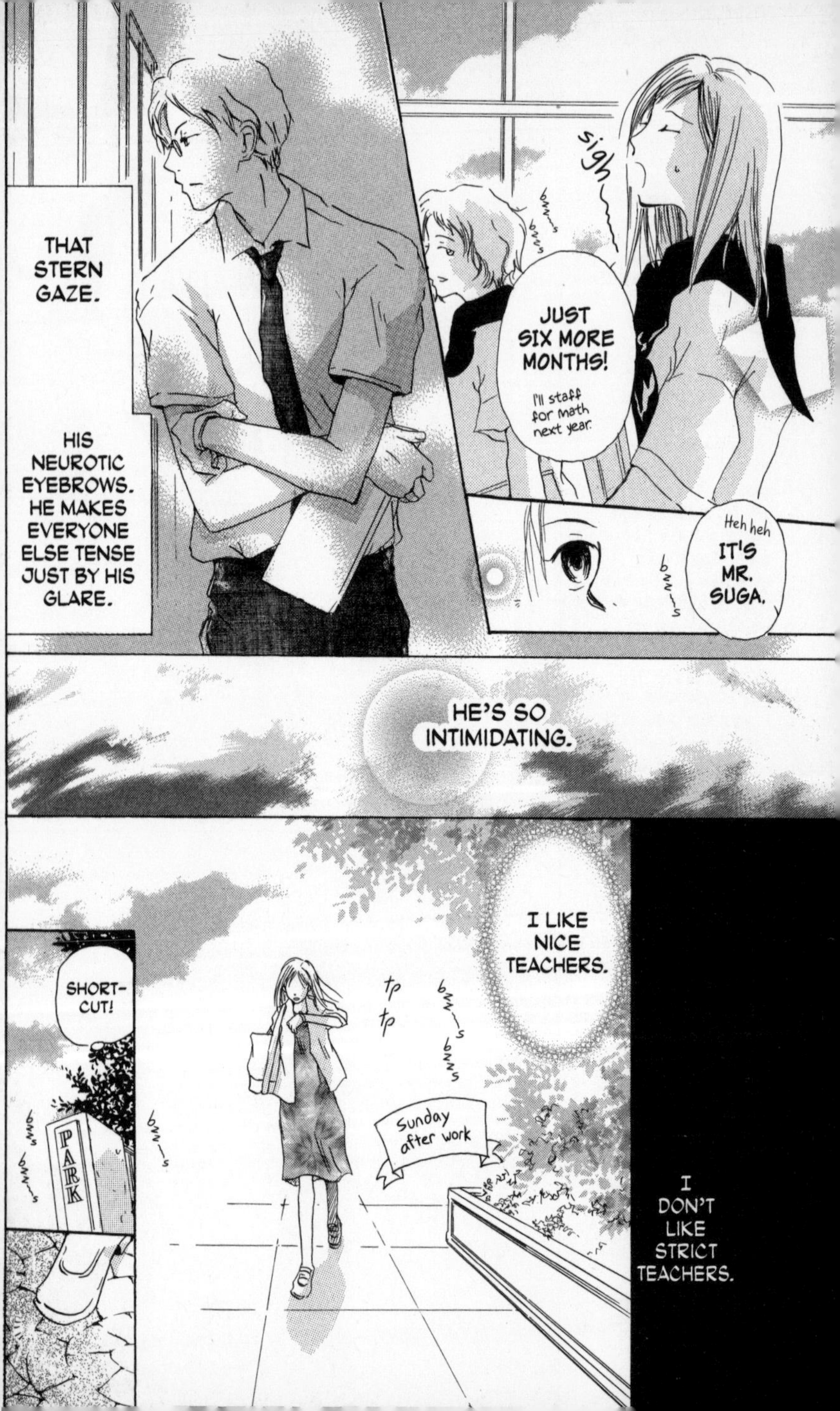
sigh
JUST SIX MORE MONTHS!
I'll staff for math next year.
Heh heh
IT'S MR. SUGA.
THAT STERN GAZE.
HIS NEUROTIC EYEBROWS. HE MAKES EVERYONE ELSE TENSE JUST BY HIS GLARE.
HE'S SO INTIMIDATING.
I DON'T LIKE STRICT TEACHERS.
I LIKE NICE TEACHERS.
tp tp
Sunday after work
SHORT-CUT!
PARK

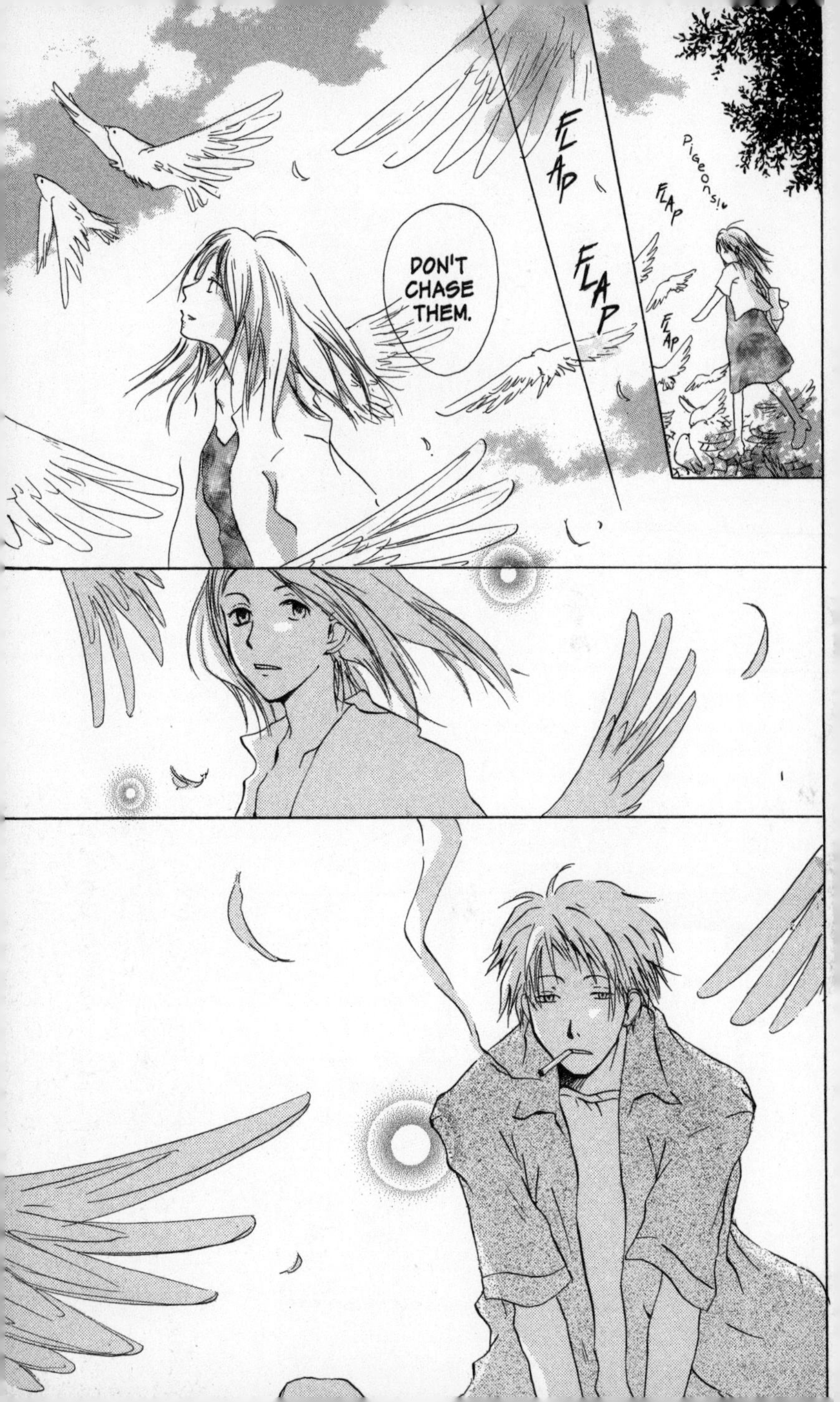
Pigeons!♡
FLAP
FLAP
FLAP
FLAP
FLAP
DON'T CHASE THEM.

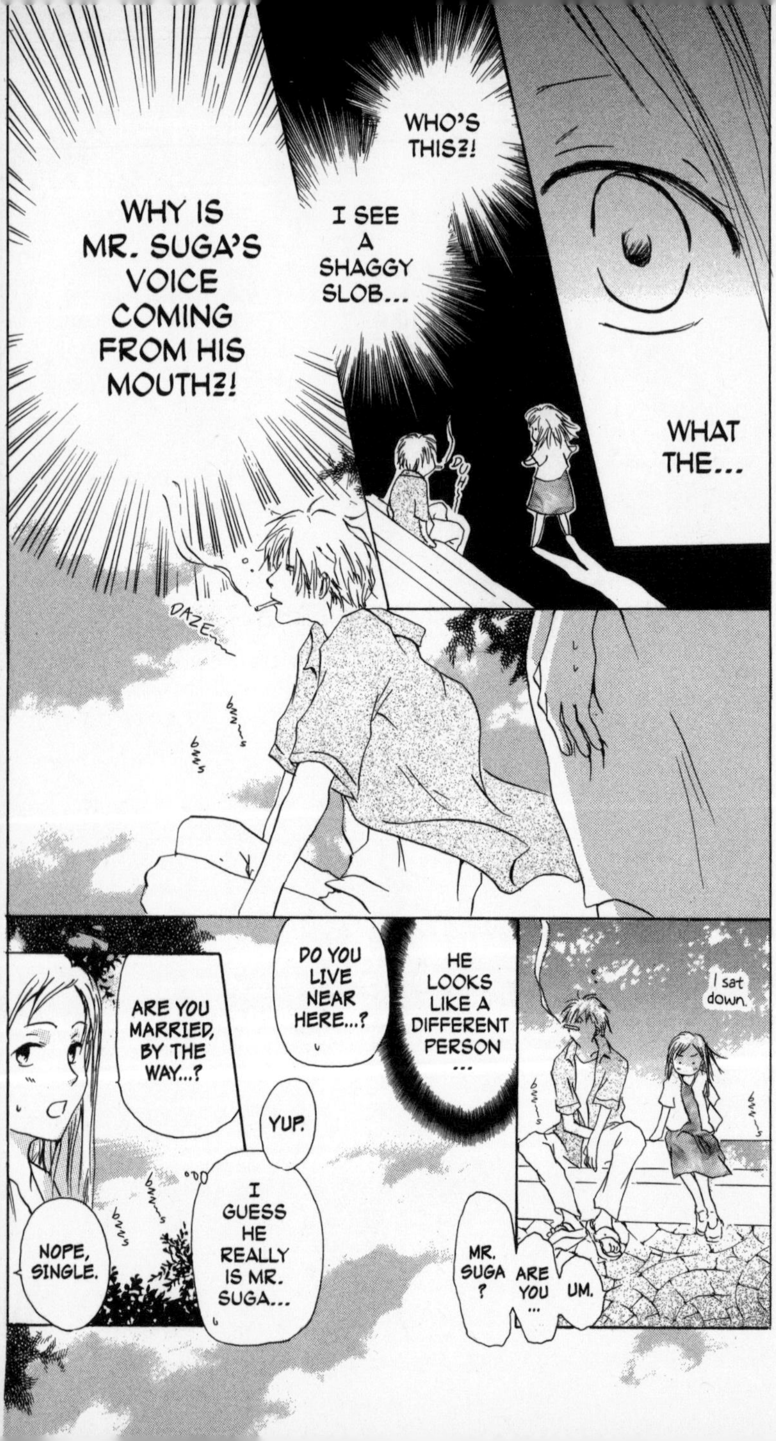
WHAT THE...
WHO'S THIS?!
I SEE A SHAGGY SLOB...
WHY IS MR. SUGA'S VOICE COMING FROM HIS MOUTH?!
DAZE~
bzz~s
bzz~s
I sat down.
bzz~s
bzz~s
UM.
ARE YOU ...
MR. SUGA ?
HE LOOKS LIKE A DIFFERENT PERSON ...
DO YOU LIVE NEAR HERE...?
YUP.
I GUESS HE REALLY IS MR. SUGA...
ARE YOU MARRIED, BY THE WAY...?
bzz~s
bzz~s
NOPE, SINGLE.

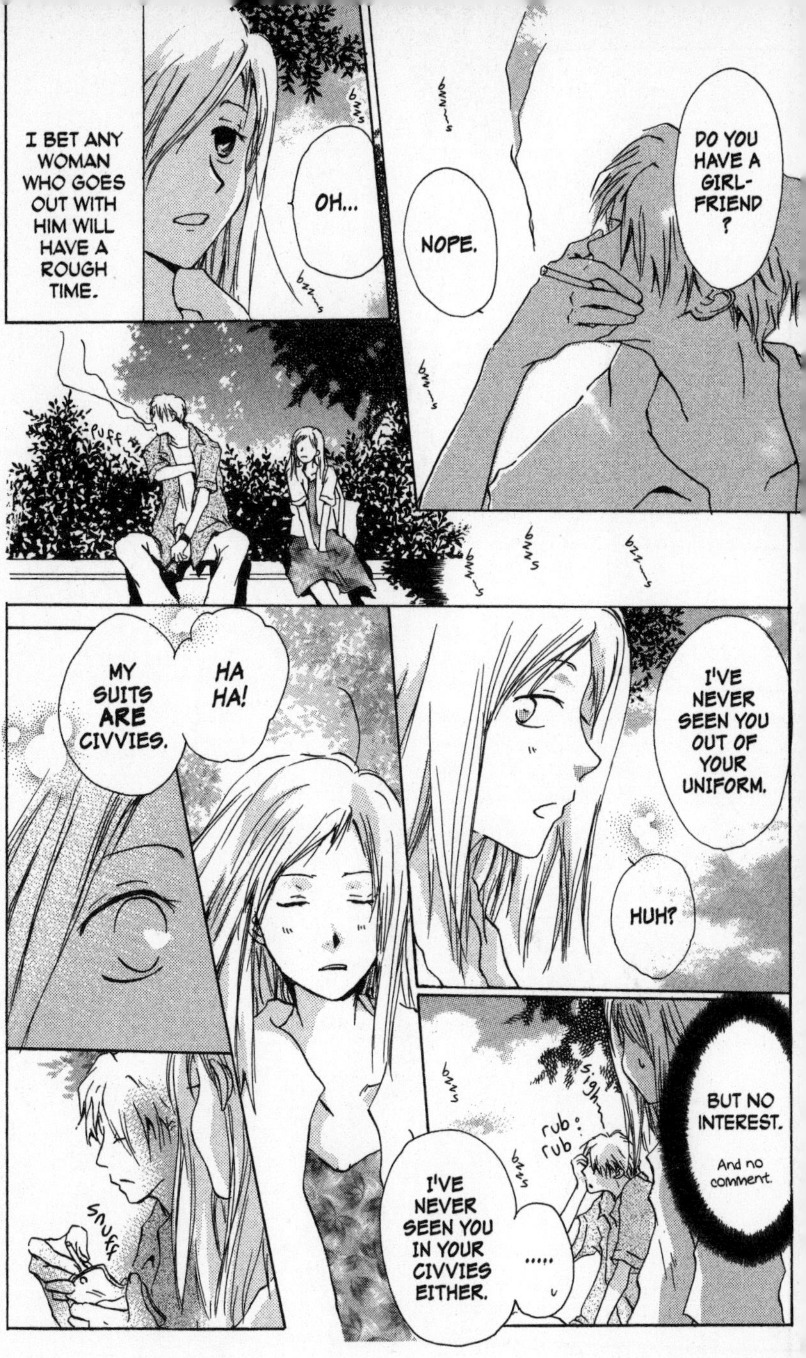
DO YOU HAVE A GIRL-FRIEND?
NOPE.
bzz~s
OH...
bzz~s
I BET ANY WOMAN WHO GOES OUT WITH HIM WILL HAVE A ROUGH TIME.
bzz~s
puff
bzz~s
I'VE NEVER SEEN YOU OUT OF YOUR UNIFORM.
HUH?
HA HA!
MY SUITS ARE CIVVIES.
BUT NO INTEREST.
And no comment.
sigh
rub rub
bzz~s
.....
I'VE NEVER SEEN YOU IN YOUR CIVVIES EITHER.
snuff

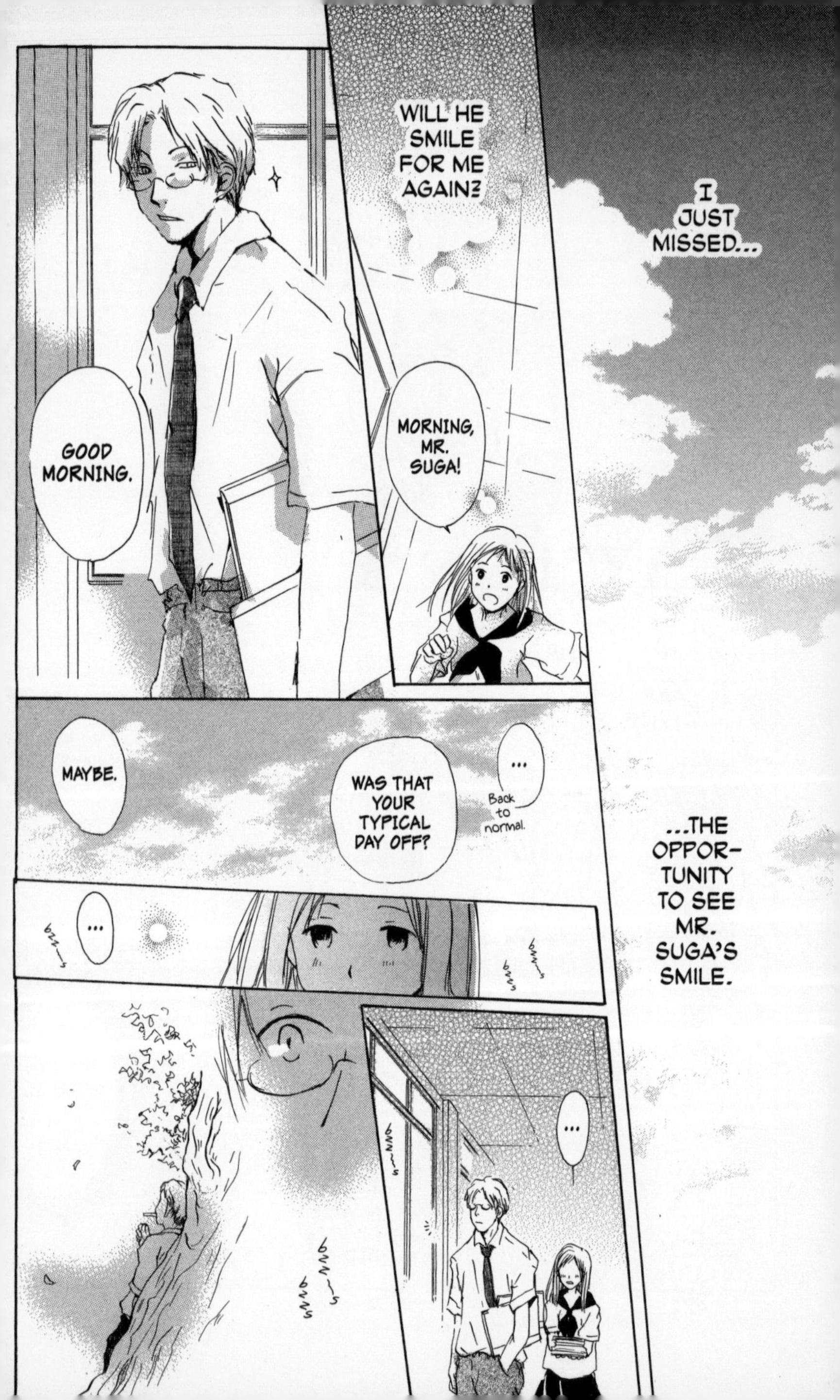

I JUST MISSED...
...THE OPPORTUNITY TO SEE MR. SUGA'S SMILE.
WILL HE SMILE FOR ME AGAIN?
MORNING, MR. SUGA!
GOOD MORNING.
...
Back to normal.
WAS THAT YOUR TYPICAL DAY OFF?
MAYBE.
...
...

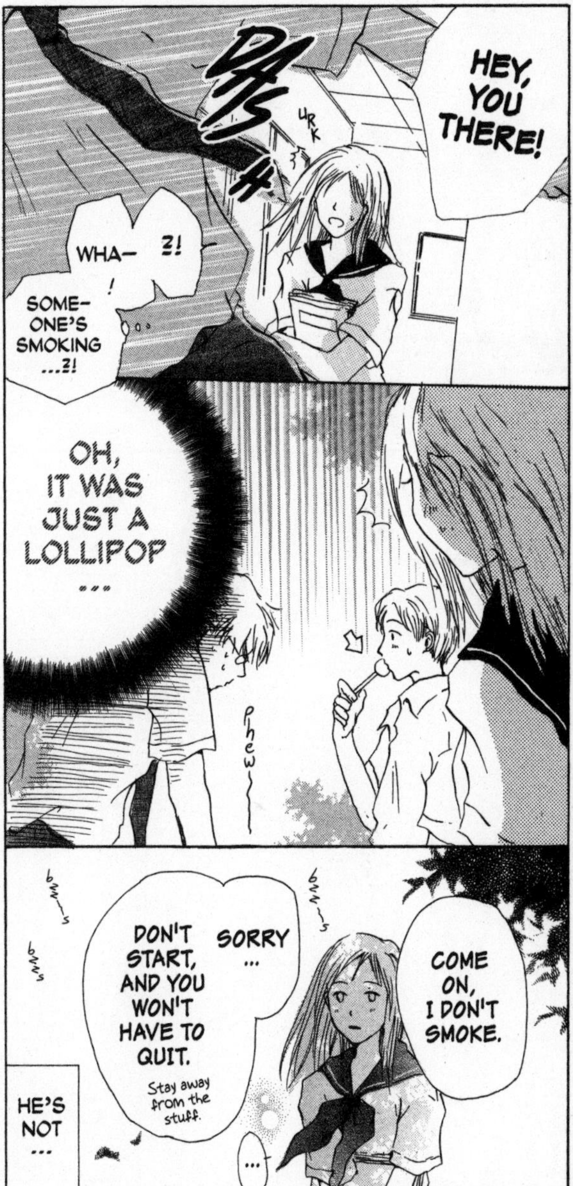
HEY, YOU THERE!
DASH
URK
WHA—?!
SOME-ONE'S SMOKING ...?!
OH, IT WAS JUST A LOLLIPOP ...
phew
bzz
COME ON, I DON'T SMOKE.
SORRY ...
DON'T START, AND YOU WON'T HAVE TO QUIT.
Stay away from the stuff.
...
HE'S NOT ...

06

❃Anime: part 3

They even let me look at the scripts. I was happy as the creator for the curve balls they threw, yet they were also careful to stay close to the original story. The content was the same as the manga, but the difference in pacing was very interesting and educational. There must be some mischievous people among the staff, since there are little glimpses of the humorous sides of Nyanko Sensei and Natsume. It's so sweet.

The director is very serious about his work. I told him he should feel free to do what he wanted with the anime, but he places great importance on the manga. I was worried that the anime would be inevitably different from the image readers had in their minds, but the staff is so sincere in their work. I feel really lucky as the creator. I hope the readers will be able to enjoy it. I'm so excited!

End of 1/4 columns.

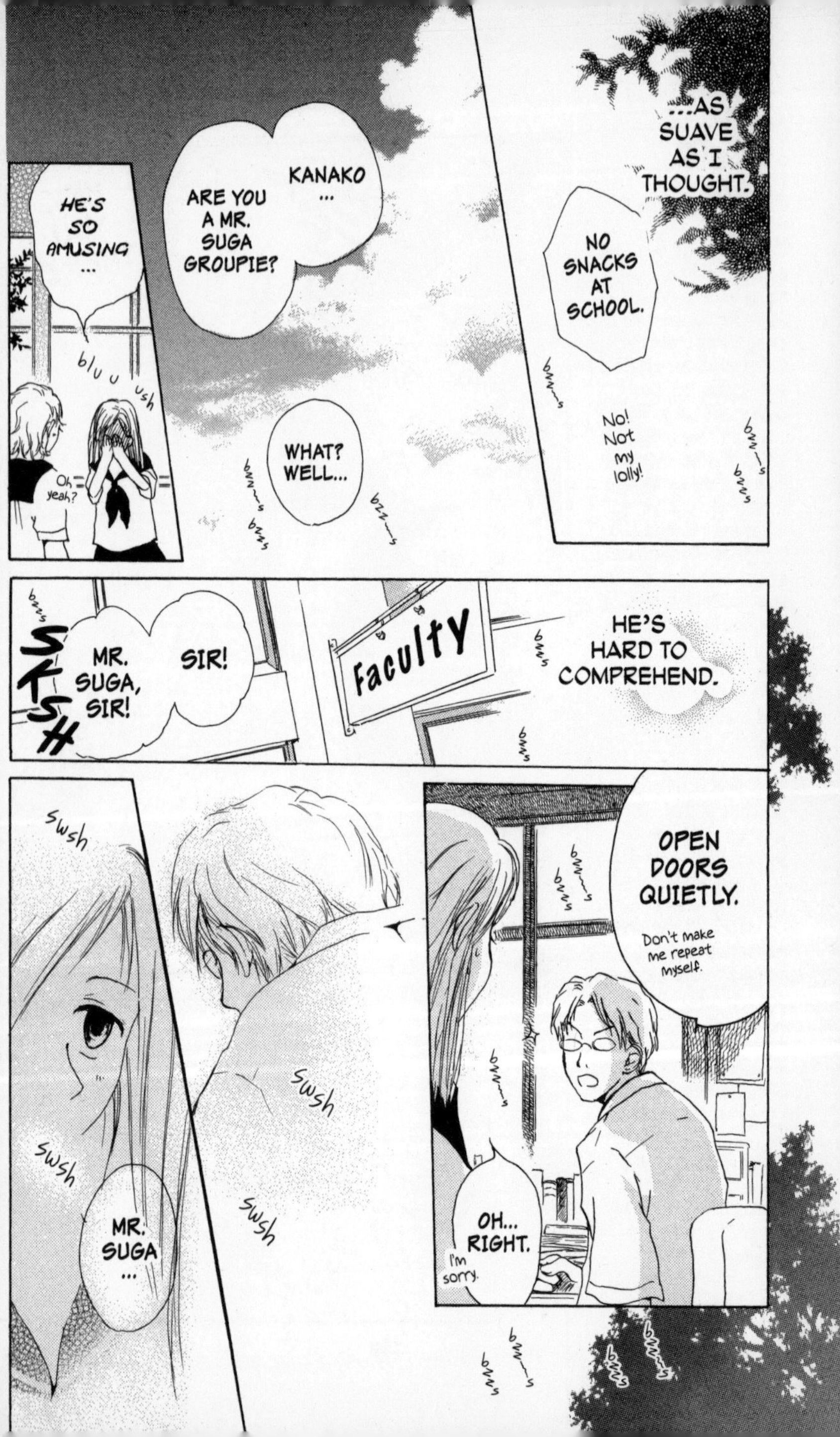
...AS SUAVE AS I THOUGHT.
NO SNACKS AT SCHOOL.
bzz
No! Not my lolly!
bzz bzz
KANAKO ...
ARE YOU A MR. SUGA GROUPIE?
WHAT? WELL...
bzz bzz
HE'S SO AMUSING ...
bluuush
Oh yeah?
HE'S HARD TO COMPREHEND.
bzz
Faculty
SIR!
MR. SUGA, SIR!
SKSH
bzz
OPEN DOORS QUIETLY.
Don't make me repeat myself.
bzz
OH... RIGHT.
I'm sorry.
swsh
swsh
MR. SUGA ...
swsh
swsh
bzz bzz

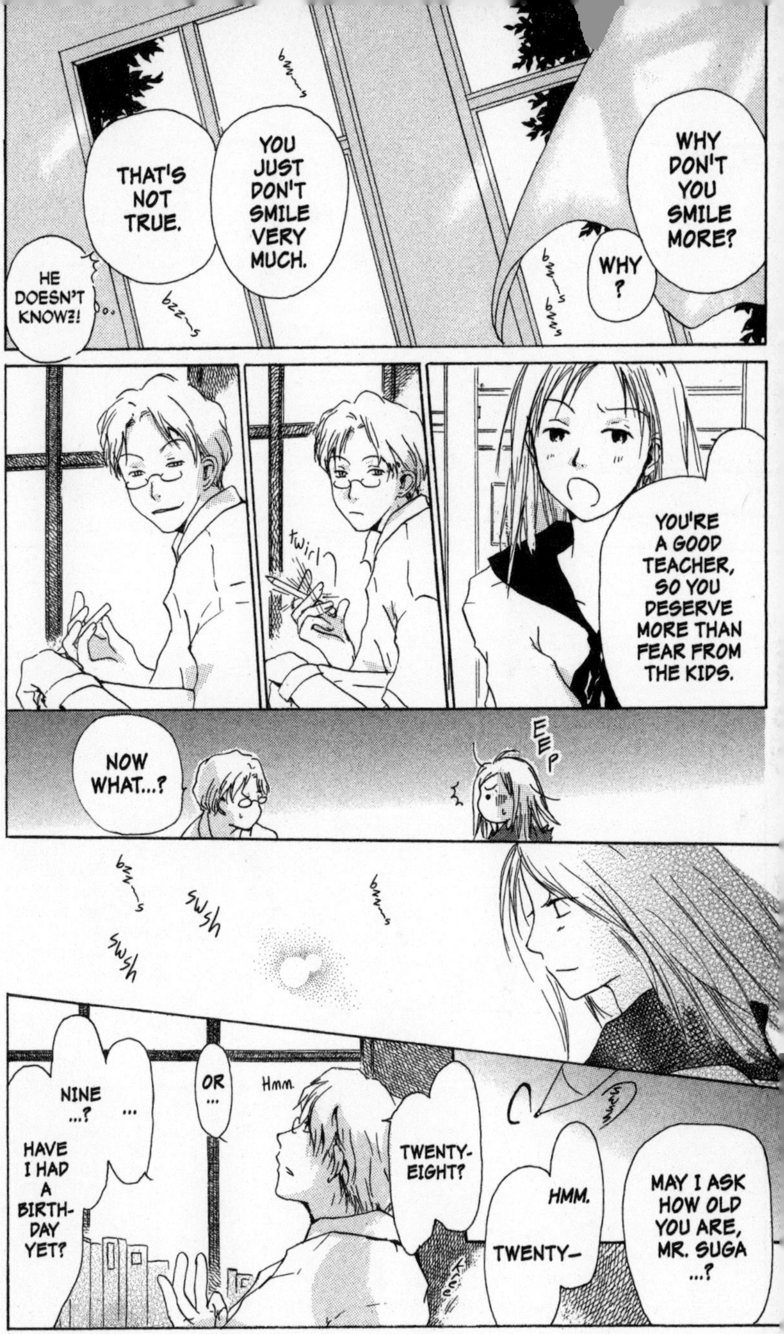
WHY DON'T YOU SMILE MORE?
WHY?
bzz~s
bzzs
YOU JUST DON'T SMILE VERY MUCH.
bzz~s
THAT'S NOT TRUE.
HE DOESN'T KNOW?!
bzz~s
YOU'RE A GOOD TEACHER, SO YOU DESERVE MORE THAN FEAR FROM THE KIDS.
twirl
EEP
NOW WHAT...?
bzz~s
swsh
bzz~s
swsh
MAY I ASK HOW OLD YOU ARE, MR. SUGA ...?
HMM.
TWENTY-
TWENTY-EIGHT?
Hmm.
OR ...
NINE ...?
...
HAVE I HAD A BIRTHDAY YET?

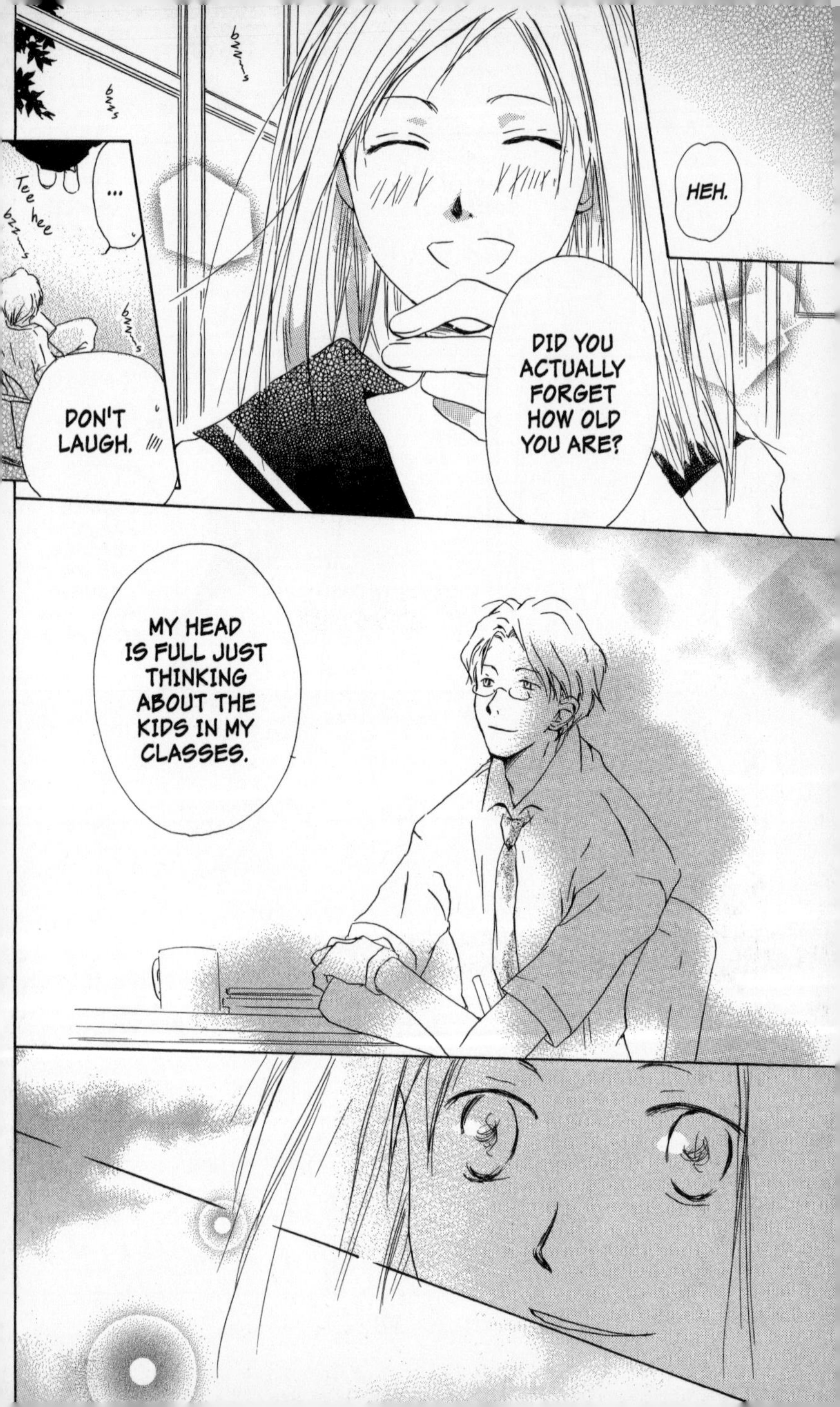
bzz
bzz
HEH.
DID YOU ACTUALLY FORGET HOW OLD YOU ARE?
...
Tee hee
bzz
bzz
DON'T LAUGH.
MY HEAD IS FULL JUST THINKING ABOUT THE KIDS IN MY CLASSES.

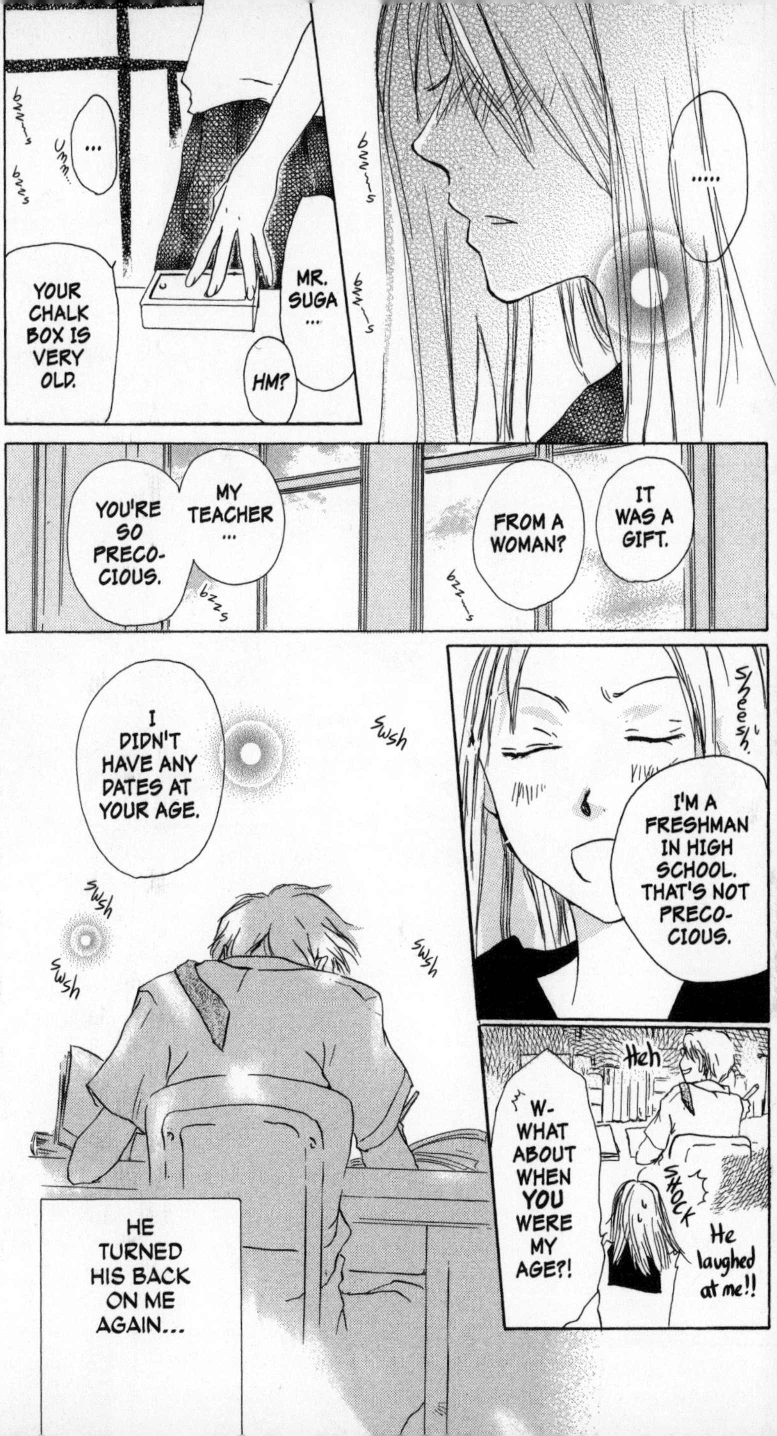
.....
...
Umm...
bzzs
bzzs
MR. SUGA ...
bzzs
bzzs
HM?
YOUR CHALK BOX IS VERY OLD.
IT WAS A GIFT.
FROM A WOMAN?
bzzs
MY TEACHER ...
YOU'RE SO PRECOCIOUS.
bzzs
Sheesh.
I'M A FRESHMAN IN HIGH SCHOOL. THAT'S NOT PRECOCIOUS.
swsh
I DIDN'T HAVE ANY DATES AT YOUR AGE.
swsh
swsh
swsh
Heh
W-WHAT ABOUT WHEN YOU WERE MY AGE?!
SHOCK
He laughed at me!!
HE TURNED HIS BACK ON ME AGAIN...

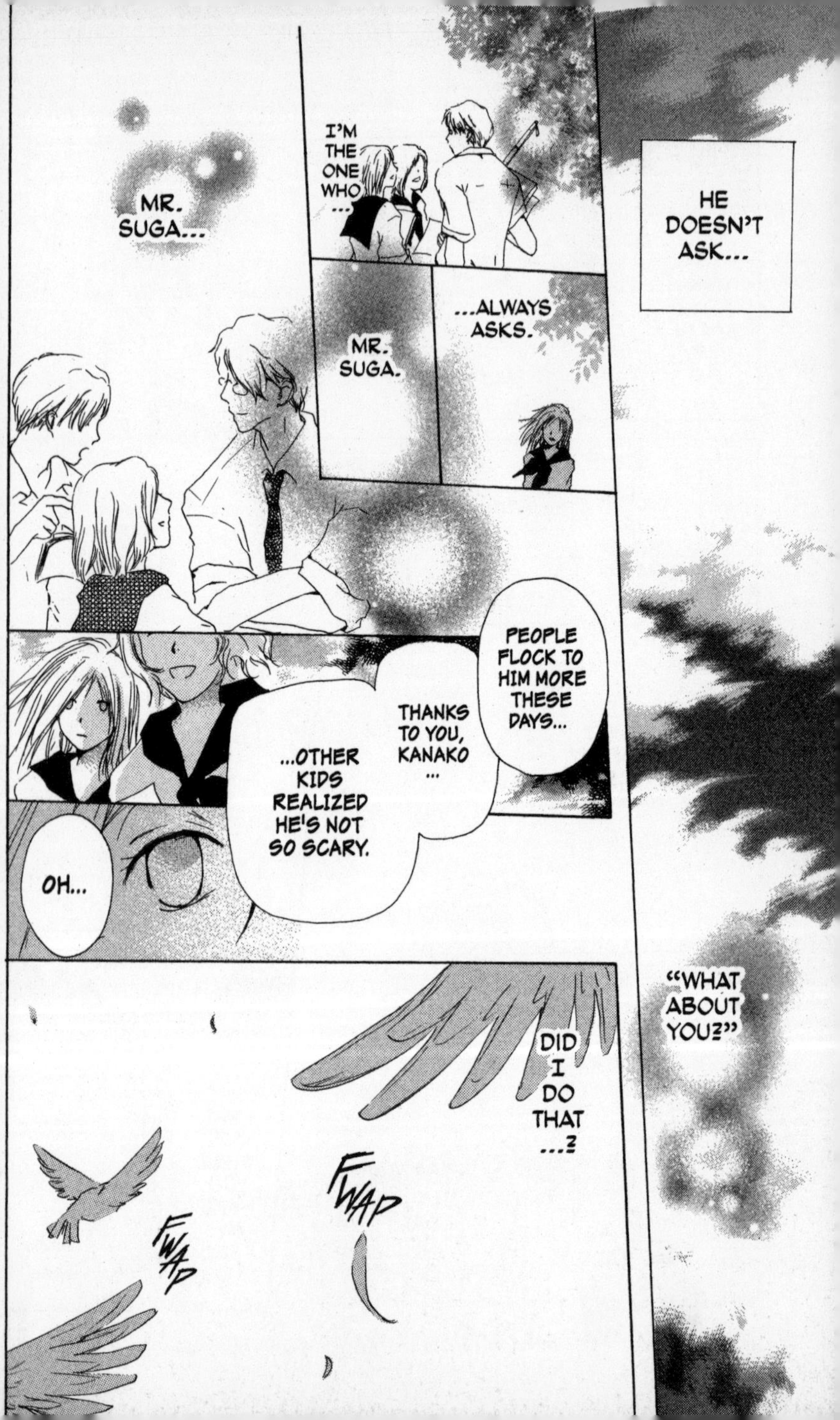
HE DOESN'T ASK...
"WHAT ABOUT YOU?"
I'M THE ONE WHO...
MR. SUGA...
...ALWAYS ASKS.
MR. SUGA.
PEOPLE FLOCK TO HIM MORE THESE DAYS...
THANKS TO YOU, KANAKO...
...OTHER KIDS REALIZED HE'S NOT SO SCARY.
OH...
DID I DO THAT...?
FWAP
FWAP

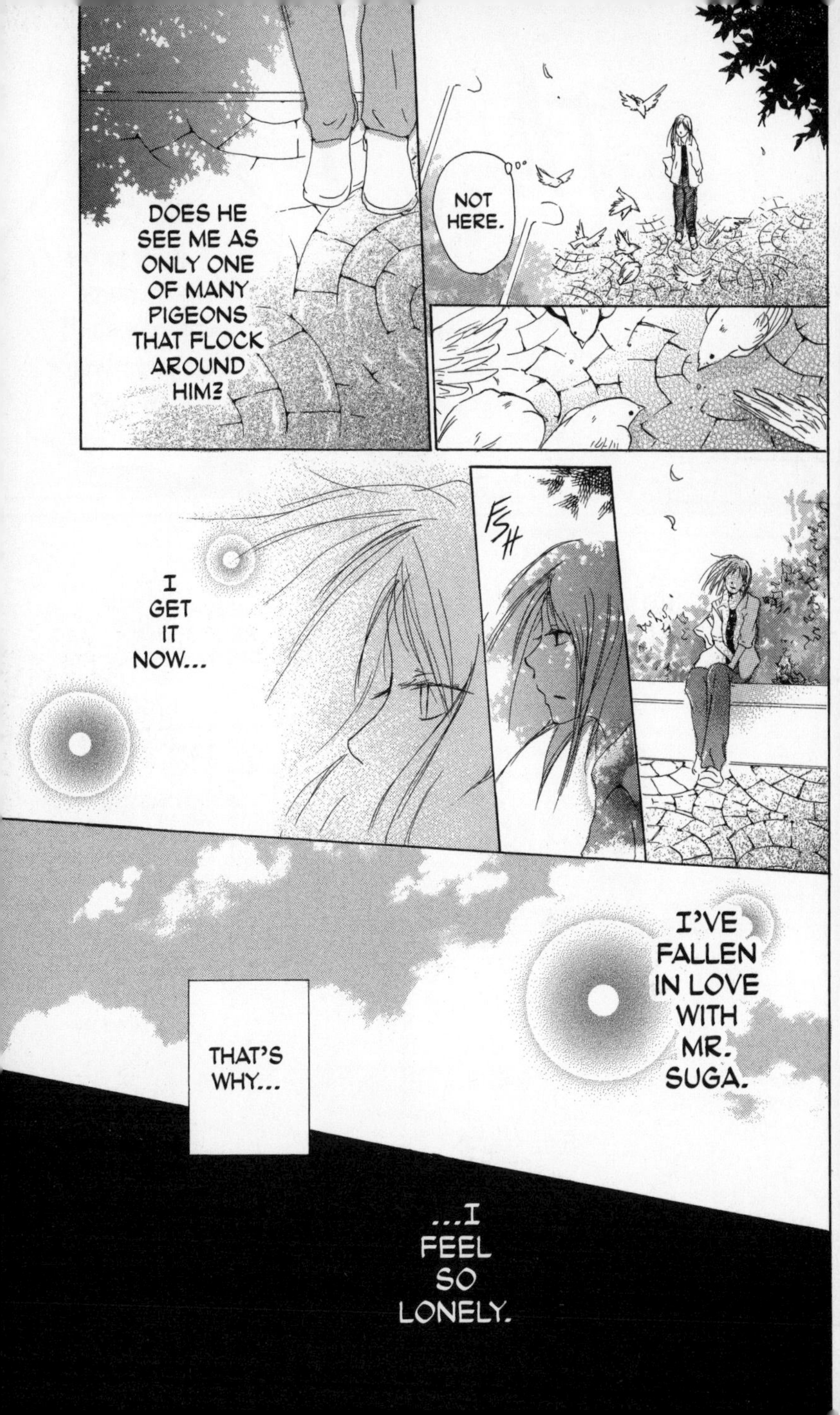
NOT HERE.
DOES HE SEE ME AS ONLY ONE OF MANY PIGEONS THAT FLOCK AROUND HIM?
FSH
I GET IT NOW...
I'VE FALLEN IN LOVE WITH MR. SUGA.
THAT'S WHY...
...I FEEL SO LONELY.

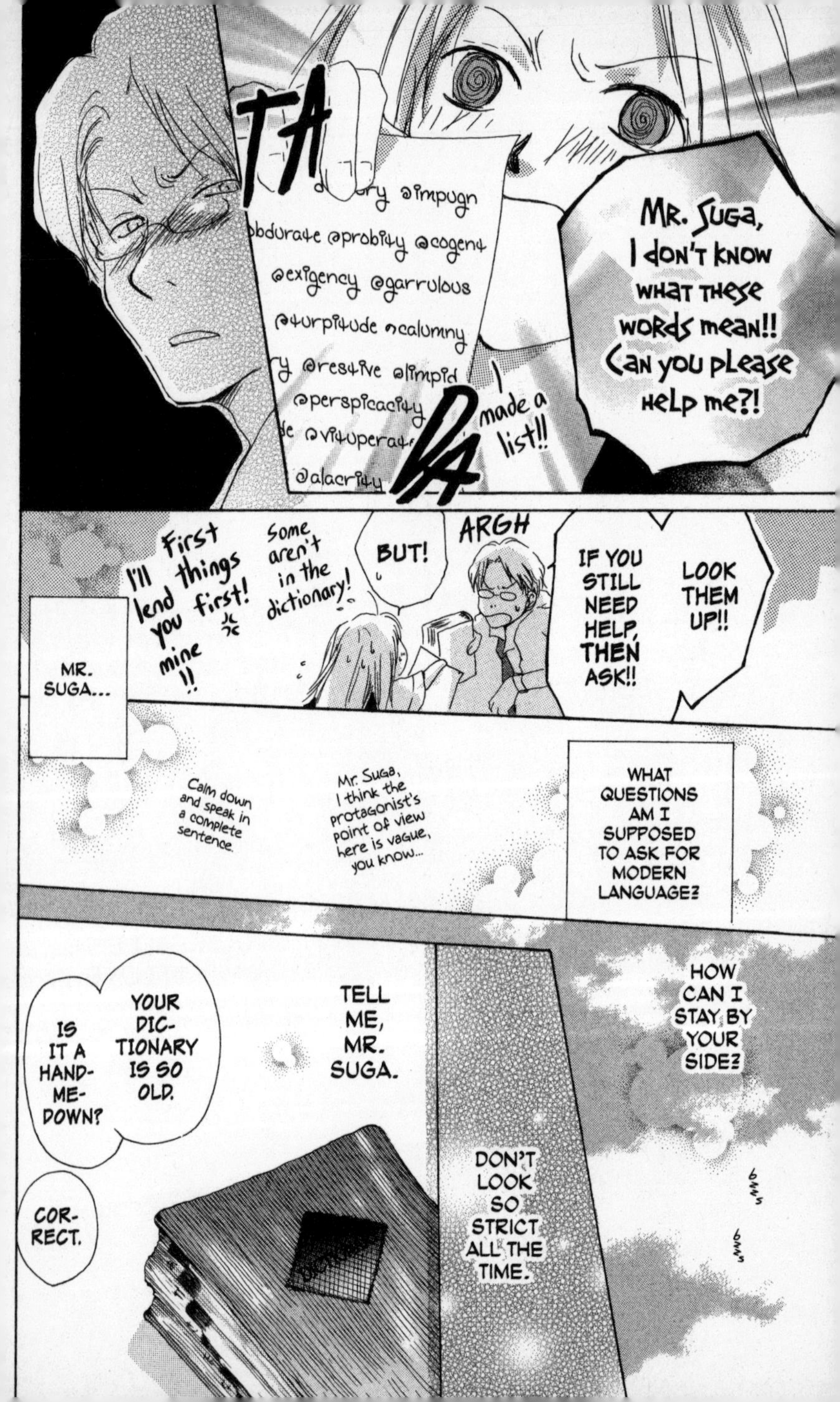
MR. SUGA, I DON'T KNOW WHAT THESE WORDS MEAN!! CAN YOU PLEASE HELP ME?!
I made a list!!
TA
DA
impugn
obdurate probity cogent
exigency garrulous
turpitude calumny
restive limpid
perspicacity
vituperate
alacrity
LOOK THEM UP!!
IF YOU STILL NEED HELP, THEN ASK!!
ARGH
BUT!
Some aren't in the dictionary!
First things first!
I'll lend you mine!!
MR. SUGA...
WHAT QUESTIONS AM I SUPPOSED TO ASK FOR MODERN LANGUAGE?
Mr. Suga, I think the protagonist's point of view here is vague, you know...
Calm down and speak in a complete sentence.
HOW CAN I STAY BY YOUR SIDE?
DON'T LOOK SO STRICT ALL THE TIME.
TELL ME, MR. SUGA.
YOUR DICTIONARY IS SO OLD.
IS IT A HAND-ME-DOWN?
CORRECT.

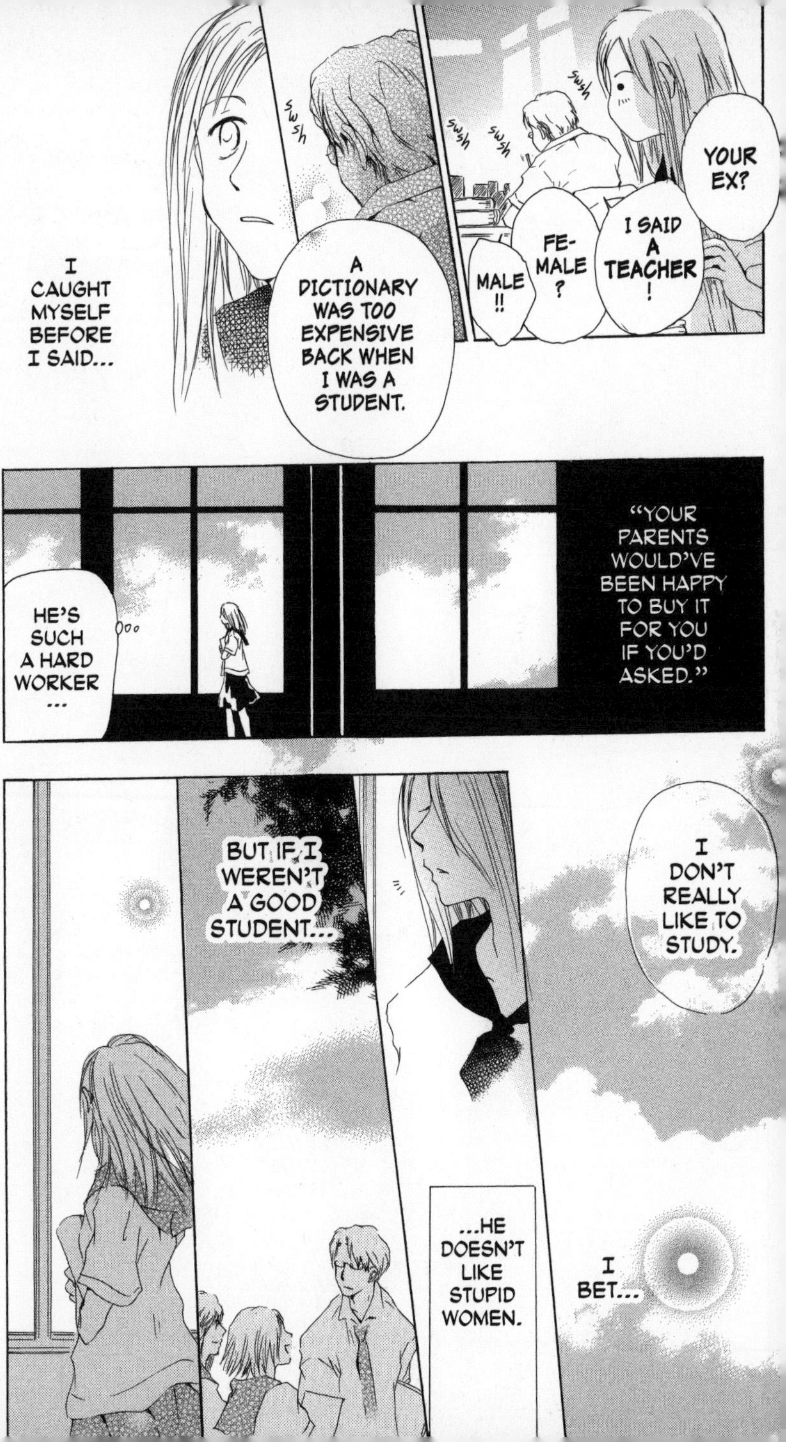
swsh
swsh
swsh
YOUR EX?
I SAID A TEACHER!
FE-MALE?
MALE!!
swsh
A DICTIONARY WAS TOO EXPENSIVE BACK WHEN I WAS A STUDENT.
I CAUGHT MYSELF BEFORE I SAID...
"YOUR PARENTS WOULD'VE BEEN HAPPY TO BUY IT FOR YOU IF YOU'D ASKED."
HE'S SUCH A HARD WORKER...
I DON'T REALLY LIKE TO STUDY.
I BET...
...HE DOESN'T LIKE STUPID WOMEN.
BUT IF I WEREN'T A GOOD STUDENT...

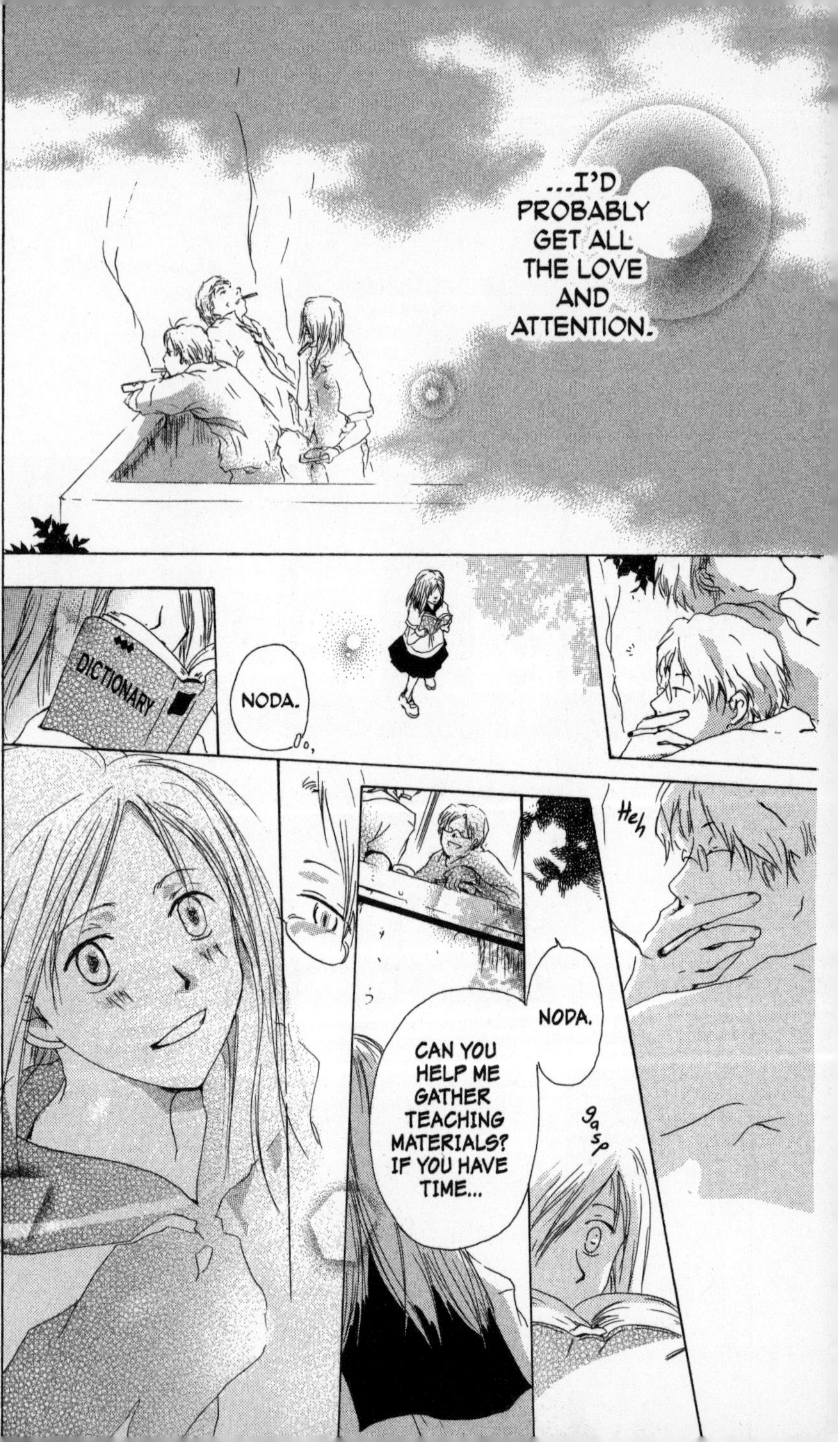
...I'D PROBABLY GET ALL THE LOVE AND ATTENTION.
NODA.
DICTIONARY
Heh
NODA.
CAN YOU HELP ME GATHER TEACHING MATERIALS? IF YOU HAVE TIME...
gasp

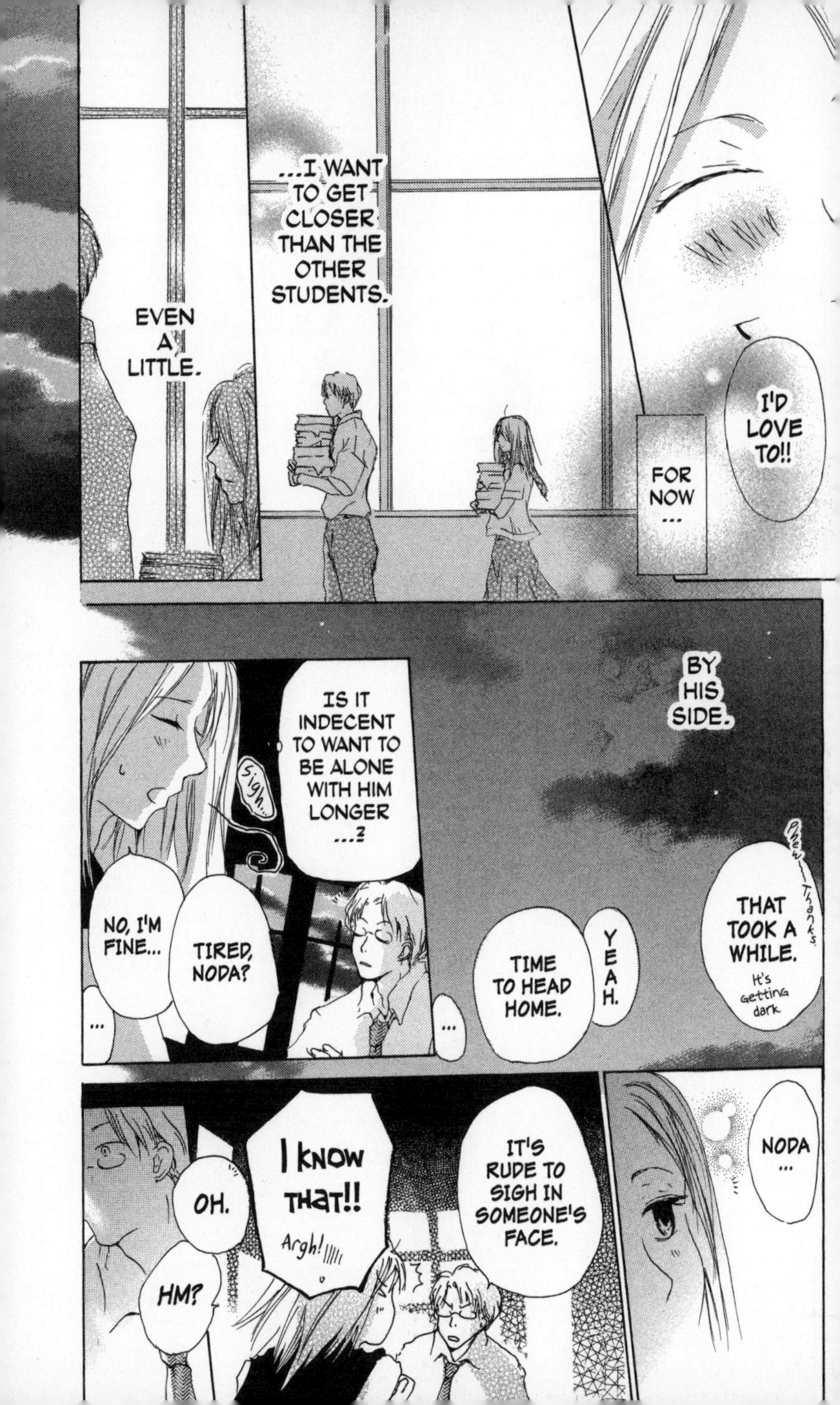
I'D LOVE TO!!
FOR NOW...
...I WANT TO GET CLOSER THAN THE OTHER STUDENTS.
EVEN A LITTLE.
BY HIS SIDE.
THAT TOOK A WHILE.
Phew—Thanks.
It's getting dark.
YEAH.
TIME TO HEAD HOME.
...
IS IT INDECENT TO WANT TO BE ALONE WITH HIM LONGER...?
Sigh...
TIRED, NODA?
NO, I'M FINE...
...
NODA...
IT'S RUDE TO SIGH IN SOMEONE'S FACE.
I KNOW THAT!!
Argh!
OH.
HM?

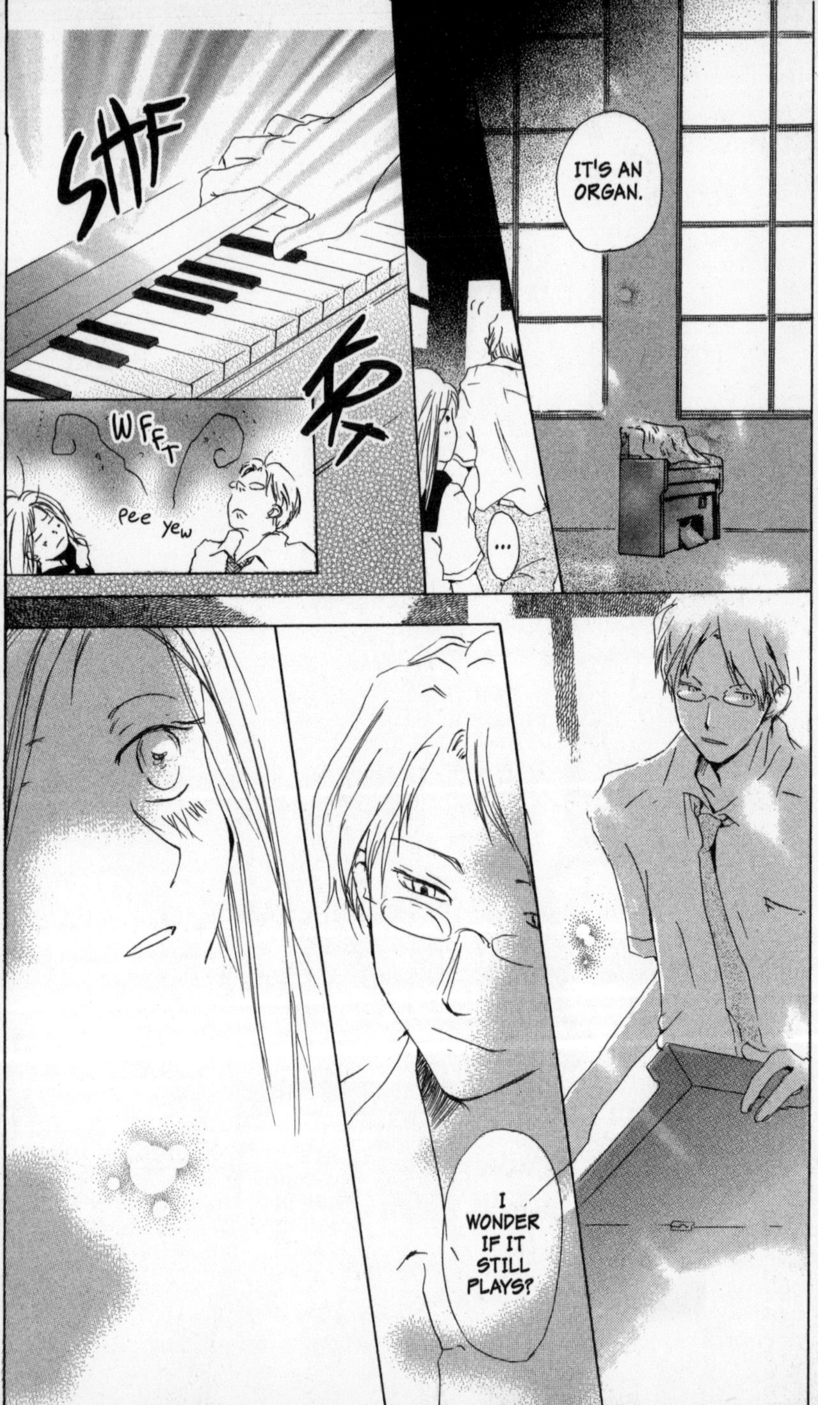
IT'S AN ORGAN.
...
SHF
KRT
WFFT
pee yew
I WONDER IF IT STILL PLAYS?

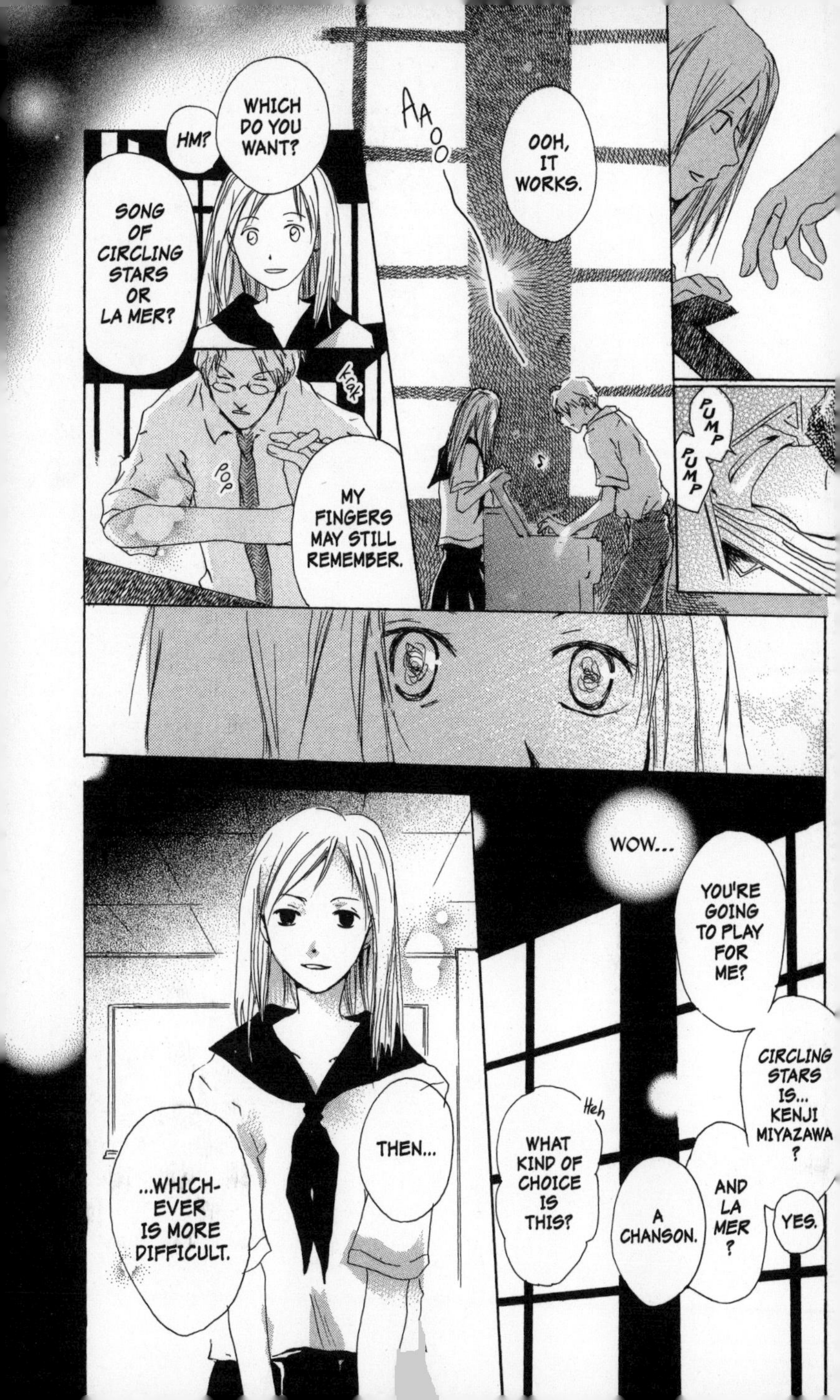
PUMP
PUMP
AAOO
OOH, IT WORKS.
WHICH DO YOU WANT?
HM?
SONG OF CIRCLING STARS OR LA MER?
krak
POP
MY FINGERS MAY STILL REMEMBER.
WOW...
YOU'RE GOING TO PLAY FOR ME?
CIRCLING STARS IS... KENJI MIYAZAWA?
YES.
AND LA MER?
A CHANSON.
Heh
WHAT KIND OF CHOICE IS THIS?
THEN...
...WHICH-EVER IS MORE DIFFICULT.

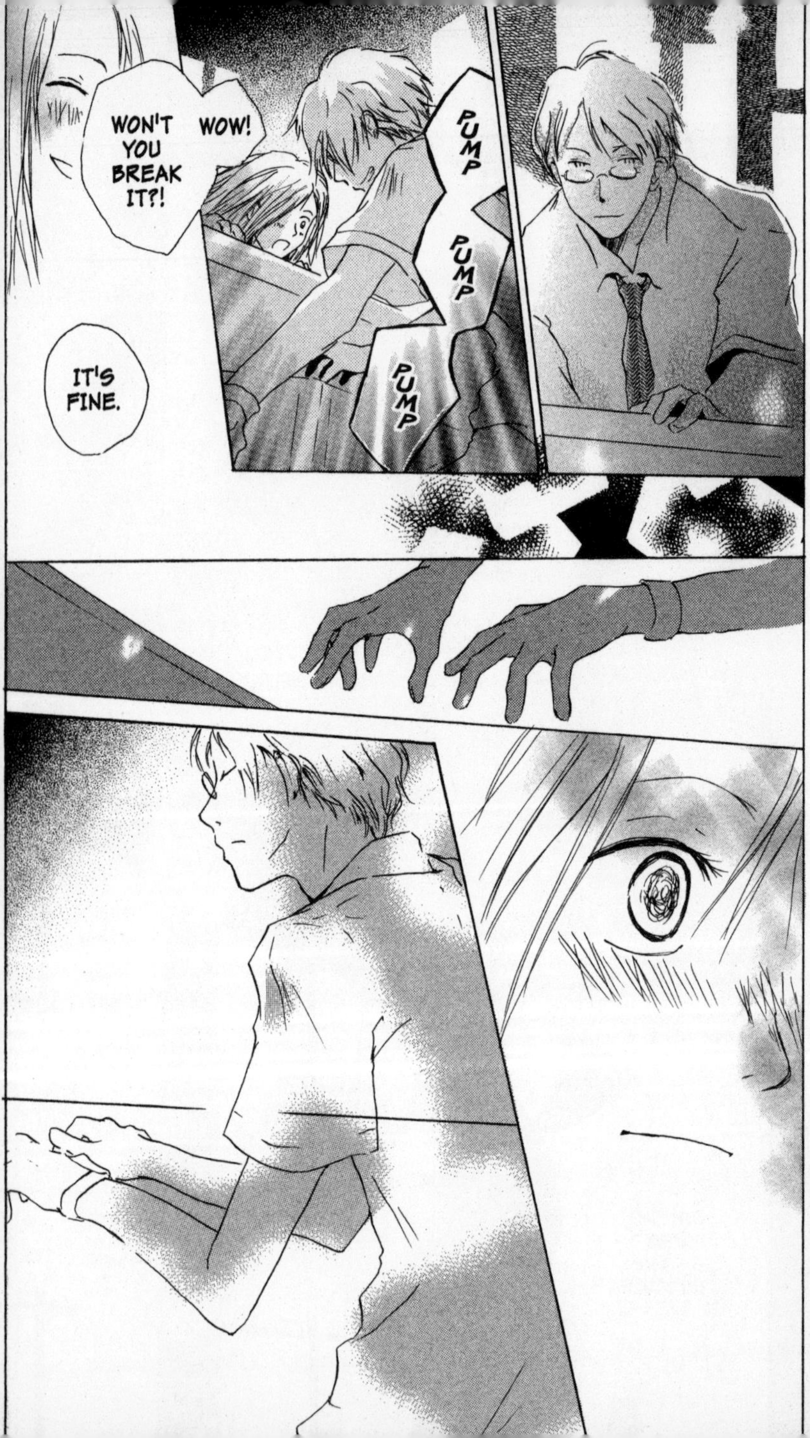
PUMP
PUMP
PUMP
WOW!
WON'T YOU BREAK IT?!
IT'S FINE.

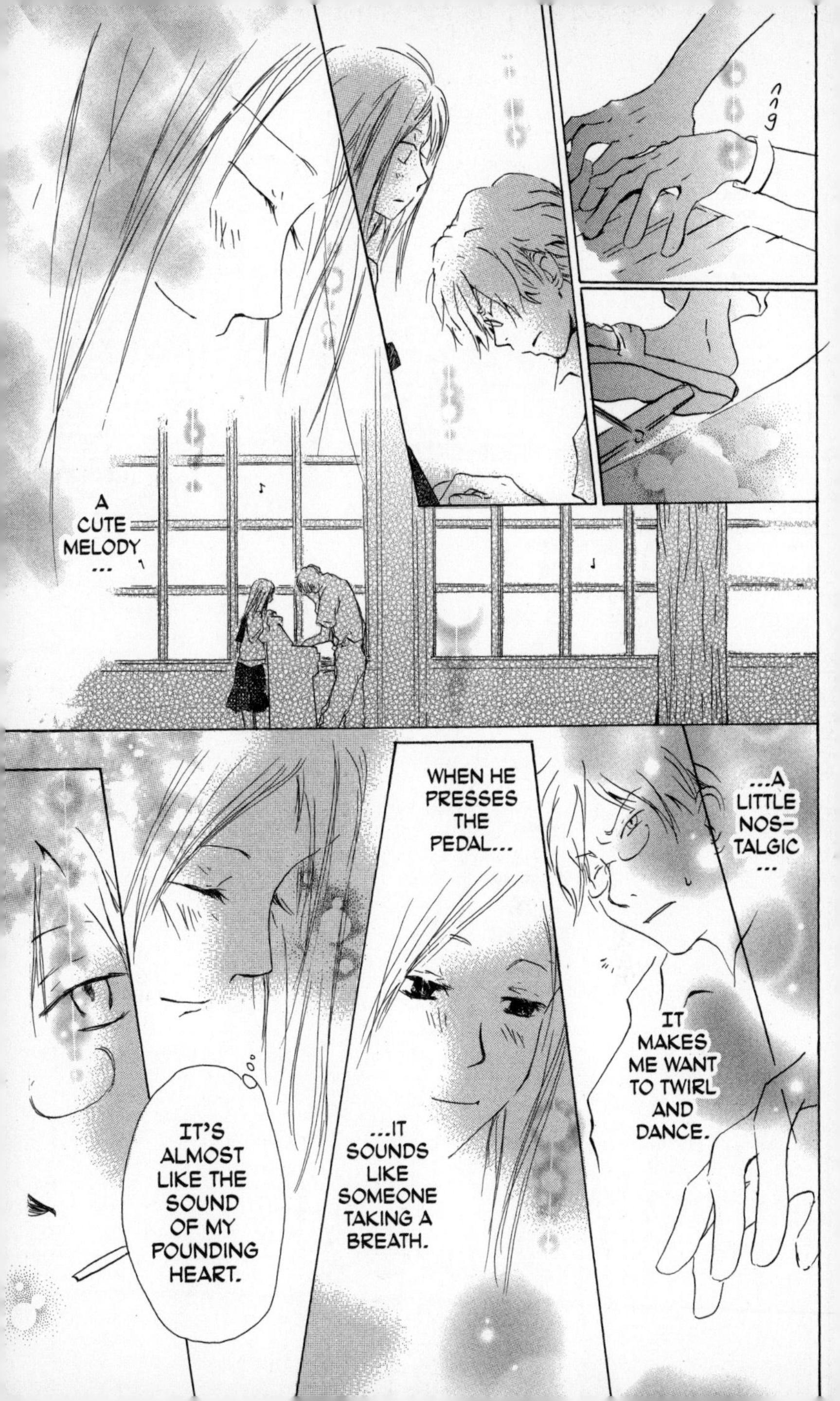
A CUTE MELODY...
...A LITTLE NOS-TALGIC...
IT MAKES ME WANT TO TWIRL AND DANCE.
WHEN HE PRESSES THE PEDAL...
...IT SOUNDS LIKE SOMEONE TAKING A BREATH.
IT'S ALMOST LIKE THE SOUND OF MY POUNDING HEART.

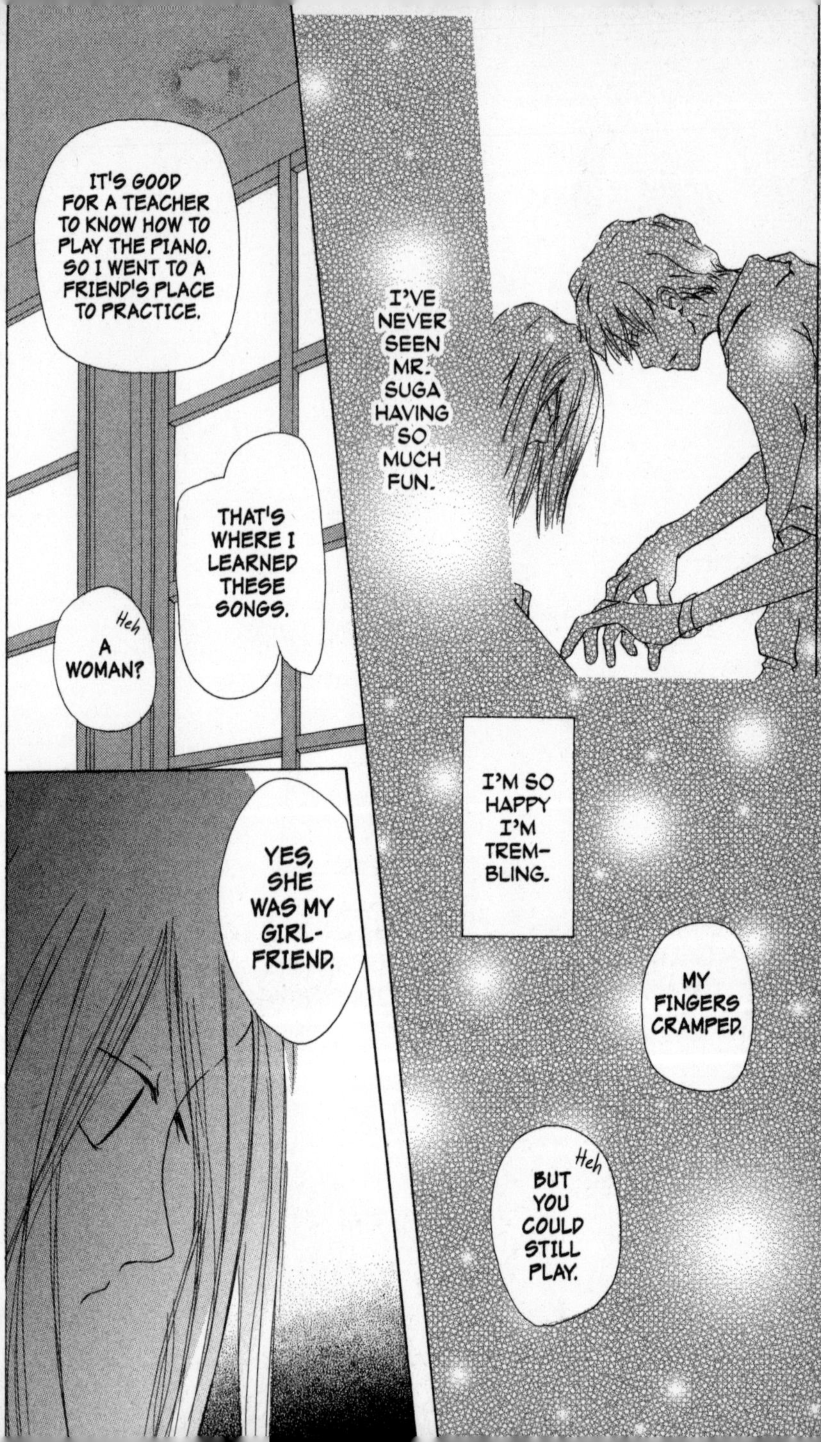
I'VE NEVER SEEN MR. SUGA HAVING SO MUCH FUN.
I'M SO HAPPY I'M TREMBLING.
MY FINGERS CRAMPED.
Heh
BUT YOU COULD STILL PLAY.
IT'S GOOD FOR A TEACHER TO KNOW HOW TO PLAY THE PIANO. SO I WENT TO A FRIEND'S PLACE TO PRACTICE.
THAT'S WHERE I LEARNED THESE SONGS.
Heh
A WOMAN?
YES, SHE WAS MY GIRL-FRIEND.

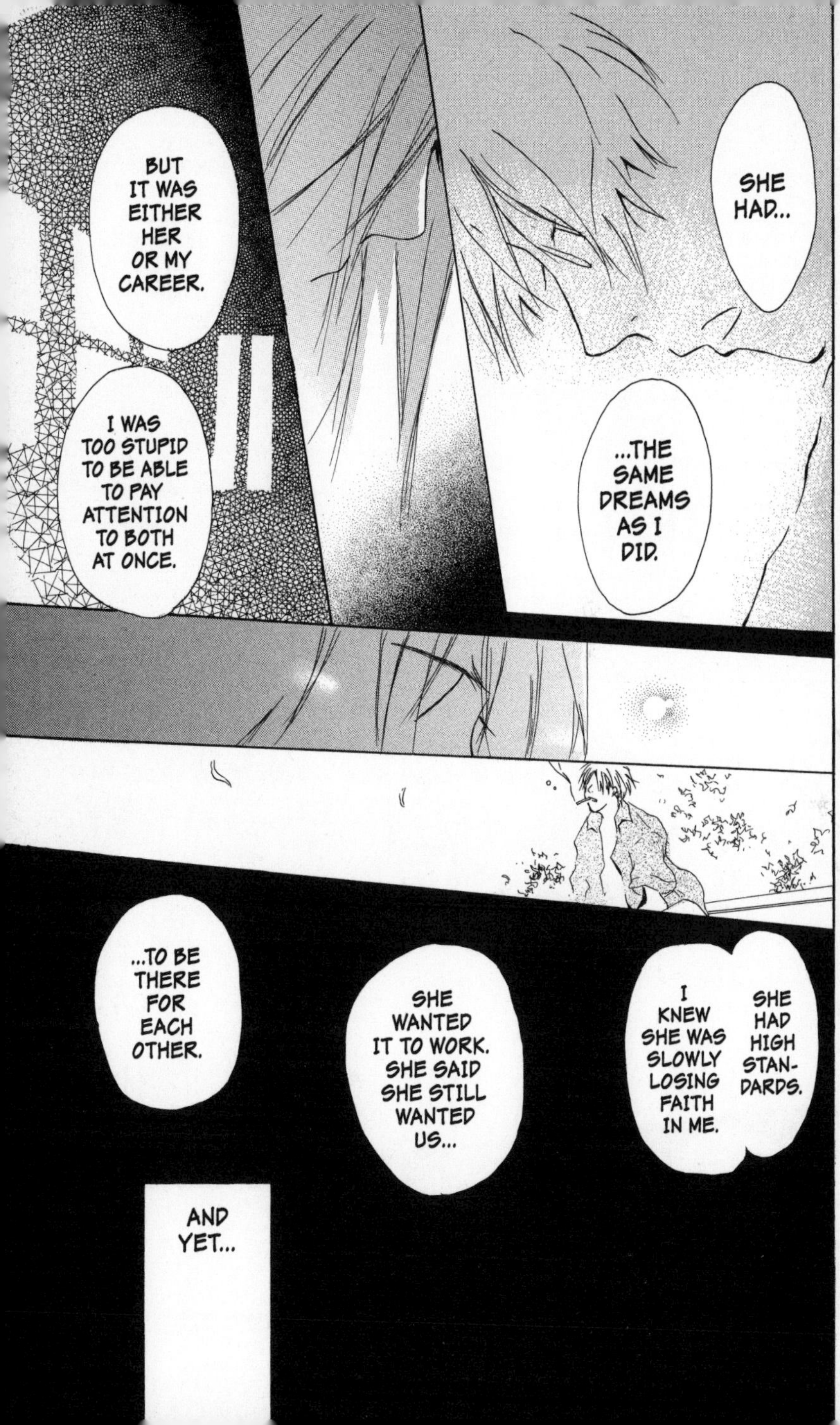
SHE HAD...
...THE SAME DREAMS AS I DID.
BUT IT WAS EITHER HER OR MY CAREER.
I WAS TOO STUPID TO BE ABLE TO PAY ATTENTION TO BOTH AT ONCE.
SHE HAD HIGH STAN-DARDS.
I KNEW SHE WAS SLOWLY LOSING FAITH IN ME.
SHE WANTED IT TO WORK. SHE SAID SHE STILL WANTED US...
...TO BE THERE FOR EACH OTHER.
AND YET...

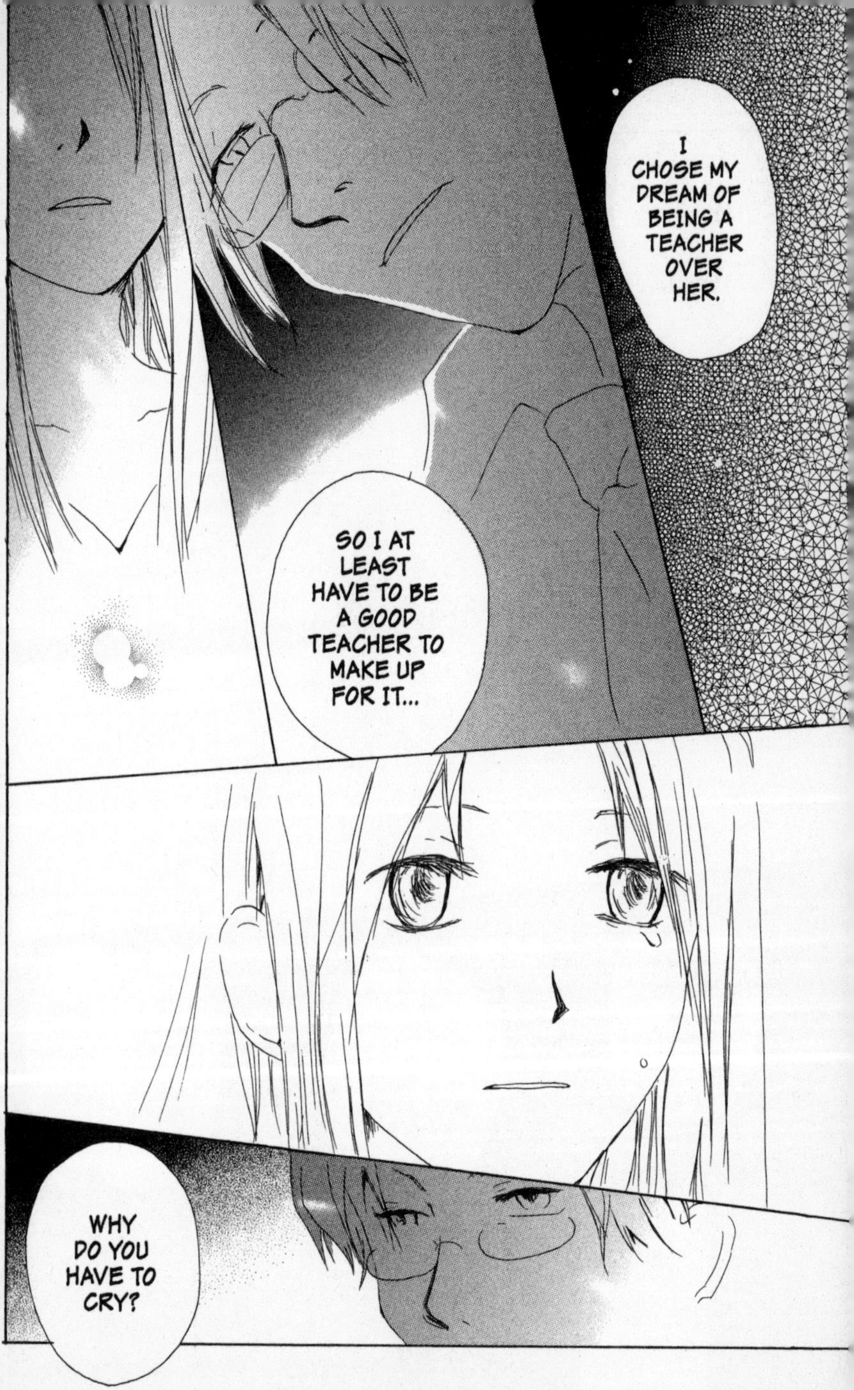
I CHOSE MY DREAM OF BEING A TEACHER OVER HER.
SO I AT LEAST HAVE TO BE A GOOD TEACHER TO MAKE UP FOR IT...
WHY DO YOU HAVE TO CRY?

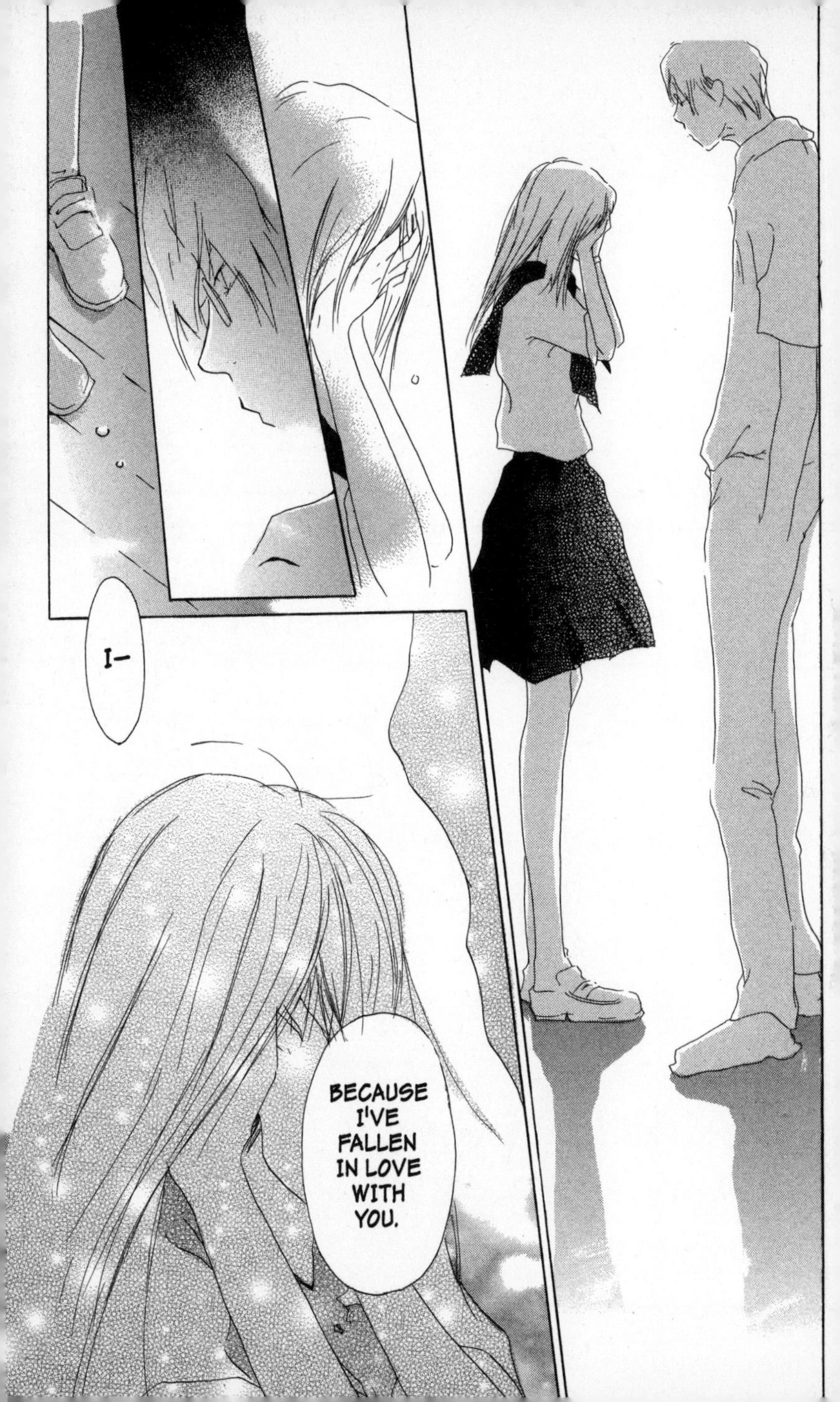
I–
BECAUSE I'VE FALLEN IN LOVE WITH YOU.

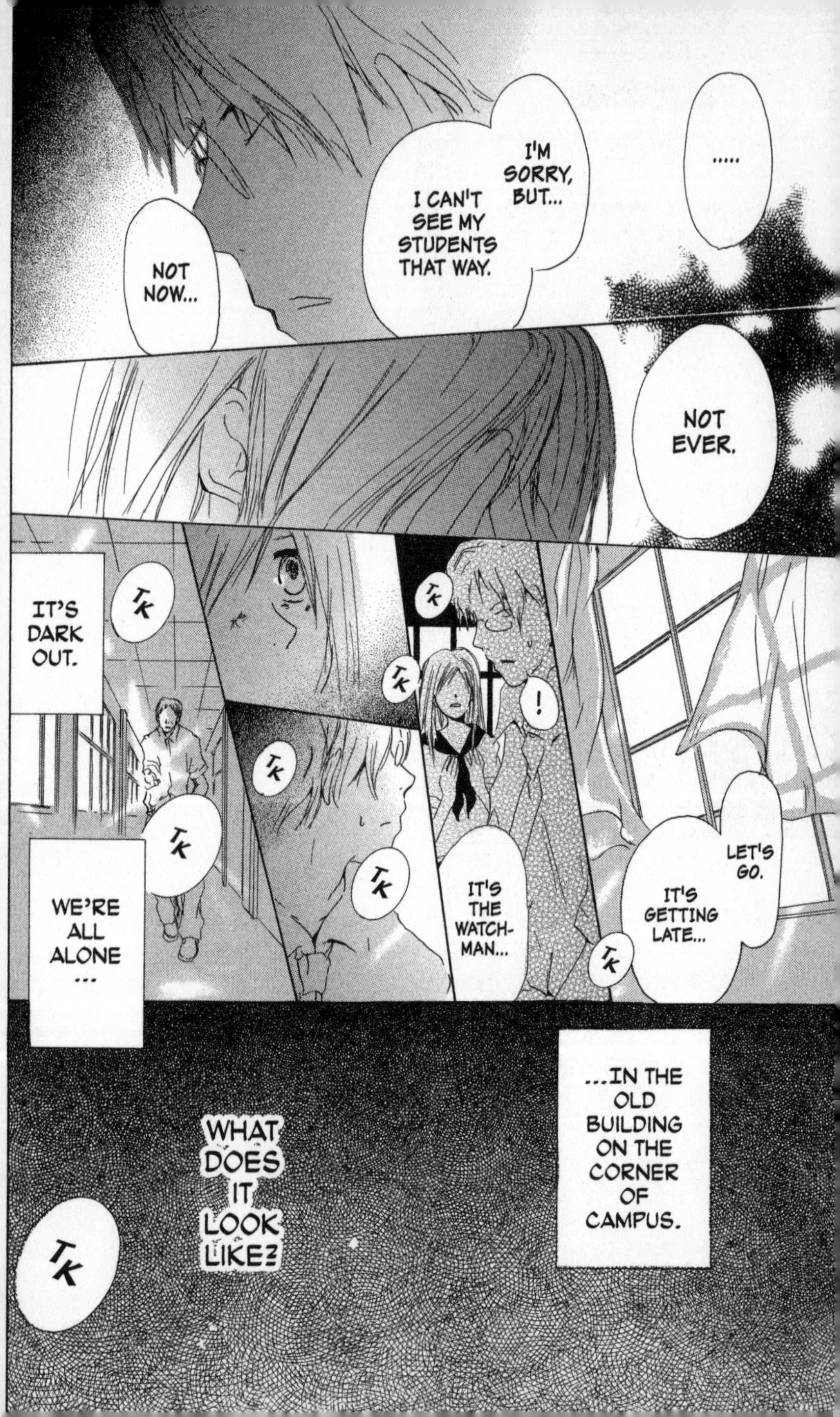
.....
I'M SORRY, BUT...
I CAN'T SEE MY STUDENTS THAT WAY.
NOT NOW...
NOT EVER.
LET'S GO.
IT'S GETTING LATE...
TK
TK
TK
!
IT'S THE WATCHMAN...
TK
TK
IT'S DARK OUT.
TK
TK
WE'RE ALL ALONE...
...IN THE OLD BUILDING ON THE CORNER OF CAMPUS.
WHAT DOES IT LOOK LIKE?
TK

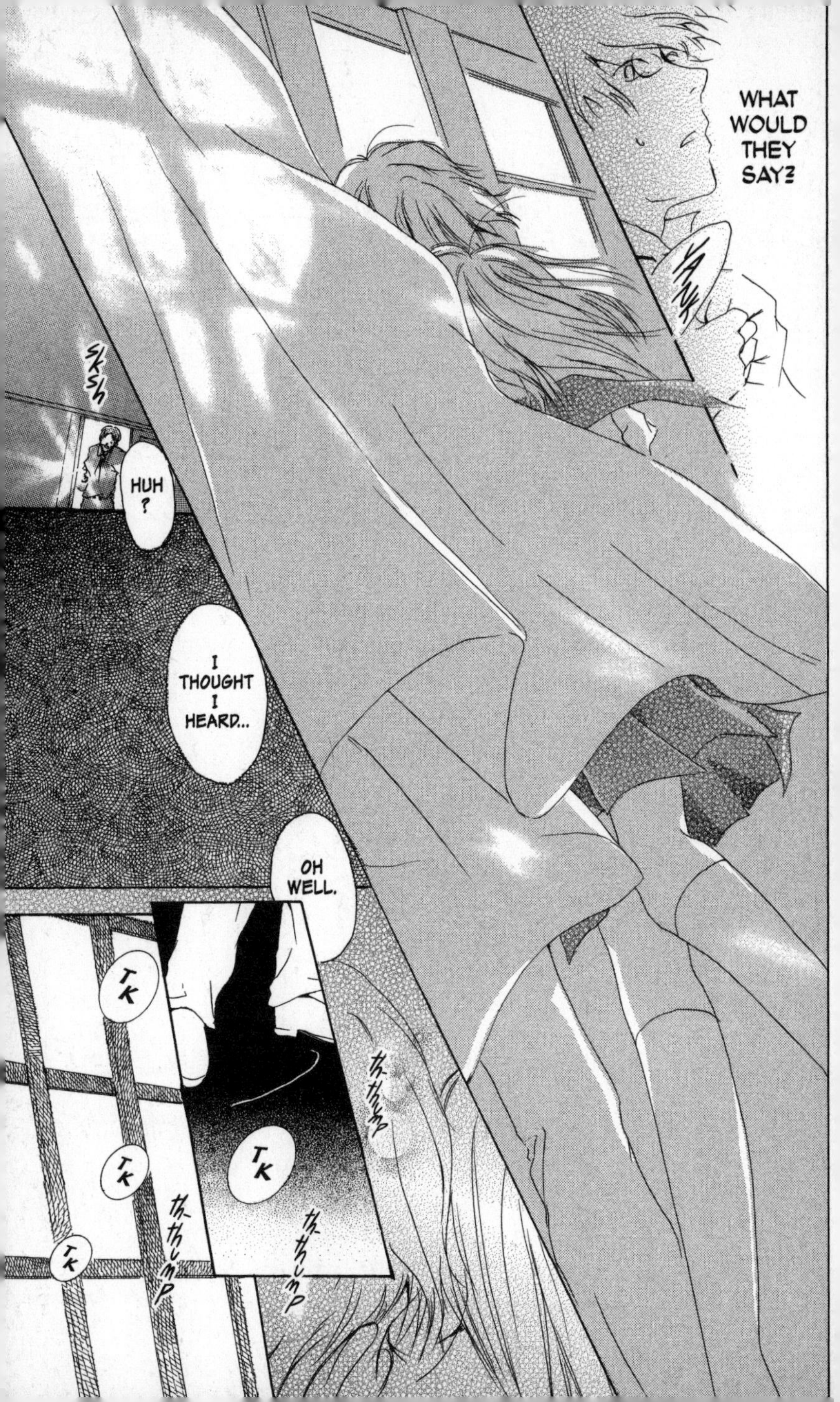
WHAT WOULD THEY SAY?
YANK
SKSH
HUH?
I THOUGHT I HEARD...
OH WELL.
THA-THUMP
THA-THUMP
TK
THA-THUMP
TK
TK
TK

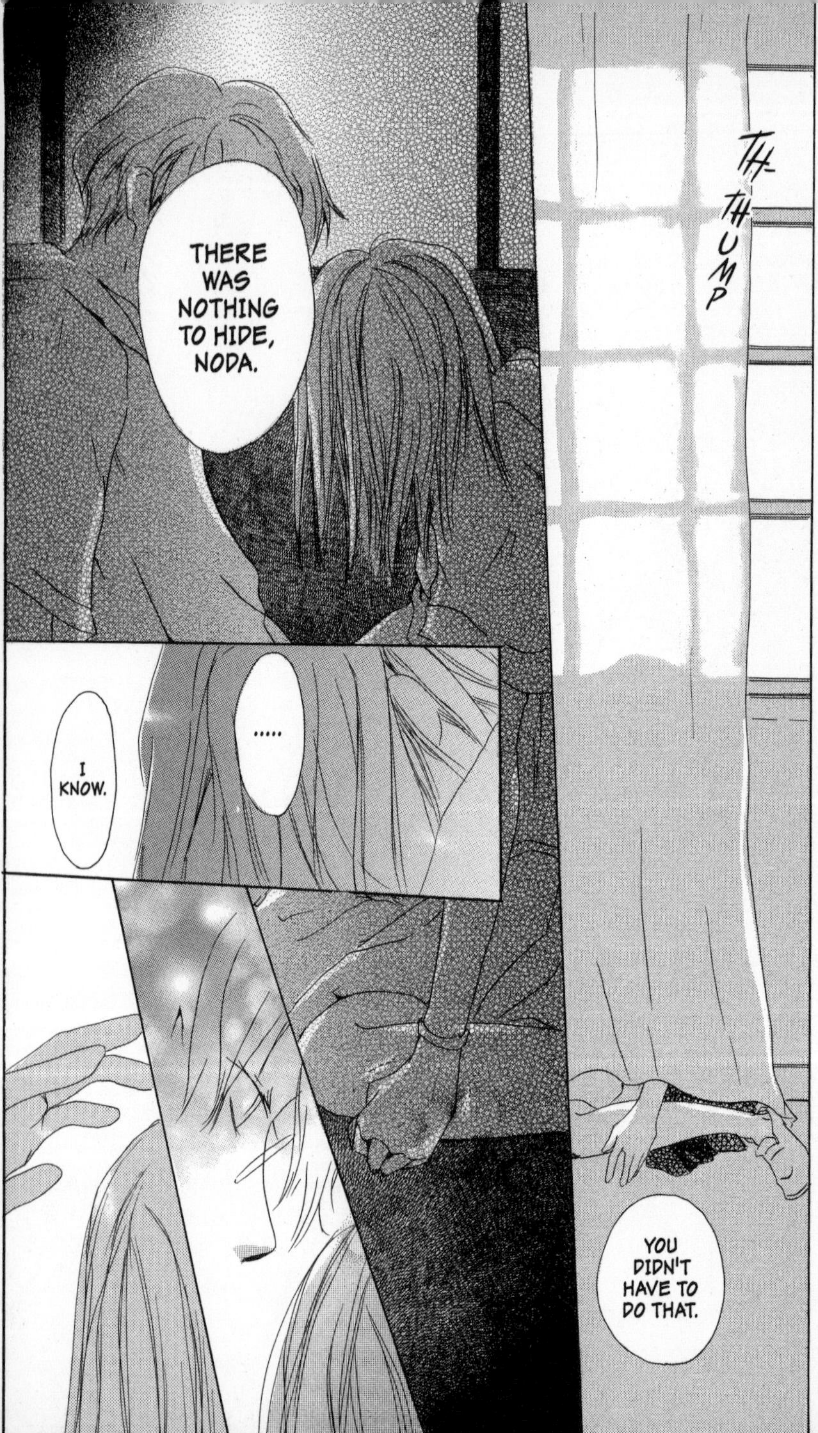

TH-THUMP
YOU DIDN'T HAVE TO DO THAT.
THERE WAS NOTHING TO HIDE, NODA.
.....
I KNOW.

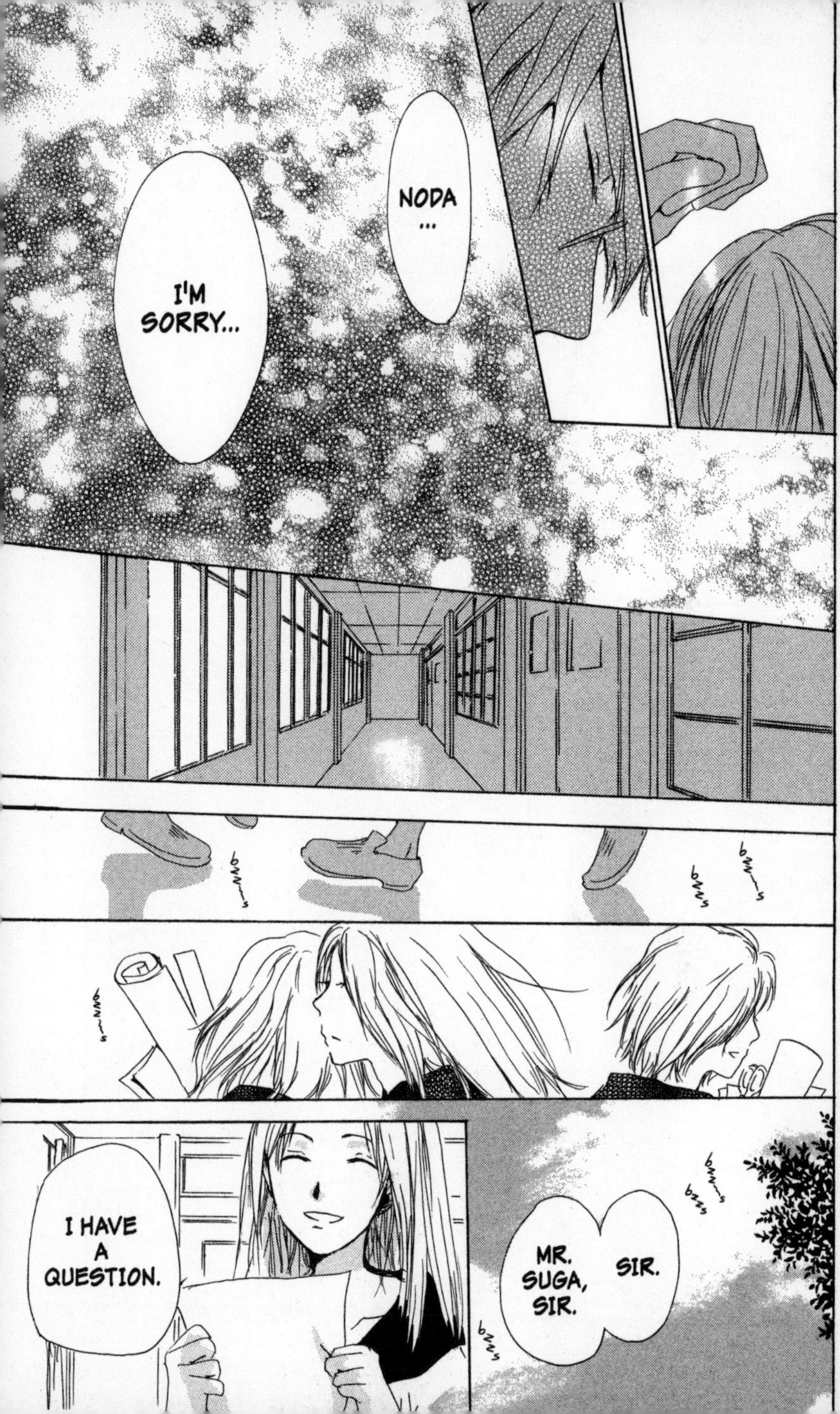
NODA ...
I'M SORRY...
bzzz~s
bzzs
bzzz~s
bzzz~s
bzzz~s
bzzs
SIR.
MR. SUGA, SIR.
bzzs
I HAVE A QUESTION.

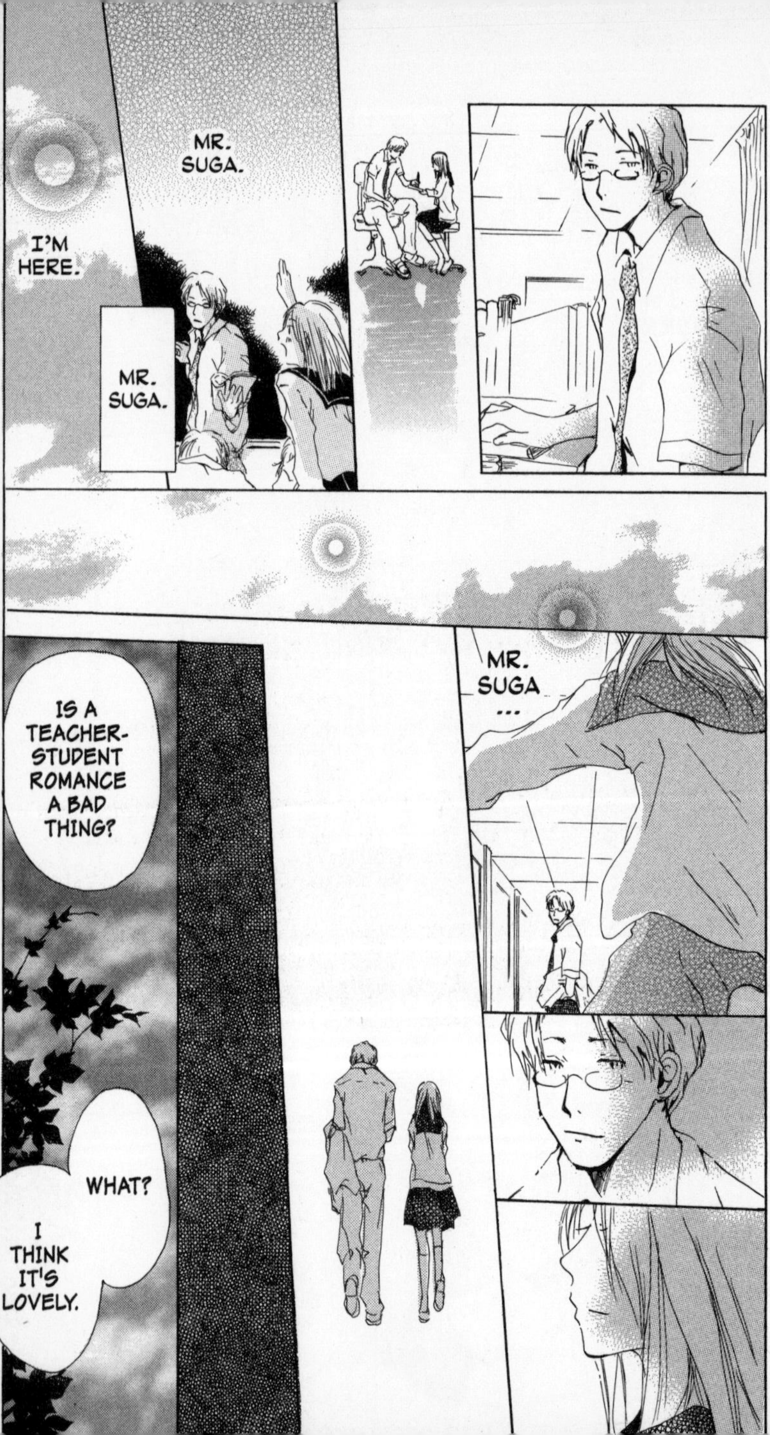
MR. SUGA.
I'M HERE.
MR. SUGA.
MR. SUGA...
IS A TEACHER-STUDENT ROMANCE A BAD THING?
WHAT?
I THINK IT'S LOVELY.

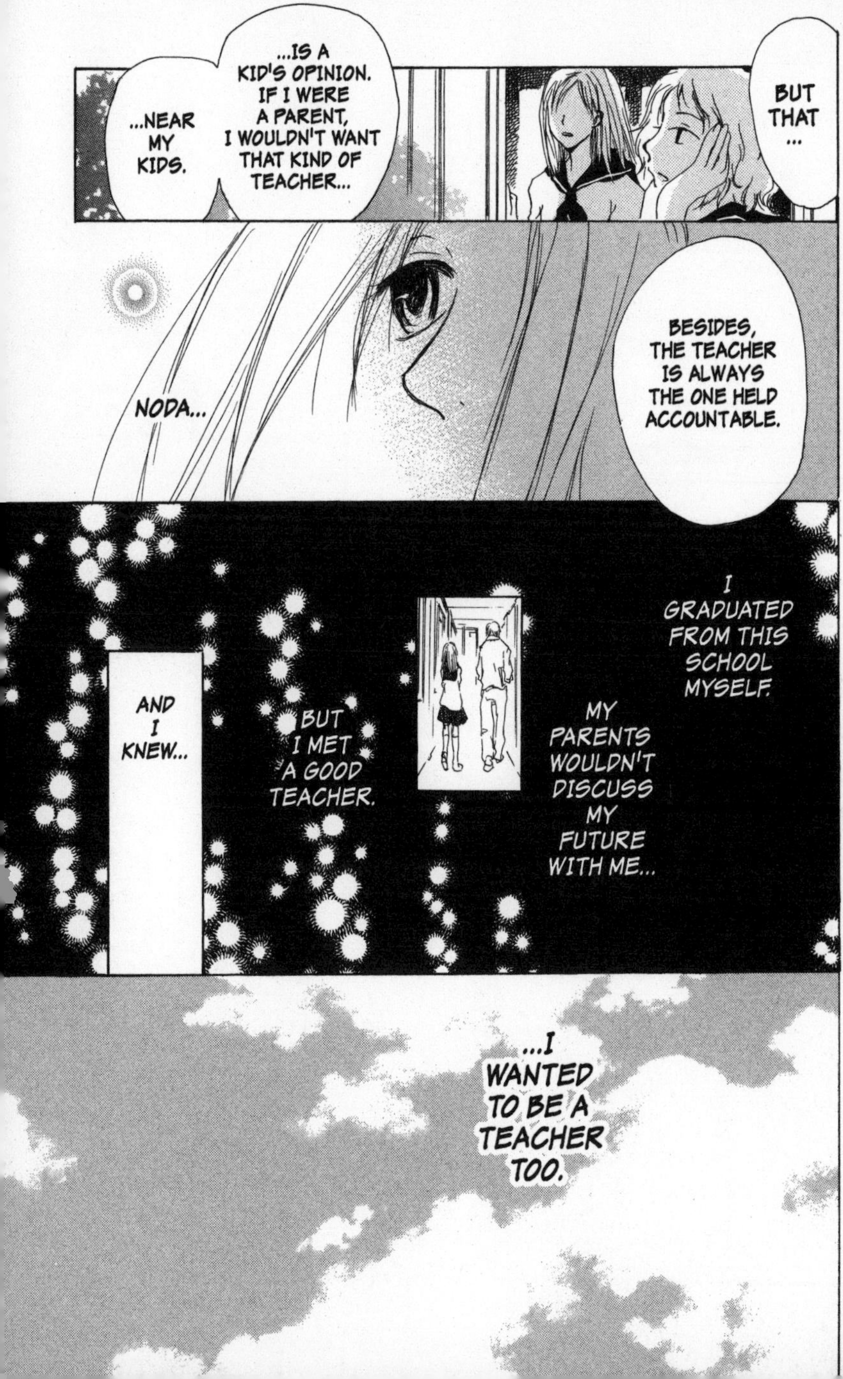
BUT THAT...
...IS A KID'S OPINION. IF I WERE A PARENT, I WOULDN'T WANT THAT KIND OF TEACHER...
...NEAR MY KIDS.
BESIDES, THE TEACHER IS ALWAYS THE ONE HELD ACCOUNTABLE.
NODA...
I GRADUATED FROM THIS SCHOOL MYSELF.
MY PARENTS WOULDN'T DISCUSS MY FUTURE WITH ME...
BUT I MET A GOOD TEACHER.
AND I KNEW...
...I WANTED TO BE A TEACHER TOO.

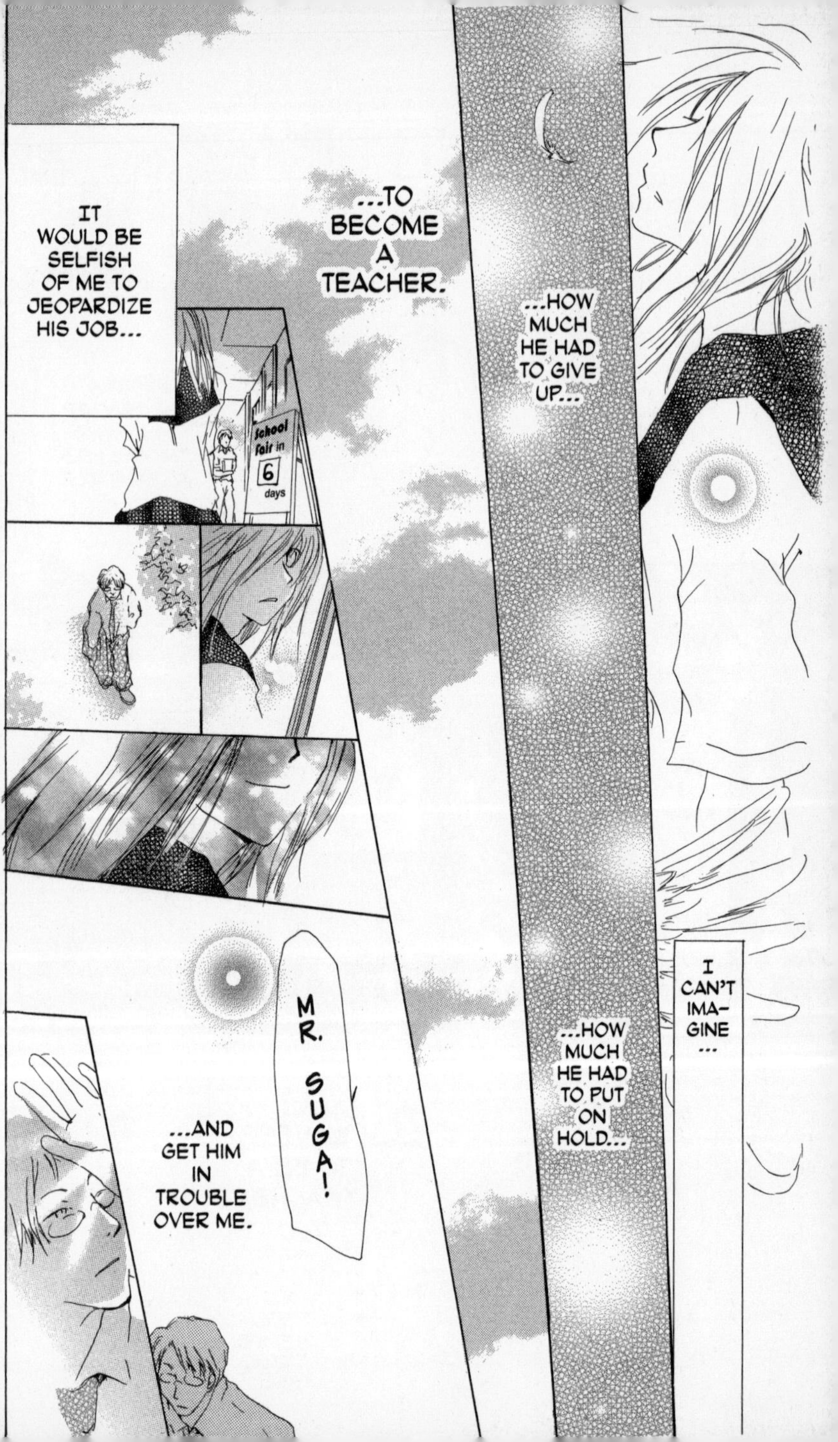
I CAN'T IMAGINE...
...HOW MUCH HE HAD TO GIVE UP...
...HOW MUCH HE HAD TO PUT ON HOLD...
...TO BECOME A TEACHER.
IT WOULD BE SELFISH OF ME TO JEOPARDIZE HIS JOB...
School fair in 6 days
MR. SUGA!
...AND GET HIM IN TROUBLE OVER ME.

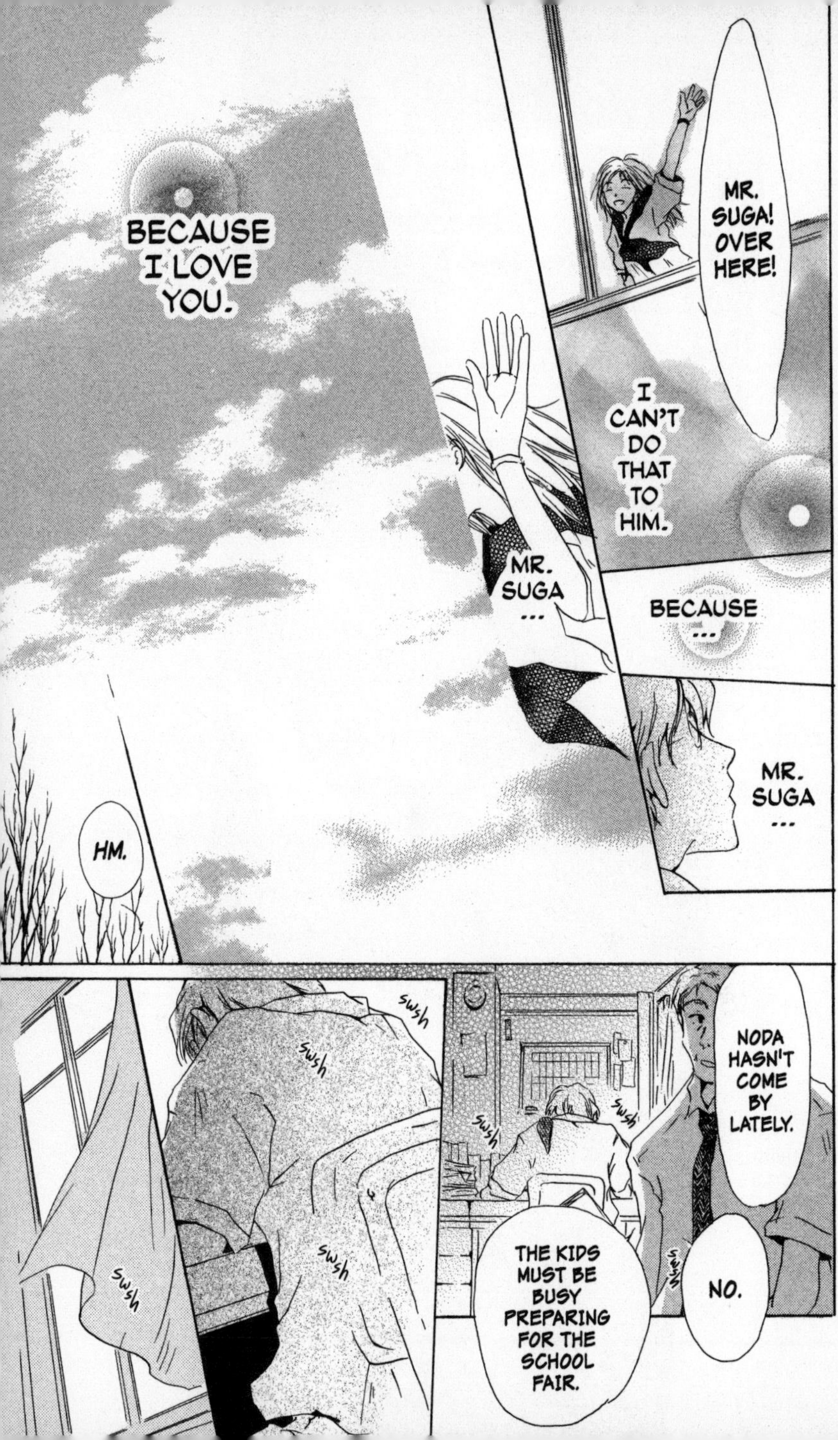
MR. SUGA! OVER HERE!
I CAN'T DO THAT TO HIM.
BECAUSE ...
MR. SUGA ...
MR. SUGA ...
BECAUSE I LOVE YOU.
HM.
NODA HASN'T COME BY LATELY.
swsh
swsh
NO.
THE KIDS MUST BE BUSY PREPARING FOR THE SCHOOL FAIR.
swsh
swsh
swsh
swsh
swsh
swsh

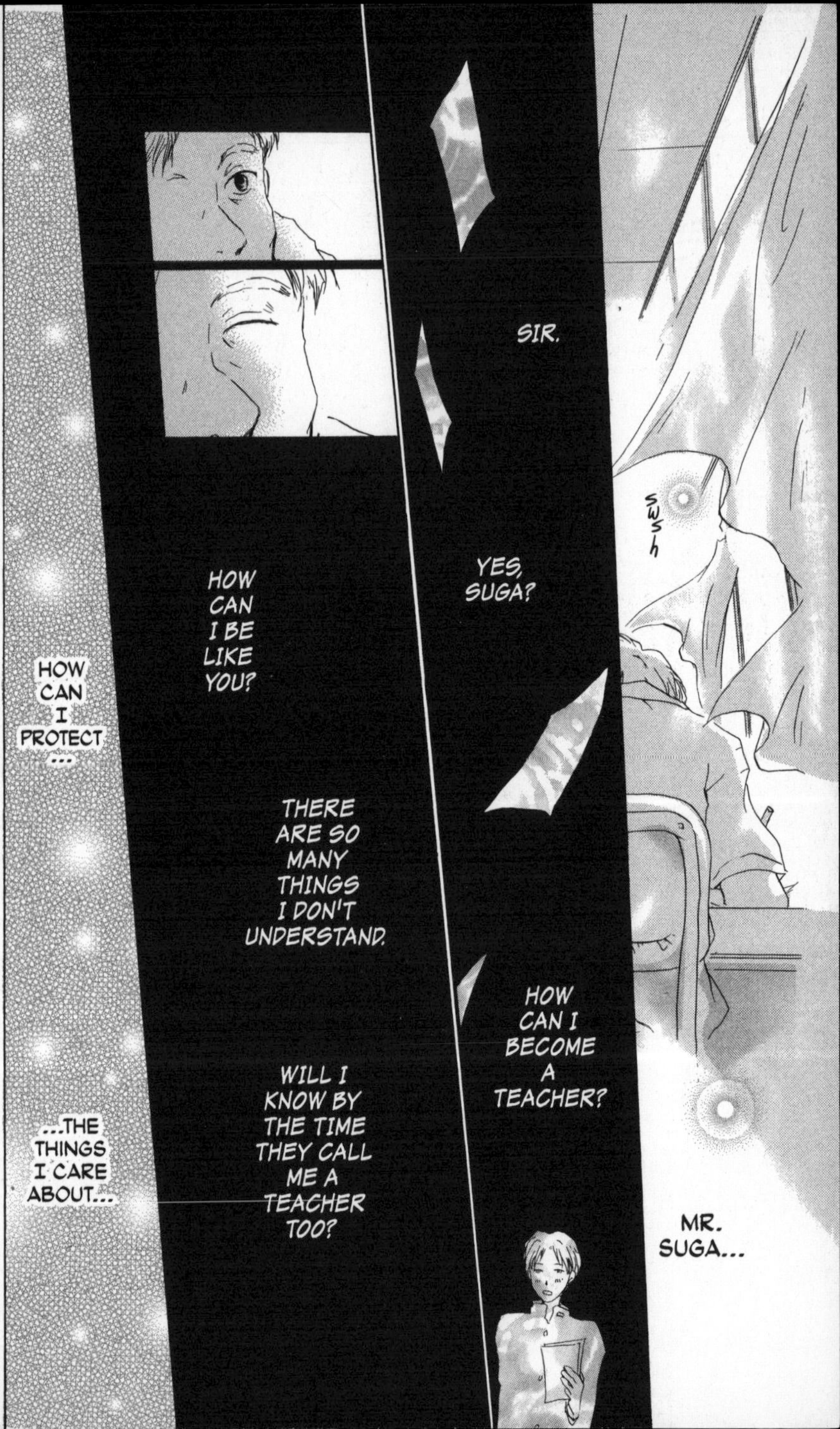
SWSH
MR. SUGA...
SIR.
YES, SUGA?
HOW CAN I BECOME A TEACHER?
HOW CAN I BE LIKE YOU?
THERE ARE SO MANY THINGS I DON'T UNDERSTAND.
WILL I KNOW BY THE TIME THEY CALL ME A TEACHER TOO?
HOW CAN I PROTECT...
...THE THINGS I CARE ABOUT...

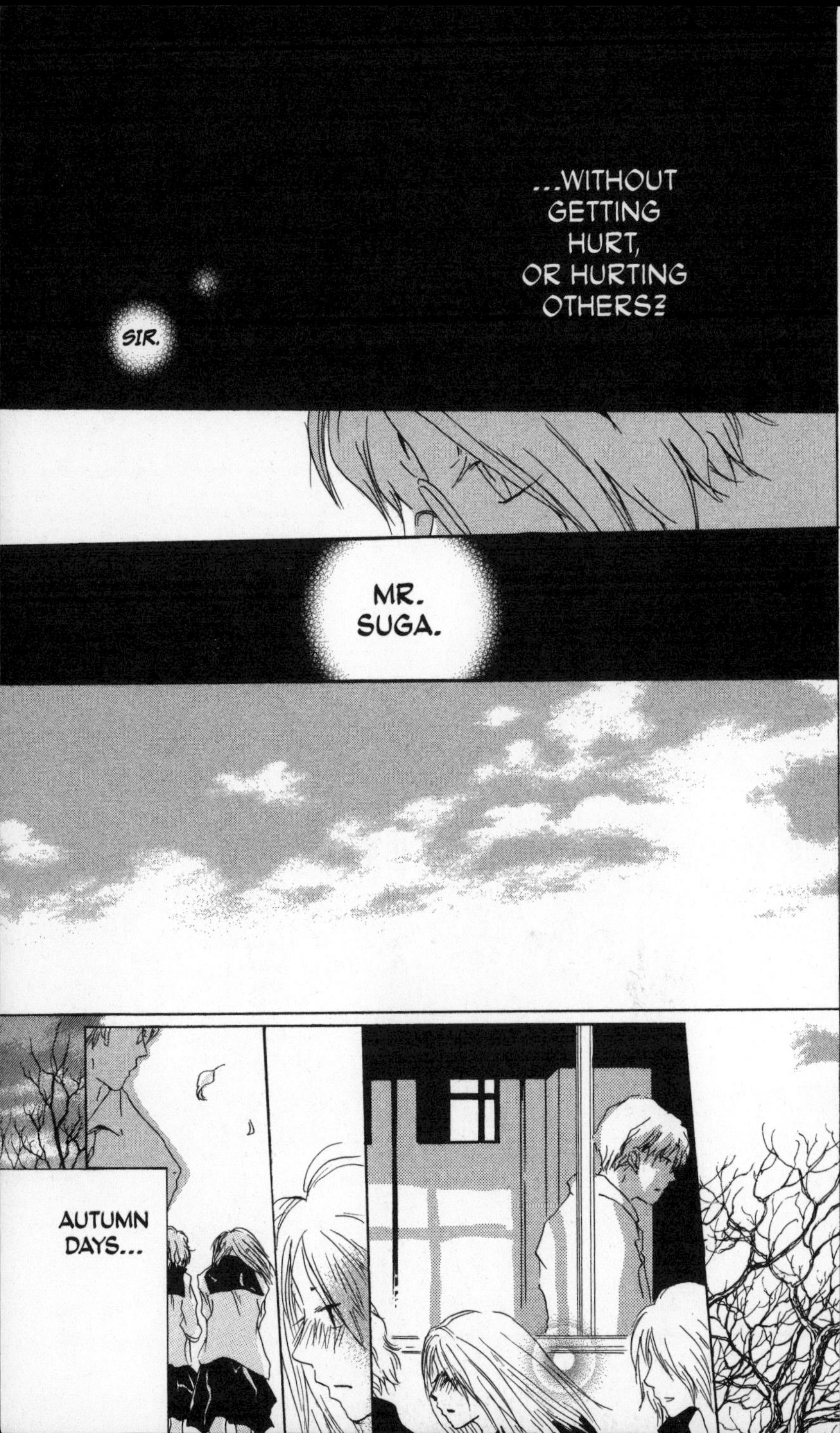
...WITHOUT GETTING HURT, OR HURTING OTHERS?
SIR.
MR. SUGA.
AUTUMN DAYS...

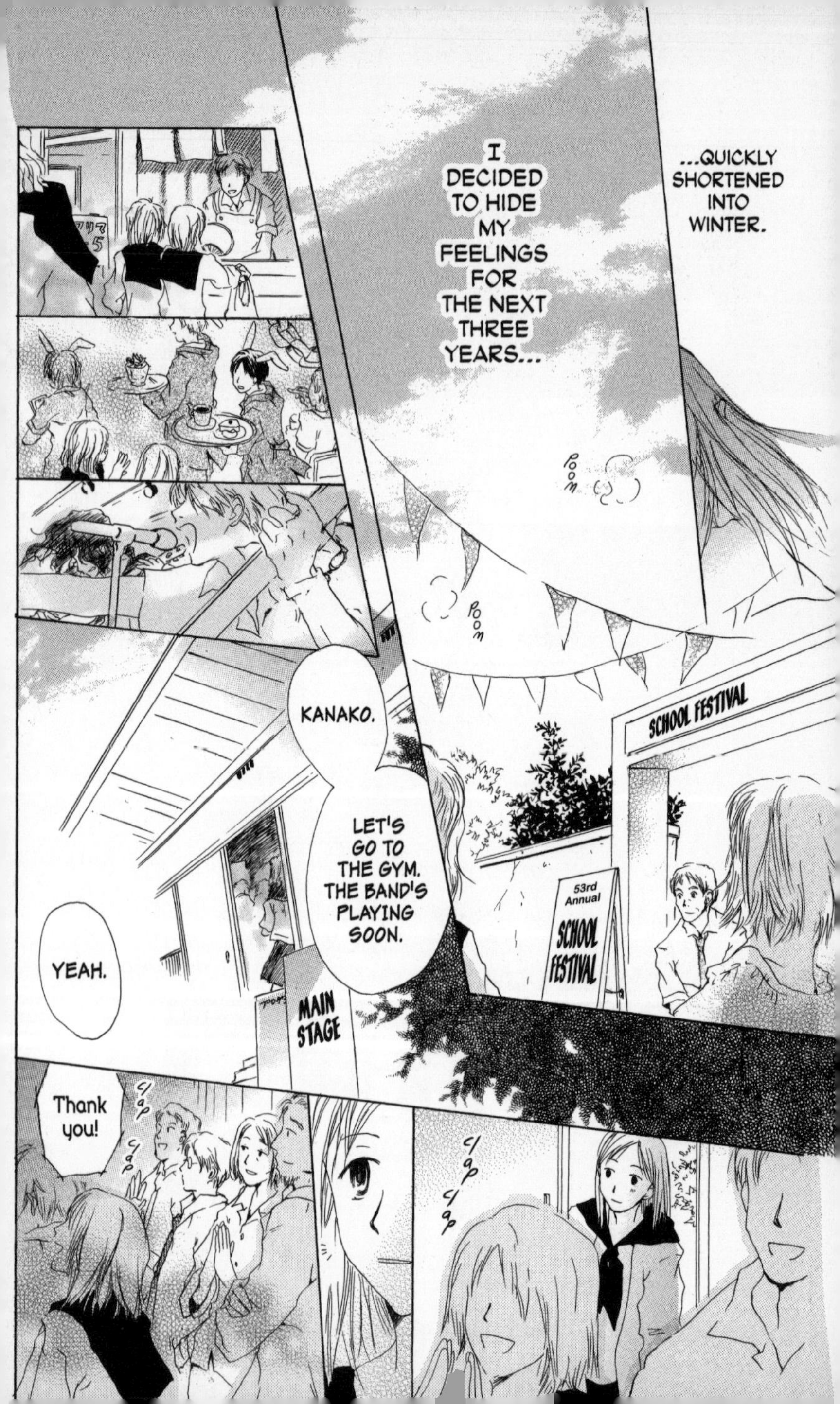
...QUICKLY SHORTENED INTO WINTER.
I DECIDED TO HIDE MY FEELINGS FOR THE NEXT THREE YEARS...
POOM
POOM
SCHOOL FESTIVAL
53rd Annual SCHOOL FESTIVAL
KANAKO.
LET'S GO TO THE GYM. THE BAND'S PLAYING SOON.
YEAH.
MAIN STAGE
clap clap
clap clap
Thank you!

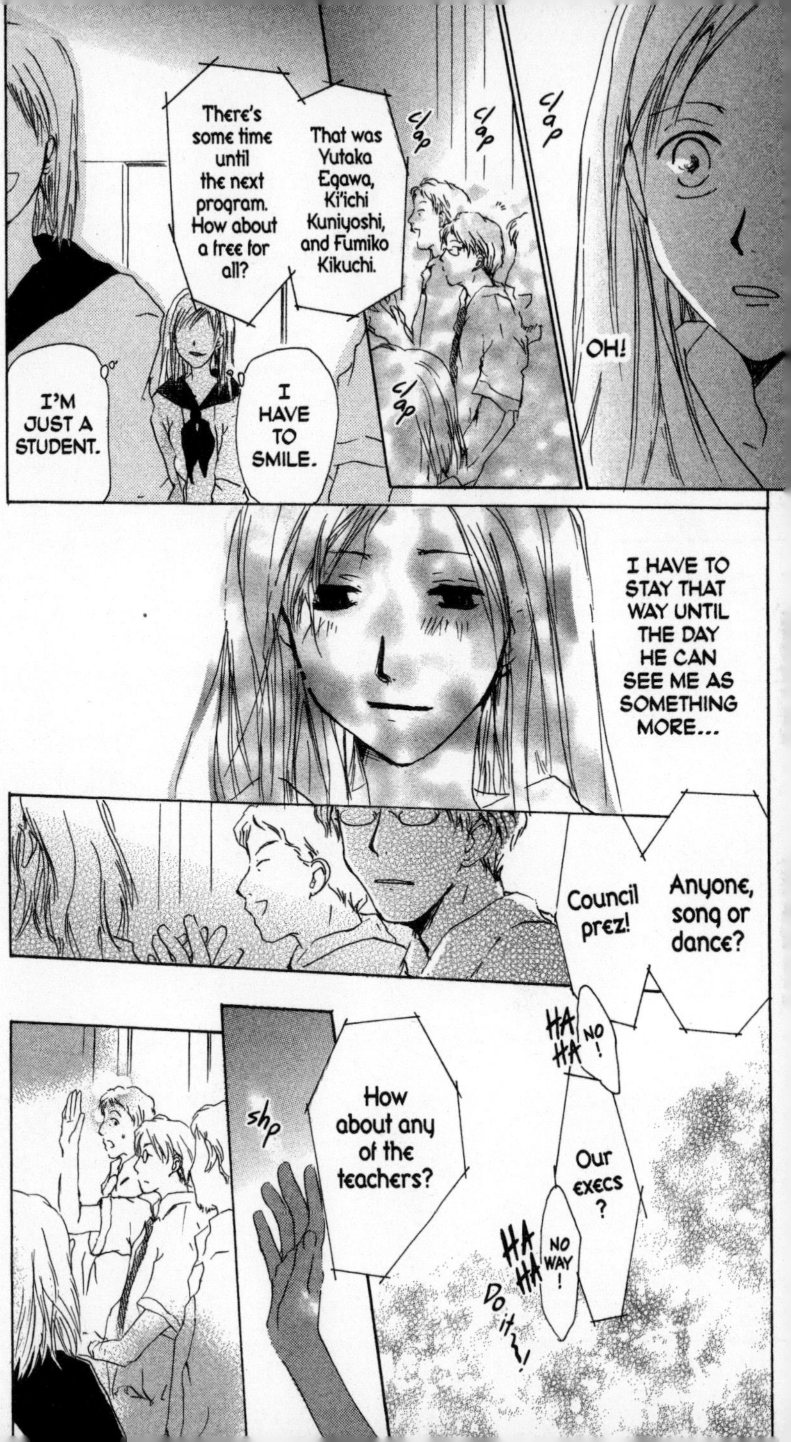

clap
OH!
clap
clap
clap
That was Yutaka Egawa, Ki'ichi Kuniyoshi, and Fumiko Kikuchi.
There's some time until the next program. How about a free for all?
I HAVE TO SMILE.
I'M JUST A STUDENT.
I HAVE TO STAY THAT WAY UNTIL THE DAY HE CAN SEE ME AS SOMETHING MORE...
Anyone, song or dance?
Council prez!
HA HA
NO!
Our execs?
HA HA
NO WAY!
Do it~!
How about any of the teachers?
shp

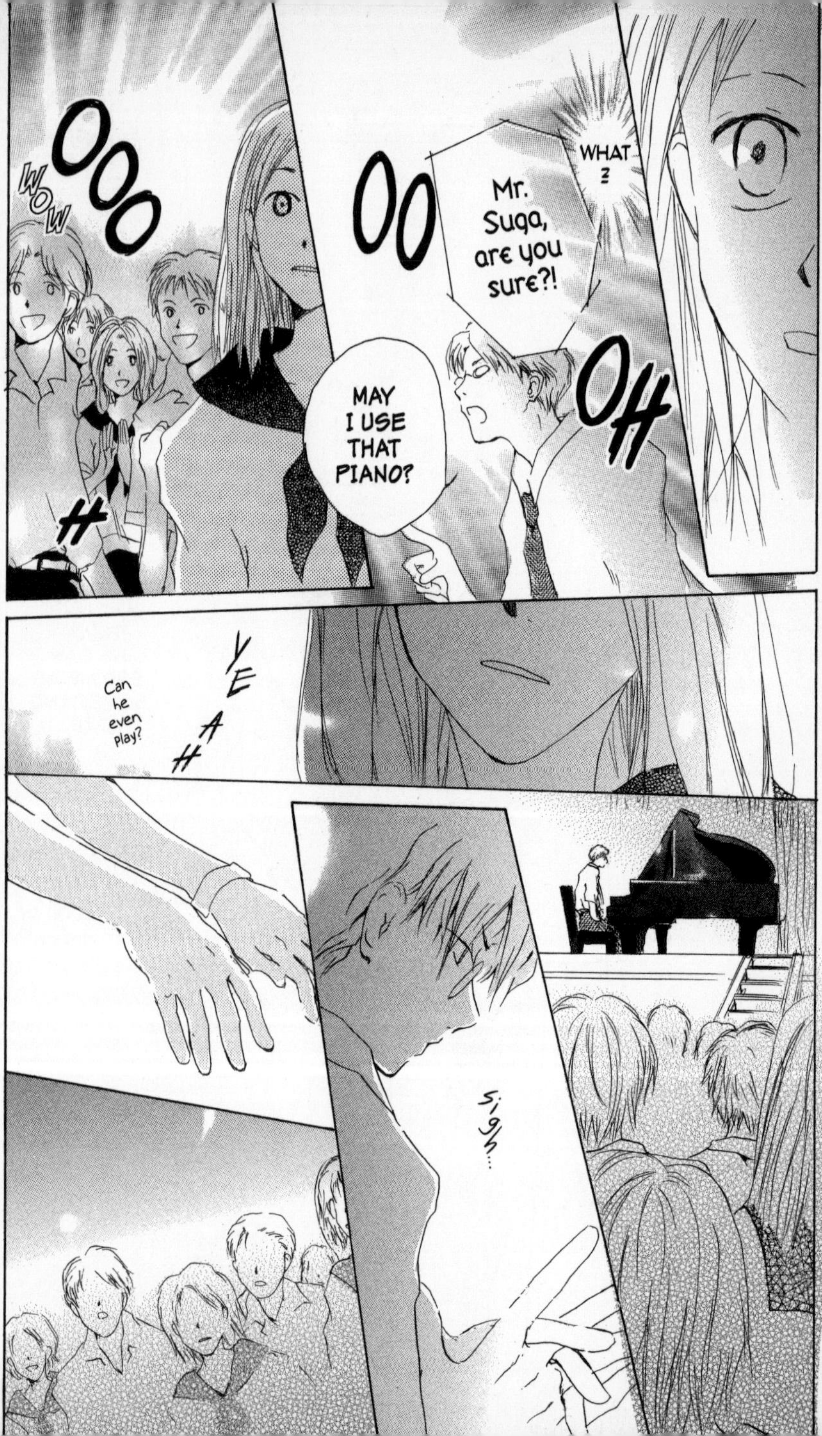
WHAT?
Mr. Suga, are you sure?!
OH
OO
MAY I USE THAT PIANO?
OOO
H
WOW
YEAH
Can he even play?
sigh...

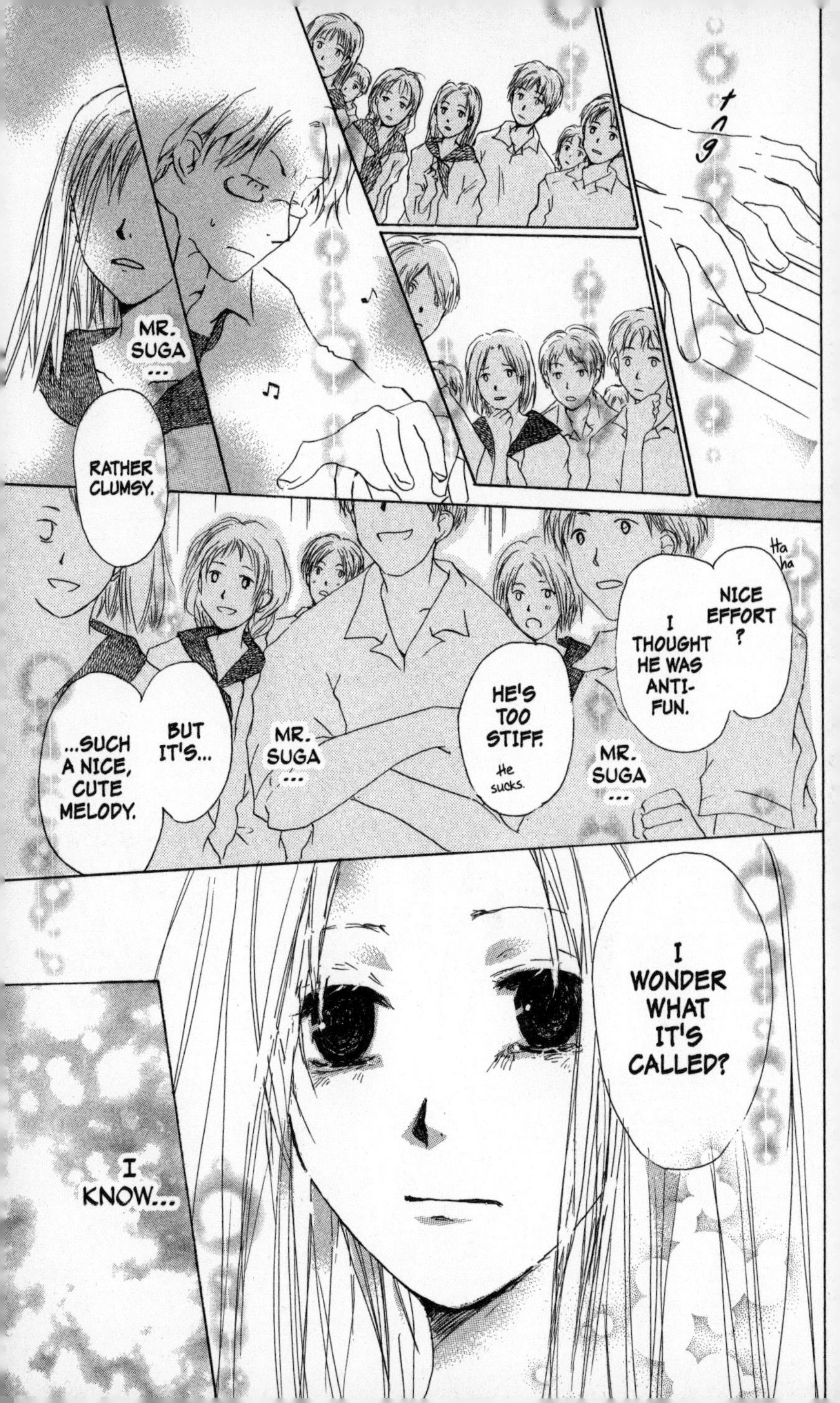
MR. SUGA ...
RATHER CLUMSY.
Ha ha
NICE EFFORT?
I THOUGHT HE WAS ANTI-FUN.
MR. SUGA ...
HE'S TOO STIFF.
He sucks.
MR. SUGA ...
BUT IT'S...
...SUCH A NICE, CUTE MELODY.
I WONDER WHAT IT'S CALLED?
I KNOW...

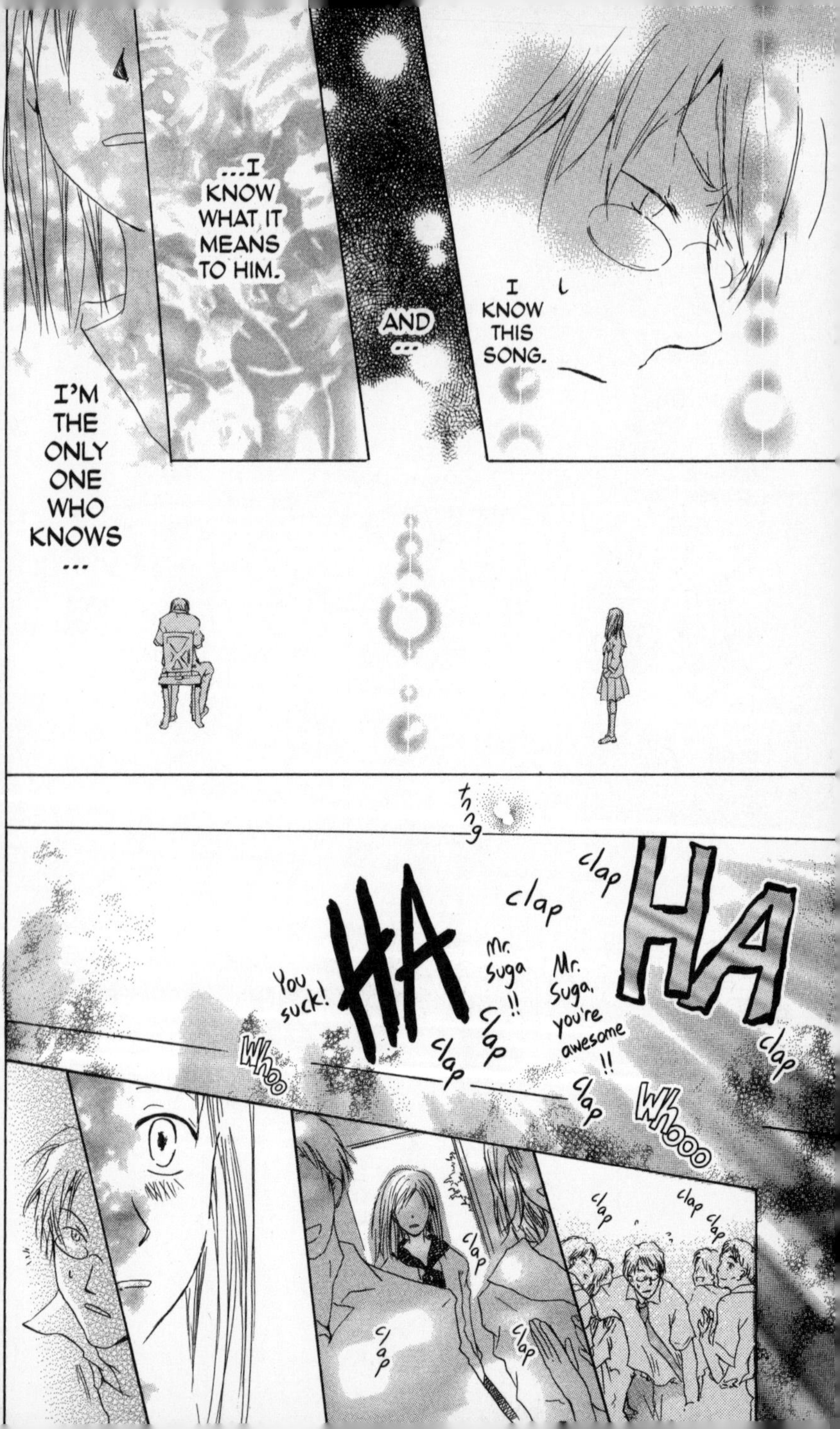

I KNOW THIS SONG.
AND ...
...I KNOW WHAT IT MEANS TO HIM.
I'M THE ONLY ONE WHO KNOWS ...
tnng
HA
clap
clap
clap
Mr. Suga, you're awesome!!
Mr. Suga!!
clap
clap
HA
You suck!
clap
Whoo
Whoo
clap
clap
clap
clap
clap
clap

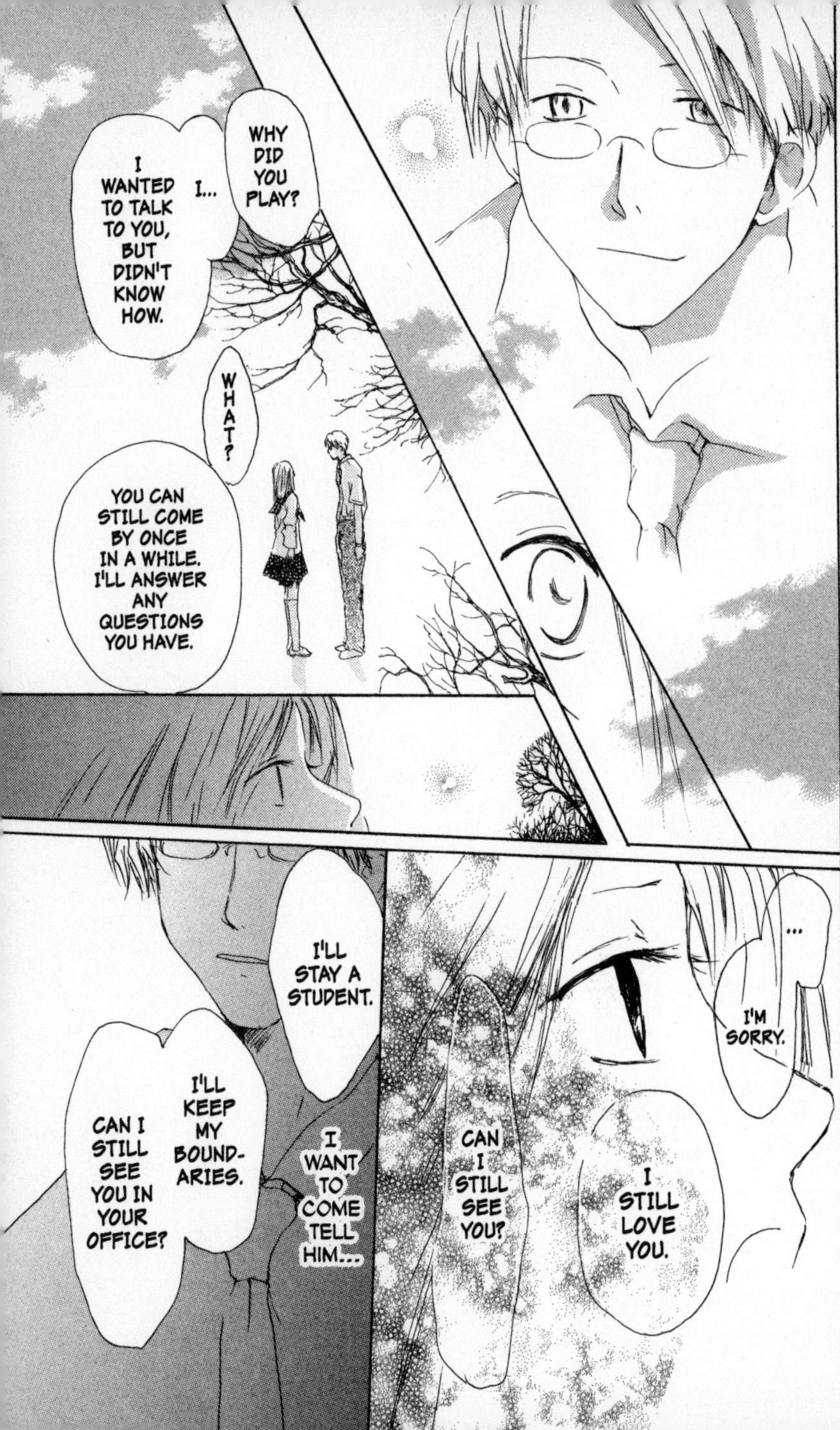
WHY DID YOU PLAY?
I...
I WANTED TO TALK TO YOU, BUT DIDN'T KNOW HOW.
WHAT?
YOU CAN STILL COME BY ONCE IN A WHILE. I'LL ANSWER ANY QUESTIONS YOU HAVE.
...
I'M SORRY.
I STILL LOVE YOU.
CAN I STILL SEE YOU?
I'LL STAY A STUDENT.
I WANT TO COME TELL HIM...
I'LL KEEP MY BOUNDARIES.
CAN I STILL SEE YOU IN YOUR OFFICE?

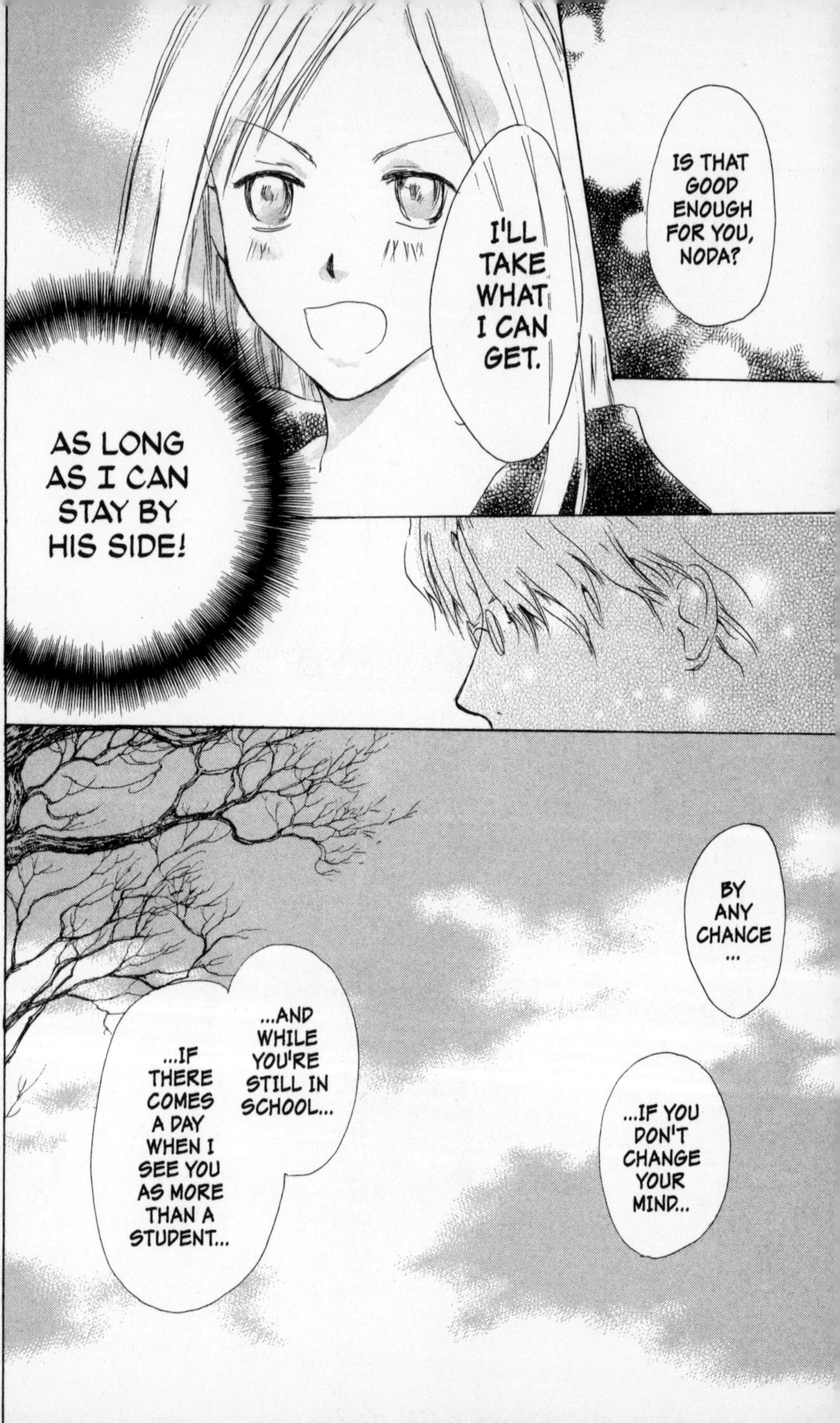
IS THAT GOOD ENOUGH FOR YOU, NODA?
I'LL TAKE WHAT I CAN GET.
AS LONG AS I CAN STAY BY HIS SIDE!
BY ANY CHANCE...
...IF YOU DON'T CHANGE YOUR MIND...
...AND WHILE YOU'RE STILL IN SCHOOL...
...IF THERE COMES A DAY WHEN I SEE YOU AS MORE THAN A STUDENT...

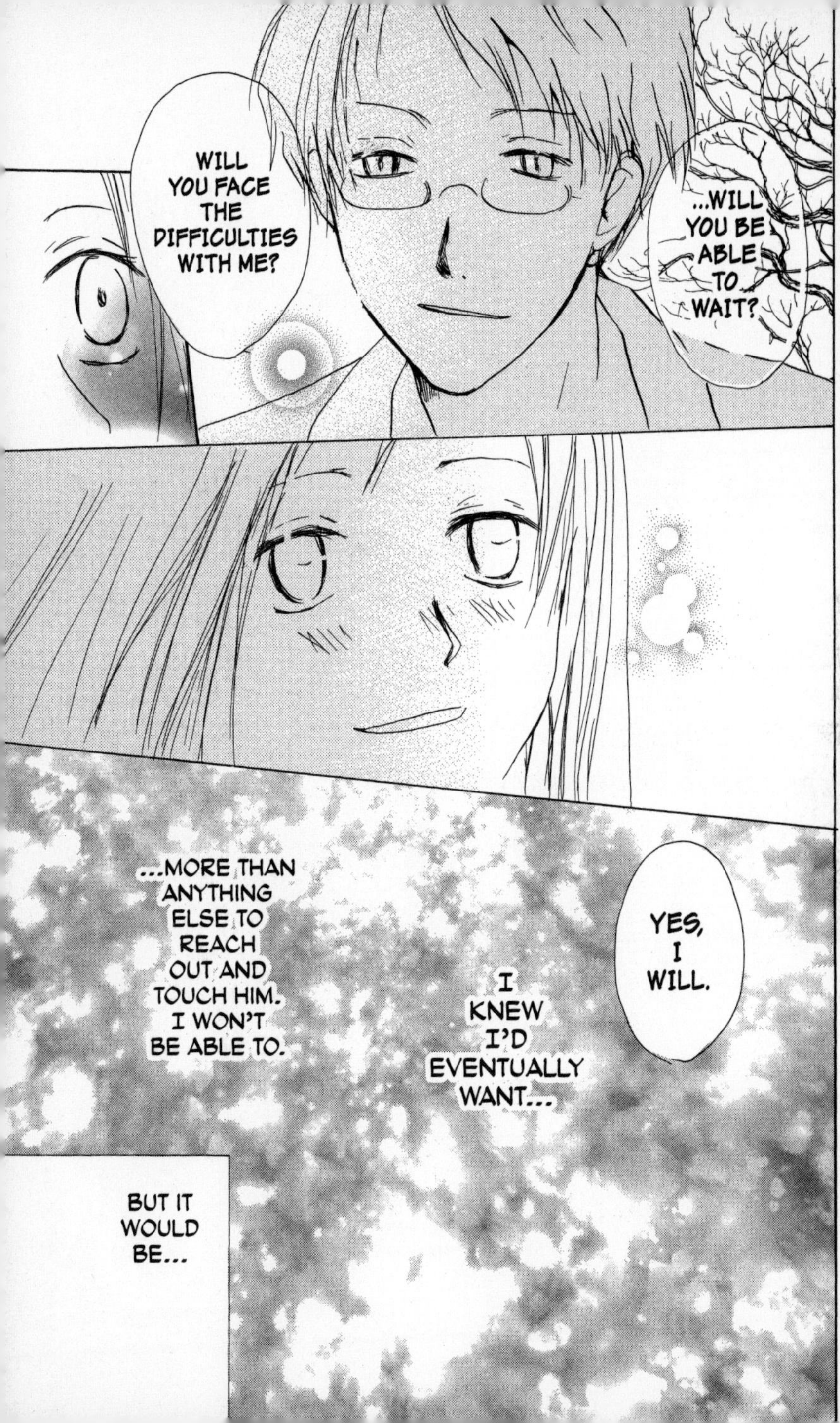
...WILL YOU BE ABLE TO WAIT?
WILL YOU FACE THE DIFFICULTIES WITH ME?
YES, I WILL.
I KNEW I'D EVENTUALLY WANT...
...MORE THAN ANYTHING ELSE TO REACH OUT AND TOUCH HIM. I WON'T BE ABLE TO.
BUT IT WOULD BE...

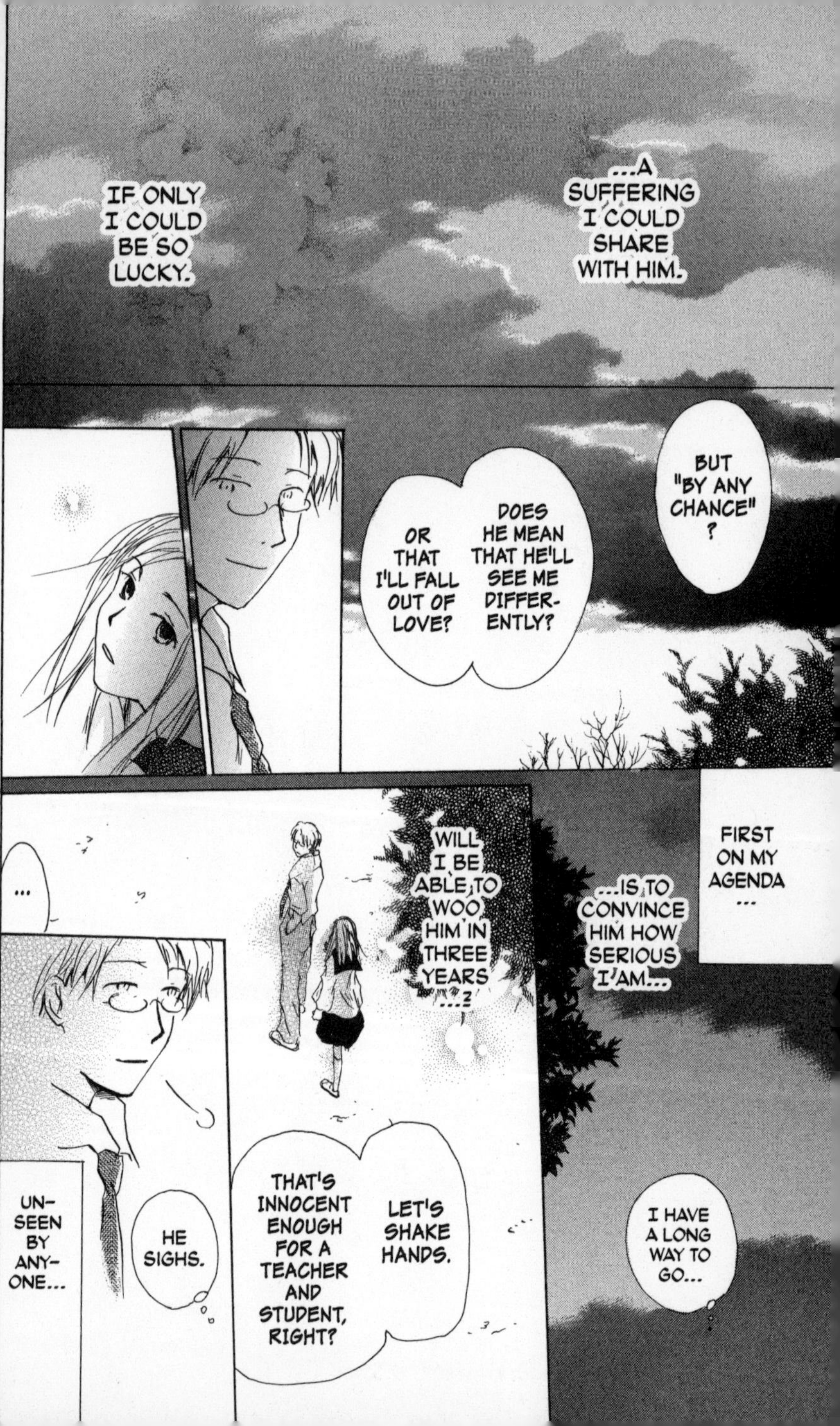
...A SUFFERING I COULD SHARE WITH HIM.
IF ONLY I COULD BE SO LUCKY.
BUT "BY ANY CHANCE"?
DOES HE MEAN THAT HE'LL SEE ME DIFFERENTLY?
OR THAT I'LL FALL OUT OF LOVE?
FIRST ON MY AGENDA...
...IS TO CONVINCE HIM HOW SERIOUS I AM...
WILL I BE ABLE TO WOO HIM IN THREE YEARS...?
...
I HAVE A LONG WAY TO GO...
LET'S SHAKE HANDS.
THAT'S INNOCENT ENOUGH FOR A TEACHER AND STUDENT, RIGHT?
HE SIGHS.
UNSEEN BY ANYONE...

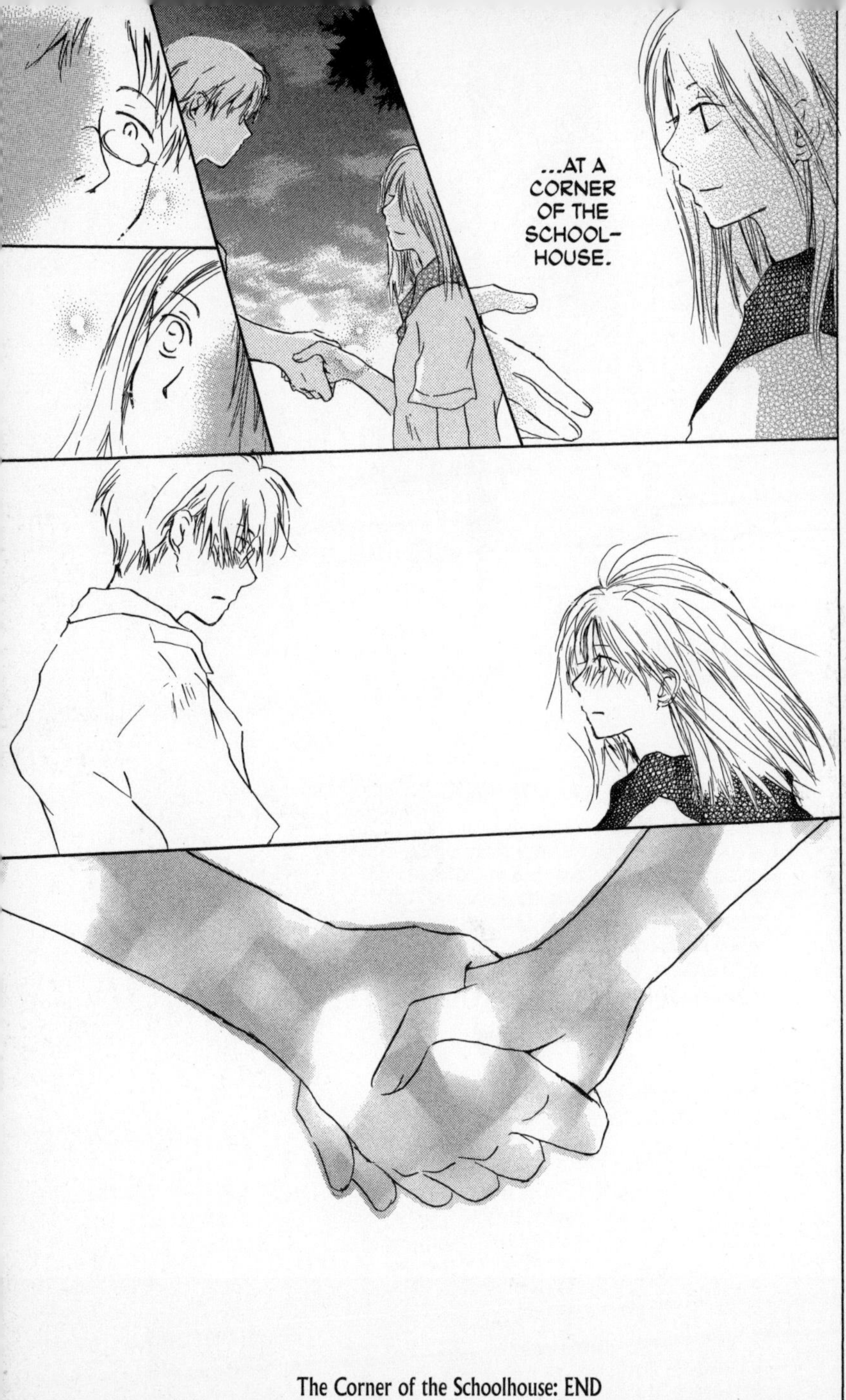
...AT A CORNER OF THE SCHOOL-HOUSE.

The Corner of the Schoolhouse: END

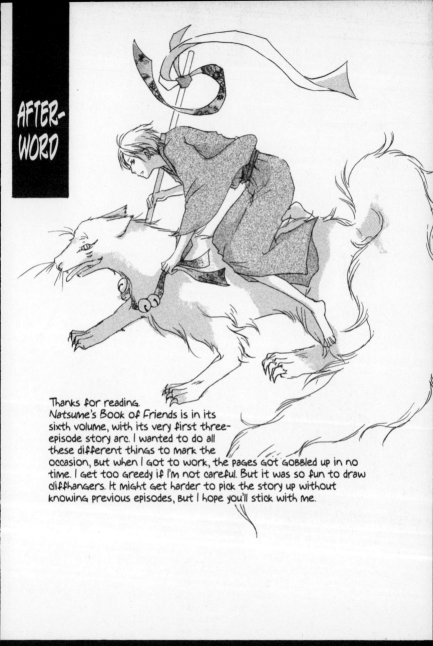

AFTER-WORD

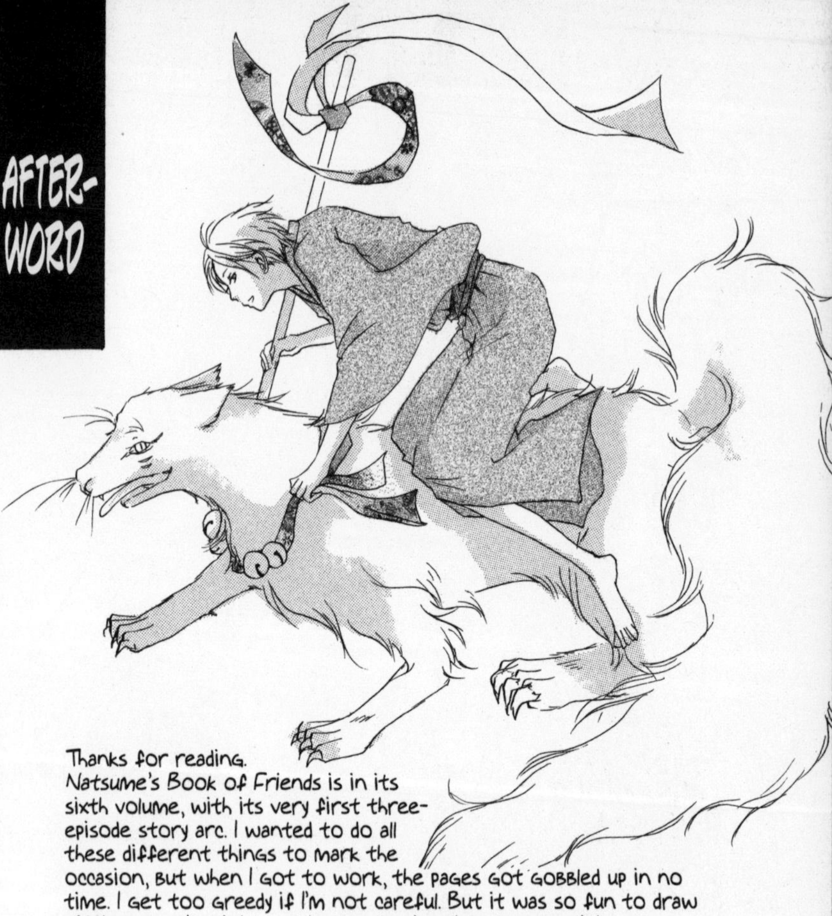

Thanks for reading.
Natsume's Book of Friends is in its sixth volume, with its very first three-episode story arc. I wanted to do all these different things to mark the occasion, but when I got to work, the pages got gobbled up in no time. I get too greedy if I'm not careful. But it was so fun to draw cliffhangers. It might get harder to pick the story up without knowing previous episodes, but I hope you'll stick with me.

CHAPTER 20, 21, 22

Takashi's Friend

Natori gets a thankless role, but I don't want to draw just kindness all the time, so he's very useful. When two awkward, clumsy people get together, things might not always end well, but I like such people anyway. It was fun to draw Taki again, and a child like Kai.

SPECIAL EPISODE 5 Natsume Observation Log

I got to draw the young fox again. It's so fun to have a small creature running all over the place. I think I drew it because I wanted a story about chasing a straw hat. I'd like to draw him again if I have the opportunity.

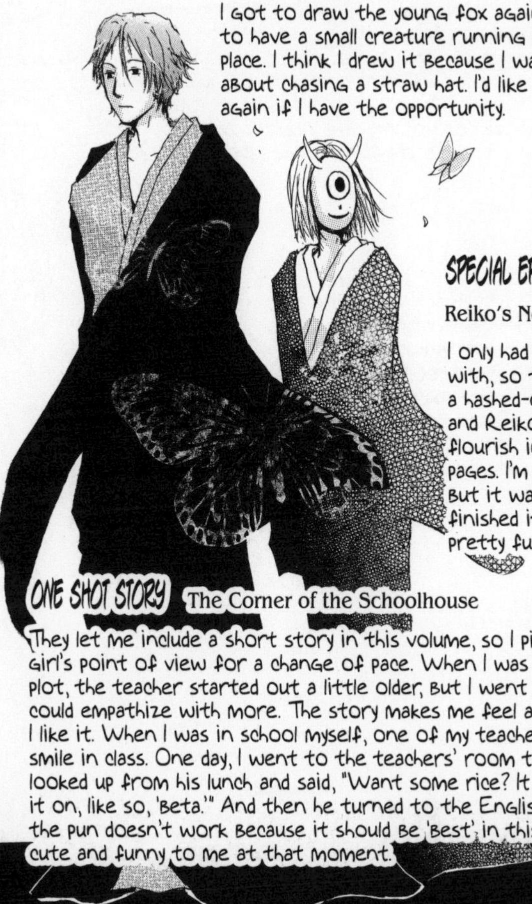

SPECIAL EPISODE 6

Reiko's Nostalgia Log

I only had eight pages to work with, so they let me work without a hashed-out plot. I figured Hinoe and Reiko would provide a bit of flourish in the short number of pages. I'm not sure about a flourish, but it was easy to work on, and I finished it up comfortably. It was pretty fun to draw a lively Reiko.

ONE SHOT STORY The Corner of the Schoolhouse

They let me include a short story in this volume, so I picked one I did from a girl's point of view for a change of pace. When I was first working on the plot, the teacher started out a little older, but I went with someone readers could empathize with more. The story makes me feel a little embarrassed, but I like it. When I was in school myself, one of my teachers never cracked a smile in class. One day, I went to the teachers' room to look for glue, and he looked up from his lunch and said, "Want some rice? It works better to stick it on, like so, 'beta.'" And then he turned to the English teacher, "I suppose the pun doesn't work because it should be 'best' in this case." He seemed so cute and funny to me at that moment.

Thanks to everyone's support, I'm able to continue Natsume for a little while longer. I want to take my time developing each story as usual.

The casting for the voices of the two main characters is the same as the drama CD voice actors. I left the rest of the casting up to the anime staff, and they picked such wonderful people. They let me come in to say hello at the recording session for the first episode, and I was able to meet the main cast. I was worried that the manga creator showing up would distract them, but it was so energizing to meet these people who are going to give life to your characters. I must work harder to make an interesting manga for not only the readers, but so people can enjoy the anime Natsume's Book of Friends.

Natsume will be in its seventh volume next time. Please let me know if you have any opinions of what you want to see happen. There are so many stories I want to depict, and I'll agonize over and enjoy every minute of it. Thank you so much for reading all the way to the end.

Yuki Midorikawa
c/o Shojo Beat
Published by VIZ Media, LLC.
P.O. Box 77010
San Francicso, CA 94107

Special thanks to:
Tamao Ohki
Chika
Mr. Sato
My sister

Thanks for reading.

Yuki Midorikawa
緑川 ゆき   June 2008

AFTERWORD: END

BOOK of FRIENDS

VOLUME 6 END NOTES

PAGE 55, PANEL 4: *Matsuzaka beef*
Beef from cows bred to have extensive marbling (fat) in their meat.

PAGE 17, PANEL 2: **200 yen, 10,000 yen**
About $2.40 and $119 USD.

PAGE 40, PANEL 5: *Soba*
Thin buckwheat noodles, often served cold with dipping sauce.

PAGE 65, AUTHOR NOTE: *Hachioji*
A city in the Tokyo metropolitan area.

PAGE 115, PANEL 3: *Tomorrow's George*
An allusion to the iconic and hugely influential boxing manga *Tomorrow's Joe* by Asao Takamori (story) and Tetsuya Chiba (art).

PAGE 136, PANEL 5: *Chu-Hi*
Shochu (an alcoholic beverage distilled from sweet potatoes, rice, wheat, or other grains) mixed with soda and citrus juice.

PAGE 161, PANEL 4: *"Song of Circling Stars"*
A song written and composed by Kenji Miyazawa, a poet and author. The song appears in the novels *Night on the Galactic Railroad* and *The Twin Stars*.

PAGE 178, PANEL 2: *School Festival*
Most Japanese high schools hold annual festivals where each class runs food booths, performs live shows, or takes part in similar things to raise money for school programs and promote the school to potential students.

PAGE 189, AUTHOR NOTE: *Beta*
A sound effect for something sticky.

Yuki Midorikawa
is the creator of *Natsume's Book of Friends*, which was nominated for the Manga Taisho (Cartoon Grand Prize). Her other titles published in Japan include *Hotarubi no Mori e* (Into the Forest of Fireflies), *Hiiro no Isu* (The Scarlet Chair) and *Akaku Saku Koe* (The Voice That Blooms Red).

NATSUME'S BOOK OF FRIENDS

Vol. 6

Shojo Beat Edition

STORY AND ART BY **Yuki Midorikawa**

Translation & Adaptation **Lillian Olsen**
Touch-up Art & Lettering **Sabrina Heep**
Design **Fawn Lau**
Editor **Pancha Diaz**

Natsume Yujincho by Yuki Midorikawa
© Yuki Midorikawa 2008
All rights reserved.
First published in Japan in 2008 by HAKUSENSHA, Inc., Tokyo.
English language translation rights arranged with HAKUSENSHA, Inc., Tokyo.

The rights of the author(s) of the work(s) in this publication to be so identified
have been asserted in accordance with the Copyright, Designs and Patents Act 1988.
A CIP catalogue record for this book is available from the British Library.

The stories, characters and incidents mentioned in this publication are entirely fictional.

Printed in the U.S.A.

Published by VIZ Media, LLC
P.O. Box 77010
San Francisco, CA 94107

10 9 8 7 6 5 4 3 2 1
First printing, April 2011

PARENTAL ADVISORY
NATSUME'S BOOK OF FRIENDS is rated T for Teen
and is recommended for ages 16 and up.
This volume contains fantasy violence.
ratings.viz.com

www.viz.com

www.shojobeat.com